DATE DUE

AP 15 02			

DEMCO 38-296

Our Joyce

Literary Modernism Series
Thomas F. Staley, Editor

Our Joyce

From Outcast to Icon

by Joseph Kelly

 University of Texas Press, Austin

Requests for permission to reproduce material from this
work should be sent to Permissions, University of Texas
Press, P.O. Box 7819, Austin, TX 78713-7819.

⊗ The paper used in this publication meets the minimum
requirements of American National Standard for Information Sciences—Permanence of Paper for Printed Library
Materials, ANSI Z39.48-1984.

Library of Congress Cataloging-in-Publication Data

Kelly, Joseph, 1962–
    Our Joyce : from outcast to icon / by Joseph Kelly. —
1st ed.
        p.   cm. — (Literary modernism series)
    Includes bibliographical references and index.
    ISBN 0-292-74331-9 (alk. paper)
    1. Joyce, James, 1882–1941—Criticism and
interpretation—History.   2. Modernism (Literature)—
Ireland.   3. Canon (Literature)
I. Title.   II. Series.
PR6019.09Z6696   1998
823'.912—dc21   97-10877

For Susan
and Spencer

Contents

Acknowledgments

I would like to thank the National Endowment for the Humanities and the Mellon Foundation for funding much of the research that went into this book. Sidney Huttner at the McFarlin Library at the University of Tulsa helped me sift through the labyrinth of Ellmann's papers. Carol Kealiher of the *James Joyce Quarterly*, also at the University of Tulsa, kindly donated much time, energy, and encouragement while I rummaged through the attic of that journal. Since the *JJQ* papers have not been organized or catalogued, Ms. Kealiher's patience and help are particularly appreciated. I would also like to thank Robert Spoo, the editor of *JJQ*, for opening the *JJQ* Archive to me. Ken Craven, Patricia Fox, and Cathy Henderson at the Harry Ransom Humanities Research Center at the University of Texas at Austin gave invaluable help with Pound's letters and especially with the Ernst papers.

As I mention in Chapter 5, Joyce criticism is a collaborative affair. That is particularly true of this book. Despite the iconoclastic nature of my argument, the Joyce community consistently has welcomed and supported me. In particular, I want to thank the Joyce scholars whom I have interviewed and corresponded with: Morris Beja (especially for his help on the Joyce Symposia), Bernard Benstock, Chester Anderson, David Hayman, Robert Scholes, Thomas Staley, and A. Walton Litz. I have referred to the unpublished letters of these and of J. S. Atherton, Maurice Beebe, Rivers Carew, Alan Cohn, Russell Cosper, Bernard Fleischman, Warren Frend, S. A. Goldman, Clive Hart, Fred Higginson, Herbert Howarth, Richard Kain, John Kelleher, Harry Levin, Philip Lyman, Joseph Prescott, Janet Salisbury, Fritz Senn, and David Ward, which are in the *James Joyce Quarterly* archive. Without these contributions my book would have been impossible. David Koch has granted me permission to use a letter by Alan Cohn, and I thank Shari Benstock especially for permission to quote letters and an unpublished memoir by Bernard Benstock.

I would like to thank Erwin Ellmann and Sidney Huttner for permission to quote unpublished material from Richard Ellmann's papers at the University of Tulsa, and Ellsworth Mason has kindly granted me permission to quote from his unpublished letters to Ellmann and to Stanislaus Joyce. I also thank Thomas Staley for allowing me to use the Mason/ Stanislaus Joyce letters. Stephanie Goldstein Bege has granted me permission to use the extensive Morris Ernst papers at the University of Texas at Austin.

Grateful acknowledgment is given to New Directions Publishing Corporation and Faber and Faber Ltd. for permission to quote from the copyrighted works of Ezra Pound. For permission to quote from Pound's contributions to *Criterion* I would like to thank the trustees of the Ezra Pound Literary Property Trust and their agent, New Directions.

Julie Gates and Miriam Tomblin both helped edit my prose; and Ali Hossaini, Leslie Tingle, and Madeleine Williams at the University of Texas Press have provided invaluable editorial help. Thomas Staley has encouraged this project for years by patiently reading many drafts, opening his personal Joyce library, and steering me toward special collections. This book could hardly have been started without his kind help. Likewise, Elizabeth Butler Cullingford has guided me again and again: her comments on many parts of the book, especially those dealing with Irish literature and with Richard Ellmann, have improved my argument tremendously. All that is praiseworthy in my treatment of the Irish context is due to her. Nor could I have done without Michael Winship's advice on textual scholarship, and I owe John Rodden thanks for reading and commenting on parts of this book. Ronald Bush helped me refine my argument about Ezra Pound. Ira Nadel advised me on biography, and I would like to thank him especially for his warm support early in this project. Thomas Hofheinz has long been a fellow traveler; and Will Godwin, William Brockman, Jayne Marek, Jan Gorak, and Bradley Clissold have all helped my research. Charles Rossman has contributed untold hours, advice, and detailed comments, as well as tons of energy and enthusiasm from his apparently endless supply of both. It is no exaggeration to say that this book would never have been completed without his help.

Finally, I would like to thank those scholars outside Joyce and Irish studies who have read and discussed portions or all of my book. Julia Eichelberger, Patricia Ward, and Nan Morrison have all made their distinct contributions. And Susan Farrell has been irreplaceable.

Whatever deficiencies, mistakes, or things of darkness you find in this book I acknowledge mine.

Portions of this book have been published in the *Journal of Social History, Joyce Studies Annual,* and the *James Joyce Literary Supplement.*

Abbreviations

Works frequently cited have been identified by
the following abbreviations:

CW James Joyce. *The Critical Writings of James Joyce.*
Eds. Ellsworth Mason and Richard Ellmann. New
York: Viking Press, 1959.

D James Joyce. *Dubliners: Text, Criticism, and Notes.*
Eds. Robert Scholes and A. Walton Litz. New
York: Viking Press, 1969.

JJ Richard Ellmann. *James Joyce.* Rev. ed. New York:
Oxford University Press, 1983.

JJA *The James Joyce Archive.* Ed. Michael Groden, et al.
New York and London: Garland Publishing,
1978–.

JJQ *James Joyce Quarterly*

JJLS *James Joyce Literary Supplement*

JSA *Joyce Studies Annual*

Letters I, II, III James Joyce. *Letters of James Joyce.* Vol. I, II, III, ed.
Stuart Gilbert. New York: Viking Press, 1957;
reissued with corrections 1966. Vols. II and III, ed.
Richard Ellmann. New York: Viking Press, 1964.

M *The United States of America v. One Book Entitled
"Ulysses" by James Joyce.* Eds. Michael Moscato
and Leslie LeBlanc. Frederick, Maryland:
University Publications of America, 1984.

MBK Stanislaus Joyce. *My Brother's Keeper: James Joyce's
Early Years.* Ed. Richard Ellmann. New York: The
Viking Press, 1958.

MFS *Modern Fiction Studies*

SH James Joyce. *Stephen Hero.* Ed. John J. Slocum and
Herbert Cahoon. New York: New Directions,
1944, 1963.

Our Joyce

Introduction

Before *Ulysses* was published Joyce showed Frank Budgen a draft of "Scylla and Charybdis," and when Budgen finished reading it Joyce asked him, "What do you think of Buck Mulligan in this episode?" "He is witty and entertaining as ever," Budgen innocently replied. Joyce was not pleased. He found himself having to explain to his reader that Buck "should begin to pall . . . as the day goes on." Budgen resisted Joyce's interpretation, at least for the length of two sentences, remarking, "The comic man usually wearies . . . if he keeps it up too long. But I can't say that Buck Mulligan wearies me." [1] Despite his objection, Budgen, who was an obliging reader, could not contradict the author for very long. It is fair to imagine he took his own attitude towards Mulligan from Joyce, since the purpose of his recalling the anecdote in his own book, *James Joyce and the Making of "Ulysses,"* was to tell us that Joyce wanted us to dislike Buck.

But the writer's influence on his or her audience is short-lived. I first read Joyce in college, before I ever had a clear picture of the writer. I knew he was Irish, and, since his works were diffused with Catholic philosophy and symbolism, I figured he was a Catholic—granted, an unusual Catholic, a modern Dante, but, like Dante, a propagator of the faith. Though I was educated by Cistercians and Dominicans and he by Jesuits, I imagined that Joyce and I shared a heritage: Irish grandparents, Aristotle, Aquinas, Latin, the adoration of the Blessed Virgin. He had been prefect of the sodality, but I had been an altar boy, so I knew where he was coming from. I constructed an image of Joyce that sustained my personal response to his books. And I, like Budgen, found Mulligan engaging. I suspected Stephen Dedalus of excessive pride and excessive guilt.

Studying Joyce in graduate school convinced me that I was wrong. I may have been right about our common heritage, but clearly I was wrong about the condition of Joyce's faith, which amounted to being wrong in my response to Stephen and Buck. Even after I discovered my error I searched for evidence of Joyce's deathbed rededication to the Church, so I could continue rejecting the significance of Stephen's apostasy. But finally I had to abandon even that notion. Richard Ellmann changed my mind. In the last, moving chapter of his biography, Ellmann reports that after Joyce's death "a Catholic priest approached Nora [his wife] and George [his son] to offer a religious service, but Nora said, 'I couldn't do that to him'" (*JJ*, 742). Here was irrefutable evidence that Joyce never reconciled with the Church. Apparently, my concept of the author had had more to do with my college education than with the biography.

These two anecdotes illustrate the point of my argument, which is based on the deceptively simple axiom that a work of literature is a social event. I am largely indebted to recent textual criticism and its sociological orientation, especially the criticism of Jerome McGann. Textual criticism has incorporated into its domain the study of publishing milieux, perhaps as a logical development from the traditional role of the textual scholar, which was, as G. Thomas Tanselle points out, to establish texts as they were intended by authors.[2] Traditional textual scholars implicitly recognize that a work of literature is a social event, at least in its original instance, because every work of literature begins as an intentional utterance from someone to someone. Less traditional scholars, like D. F. McKenzie and Jerome McGann, have for the first time directed attention to the social character of a literary work throughout its entire life. In fact, it was McGann who proposed that we consider literature as a social event:

[S]pecific poetic utterances—specific poems—are human acts occupying social space; as such, they most certainly are involved with extra-poetic operations. For poetry is itself one form of social activity, and no proper understanding of the nature of poetry can be made if the poem is abstracted from the experience of the poem, either at its point of origin or at any subsequent period.[3]

A poem, or any work of literature for that matter, can be properly understood only within the social contexts of each of its publications. Thus the "experience" of the poem is complex, and McGann proposes that we begin reconstructing it by dividing a work's life into two periods, the first its point of origin and the second that period when the work "passes entirely beyond the purposive control of the author."[4]

A study of the first period, which McGann calls the "originary textual moment,"[5] would focus on the author's "expressed intentions," indicated not only by his publication choices (the physical aspects of the book) but also in his "statements about his work."[6] And it would consider "other persons or groups involved in the initial process of production (e.g., collaborators, persons who may have commissioned the work, editors or amanuenses, etc.)."[7]

Frank Budgen's story, apparently, supplies us with evidence about the originary moment of *Ulysses,* because it assumes that *Ulysses* was still under Joyce's "purposive control." In fact, the story seems to extend Joyce's control over the novel, because Budgen expected his own readers to defer to Joyce's opinion of Buck. Writers, then, can influence distant readers—those out of earshot, so to speak—in any number of such ordinary ways. The packaging of the book, the writer's publicized comments on the text, the writer's public image—all influence the reader's understanding of the text. They are clues to the writer's attitude, just as surely as a speaker's tone, gestures, and facial expressions influence how a hearer interprets his or her speech. To treat literature as a social event, then, means that each work is an intentional utterance, that the writer meant to say something to a particular group of people. That utterance is interpreted properly to the degree that we understand the writer's intention.

But what happens when the writer is not present even in these ordinary ways? At the end of his lecture "What Is an Author?" Michel Foucault looks forward to the happy day when "tiresome" questions about authorship like "What has [the author] revealed of his most profound self in his language?" will be replaced by new questions like "Who controls . . . the modes of existence of this discourse?"[8] The old question becomes unimportant, and the new question can be asked because Foucault does not situate the "author" in the person of a writer who lived, died, perhaps married, put pen to paper, ate dinner, and drank a lot or a little or not at all. The author is a function of a discourse, a figure readers construct to enable certain attitudes to texts, a figure who has little to do with the historical writer:

These aspects of an individual, which we designate as an author (or which comprise an individual as an author), are projections, in terms always more or less psychological, of our way of handling texts: in the comparisons we make, the traits we extract as pertinent, the continuities we assign, or the exclusions we practice.[9]

In other words, the way we are used to reading books will dictate the way we imagine the "authors" of those books.

John Rodden has demonstrated this process of literary biography in his study of George Orwell's reputation. Rodden holds that Orwell's various reputations, the "rebel," the "common man," the "prophet," and the "saint," have as much to do with the uses to which particular groups of readers put his texts as with accurate biography. Liberals projected one intention on Orwell, and conservatives projected another, both by sifting the biographical data through their own sieve. Since the writer was not present, his readers were free to supply their own notion of the author.[10] This process is the transfer of authority McGann calls a work's secondary moment—that period when the work passes beyond the purposive control of the author and into the purposive control of someone else. The "author," after his or her death or departure from public life, becomes a "critical and historical reconstruction."[11] My own anecdote illustrates a secondary moment of *Ulysses*. In 1984 when I first entered graduate school, Joyce could no longer control anything. His work was authored by Ellmann, so to speak, for in this later context, forty-three years after Joyce died, Ellmann supplied the author's tone, gestures, and facial expressions.

But there is no reason to hold that works pass out of the author's control only after death. They might slip out of an author's control long before death, or the legacy of an author's self-fashioned image might linger long after. Thus, after a careful consideration of Budgen's book, we should recognize that his anecdote probably does not extend Joyce's authority at all. It might have nothing to do with Joyce. It might be Budgen's own attempt to control readers by manipulating their image of Joyce. At any rate, since it is hearsay recalled more than a decade after the event, we should not treat it as very likely evidence of Joyce's intention, for it is not nearly so weighty as Joyce's letters, for example, or a contemporary account, like Stuart Gilbert's diary entries that describe the composition process of *Finnegans Wake*. It reflects Budgen's intentions in 1934 rather than Joyce's intentions in 1922.

A McGannian analysis, then, must take a circuitous route, since it depends on a reconstruction of the "author," who is invented by whoever has authority over the author's reputation. It also requires a reconstruction of readers, because, just as we replace writers with our own version of the "author," we replace readers. Jon Klancher argues that "[t]he figure of the 'reader,' ubiquitous in contemporary criticism, most often appears in the fleshed-out principle of linguistic or literary competence, dressed as the implied, ideal, or projected reader of reader-response theory and *Rezeptionkritik*." [12] The figure of the reader, really a projection of the critic, will read texts with the assumption that authors mean their works to be read in the method prescribed by whatever fleshed-out principle of literary competence the critic subscribes to. The readers who haunt the minds of critics do not read books the same way real people read books. These specters read the way critics read. Klancher's purpose, which I find reasonable, is to replace these ubiquitous and insubstantial figures with flesh and bone.

This, then, is the difference between a reputation history and a literary biography. A biography projects onto a writer the prejudices of the biographer. The successful biography will assume authority over a writer's texts by constructing an author who justifies the biographer's way of reading. More often than not, and certainly in Joyce studies, biography reduces literature to a private act, not a social act. It gives us an author who seems to be speaking to friends, family, or to himself. Ellmann's biography begins with this very premise: "This book enters Joyce's life to reflect his complex, incessant joining of event and composition. The life of an artist, but particularly of Joyce, differs from the lives of other persons in that its events are becoming artistic sources even as they command his present attention" (*JJ*, 3). Reputation history holds that Joyce's relationship to his readers is far more important than his relationship to father, mother, wife, brothers, sisters, children, or friends, so the reputation history enters a writer's life not to reflect the incessant joining of private history and personal art but to reflect the interaction between published art and public history. A reputation history will reconstruct Joyce's knowledge of and attitude towards readers, and readers' knowledge of and attitude towards him. It will demonstrate how all representations of Joyce are attempts to garner authority over his work. Since fiction, like drama, is reinterpreted by each of its "productions," [13] each publication changes the meaning of a work not only because of the changed physical aspects of the text (although these changes are significant) but also because the social context of the work changes with each new publication. The readership changes. The historical context surrounding a work changes. And the author changes—not literally, of course, but the reputation of the writer, established by various authorities, changes. Reputation and reception histories are not only germane to textual studies, but they are also fundamental to any critical assessment of a work.[14]

Such a project is close to the new historicist reconstruction of "discourse," so I would classify my project as new historicist. What exactly defines the boundaries of a "discourse" is a debated issue. As Carolyn Porter points out, "framing the discursive field" is the issue "new historicists most urgently need to discuss."[15] Typically, new historicists treat "discourse" as coercive ideology, and they frame the discourse by studying extant texts, not only literary but also scientific, legal, religious, and popular texts. To define a discourse is to map out a power struggle or at least to expose the hidden exercise of power. The reconstruction of a discourse, then, should come close to defining the context in which a given work is published, read, and interpreted, because that context determines who exercises power through the work.

There is, of course, a danger that rather than attending to historical authors and readers, new historicists will project their own prejudices into their criticism. Frank Lentricchia suggests that new historicist studies do little more than reflect "the American academic intellectual in the contemporary moment of literary theory." Lentricchia attributes the determinism he sees in new historicists not to historical evidence but to "the typically anxious expression of post-Watergate American humanist intellectuals."[16] Richard Levin identifies certain new historicist maneuvers that seem to confirm Lentricchia's accusation. Authorial intention is replaced, Levin demonstrates, by the fiction of textual intention: "as a result of its new status as authorial surrogate, the text acquires a repertoire of new activities." Levin catalogues the repertoire: "the text has a project" (usually the reaffirmation of an oppressive ideology); "the text has strategies" (the techniques the text uses to win our sympathy for that ideology); "the text displaces" real conflicts with sham conflicts; "the text conceals . . . contradictions in its own ideological project"; "the text offers an imaginary resolution" (while the real conflicts remain unresolved); "the text offers pleasure" (in a sort of bread-and-circuses strategy); "the text [inadvertently] reveals . . . precisely what it was trying to conceal or suppress, its ideological contradictions or feminine subtext."[17] As Levin points out, subtexts will always reflect what the critic is looking for—class struggle in the case of Marxists; gender struggle in the case of feminists. The critic's intention takes the place of the writer's intention.

Let me examine one example of what I consider to be a valuable work of recent Joyce criticism to demonstrate how even at our best we still efface writers and readers. Richard Brown's *James Joyce and Sexuality* proposes to reconstruct the discourse of sexuality in which Joyce's fiction was published. Brown sets up his project by dismissing certain popular critical concerns, like "epiphany" and "exile," because of their irrelevance to "contemporary issues and to a contemporary reading public." He proposes that Joyce criticism ought to elucidate "the implication of his fiction in . . . the relevant context of contemporary ideas." Brown places his own project in the company of Michel Foucault's work on the discourse of sexuality, because Foucault "encourages us to attend to a new sense of the relationship between spoken and written attitudes and social and political constraints." So far, so good. But Brown diminishes the need for historical evidence: "For [Foucault] conventional social history is not so important as is trying to identify the ways in which sexuality is 'put into discourse.'" By dismissing historical methods in his historical study of "contemporary issues" and "a contemporary reading public," Brown can rely on written texts, especially books, which is a typical new historicist tendency. Brown ascertains sexual "attitudes" by reconstructing a discourse of sexuality, which he finds embodied in the books in Joyce's personal library. Through such a method, Brown claims, "it is possible to discern the attitudes that Joyce's fiction takes on important contemporary issues." [18] Though Brown does not completely divorce Joyce from his texts (for example, he does consult Joyce's letters, as Jerome McGann advocates he should if he were to treat Joyce's fiction as a social event), note that in Brown's sentence Joyce's fiction, not Joyce himself, adopts an "attitude" on contemporary issues. Brown employs one of the rhetorical maneuvers Levin exposed.

That sleight of speech is important, because discerning the "attitude" of Joyce's fiction can then be limited to a discourse defined solely by books published near the turn of the century and available in Europe. Brown carefully reconstructs a "discourse" of sexuality contained by such books, but his focus on these books leads him to statements such as, "During the nineteenth century few questions were so high on the agenda for discussion and reform as questions of marriage." [19] The historian might sensibly ask, *Whose* agenda? Brown ascribes the agenda to a period and narrows it no further, leaving us to understand that it belongs to the nineteenth century itself—an attribution so broad that it is nearly meaningless. In the next sentence Brown points out that Charles Dickens dealt with marriage in *Hard Times,* and that Dickens's interest in marriage "gives us some indication of the felt importance of the marriage issue at the time." It does give us some indication, but to define the boundaries of this "discourse" we would have to discover who actually read Dickens. Brown implies that everyone did: "at the time" has the same rhetorical effect as the personification of the nineteenth century. Brown reconstructs the discourse of sexuality through a limited number of printed texts, and he projects that discourse onto the "attitudes" of populations so large that they go undefined. If there was any "agenda," it belonged to Joyce's library, not to a definable population. Brown's statement really means that among books in Joyce's personal collection few issues come up as often as marriage and marriage reform.

The tendency to replace authorial intention with textual intention helps Brown sidestep complicated historical verification, which otherwise would qualify his assertions.[20] This helps simplify the process of reconstructing a "discourse" immensely, because excluding the author invariably leads to excluding readers. So long as Joyce's fiction adopts an attitude, we can stay in the libraries—a relatively finite project—to discern the discourse. But once we consider Joyce's attitude, the boundaries of the discourse explode into realms literary critics usually avoid.

For example, the demographic history of Ireland (especially the unusual demographics of marriage in that country) must have contributed to Joyce's attitude "on contemporary issues." Brown makes no attempt to account for this remarkable social history. But this history is probably more important to reconstructing the social milieu (at least among Joyce's Irish readers) than are any of the books Brown discusses. That Dublin had an undersupply of eligible bachelors in 1900 was probably more important to Joyce's attitude towards marriage than was Dickens's *Hard Times*. Any number of such extratextual factors must have influenced Joyce, and, likewise, the discourse Joyce's readers shared cannot reasonably be defined by books in Joyce's personal library. The discourse of sexuality Brown discovers may never have existed except, perhaps, among those with regular access to Joyce's library. In other words, Brown reconstructs the contemporary issues surrounding Joyce's work without attaching those issues to any contemporary reading public. The unfortunate consequence is that Brown's author probably is no more accurate than any conventional biographer's, because it is a fiction invented to sustain his method of criticism.

My book, I hope, avoids this pitfall by restoring real intentions to the literary act—first the author's and later others'. I tell the story of four important episodes in the history of Joyce's reputation. Chapter 1 sets the stage for these episodes by reconstructing an accurate version of Joyce's intentions, at least in his early career, which serves as the standard against which I compare subsequent versions of the author. Most of the evidence suggests that before 1914, Joyce believed his main audience was the Dublin middle class. As a consequence of necessity, he published in London, but this circumstance of the book trade did not seriously influence his first purpose. He wrote to improve his country. He felt that he was rescuing his own class—the newly enfranchised but economically stagnant, educated, urban Catholics—from what he considered a disabling cultural nationalism. In 1904 serious Irish writers could not escape the political battles that saturated Dublin's culture, and Joyce never tried. He wanted his art to have the kind of persuasive effect on readers that we today consider rhetorical as opposed to literary. His weapon— not yet silence, exile, or cunning—was an uncompromising, unromantic, hard-featured realism.

But in 1914 Joyce fell into the hands of Ezra Pound, T. S. Eliot, and their readers, first in *The Egoist* and later in *Criterion*. This event dramatically shifted Joyce's fortunes: he finally got into print and secured an audience. Strictly speaking, this might not constitute a "secondary textual moment," because Joyce was still alive, he was at least partially complicit in the change, and he had not yet begun writing his most celebrated book. Nevertheless, Joyce had to surrender his literary reputation, which never again would be under his complete control. Chapter 2 reveals how Ezra Pound and T. S. Eliot changed Joyce from an Irish writer into an avant-garde, cosmopolitan writer, shucking off his parochial husk to make him serve their literary movement. It has become something of a given in Joyce criticism to treat Pound and Eliot as the initiators of two competing schools of Joyce criticism, one descending from Eliot to Hugh Kenner and the other from Pound to Richard Ellmann.[21] But outside the small courts of criticism these opponents look very much alike. Despite their differences, Pound and Eliot collaborated to present Joyce as a writer disengaged with politics and wholly unconcerned with the effect of his fiction on readers. In short, their Joyce was an egoist, a writer writing not to his fellow countrymen but to other writers, the great living and the greater dead.

Pound and Eliot launched Joyce's reputation on a trajectory that would take it through this century. In the 1930s Morris Ernst, who defended *Ulysses* in its celebrated obscenity trials, originally meant to legalize the book on the grounds of its social utility. Borrowing a strategy he had used before—in his defense of Radclyffe Hall's *The Well of Loneli-*

ness, for example—he hoped to convince the courts that *Ulysses* was useful to society as a rare and realistic psychological document. But, as the Ernst archives at the University of Texas show, very quickly he discovered that his best defense was to promote Pound's and Eliot's Joyce, because the law believed that elevated, isolated, geniuses were incapable of obscenity. This judicial attitude, which I detail in Chapter 3, depends on a peculiar characterization of the relationship between a writer and readers. The "classic"—for so books by geniuses were labeled—is incomprehensible except to a safe coterie of educated and wealthy readers. Because this version of Joyce was false, Ernst was obliged to support his case with misleading and sometimes invented evidence. Woolsey's famous decision in 1933 gained Joyce a wider circulation, but at the price of a reputation that continued to strip his work of the ability to affect people, for if readers cannot be aroused neither can they be rescued from a disabling ideology.

Chapter 4 evaluates the most enduring influence on Joyce's reputation, Richard Ellmann's *James Joyce*. The Ellmann papers at the University of Tulsa and a collection of letters between Stanislaus Joyce and Ellmann's friend, Ellsworth Mason, provide a revealing glimpse into the making of that biography. I argue that Ellmann's critical biases—biases he shared with the profession at large—were projected onto his subject. Ellmann's Joyce looks very much like an American liberal during the Cold War, a champion of tolerance and civil liberties, but lukewarm and ineffectual as a socialist reformer. Ellmann's biography, which treats Joyce's fiction mainly as a refashioning of his life, supposes that Joyce was in conversation with himself, sometimes with his wife, but never really with a reading public.

This version of Joyce served the needs of the Joyce Industry in the 1950s and '60s, which, following general trends in the American academy, tended to remove literature from the historical contexts of its publication. Chapter 5 narrates the story of Joyce's canonization, which transferred authority over his reputation to the academy. Naturally, academics were drawn to the image of Joyce the Genius, and so they further refined and solidified that reputation, until it seemed that Joyce intended professors to be his readers. This version of Joyce served the Industry's needs: mainly the need to publish. Criticism, of course, has changed a great deal since the early years of the Joyce Industry, so we find today that this image, bequeathed to us by Pound and Eliot, inhibits what we do with his fiction. Ultimately, then, this book should be taken as an argument for abandoning the author who we, for so long, have believed wrote Joyce's books.

That argument should not be construed as an assault on critics. As will be obvious in Chapter 5, I could not have made this argument without the generous and frank help of many Joyce critics. What is not evident is the encouragement and guidance many critics gave me, especially when I presented sections of this book at conferences in Seville, Dublin, Miami, and Vancouver. Joyce criticism, like the whole profession, is dynamic, perhaps even progressive. I believe that the enduring image of Joyce has stalled change, so it was in the spirit of critical progress that I wrote this book.

I certainly am not taking the first step in this direction. I put my work into the context of many new, historical considerations of Joyce and his work, including recent books by Emer Nolan, Robert Spoo, Thomas Hofheinz, Maria Tymoczko, Enda Duffy, Vincent Cheng, and James Fairhall.[22] More specifically, Jeffrey Segall's 1993 *Joyce in America* analyzes Joyce's reputation, and Edward L. Bishop's 1994 article, "Re: Covering *Ulysses*," treats that novel in each of its publishing contexts.[23] Though portions of the present study were written before Segall's and Bishop's work came out, it should be considered a response to theirs, disputing them, confirming them, filling gaps they left. Plenty of gaps are left yet. Two I considered but, in the end, purposely left out. The first is the story of Joyce's own role in promoting his public image. Though it has been touched on here and there, that topic is ripe for research. For example, discussing Paul Leon's (and, presumably, Joyce's) insistence that Bennett Cerf not include the Linati scheme in the American edition of *Ulysses*, Bishop cites "the delicate relationship between cultural capital and real capital."[24] He implies that by constructing a public image of the autonomous artist, Joyce increased his cultural value, which preserved his stature while increasing his share of the book market. But Bishop does not pursue the issue beyond a couple of pages. Another gap is the story of the Joyce Industry outside America. Fritz Senn has publicly encouraged scholars to use the records he has collected in Zurich concerning Joyce studies in the 1960s and '70s. My failure to address Joyce's European reputation was brought to my attention when I presented a part of Chapter 5 at the Joyce Symposium in Seville in 1994. With some regret, I leave that issue to an abler scholar. As the proverb goes, these two episodes are another story. I make no pretense to have exhausted the topic. I hope I have helped open the topic up.

Joyce the Propagandist

1

"Propagandist" is a deceptive term, so I want to dismiss a couple of its associations before I label Joyce one. We usually think of propaganda as bad and short-lived (like the Nazi movies and communist novels), as opposed to "art," which, having no clear political end, is good and timeless. William Wimsatt and Cleanth Brooks use this meaning of "propagandist" in their influential history, *Literary Criticism,* which applies the term to nineteenth-century realists. Wimsatt and Brooks discredit Tolstoy and Zola (and, incidentally, Marxist literary critics) with the opprobrium "propagandist[s] for social progress," because the realists considered themselves to be social activists and their literary works to be socially active, and Wimsatt and Brooks felt that social action was not a proper end of art.[1] I do accept their link between "activism" and "realism." After all, Zola and Ibsen and Tolstoy openly professed the political intentions of their literature. But I reject the slur against propaganda, because I admire Joyce and know that he considered himself to be an advocate of social progress and that he wanted the publication of *Dubliners* to change society. This claim is not as radical as it sounds. In the last ten years or so a new school of criticism—what we might call the "realist" school—has grown up around *Dubliners.* Essays by Paul Delany, Robert Scholes, James Fairhall, Florence Walzl, Margaret Chestnutt, and Trevor Williams demand that we reassess Joyce's literary reputation.

That reputation, at least insomuch as it regards

Dubliners, was more or less settled for forty years. Ever since Richard Levin and Charles Shattuck compared *Dubliners* to *Ulysses* in their 1944 essay, "First Flight to Ithaca," the critical community has treated Joyce's earlier book as the first shot fired in a revolution of the word.[2] So we are used to thinking of Joyce's early work as the embryonic stage of his later high modernist texts. Interpreting the literal or naturalistic level of *Dubliners* has come to be viewed as less important, less sophisticated, and less valuable than explicating what is called the "symbolic" or deeper levels. This prejudice was institutionalized by New Criticism in the 1950s. Richard Kain and Marvin Magalaner, for example, were among the first to fault Joyce's early readers for ignoring the symbols: "Beneath the 'awkward' and faltering surface of his naturalistic dung heap, Joyce included much more . . . than most sophisticated contemporary critics give him credit for."[3] Magalaner went so far as to suggest that readers who do not explicate "all possible levels of meaning in the works of a complex writer" were "bumbling commentators."[4] By 1956, when Brewster Ghiselin's seminal "The Unity of Joyce's *Dubliners*" appeared, the stupidity of "realistic" readings was cemented in the minds of critics.[5] Even Robert Scholes and A. Walton Litz, in their fine critical edition of *Dubliners,* censured early readers of *Dubliners* for not recognizing the "highly developed symbolic pattern" with which they believed Joyce structured the book (*D,* 298).

We have come a long way since New Criticism. No one has called Paul Delany or Florence Walzl a bumbler. But we have retained this prejudice against realism, as if suggesting that Joyce was a realist were equal to confessing that he was a bad artist. Brenda Maddox, in her introduction to the 1990 Bantam Classic edition of *Dubliners,* wrote that "[a]t first glance, the book is a fine example of late-nineteenth-century naturalism. . . . Yet beneath the naturalistic surface lies a revolutionary modernist text." And so she alludes to the naïveté of George Roberts, the Dublin publisher who accepted, and then, repenting, rejected and burned the book in 1910.[6] As recently as 1993, John S. Kelly, in his afterword to Hans Gabler's *Dubliners,* construed Joyce's "mean" style as an attempt to maximize the "symbolic and mythical resonances" of his allusions.[7] Most of the articles in the recent *Dubliners* issue of *Style* are written with this attitude.[8] The 1991 special issue of *JJQ* on *Dubliners* is a mixed bag—about half of the contributors seem to have complacently acquiesced to the prejudice against realism, and nearly all deny the possibility that the stories are straightforward. Critics of *Dubliners* nearly always begin their essays with the axiom that the stories are deceptively transparent.[9] That they are merely transparent is unthinkable, because clarity is bad. Joyce must have intended them to be opaque.

Joyce's private notes about Aquinas and Aristotle in the Paris notebooks and Richard Ellmann's biography have been the most influential extratextual evidence of intention. But, as I will indicate below, I believe the notebooks are less important than Joyce's published critical writings, and Ellmann's biography was itself a product of 1950s criticism. Despite the work of recent critics, then, New Criticism's characterization of Joyce's early artistic intentions has been settled since the debates about his aesthetics in the 1950s. But that view of Joyce is wrong. Between 1904 and 1907, when he was writing *Dubliners* and *Stephen Hero,* Joyce was a political writer trying to establish a tradition of realism in Ireland.

Joyce's First Readers

Perhaps this implication has been missed because we tend to forget that Joyce was not writing for literary critics. We forget that before 1914 his primary audience was the Irish. According to Stanislaus, Joyce "always thought that his stories could interest only Dubliners and he struggled desperately to have his book published in Dublin." [10] In the summer of 1904, just before Joyce left Dublin for Paris and eventually Trieste, he began writing sketches for *The Irish Homestead.* Three were published in the late summer and fall of 1904: "The Sisters," "Eveline," and "After the Race." A fourth, "Hallow Eve" (which became "Clay"), was rejected or postponed by the editor in January or February of 1905 (*Letters II,* 83). This fourth story was the last Joyce tried to get published in Irish periodicals, because by April he apparently began to conceive of a wider circulation.

He told Stanislaus he planned to offer "Hallow Eve" to the London *Daily Mail* (*Letters II,* 87), and in July he instructed Stanislaus to try to place the fifth story, "The Boarding House," in "an English or American paper" (*Letters II,* 92). Apparently this letter reflects a shift in his publishing intentions. For the first time, he spoke of offering the stories to the English public in a book: "when *Dubliners* is complete I intend to offer it to Heinemann" (*Letters II,* 97). But William Heinemann, one of the new, progressive, small publishers in London, rejected it, so on 15 October 1905, when the collection numbered twelve (of its eventual fifteen) stories, Joyce offered it to Grant Richards, another London publisher. He implied to Richards that he was aiming for an international audience: "The second book I have ready is called *Dubliners.* . . . I do not think that any writer has yet presented Dublin to the world" (*Letters II*, 122). Joyce went on in his letter to contest the English stereotype of Dublin, which suggests that he wanted the book to affect English readers. And elsewhere Joyce mentioned sales in England and America (*Letters II*, 131) and the timeliness of Irish issues in England (*Letters II*, 129, 177).

But Joyce seems to have made these points to sell his book to London publishers rather than to describe his artistic intentions. As I will discuss below, such concessions to the English market were inevitable for Irish writers, if they wanted their books to be available in Ireland.[11] When push came to shove, when he defended the book against criticism by the printer, Joyce made it clear that the decision to send the manuscript to London instead of Dublin was almost surely a matter of practical necessity and did not represent a revision of his target audience:

> The printer denounces *Two Gallants* and *Counterparts*. A Dubliner would denounce *Ivy Day in the Committee Room*. . . . The Irish priest will denounce *The Sisters*. The Irish boarding-house keeper will denounce *The Boarding-house*. (*Letters II*, 134)

Richards, with good reason, was concerned with the English reception, while Joyce cited the inevitable reaction of Irish readers. English readers, apparently, were little more than eavesdroppers on his conversation with his compatriots.[12]

Our failure to recognize Joyce's patient has led us to misunderstand his diagnosis. Joyce told Constantine Curran that he wanted *Dubliners* to "betray the soul of . . . paralysis which many consider a city," and he told Richards that "I chose Dublin for the scene because that city seemed to me the centre of paralysis" (*Letters I*, 55, and *Letters II*, 134). With few exceptions, critics tend to regard paralysis as a moral or spiritual failing general to humankind in the modern world, a disease fundamental to our modern age.[13] But globalizing paralysis denies any real possibility of curing the disease and, therefore, of any persuasive or exhortative purpose for Joyce's book; and it denies that paralysis was unique in Ireland, or at least unique to small, Catholic, colonized countries struggling to achieve democracy and industry. But the paralysis Joyce exposes in *Dubliners* is specific. It affects only his own class, the rising Catholic middle class in Ireland.[14] The book should not be applied to populations in England, to populations in America, or to the general human condition in the modern world, because the paralysis derived from Ireland's unique conditions and from the unique way the Irish dealt with those conditions.

First and foremost, paralysis was economic. In 1907 Joyce wrote that the "backdrop to this sad comedy" of home rule politics

> is the spectacle of a population which diminishes year by year with mathematical regularity, of the uninterrupted emigration to the United States or Europe of Irishmen for whom *the economic and intellectual conditions* of their native land are unbearable. (*CW*, 190) [emphasis added]

Joyce was not alone in thus characterizing Irish society. As Kevin Sullivan has pointed out, Joyce's friend Tom Kettle, the most promising and admired of the young men in Joyce's University College of Dublin crowd, a future member of Parliament for Tyrone and a professor of economics, wrote: "Ireland is admitted by all to be unprogressive: as witness, when it is half-past twelve in London it is only five minutes past twelve in Dublin." [15] In a more serious vein Kettle accused Dublin of having "the weakest . . . economic structure" among "all the great cities of the United Kingdom." Its problem was that wealth was concentrated in a parasitical class of "government officials, professional men, annuitants" who drew their incomes "not from the volume of local production, but from that larger stream of national production." [16] Describing the labor strikes of 1913, Kettle echoed not only Joyce's concern with self-delusion, but the metaphor of an ignorant, diseased society:

> In the perplexity spoken of there is probably a considerable leaven of self-deception. The dead weight of details overwhelms us, largely because we lack the courage of the obvious. We are muscle-bound, not precisely by downright egotism or dullness, *but by that unaccountable palsy,* sometimes experienced, in which mind and brain seem to be cloven into unrelated halves. . . . The simple truth is that, in contemporary conditions, what we call the Labour Unrest is just as normal *as pain in a disease.*[17] [emphasis added]

Kettle's prescription for the palsy differed from Joyce's (Kettle joined the Parliamentary Party), but the diagnoses by the two University College of Dublin graduates are strikingly similar. The country's progress—especially its economic progress, after which all else would follow—was paralyzed.

Joyce depicted this paralysis in a number of his cityscapes. For example, James Duffy's room looks out on a "disused distillery" (*D*, 107). The one distiller we meet in *Dubliners,* Cotter in "The Sisters," is, appropriately enough, old and probably retired. At the turn of the century, distilling was a decaying industry in Dublin. The decay was partly the effect of large-scale production and partly the effect of the market, which was dampened by temperance drives. In 1840, eighty-six distilleries flourished in Ireland, but by the 1860s that number had dwindled to twenty-two. Through the '70s, '80s, and '90s, the industry rebounded, largely through exports, which had increased eightfold by 1907. But competitive export required large-scale production, and small distilleries were squeezed out. Furthermore, in the 1890s, blended whiskeys, which were distilled in Belfast (Dublin distilleries made pot-still whiskeys), accounted for most of the increases in export. By 1907 Belfast accounted for 63 percent of exported whiskey. Likewise, the beer-brewing industry increased its exports in the last decades of the century, but brewers employed fewer and fewer workers as large-scale operations took over the industry. In 1837 Ireland had 247 breweries; in 1901 that number had dropped to 41. Guinness accounted for more and more of the domestic and especially the export market, so Dublin brewed 96 percent of Ireland's exported beer, which reversed the trend in distilling. But the boom in exports in other industries directly contributed to the decay of Dublin: "The effects of the export boom were . . . narrow in their diffusion—diffused among a comparatively small number of firms more especially in the north." [18]

Dublin, literally, was falling down.[19] Factories were disused. Shops fell into disrepair. And the large mansions that once housed the city's moneyed class had become slums. The latter appear in Little Chandler's perambulations, which bring him "under the shadow of the gaunt spectral mansions in which the old nobility of Dublin had roistered" (D, 72).[20] By 1891, the demographics of the city reflected its economic collapse. According to L. M. Cullen, nearly four-fifths of the city's workers lived in the inner city, while half of its clerks and two-thirds of its "gentlefolk" lived in the suburbs.[21]

Only a generation before Joyce the material prospects of the Catholic middle class had been much rosier. As John Hutchinson explains, in the nineteenth century Britain was compelled "to educate increasing proportions of [its] populations for technical positions in the military and civil apparatus" of the empire. Previously the exclusive domain of Protestants, the Indian civil service was opened to Catholics in 1855; in 1870 the home civil service, parts of the Irish civil service, and the army were opened to Irish Catholics. Joyce was in this rising tide, and he was on the wave's crest: one of "those who attended [preparatory] schools such as Castleknock, Clongowes and Belvedere and the university colleges."

Joyce's education promised him a place among the relatively small number of Catholics educated at a university.[22]

But the schools of higher learning were still, even in Joyce's day, essentially segregated. The middle decades of the 1800s would be taken up with the "university question" because Trinity College, which was a Protestant institution, enjoyed a virtual monopoly on higher education in Ireland. The problem, as F. S. L. Lyons points out, was that the Catholic hierarchy, on religious grounds, discouraged Catholics from attending both Trinity College and the secular Queen's colleges established by Sir Robert Peel in the 1840s. Trinity, contributing to its unpopularity among Catholics, tried its hardest to disown native Irishness (which meant "Catholic" Ireland). Meanwhile, the Unionists opposed any public support of a Catholic university on the grounds that it would support home rule, which, in their eyes, was equivalent to Rome rule.[23] In 1854 Archbishop Cullen succeeded in founding the Catholic University in Dublin, and he succeeded also in securing Cardinal Newman as rector. But the denial of public funds and the refusal of the government to recognize degrees conferred by the young university ensured that its graduates would not be able to compete with Protestants for civil service and professional careers.[24]

The University Education (Ireland) Act of 1879, sponsored by the conservative prime minister Disraeli, combined the Queen's colleges and Catholic University into one nondenominational Royal University. In 1883 administration of the Dublin branch—University College, Dublin, or UCD—was taken over by the Jesuits, although they were severely restricted in what they could do. As Sullivan describes it, the curriculum Joyce himself took at UCD, compared to, say, the curriculum at Trinity, or even at the high school–level Belvedere and Clongowes, was a joke.[25] (The only respectable branch of UCD was the medical school in Cecilia Street, which, as the surest avenue of success, naturally enough attracted the best talents among students.) But if the education at UCD was subpar, most commentators agree that the vitality of student life in the decade between 1895 and 1905 was exceptional. As Sullivan puts it, the "true center of intellectual vitality at University college" was the "undergraduate societies and academies" that the students organized, not the formal education offered by the school.[26] The students took the burden of education upon their own shoulders. The litany of Joyce's fellow students, familiar not only to Joyceans but also to Irish historians, demonstrates how extraordinary was Joyce's company at UCD: Tom Kettle, journalist, economist, and M.P.; Francis Sheehy-Skeffington, feminist, pacifist, and journalist; Hugh Kennedy, Chief Justice of Ireland; Arthur Clery, professor of law; Constantine Curran, literary critic and professor; John O'Sullivan, Minister of Education; George Clancy, mayor of Limerick; Hannah Sheehy, feminist, journalist, and educator.[27] An exceptional group of young men and women, the sons and daughters of the first generation of a Catholic professional class, were thrown together in the main Catholic university in the country, bad as it was.

Despite his education and the success of the previous generation, Joyce's prospects under the status quo were not good. The graduates of UCD should have acquired better positions than as workers, farmers, clerks, and schoolteachers, but they were not assured a place among the prosperous because they competed with the children of an established class of Protestant professionals, educated at Trinity, who held the inside track to success.[28] Even as late as 1901, Catholics were underrepresented in the more prestigious professions. While Catholics accounted for 75 percent of the general population, only 44 percent of the barristers and solicitors, 43 percent of the physicians, and 42 percent of the architects, accountants, and civil engineers were Catholic. These percentages reflect little improvement over conditions in 1881 and only a 10 percent improvement over 1871. The number of jobs in the legal profession in 1901 was nearly the same as in 1871 (2,216 and 2,215). Medical jobs actually decreased in number (from 2,441 in 1871 to 2,221 in 1901). In thirty years, certainly during Joyce's youth, the expanding Catholic middle class could make little headway into the stagnant higher professions. Admittedly, the population of the entire country was falling in these thirty years, but that decline itself indicates an undersupply of jobs for the new generation of highly educated Catholic men and women, many of whom sought work abroad. According to the 1901 census, only 3,376 Catholics out of 3,308,661, about 0.1 percent, held jobs that required a university education (barristers and solicitors, doctors, architects, accountants, and civil engineers).[29] The only Catholic businessmen who regularly advanced to prosperity were vintners and publicans; "only the lower grades" of the Irish civil service and of business were "in practice" open to Catholics; and, according to one historian, below "the better salaried white-collars . . . there were virtually no Protestants."[30] Suffering discrimination, "young Catholic graduates were faced with unemployment or underemployment, or were forced to accept lower status positions in the Irish civil service or in the teaching profession."[31]

Despite these poor employment prospects, middle-class Catholics were going to run the country. The Local Government Act of 1898, a dramatic attempt at conciliation by the Balfour government, reformed local government in Ireland. Hitherto dominated by the Ascendancy, local government passed into the hands of "the Catholic and nationalist majority." As F. S. L. Lyons writes,

> The Local Government Act was not far short of revolutionary, for it marked a decisive shift in power and influence over the country at large away from the landlord ascendancy class and toward "the democracy" of farmers, shopkeepers and publicans.[32]

At stake during the revolution was how this new class of Catholics would view itself, and that self-image, at least partially constructed by literary culture, would direct Ireland's political policies for at least the next generation.

Politics and the Literary Industry in Ireland

Irish readers in the nineteenth century did not think of themselves as a population separate from English readers. They could hardly have done so, since a native Irish publishing industry simply did not exist. Publishing had flourished once. Before the 1801 Act of Union, Dublin publishers produced cheap reprint editions to sell in Ireland, England, and especially in America after the revolution.[33] The Irish trade peaked between 1780 and 1785, when exports topped £10,000 per year and imported books were valued at less than £3,000 per year. M. Pollard's analysis of the books listed by Irish traders in the middle of the eighteenth century indicates that many Irish publications had been written by the Irish themselves. In fact, two-thirds of the subscription trade (which dominated the Irish industry) presented original works by Irish writers—in the fields of literature, history, religion, science, and law—written for Irish readers.[34] These readers were not exclusively of the noble, gentlemanly, legislative, or wealthy classes. According to Richard Cole's list of 203 private libraries sold in the late eighteenth century (many sold because their owners were leaving the country), only 67 belonged to the landed nobility and gentry; only twelve others belonged to government workers. Though we cannot assume this sample accurately represents the Irish reading culture, it is our best estimate, and it includes 64 clergy (39 Protestant, 25 Catholic); 36 lawyers; 11 men of letters; 5 physicians; 4 merchants; and 4 soldiers. These libraries represent a vibrant reading culture in Dublin before the Act of Union.

Even so, the Irish readership cultivated by the native book industry were neither "Gaelic" nor "Catholic." Practically no books were printed in the Irish language, and the inventories of libraries owned by Catholics are distinguished by their lack of books printed in Ireland.[35] French and Latin books, especially books on theology, dominated the shelves of Catholics, while the Irish reprints of popular English authors, from Johnson to Gibbon, were hardly represented. To the extent that the Irish publishing industry did nourish an Irish readership, those readers were decidedly Protestant. And, despite the subscription trade, most of the writers were English. Cole's list of the most popular books in 203 Irish private libraries is headed by Johnson's *Dictionary, Lives of the Poets, Rambler, Works,* and his edition of Shakespeare's plays; Gibbon's *Decline and Fall of the Roman Empire* and *Miscellaneous Works;* Sterne's *Works, Tristram Shandy,* and *Sentimental Journey;* Boswell's *Life of Johnson* and *An Account of Corsica;* and Smollett's *History of England* and *Don Quixote.* Goldsmith's *History of the Earth* and *Roman History* are the only Irish contributions to the list of best-sellers. Likewise, Pollard's examination of Arthur Browne's library, sold in 1805, indicates that 52 percent of his books were printed in England, 26 percent in Ireland, and 21 percent on the Continent.[36] So, despite the undeniable sense of political independence shared by Dublin's readers, even before the Act of Union, Dublin's literary culture was dominated by London.

The Union extended England's dominance by destroying the Irish publishing industry. After 1801, exports fell below £3,000, while imports soared to over £20,000 per year.[37] Copyright law made the reprint business illegal, and special tariffs made it nearly impossible to import paper to Ireland.[38] The political climate and these restrictions dispatched the last of three waves of Irish bookmen to America, and this wave completely drained the Irish industry.[39] That many of these emigrants were patriots compelled to leave because they lost the 1798 Rebellion suggests how thoroughly the native publishing industry was involved in nationalist politics even if it was not culturally separated from England. As we might expect, the catastrophe that fell on the Irish bookmen ruined any distinctly Irish community of readers. Those who had not been obliged to flee to America—the remaining "nobility, gentry, members of Parliament, and people of wealth and culture in general"—flocked to London. "The Union," according to Cole, "deprived the Irish book trade of large numbers of its audience."[40] Citing nineteenth-century Irish historians, Cole asserts that the loss of Ireland's independent parliament made Dublin an intellectual "backwater" of London. Although Cole does not develop the point, the clear implication is that Irish intellectual culture, which had been self-consciously independent of (if not very different from) England in the heady years while the parliament and book trade flourished, withered after the Act of Union.

The destruction of the Irish printing industry ensured English cultural dominance for another century. Nineteenth-century Irish readers had nothing to buy except English and American books. To the extent that it participated in a literary culture, nineteenth-century Ireland was indeed an English backwater. Without a native publishing industry, the Irish reading public would be hard put to identify itself as a group politically or culturally separate from the English reading public. The arrival of Catholics in the civil service and the national schools in Ireland, which for a couple of decades in the middle of the century succeeded in teaching Protestants and Catholics in the same classrooms four days each week, contributed to the homogenization of cultures. Whatever the cause, the rising middle class looked to England for its literary culture. With a few notable exceptions, like the Young Ireland contributors to *The Nation* (which explicitly encouraged separatist politics), Irish writers still wrote for English publishers and, consequently, for English readers. The inevitable departure from Ireland and arrival in London of Irish men of letters bears testimony to this fact as late as the 1880s, when writers like Yeats and George Moore depended on England to publish and sell their books. As Grattan Freyer puts it, "It was unpalatable [for Yeats] but true that poetry and prose by Irish writers must aim at being read largely by an English audience or not at all."[41] Chandler in Joyce's "A Little Cloud" recognizes this point, though he does not share Yeats's distaste for it:

> He would never be popular: he saw that. He could not sway the crowd but he might appeal to a little circle of kindred minds. The English critics, perhaps, would recognize him as one of the Celtic school by reason of the melancholy tone of his poems. (*D*, 74)

Not only is Chandler's imagined poetry read and assessed by the English, those critics reduce it to a mere branch or "school" of English poetry that is defined by a colonial stereotype: Irish melancholy. Chandler is so drowned in English literary culture that he longs to be its adjunct. He does not or cannot conceive of writing exclusively to his fellow Dubliners.

The literary revivalists understood this problem, so they created an *Irish* readership—a population of readers conscious of being culturally distinct from the English.[42] They founded the Irish Literary Society (in London, attended by Irish émigrés) and the National Literary Societies (in Ireland) in 1891 and 1892 to promote the reading and discussion of Irish texts, and they established The Cuala Press and the Maunsel Company to publish the books demanded by these readers.[43] They organized lending libraries to supply books to the societies (and to supply subscriptions to the new publishers). As John Hutchinson puts it, the revivalists were trying to create "a national public opinion educated in Irish literature, legends and folklore."[44] The societies, significantly enough, "found their constituency among the middle-class Catholic antiquarians and littérateurs to whom Young Ireland was sacred."[45] In 1899, Yeats established the Irish Literary Theatre with the express hope of securing "a wider audience" among these people.[46] The efforts to promote an Irish culture did not entirely and immediately succeed. Douglas Hyde's now famous speech, "On the necessity of de-Anglicizing Ireland," was greeted with "polite incredulity" by the National Literary Society in 1892.[47] But by 1900, for the first time in generations, Irish writers could write to an Irish rather than an English audience. And that audience, the public whose opinion the revival sought to influence, was the Catholic middle class.

Conflicts within the new literary industry, then, should be viewed as competing efforts to fashion this class's consciousness. As Yeats's contempt for the middle class demonstrates, the literary revival tried to impose a consciousness from outside. According to Denis Donoghue, Yeats wanted to

> suppress—or at least intimidate—the new, petit-bourgeois class, the small shopkeepers "fumbling in a greasy till," which Yeats despised and feared. These were the people to whom Daniel O'Connell gave voice; Catholic, but not at all emancipated from the penury of their daily interests.[48]

Other members of the revival might have been less secure in their prejudice, and Donoghue may exaggerate when he asserts that Yeats meant to "suppress" or "intimidate" this class. After all, he knew they were his audience, so it is more likely he expected to change them utterly. But what cannot be denied is that the revival tried to impose on its audience an alien culture. The revival is attacked today by the Field Day group of Irish critics for the legacy of its success—cultural nationalism.[49]

I should distinguish here political nationalism from cultural nationalism, because this difference accounts for the difference between Joyce's politics and the politics of the literary revival.[50] The revival was culturally nationalist, while the Nationalist Party, first under Parnell and later under John Redmond, is usually described as politically nationalist. While few commentators make much of this distinction, Hutchinson draws instructive differences between the two groups, not only in Ireland but in all nationalist movements. The goal of the failed political nationalists, like Parnell, had been "Ireland's normalization among the nations of the world by the regaining of her independent *statehood*."[51] Political nationalism, unlike cultural nationalism, does not recognize essential distinctions between nations. Growing out of rational, liberal eighteenth-century political thought, it held a "conception of the nation that looks forward ultimately to a common humanity transcending cultural differences."[52] The parliamentarians, from Parnell to Redmond, wanted to liberate Ireland's politics, not its culture, from England. The political nationalist saw no need to de-Anglicize Ireland.

But the English way of doing things threatened cultural nationalists, because England was modern. Cultural nationalism "is a response to the erosion of traditional identities and status orders by the modernization process," which Hutchinson defines as "those changes that occur in economic, cultural, political and military institutions when scientific principles are applied to solve problems of social and natural life."[53] In other words, "modernization" is nearly synonymous with the liberal political philosophy that dominated European politics in the second half of the nineteenth century. Because they took as their opponent not foreign sovereignty but modernity, and because modernity was personified for the Irish by the English, the cultural nationalists undertook a program of de-Anglicizing Ireland by promoting "historico-cultural revivals in order to propound the idea of the nation as a moral community."[54] This kind of moral regeneration resurrects a culture's supposed dormant and ancient morality as an antidote to the demoralizing effects of modern life. The chief goal of the cultural nationalists, then, was to resurrect (or create) an Irish culture distinct from the modern English culture that threatened the nation. Political autonomy may or may not be achieved in the process— at any rate it was a secondary concern. Thus Unionists (like Horace Plunkett) and separatists (like Yeats) could be united in a single *cultural* project.

Hutchinson claims that cultural nationalists always use "myths and legends" to create a collective national identity.[55] It was particularly in the interests of the literary revival to de-Anglicize Ireland with Gaelic myths, because such an ancient heritage would not vilify the Anglo-Irish, while the historical memory of the rising Catholic class, mindful of the penal laws and the land wars, could hardly benefit men and women like

Yeats and Lady Gregory. If the literary revivalists, who were mostly older Anglo-Irish, were to have any place in the new Ireland, Irishness had to go deeper than the Roman brand of Christianity.

This cultural program attracted many of the Catholic UCD students. For example, the Irish language movement, officially apolitical according to Douglas Hyde but openly nationalist in character, was supported by the president of UCD, Father Delany. He led students in Gaelic League marches, provided prizes for the School of Irish Learning, and invited Eoin O'Neill (later leader of the Irish Republican Brotherhood) and Patrick Pearse (later a leader of the Easter Uprising) to lecture in the evenings at the university.[56] Arthur Clery, a Joyce contemporary, recalled that "the Gaelic League was beginning to get into its stride, and nowhere was the new movement accepted with more enthusiasm than among the students of University College."[57] At the 1903 commencement exercises, a number of students abducted the organ rather than let "God Save the King" (a "party tune of a Unionist Ascendancy clique") be played on it. The Literary and Historical Society (the L & H), defended the demonstration, only to be suppressed. According to Joyce's classmate, Eugene Sheehy, nationalism enjoyed a resurgence among Catholic students in 1903, but the resurgence took place outside the Parliamentary Party, whose political nationalism was much tamer than the radical cultural nationalism that appealed to many students.[58] In fact, Joyce's generation linked the interests of the Parliamentary Party to the status quo. By 1901, the Parliamentary Party was a monopolistic political machine that controlled many government appointments, and nepotism rather than merit dictated its selections.[59] As Hutchinson puts it, the native political institutions, "although 'formally' nationalist, seemed to have degenerated into an outlet for careerists, indifferent to the gross problems of emigration, urban poverty and alcoholism."[60] Joyce, whose own father had been first a beneficiary and then a casualty of the party's nepotism, attacked the mercenary nature of the Irish political machine:

> The representatives themselves have improved their own lot, aside from small discomforts like a few months in prison and some lengthy sittings. From the sons of ordinary citizens, pedlars, and lawyers without clients they have become well-paid syndics, directors of factories and commercial houses, newspaper owners, and large landholders. (CW, 196)

The Parliamentary Party ossified into a reflection of "the norms of the dominant state" and laid "a dead hand on the national community, attempting to stifle any extraparliamentary movements outside its control."[61] So the Parliamentary Party, once the organ of political nationalism, did not offer much change, while cultural nationalism excited discontented students with its anti-English rhetoric and its vague and romantic promises of change.

Yeats and George Russell (AE) set out to cultivate the more promising literary talents of the UCD set, inviting them to their salons, introducing them to the National Theatre clique, opening doors in the publishing business.[62] In August 1902 Russell first asked Joyce to meet with him,[63] and apparently he was impressed with what he saw, for he recommended Joyce to Lady Gregory and Yeats, remarking that the youth "writes amazingly well" and that George Moore "says [he is] preposterously clever."[64] Russell told Yeats that Joyce "belongs to your clan more than to mine and still more to himself. But he has all the intellectual equipment—culture and education, which all our other clever friends here lack" (*JJ*, 100). Joyce, along with Padraic Colum, seemed the most promising young talent in Dublin, and Russell did what he could to encourage them both. In March 1903 he praised them to an American publisher, Thomas Bird Mosher: "The tendency here [in Dublin] is to deal more with spiritual subjects and the spiritual side of nationality. One of the young writers[,] Padraic Colum[,] will I think be our next great literary figure in Ireland." Russell seemed a bit less enthusiastic of Joyce: "Another boy . . . writes with perfect art poems as delicate and dainty as Watteau pictures."[65] Two years later the two young Catholics seemed to have exchanged places in Russell's estimation. Colum was "a talent" he thought Europe would "one day . . . recognize." But Joyce was "a young scamp . . . who writes with a more perfect art than anyone except Yeats." His portrait of Joyce concludes with the colorful observation that "the poet has decamped to the continent with a barmaid."[66]

Clearly Russell took a special interest in Joyce, and there is some evidence that Joyce condescended to accept the older man's patronage. In the fall of 1902, for example, on the eve of his move to Paris, he used Russell to meet with Yeats and to secure literary contacts abroad. But Joyce eventually rejected Russell and his ilk entirely in his 1907 broadside, "The Holy Office," which referred to them as "that mumming company" among whom Joyce refused to be "accounted" (*CW*, 150).

Critics usually characterize Joyce's dissociation from the revival as a matter of egoism or of artistic independence. Ellsworth Mason, in his introduction to Joyce's review of Lady Gregory's book, regarded Joyce's criticisms as "preliminary skirmishings in his battle for artistic independence" (*CW*, 102). Richard Ellmann explored a more complex maze of motivations, ultimately concluding that the social snubs Joyce suffered from George Moore and Lady Gregory left him "resentful and inert, angry and indifferent" (*JJ*, 135). Ulick O'Connor, at pains to trivialize Joyce's objections to the literary revival, speculates that Joyce "regarded [the revival] with the intolerance of the young toward the middle-aged."[67] No doubt these all contributed to Joyce's rejection of the revival, but, if we take the young Joyce more seriously, we should acknowledge that he had political scruples that required him to reject the revival's aesthetic program. Joyce was a political nationalist committed to the liberal progress of Irish society. His rejection of the literary revival was not merely egoistic, nor merely aesthetic. It was political.

His most explicit rejection of the literary revival, "The Day of the Rabblement," bears this out. The occasion of the article was the Literary Theatre's 1901 adoption of two parochial plays—one in Irish by Douglas Hyde and the other, by George Moore and W. B. Yeats, based on Irish folklore. These productions indicated to Joyce that the theater had rejected modern dramaturgy. The preference for parochial Irish plays over "European masterpieces" of realism (like Ibsen's *Ghosts*) was not merely a matter of aesthetic preference. The rejection of realism, according to Joyce, undermined the theater's role as "the champion of progress" (*CW*, 70). Joyce's tirade against the theater is shot through with liberal political rhetoric. The production of realistic plays, Joyce declared, "was absolutely necessary" because "nothing *can be done* until the forces that dictate public judgement are calmly confronted" (*CW*, 70) [emphasis added]. Joyce's phrase recalls Tolstoy's book, *What Are We To Do?*, to which Joyce had alluded a year and a half earlier in a speech to the L & H. Joyce enumerated what he thought should be done:

> First, clear our minds of cant and later the falsehoods to which we
> have lent our support. Let us criticize in the manner of free people, as
> a free race, recking little of ferula and formula. (*CW*, 42)

"The Day of the Rabblement" proposes that art should demystify the public. Mason was not far off the mark, then, when he said that Joyce's complaint against the revival was their aversion to frankness: "Joyce, who had always prided himself on his candour and honesty, and was now demonstrating those qualities in *Stephen Hero* and the first stories of *Dubliners*, yokes Aristotle to Christian ritual to claim that his own office is Katharsis, *the revelation of what the mummers hide*" (*CW*, 149) [emphasis added]. Joyce hates the multitude for "the contagion of its fetichism and deliberate self-deception," and he condemns all the more the artist who panders to it (*CW,* 71). The Irish Literary Theatre, by playing to the multitude's love of self-aggrandizement (in the form of plays extolling the virtues of native Ireland), "cut itself adrift from the line of advancement" (*CW,* 71). "Progress," "the line of advancement," the demolishing of traditional "ferula and formula," criticizing "in the manner of a free people" are all liberal slogans. In Joyce's mind, the literary revival failed because it refused to liberalize Irish society. Instead, it set society in the opposite direction (*CW,* 72).

So Joyce rejected the literary revival for political reasons. He was not entirely alone. A movement made up largely of Catholic writers from Joyce's generation opposed the Gaelic revival. While the literary revival revolved around Lady Gregory's coterie and the patronage of high society, the writers in this countermovement revolved, at least to some extent, around Arthur Griffith. Party lines are hard to draw. For example, Joyce sometimes praised Yeats, and Yeats promoted Joyce's work even after Joyce rejected the revival. And Griffith had no problem using the revival, until it threatened his nationalist program. His paper, the *United Irishmen,* even published Yeats and Russell. Furthermore, the Catholic hierarchy was not fond of Griffith. But Catholic writers were attracted to Griffith because his program of replacing the imperial apparatus of government—the courts, the bureaucracies, etc.—with native apparatuses would have benefited their class. So, despite the blurring of party loyalties, we can divide the Dublin literary scene along these lines. The division reveals a class conflict.

Griffith's group were writers from Joyce's milieu—young, Catholic, middle- or working-class, mostly without Trinity or Oxbridge connections. Joyce's friend Oliver Gogarty was the most patrician among them, but at least he was Catholic and, in reality, his family was *nouveau riche*—the medical profession had been its road to success. Gogarty represented the successful Catholic experience. James Stephens was Protestant, but he was poor, urban, and modestly educated. He had more in common with Joyce than he had with Yeats. Seamus O'Kelly, a rural Catholic newspaperman, came under Griffith's wing also. Daniel Corkery, who was to teach both Sean O'Faolain and Frank O'Connor their craft, might not have been a Griffith protégé, but he was a member of this class. The chief distinguishing characteristic of this group of writers was that they did not fit in with the Protestant, largely upper-class literary revival.[68] And together, though perhaps not in a coordinated effort, they presented to the middle class a self-image that disputed the revival's image. By and large, theirs was a realistic image—an honest picture of their own experience.

George Moore, always uneasy playing the role assigned him by the revival, introduced a new strain in Irish letters when he published his collection of stories, *The Untilled Field,* in 1903. As Richard Fallis puts it, Moore "gave to Anglo-Irish literature its first collection of tales in the modern mode." [69] By "modern mode" Fallis means simply that Moore's stories departed from the Gaelic style of the revival. It was a modest beginning. *The Untilled Field* could hardly be described as a severe break with the revival. In fact, Moore expected the stories to be translated into Irish so they could serve as lessons for students in Gaelic League classes.[70] Nevertheless, the stories celebrate neither the aristocracy nor the peasantry and seem to suggest that what is needed in Ireland is a good dose of middle-class social progress. They accomplish this message through a realistic style, which demolishes the mythical version of rural life portrayed by the revival. Moore is so unflinching in his excoriation of rural Ireland that, more than anything, the book advocates exile.[71] The thematic and stylistic connections to Joyce's own *Dubliners,* begun a year after the appearance of *The Untilled Field,* are obvious, especially the theme of paralysis.

Deborah Averill sums up those connections in her sketch of the lineage of Irish realism:

> James Joyce's *Dubliners* (1914) and the stories of Seamus O'Kelly and Daniel Corkery followed Moore's book and provided links in the growing tradition, which was most fully realized in the work of post-Revolutionary writers Liam O'Flaherty, Sean O'Faolain, and Frank O'Connor. These short story writers differed from the Renaissance poets and dramatists [because] . . . [t]heir stories were realistic in mood and dealt mainly with contemporary Irish Catholic society rather than aristocratic tradition or mythology and folklore. The mundane perspective of their stories countered the more romantic and heroic perspectives of the poetry and drama.[72]

Patrick Rafroidi carefully points out that the Moore/Joyce school of realism differed from that of nineteenth-century Irish realists, like Somerville and Ross, who were themselves part of the Ascendancy and wrote about aristocratic Protestants.[73] Despite the Anglo-Irish realist tradition in the 1800s, the style had to be reinvented in Ireland in 1903.

Since they "dealt mainly with contemporary Irish Catholic society," the twentieth-century realists appealed to the new, Catholic readership.[74]

These writers interpreted the experience of the emergent Catholic middle class from within it, and time and again they identified social paralysis as a political problem. Because the literary revival opposed middle-class progress and because it diagnosed Ireland's problems as cultural rather than political, it was perceived as contributing to that paralysis. From the perspective of Irish literary history, then, Joyce, at least in his early career, was a realist. The stories in *Dubliners* may contain a number of symbols, epiphanies, lyrical extravagances, etc. But these are not innovations. They do not point to the new symbolic style being pioneered in London and Paris. They are a holdover, a remnant of the Gaelic style. To the reader used to Synge and Yeats and Gregory and AE, lyrical and symbolic passages like the falling snow in "The Dead" were not unusual or particularly remarkable. To the Irish reader, *Dubliners* was remarkable wherever it was mundane, quotidian, realistic, even banal.[75]

Most American critics of Joyce still misunderstand what was innovative about Joyce's stories. For example, Lea Baechler's recent study of narrative style in "Araby" and "A Little Cloud" identifies two narrative styles in the stories: "the deceptively transparent surface of any given story and the presence of non-narrative figurations." The "surface" of the stories is the conventional realistic narrative which "adhere[s] to expected narrative sequence, in which time passes and change occurs."[76] The "non-narrative figurations" are the lyrical passages, which Baechler identifies as "intrusion[s]" into the surface. Because she holds that these "figurations" are unexpected, Baechler hypothesizes that the intrusions will subvert the realism in the stories.[77] Likewise, Michael Faherty distinguishes two narrative styles—one he calls the "narrative objectivity and realism" that open the stories and the other he calls the "rhetorical climax and authorial comment" that conclude the stories—categories which correspond, more or less, to Baechler's description. While Faherty is careful to point out that the "rhetorical climaxes" are not "due to any particularly poetic turn of phrase or lyrical moment," he does hold that their effect depends on their being unexpected. Both critics, having disregarded Joyce's original audience, misidentify the "expected" and "unexpected" styles in the stories. To a reader of *The Irish Homestead,* the rural paper in which Joyce's stories first appeared, the lyrical passages were conventional; these passages were transparent because of their normalcy. The passages that called attention to themselves were the realistic passages. In fact, when we talk about "departures" and the "unexpected" in Joyce's stories, we should discuss those passages we consider the "surface" of the stories, because the realistic passages departed from

the conventions of narrative that Joyce's readers expected. This point—
that the stories in *Dubliners* introduced realism to Ireland—becomes
more obvious when we put the earliest stories back into their original
publishing context.

The Irish Homestead and the Rural Middle Class

The Irish Homestead was the publication of the Irish Agricultural Organization Society. The I.A.O.S. was the fruit of an agricultural reform orchestrated by the vituperative Horace Plunkett. Plunkett, the third son of
the sixteenth Lord Dunsany, was a member of the land-holding Irish Ascendancy. As such he was counted among Unionists. He was even elected
to the English Parliament as the Unionist member from South Dublin for
two terms in the 1890s. But he was as quick to criticize the Ulster Pres-
byterians and his fellow Unionists as he was to criticize nationalists and
Catholics. His own policy tried to avoid the coercion of Unionism and
the demagoguery of nationalism by promoting an "apolitical" program
for the modernization of Irish agriculture. His chief innovation was the
establishment of dairy cooperatives that would give the small, proprietary farmers access to modern dairy machines. Thus Irish agriculture
could establish a consistent quality for its products and compete with the
more advanced Dutch farms for the English markets. In 1894 the cooperatives amalgamated into the I.A.O.S.[78]

George Russell began working for the I.A.O.S in November 1897, as a
bank organizer in the Congested Districts of West Ireland. In the early
1900s he seemed to have been exercising considerable influence over *The
Irish Homestead* through its editor, H. F. Norman, who was a fellow
member of the Theosophical Society. In August 1905 what he had been
doing unofficially was made official: Russell was appointed editor of the
paper, a position he would hold for years. He took the I.A.O.S.'s neutrality seriously, so seriously, in fact, that in 1914, when Horace Plunkett not
only moved toward home rule but actually advocated it at co-operative
meetings, Russell informed him that his arguments "violated the principle of neutrality you yourself set up." Russell threatened to resign his
post if Plunkett continued to politicize the movement.[79]

Despite this official commitment to neutrality, the I.A.O.S. advocated
changes that had profound political consequences. Lyons suggests that
the I.A.O.S. could have succeeded only in the political atmosphere of the
1890s, after Parnell's fall split the nationalists. Until 1890 progressive reforms were subordinated to the progress of home rule. To forge new institutions of progress under the auspices of Westminster would be tacit

disapproval or at least disbelief in the eventual success of the push for home rule. The dormancy of the home rule movement in the '90s opened the door for reforms instituted by the more progressive of the Unionists, like Plunkett, who sought to preserve the Union not through coercion but through an amelioration of the conditions that led to nationalist agitation. The I.A.O.S. complemented the conciliatory policy of the Conservative Irish Secretaries Gerald Balfour and George Wyndham. By promoting rural prosperity, not only through improved agricultural technique but through land reforms that turned militant tenant farmers into property owners, conciliation would rob nationalism of a large base of support.[80] According to Lyons, while

> economic circumstances before 1850 had conspired to produce a rural proletariat, improved conditions in the second half of the nineteenth century, combined with the rudiments of education and the ability to accumulate a little capital, had begun to transform that proletariat into a bourgeoisie.[81]

The Wyndham Act, the last and most successful of the land reforms, which transferred large Ascendancy estates to the tenantry by financing low-interest long-term loans, was passed in 1903, one year before Joyce started writing for *The Irish Homestead*.[82] The 1890s and 1900s, then, saw the formation of a rural, Catholic middle class, and this class showed signs of middle-class consciousness, including expectations of ever increasing living standards and increased buying power.[83] Since this class was a growing power base in Irish politics, Plunkett's program, though officially apolitical, undermined radical political reform.

The Irish Homestead mirrored the politics of its parent organization. It advertised itself as a

> [w]eekly Paper for all Classes, all Creeds, and all Parties. . . . A paper of general interest and utility to all concerned in the promotion of Irish Agriculture and Industries, in the advancement of practical and technical education, the development of Ireland's resources generally, and in all forms of effort for raising the economic and social condition of Irish men and women.[84]

Eager to keep its distance from the government, the paper insisted on its back cover that it was "supported entirely by voluntary subscriptions and donations."

Those subscriptions translated into a large readership. Plunkett reported that in 1904 the I.A.O.S. was constituted by 876 cooperative so-

cieties throughout Ireland. The paper was mostly devoted to technical issues concerning farming, especially dairy farming, and its advertisements
clearly were aimed at the proprietary farmers. For example, "The Sisters," published in the 13 August 1904 issue, shared a page with an
advertisement by the Dairy Supply Co., Ltd., of Belfast and Cork for
"Dairy machinery and appliances of every description," including cream
separators, refrigerating machines, and milk pumps.[85] So by promoting
progress in the industry, the paper supported the government's policies of
conciliation. In fact, the I.A.O.S. actually paved the way for the Department of Agriculture and Technical Instruction for Ireland in 1899, a government agency that maintained educational institutions and a circuit of
lecturers, experimented with agricultural production, administered agricultural loans, and fought animal diseases.[86] But, as Henry Summerfield
points out, "since Plunkett advocated 'better living' to complement 'better farming' and 'better business,' the paper also devoted a little of its
space to the arts."[87] The list of contributors to the 1902 Christmas issue
included Eva Gore-Booth, George Roberts, Padraic Colum, AE, Jack
Yeats, Lady Gregory, W. B. Yeats, and Douglas Hyde—practically a role
call for the literary revival.

It might seem contradictory to claim at once that the paper served
conciliation and the revival, but it is important to remember that the revival was largely a culturally separatist movement, not a politically separatist movement. It reacted more against English modernity than English
authority. For example, Hutchinson reminds us that Russell believed that
"promoting the establishment of local libraries and Irish literature as
well as modern methods in the production, marketing and distribution of
dairy products" would create his ideal "Celtic rural communalist civilization." *The Irish Homestead* would help establish "the modern democratic equivalent of the old Celtic social order."[88] Russell, then, thought
the paper was a device for molding class consciousness.

Others did too. Most contemporaries viewed agricultural reform in
Ireland as a site of cultural conflict. Catholic revivalists of the 1880s, by
"rejecting the association of Catholicism with rural backwardness," distinguished "the future Ireland from British mass industrial society [by
imagining] a superior Democratic nation based on the conservative
virtues of a prosperous peasant proprietary." W. P. Ryan's paper, the
Irish Peasant, "like mainstream revivalists, envisaged a secular rural
Gaelic nation, with much of the population of the cities resettled on the
land."[89] The I.A.O.S. used *The Irish Homestead* to foster in its readers a
sense that they belonged to a secular Gaelic society.

True to official neutrality, the typical *Irish Homestead* story avoided overt politics and instead immersed readers in the purple haze of the Celtic Twilight, presenting mysterious, mystical, or at least romantic landscapes and populating Ireland with ghosts, fairies, and folkloric characters. For example, Lady Gregory's "A Story of the Country of the Dead" begins with a narrative frame characteristic of revival fiction: a marvelous tale told by some provincial to the urbane narrator at some remote farm.

> This is a story I was told a little time ago, in Irish, by an old man. Another old man helped me to "put English on it." [90]

The frame is a self-conscious display of Irish fiction's folk roots. Vivien Mercier points out that this oral trait practically defines the Irish short story, which derives its dramatic quality from the "theatrical atmosphere of a traditional *ceilidhe* or story-telling session." [91] After the opening frame, Gregory's story begins,

> There was a farmer one time had one son only, and the son died, and the father would not go to the funeral, where he had had some dispute with him. And, after a while, a neighbor died, and he went to his funeral; and a while after that again he was in the churchyard looking at the grave, and he took up a skull that was lying there.[92]

This opening offers no causal link between the events—the son's death, the neighbor's funeral, the visiting of the churchyard, the picking up of the skull. The narrator resorts to the phatic "and, after a while" to string the events together. The style is identical to the "non-narrative figurations" that Baechler found so remarkable in Joyce's stories. Gregory's story has a fairy- or folktale atmosphere: places are barely sketched or appear fantastic, the skull speaks, ghosts appear.

In the culminating act of his dubious mentorship, Russell suggested early in the summer of 1904 that Joyce write some stories for *The Irish Homestead*:

> Look at the story in this paper The Irish Homestead. Could you write anything simple, rural?, livemaking?, pathos?, which could be inserted so as not to shock the readers. . . . The editor will pay £1. It is easily earned money if you can write fluently and don't mind playing to the common understanding and liking for once in a way. (*Letters II,* 43)

Russell was trying to put a few pounds in Joyce's pockets, money he could certainly use, and, in his genuinely helpful way he was trying to establish the promising, young, unpublished writer.

Joyce shared a lot more in common with Russell than he ever realized, especially their sympathies with labor. If Joyce had stayed in Ireland, I imagine he and Russell would have stood on the same side of the barricades in the general strike of 1913. But in 1904 Joyce must have seen Russell as part of a campaign to foist a romantic and unprogressive ideology on the new rural middle class.

The stories he submitted to the *Homestead* suggest as much. "The Sisters," told in the first person, retains vestiges of the oral tradition, but Joyce dropped the first person narrator altogether in "Eveline" and "After the Race." *Dubliners* is remarkable, as Averill points out, for showing "no awareness of a listening audience."[93] His landscapes are unromantic. Joyce presented a quotidian, urban world. And far from obscuring or avoiding causality, his stories expose it. Events are linked in a logical temporal and spatial sequence. For example, consider the opening of "After the Race":

> The cars came scudding in toward Dublin, running evenly like pellets in the groove of Naas-road. At the crest of the hill at Inchicore the sightseers had gathered in clumps to watch the cars careering homeward, and through this channel of poverty and inaction the Continent sped its wealth and industry. Now and again the clumps of people raised the cheer of the gratefully oppressed.[94]

The other stories, "The Sisters" and "Eveline" are much more conventional—that is, they are more like Lady Gregory's opening. In "The Sisters" a mysterious "Providence" is invoked four times, directing the boy, who finds himself a "prophet" when he foresees the "ceremonious candles in whose light the Christian must take his last sleep."[95] Father Flynn's life and death, which pervade the story, exude the same mysterious atmosphere as Lady Gregory's tale. He was "always a little queer," and his sister reports, "Even when we were all growing up together he was queer. One time he didn't speak for a whole month." The boy's aunt suggests that the priest "read too much," while Eliza opines that "the duties of the priesthood were too much for him."[96] No one is sure what went wrong with him, but they consider him a fantastic character. This is confirmed by the boy's description of him, which emphasizes his premature age, his automatic, lifeless gestures, and his aged, "everlasting" clothes. The story leaves readers with the macabre image of the priest "sitting in his confession-box in the dark, wide awake, and laughing like softly to himself."[97] When Joyce reworked the story for publication in *Dubliners,* he retained and even added some revivalist elements. The boy's vision of the priest's ghost returned from the dead to confess his sins creates the romantic atmosphere of the typical *Homestead* story (*D,* 11).

"Eveline" begins with ghosts of a sort, as the title character remembers, in a melancholic revery, her dead mother, the dead Mrs. Dunn, and her own lost childhood. Buenos Aires figures as an indistinct, fantastic place in Eveline's imagination, which is fired by Frank's "tales of distant countries."[98] Joyce's readers may have wondered why these stories were set in the city ("The Sisters" is set on a specific street) instead of at some indistinct farm in a remote county. Otherwise the atmosphere of the first two stories would not jar their expectations. The dead room in "The Sisters" (which is "suffused with a dusky golden light") and the quay in "Eveline" (at which is glimpsed "the black mass of the boat lying in . . . with illumed portholes" and which blows "a long mournful whistle into the mist") seem to be merely urban translations of fantastic folktale locales.

Joyce never gave up this style completely. Even as late as "The Dead," elements of *The Irish Homestead* style appear in his prose. Gabriel's journey to the dead resembles the farmer's journey in Lady Gregory's story, and their results are nearly identical. Gabriel is transported to a "gray impalpable world" inhabited by "the vast hosts of the dead" (*D,* 223). "The solid world itself which these dead had one time reared and lived in was dissolving and dwindling" (*D,* 223). In Lady Gregory's story, the farmer is magically transported to "the country of the dead," where he perceives the spirits of farmers and wives. His own world withers away, for he has spent 700 years on his journey, and when he goes back to the graveyard where his son is buried, "no house or village where [he] came from" remains. Like Gabriel, the farmer communes with the dead—his son actually reaches out from the grave, takes his hand, and together "he and the son went up to heaven."[99]

Actually, only in a few places do Joyce's first two stories seem to shake off *The Irish Homestead* style. Yet even these stories proved Joyce was not a revivalist. For example, K. F. Purdon's "Match-Making in Ardenoo," published in the 1902 Christmas issue of the paper, shares a number of themes with "Eveline," but Joyce's story seems radical in comparison.[100] Purdon's protagonist, Kitty Dempsey, is a young, single woman, whose romance with a young man is impeded by her mother. The woman's paramour, Dan, is compelled by his poverty to emigrate, leaving Kitty behind. Kitty's father dies, and she bears the brunt of keeping the farm. When her pestering mother is stricken with paralysis, Kitty's domestic burden increases. Forced by the need to pay two years of back rent, she consents to marry a rich old man. While Kitty frets awaiting the wedding, Dan returns from America with a fortune. Kitty sneaks out of the wedding party to marry Dan, and everyone is happy, even the jilted bridegroom.[101]

"Match-Making in Ardenoo" does not expose any of the circumstances that direct the actions of the characters. Kitty is applauded for the abject selflessness that allows her to slave for, and then to care for, her mean mother. The story accepts Dan's emigration without indicting the forces that compelled him to leave, and his return from exile with a pot of money preempts any inquiry into the causes of his poverty. In fact, the happy, fairy-tale ending to the story defuses any criticism of the status quo. The impediments to happiness in the story—Kitty's mother's tyrannical domination, and Dan and Kitty's poverty—figure as fairy-tale antagonists. They are accepted without interrogation, like evil witches and nasty stepmothers. The story romanticized the problems confronting its readers, and thus it served the Conservative policy of conciliation.

"Eveline," in contrast, clearly criticized the domestic forces—Eveline's loyalty to her dead mother and her domination by a bullying father—that impede her marriage to Frank. By refusing to romanticize Eveline's domestic situation, Joyce indicted the forces that trap her, which, as Florence Walzl has pointed out about most of the women in *Dubliners,* derive from her enforced economic dependence.[102] The character of "Irishness" in "Eveline," treated realistically, contradicts the romanticization of "Irishness" in other *Irish Homestead* stories. And certainly by the time "After the Race" was published, Joyce's message had become overt. "Irishness" is a matter of scorn—embodied in the gratefully oppressed masses and the "advanced Nationalist," Jimmy's father, who modified his patriotism in order to pursue his vocation as merchant prince.

Joyce was aware of the effect of his stories. In January 1905, a month after "After the Race" was published, he wrote his brother: "I send you the fourth story of 'Dubliners'—'Hallow Eve' [later 'Clay']—which I want you to offer at once to the Editor of the Irish Homestead. Perhaps they are annoyed with me and won't honour me by printing any more" (*Letters II,* 77). According to Hugh Kenner, readers were complaining, and so Norman rejected "Hallows Eve."[103] We might surmise that what had appeared as brief lapses of convention in his first two contributions had become a principle of Joyce's compositional choices by his third and fourth. By the time he submitted "Clay," it was clear that anti-revival elements—his overt criticism of social institutions, like the Church (in "The Sisters") and the "merchant princes" (in "After the Race")—dominated his art. He wanted to and succeeded in shocking his readers.

While Joyce first wrote these stories to rural readers, he must have been conscious of his urban readers even as early as 1904. Russell suggested that Joyce sign the stories with a pseudonym, and Stanislaus reported to Richard Ellmann that Joyce did so "because he was ashamed of publishing in 'the pigs' paper'" (*JJ*, 164). Joyce need hardly have been ashamed—he was in good company in that particular "pigs' paper"— but the use of a pseudonym suggests that he expected people he knew to read the paper and that he wished to be disassociated from the likes of Yeats and Russell. What effect would his stories have on the people Joyce knew? His brother Stanislaus Joyce describes the significance of the stories in their urban context:

> They were the first signs of his [Joyce's] revolt against the environment which had produced him, and which at its best was a kind of debased romanticism, agitated by embittered party politics, spiritualised by sentimental drawing-room ballads, and enlightened by amiable illusions with regard to foreign nations.[104]

By presenting a realist's view of Dublin in a revivalist paper, Joyce's stories undermined the version of Ireland promoted by the revival. He chose to shock his readers—both rural and urban—by treating their problems seriously. By frankly identifying these problems and their causes, Joyce hoped to lead his readers to a socialist rather than a revivalist sensibility.

Joyce's Politics

Joyce deplored the revival's version of Ireland because it offered his class an antiquated romantic image of itself that served the feudal structures of the old Ascendancy. This version of Ireland, as Joyce saw it, created the class snobbery he detected among his schoolmates. Unlike Yeats, Joyce seems to have been entirely unconcerned with the need to de-Anglicize Ireland. His visions of the future Ireland mention nothing of cultural autonomy. Rather, they look like Hutchinson's description of political nationalism: "Ireland's normalization among the nations of the world by the regaining of her independent statehood." When he imagined an independent Ireland, Joyce pictured the economic effects of the appearance of a rival island near England, a bilingual, republican, self-centered, and enterprising island with its own commercial fleet, and its own consuls in every port of the world. (*CW*, 173)

Ireland would act not like a colony but like other independent nations, sending its own consuls to foreign ports, sending its own ships out to trade, and governing itself. These goals were the heart of Joyce's liberal politics. I do not mean to complicate Ireland's already complex politics by labeling Joyce a "political nationalist liberal." Nor do I mean to imply that Joyce felt an association either with the English Liberal Party or with the Parnell's Irish Party. But the term does seem to describe accurately Joyce's politics, and if it does not describe the platform of any political party in Ireland, that deficiency—not any supposed artistic disengagement—accounts for his nonpartisanship.[105]

Clearly Joyce was, as was his father, disillusioned with both the Liberal and Parliamentary parties after Gladstone coerced the parliamentarians into cutting off their own head to spite their limbs. The Liberals abused Parnell as much as the Catholic Church, and his fall impressed on Joyce's young mind the merely opportunist motives of the liberal Gladstone. Gladstone feigned support of home rule to swing the vote of Parnell's formidable block of Irish M.P.'s, and he felled Parnell when home rule threatened to succeed. That was Joyce's view while he was writing *Dubliners*. In 1907 Joyce wrote in the Trieste press:

The most powerful weapons that England can use against Ireland are no longer Conservatism, but those of Liberalism and Vaticanism. . . . It takes little intelligence to understand that Gladstone has done Ireland greater damage than Disraeli did. (*CW*, 195)

Again in 1910 he dissected the "Liberal strategy" in Ireland as conciliation "which aims to wear down the separatist sentiment slowly and secretly, while creating a new, eager social class, dependent, and free from dangerous enthusiasms" (*CW*, 212). But Joyce was a political nationalist in the sense that he adhered to the general liberal political philosophy, or what he took for the liberal philosophy, of Parnell's Irish Party.

Joyce's admiration for Parnell, like his admiration for Ibsen, is famous and hardly needs proving here. But what does merit discussion is whether Joyce's admiration was born of his attraction to Parnell's mythical status as the latest and greatest in the line of Ireland's betrayed saviors or of his attraction to Parnell's parliamentarianism. It is difficult to pin down

Parnell's own position. Equivocation might be expected of a debt-ridden Protestant landlord, committed to working within the English constitution, who also led a coalition of separatist, reforming nationalists. And Parnell equivocated. As R. F. Foster points out,

> Dazzling as the political structure of Parnellism had been, it had never really defined what Home Rule meant. . . . The Home Rulers, it has been neatly said, were "not a party with a policy, but a movement with an ultimate objective." [106]

It might be difficult to say unequivocally whether Parnell was a cultural or a political nationalist, but it is not so difficult to recognize that Joyce's hope for a politically independent Ireland, not a culturally independent Ireland, attracted him to Parnell.

On the surface, Joyce may seem to have believed that Ireland was different from other nations essentially, racially, and culturally. In a lecture he delivered at the Università Populare in Trieste, "Ireland, Island of Saints and Sages," he did define the Irish nation along lines that sound essentialist to us today: "Nations have their ego, just like individuals" (*CW*, 154). In a lecture on James Clarence Mangan he stated that "Mangan . . . sums up in himself the soul of a country and an era" (*CW*, 184). In an article written in 1907 on the death of the Fenian John O'Leary, he identified the Irish character as dominated by a tendency toward betrayal (*CW*, 189). And in the "Home Rule Comet," written in 1910, the year of Halley's comet, Joyce personified Ireland as a betrayer:

> She abandoned her own language. . . . She has betrayed her heroes, always in the hour of need and always without gaining recompense. She has hounded her spiritual creators into exile only to boast about them. (*CW*, 213)

This reduction of all differences into a single Irish soul or character seems to indicate that Joyce, like the cultural nationalists, imagined a homogeneous Ireland essentially distinct from England. But Joyce's version of the Irish nation excluded the Unionists: "The Irish attitude and the Irish character," he declared in one sweeping generalization, "were antipathetic to the queen [Victoria], who was fed on the aristocratic and imperialistic theories of Benjamin Disraeli, her favorite minister" (*CW*, 164).

Nevertheless, when we put these metaphors in context, we must conclude that Joyce used them without recognizing their import. A thorough reading of Joyce's critical writings indicates that he consistently rejected the idea that nations could be defined along racial or cultural lines. As

Manganiello points out, Joyce, in his "Island of Saints and Sages" lecture, claimed that

> To exclude from the present [Irish] nation all who are descended
> from foreign families would be impossible, and to deny the name of
> patriot to all those who are not of Irish stock would be to deny it
> almost all the heroes of the modern movement. (CW, 162)

Indeed, Joyce described the Irish race as a mix of Celtic, Scandinavian, Anglo-Saxon, Norman, and Danish strains (CW, 161). (Recall that Leopold Bloom defined a nation as "the same people living in the same place . . . or also living in different places," which is a definition broad enough to make an Irishman out of the son of a Hungarian Jew.) [107] Also, in a letter to Stanislaus Joyce that generally praised Arthur Griffith, Sinn Fein, and the *United Irishmen,* Joyce wrote: "What I object to most of all in his [Griffith's] paper [*United Irishmen*] is that it is educating the people of Ireland on the old pap of racial hatred" (*Letters II,* 167). Joyce also rejected the resurrection of an ancient Gaelic culture: "Ancient Ireland is dead just as ancient Egypt is dead" (CW, 173).

To be sure, Joyce had little respect for Redmond and the parliamentarians when he was writing *Dubliners.* In 1907 he thought parliamentarianism was as ineffective as Fenian terrorism, and, as I mentioned above, he decried the patronage system of the parliamentarians' party-machine (CW, 190, 196). Also, he was still bitter about their betrayal of Parnell (CW, 196). Meanwhile, he praised Sinn Fein for its political and commercial separatist policies:

> He [Griffith] was the first person in Ireland to revive the separatist
> idea on modern lines nine years ago. He wants the creation of an
> Irish consular service abroad, and of an Irish bank at home. . . . A
> great deal of his programme perhaps is absurd but at least it tries to
> inaugurate some commercial life for Ireland. (*Letters II,* 167)

In the Trieste newspaper, *Il Piccolo della Sera,* he compared Sinn Feiners somewhat favorably to the Fenians, choosing to praise their political and economic separatism:

> They aim to make Ireland a bi-lingual Republic, and to this end
> they have established a direct steamship service between Ireland and
> France. They practice boycotts against English goods; they refuse to
> become soldiers or take the oath of loyalty to the English crown; they
> are trying to develop industries throughout the entire island; and

instead of paying out a million and a quarter annually for the maintenance of eighty representatives in the English Parliament, they want to inaugurate a consular service in the principal ports of the world for the purpose of selling their industrial products without the intervention of England. (*CW*, 191)

While it cannot be denied that Sinn Fein was a culturally nationalist organization that supported the de-Anglicization of Ireland (*Letters II*, 187), its cultural policies were exactly what Joyce objected to: "if the Irish programme did not insist on the Irish language I suppose I could call myself a nationalist" (*Letters II*, 187). Joyce believed that Sinn Fein was capable of liberating Ireland not only from English politics but also from Catholic ideology. Griffith, Joyce thought, held

> out some secular liberty to the people and the Church doesn't approve of that. I quite see, of course, that the Church is still, as it was in the time of Adrian IV [the English pope that authorized the first Norman invasion of Ireland], the enemy of Ireland: but, I think, her time is almost up. For either *Sinn Fein* or Imperialism will conquer the present Ireland. (*Letters II*, 187)

While the tone of Joyce's letter indicates that he recognized the dangers in Sinn Fein, he also praised it as a socially liberating institution. We can say with confidence that Joyce had clear political hopes for Ireland and that these goals amounted to a program of political nationalism: Joyce wanted Ireland to win its political autonomy and establish a government that would work toward a progressive liberal reform of Irish society. His decision to write in the style of nineteenth-century Continental realism derived from this political stance.

Class Conflict in *Dubliners*

Joyce wrote *Dubliners* to aid reform. Nearly all the stories depict middle-class Catholics drowning in poverty, yet clinging to a spar of middle-class respectability. They must hold themselves above the working class no matter what the cost. Well into the twentieth century Dublin was hierarchical, and most citizens had a keen awareness of their place in society. Alexander Humphrey attributes the hierarchy to the legacy of "the days of the Ascendancy, its relative rigidity and the generally subordinate position of Catholics within it":

> Despite this subordination, if not because of it, among Catholics, and even among the lower classes of Catholics, lines of distinction and

their corresponding sentiments existed before 1922 whose strength was quite disproportionate to the grounds upon which they were based.[108]

A class consciousness based, in 1900, on the vestiges of quasifeudal structures (like ladies and gentlemen) and held by a population struggling to secure its place in the middle class may sound a bit far-fetched. By 1900 such ideological conflicts were well over in most western European countries. But Dublin was an anachronism. Class conflicts fought in the early nineteenth century on the Continent were fought in Ireland at the century's end. Responding to George Moore's famous quip that "Ireland [was] feudal in the 1870s," James Meenan remarks that just "thirty years later something resembling a middle class had emerged."[109] As usual, that class wrapped itself in the trappings of the aristocracy it meant to replace. Paul Delany reminds us that Joyce expressed a similar view: "Ireland was 'an aristocratic country without an aristocracy'; the knights of *Dubliners* are neither gentle nor gallant."[110] That social revolution, which had been the subject of realism for generations on the Continent, the rise of a middle class and the dismantling of a landed aristocracy, had come to Ireland only in Joyce's lifetime. Ireland was, perhaps, the last place in western Europe where a genteel class consciousness would be worth discrediting.

Dominic Manganiello presents a compelling case that feudalism was on Joyce's mind when he wrote *Stephen Hero*. Quoting from that fragment, Manganiello writes,

> Stephen finds in his godfather, Mr. Fulham, the same aristocratic notions, respect for the feudal distinctions and "natural submission to what he regarded as the dispenser of these distinctions" as displayed by his father. . . . Mr. Fulham, moreover, had affection for the "feudal machinery and desired nothing better than it should crush him . . ." Stephen detests these attitudes he regards as symptomatic of "the pride of the burgher." The feudal aristocracy has given way to a rural burgher class which he finds equally obnoxious.[111]

The oppressor in *Stephen Hero* is an amalgamation of "feudal machinery" and "feudal distinctions" retained not to the benefit of a genuine aristocracy but to a new "rural burgher class." The retention of these distinctions is ironic, for Mr. Fulham enjoys "the fruits of nationalist agitation" (*SH,* 247), which, since it was republican, was decidedly anti-aristocratic. Mr. Fulham adopts the elitist attitude of the Protestant aristocracy whose decline enabled his own rise.

Dubliners concerns the urban burghers. The richest Irishman in *Dubliners,* Jimmy Doyle in "After the Race," learns his elitism in school. In fact, his father, a self-made "merchant prince," sent Jimmy to college more with the purpose of raising the Doyles into a higher class than of giving him any book learning. Jimmy attended Trinity College in Dublin "to study law," and was sent to Cambridge "to see life a little" (*D*, 43). His father is unconcerned when Jimmy neglects his studies and is "covertly proud" of Jimmy's excesses and the bills he runs up. His father measures Jimmy's achievement at the university by the company he learns to keep:

> It was at Cambridge that Jimmy met Segouin. . . . Jimmy found great pleasure in the society of one who had seen so much of the world and was reputed to own some of the biggest hotels in France. Such a person (as his father agreed) was well worth knowing. (*D*, 44)

Villona, "a brilliant pianist—but, unfortunately, very poor," was, according to this accounting, not "worth" knowing (*D*, 45). With reason, if without compassion, Jimmy looks down on the "profane world of spectators," the "gratefully oppressed" working class of Dublin who admire him and his friends in the automobile. Although it is unstated, the source of the older Doyle's pride is easy to infer: though he is a member of the *nouveau riche,* Jimmy is acting like a native of the landed Protestant caste: a *nouveau* prince.

Dubliners consistently attacks education as a source of elitism. For example, the early stories about childhood indict the prestigious schools for teaching students to feel superior. In "An Encounter," Father Butler, who had just discovered a comic book in one boy's pocket, reminds his students of their privilege: "I'm surprised at boys like you, educated, reading such stuff. I could understand it if you were . . . National School boys" (*D*, 20). Later in the story, the narrator and his friend Mahoney are taken for upper-class Protestants because of the "silver badge of a cricket club" that Mahoney wears in his cap (*D*, 22). And the narrator indicates his own pride in privilege when he thinks of telling the pederast that he and Mahoney "were not National School boys to be *whipped,* as he called it" (*D*, 27). Boys who attended the prestigious Catholic schools, unlike students of the public schools, were on a track to join the Protestant professional class. They were not common school children. They were taught by the Jesuits, who "cater for the upper classes" (*D*, 164).

Little Chandler is one of these boys grown up. He is well-educated and considers himself, with some justification, a sophisticate. But since he earns his living as a clerk, part of the lower tier of professionals, he is hardly successful. He and his wife are too poor to afford a servant—roughly equivalent to owning an automatic dishwasher today—which indicates an economic (if not educational) distance between the Chandlers and the middle class (D, 82). In a cut-rate attempt to live like the gentry, the Chandlers fill their house with rent-to-own furniture (D, 83). But Chandler himself is not fooled. He is conscious that to have succeeded financially he would have had to have left Dublin, which expresses the sentiments of UCD graduates succinctly: "if you wanted to succeed you had to go away. You could do nothing in Dublin" (D, 73).[112] Doctors graduating from the medical school in Cecilia Street generally could find work if they were willing to emigrate to India or other parts of the empire, but success was less assured for young Catholic lawyers. And, though the Irish civil service was still expanding, it offered few top-level positions, and those, appointed by the chief secretary, went to Protestants.[113] Chandler's friend Hogan, who had secured a "good sit" in the new Land Commission, that stepchild of the I.A.O.S., was unusual among Chandler's crowd (D, 75).

Despite his poverty and poor prospects, Chandler retains a deplorable sense of superiority over working-class Dublin, which he regards as "all that minute vermin-like life" (D, 71). Even his feelings of superiority over Gallaher, Chandler's "inferior in birth and education" (D, 80), are expressed in terms of class: "there was something *vulgar* in his friend which he had not observed before" (D, 77) [emphasis added]. Chandler's sense of superiority, according to Joyce, only increases his sense of indignity: "He felt acutely the contrast between his own life and his friend's, and it seemed to him unjust" (D, 80). While Gallaher lives bravely in London, the exigencies of domestic life in a depressed Dublin require all of Chandler's energy. Certainly Gallaher's (apparently) exciting life would have its appeals even for the successful middle-class man, but Chandler's dissatisfaction with his own life stems not from its conventionality but from its meanness. He is poor, but his birth and education promised him he would be comfortably well-off. He thinks he ought to be more than a petty clerk. He thinks he ought to be able to afford the leisure to write poems. Instead, he is consumed by the difficult struggle to surround himself with the trappings of the gentry, and he directs his invective not at the causes of his poverty but at the working class, to which he is in danger of succumbing.

The precarious economy naturally makes these characters feel insecure in their status, and this insecurity, according to Joyce, leads them to insist on their own gentility more tenaciously. For example, Mrs. Kearney, one of the few monied characters in the book, probably displays her success so insistently because she is aware that her husband's industry, bootmaking, is in a dangerous position. As L. M. Cullen reports, "The sewing machine had made possible the factory boot, and cheap boots from the factories reduced the number of bootmakers by over a third between 1871 and 1891, and by the same proportion again between 1891 and 1911."[114] Judging by the savings account he set up for his daughters' dowries, which totaled only £100 each after twenty-four years of "paying a small sum every week" (D, 137), we should infer that Mr. Kearney is not a factory owner. More likely he is an owner of one of those small shops that were becoming more obsolete each year. Nothing makes one conscious of status more than the threat of its loss, so it is no surprise that Mrs. Kearney is defensive about her rights. The matter of her daughter's contract as an accompanist for a nationalist variety show, which the "committee" apparently means to violate when it cancels one of the performances, means more to Mrs. Kearney than the lost two guineas. She feels she was "treated scandalously" (D, 148), because, in her mind, the refusal of payment denies her class status by upsetting her sense of her own importance. Ironically, by insisting on the money, she only further demonstrates that she is not a gentlewoman. Though she struggles to remain "ladylike" (D, 141) and strives "to be polite" (D, 144), the low-class character of the whole affair distresses her precisely because her sense of being a lady is contingent on such showy signs. For example, she is disturbed that none of the stewards at the concert hall wore "evening dress," that the acts were merely "mediocre items," and that "the audience behaved indecorously" (D, 139–140), things that someone more secure in her position would have the luxury of overlooking. Mr. Holohan reiterates her dubious status with the unanswerable insult: "I thought you were a lady" (D, 149).[115]

The characters in "Grace" all display Mrs. Kearney's anxiety. They refer to the policeman who discovered Kernan unconscious on the floor of the bar as a "country bumpkin," an "ignorant bastoon," a "thundering big country fellow," an "omadhaun," and a "yahoo" (D, 160–161). Conversely, Mr. Kernan admires the Jesuits for being "an educated order" (as opposed to "ignorant, bumptious" secular priests), and the whole lot of gentlemen admire the Jesuits especially for catering "for the upper classes" (D, 164). Mr. Power, Mr. Cunningham, Mr. Kernan, and Mr. M'Coy all feel an upper-class consciousness and are at pains to display it in their dress and erudition. The story's humor largely depends on the falseness of their erudition, which reveals not their gentility but their pretensions. Their clothes, manners, and education all aspire to gentility, to grace. Mr. Fogarty, the grocer, has it: "He bore himself with a certain grace, complimented little children and spoke with a neat enunciation. He was not without culture" (D, 166). Mr. Kernan also has it and "was keenly conscious of his citizenship [and] wished to live with his city on terms mutually honourable" (D, 160). Mr. M'Coy is provisionally accepted, being the type who would condescend to a "low playing of the game," as Mr. Cunningham would put it (D, 160). The uniformed policeman, being a country bumkin, does not have it.

With as little justification but with the same conviction, other characters in *Dubliners* feel superior to the working class. Maria, the housekeeper at a laundry, really a member of the working class herself, accepts Ginger Mooney's toast even as she distances herself from Mooney's low-class allusion to "a sup of porter": Maria "knew that Mooney meant well though, of course, she had the notions of a common woman" (D, 101). Later, on the tram, Maria notes the difference between the "young men" who ungallantly keep their seats and a polite "elderly gentleman" who gives his up (D, 102–103). The young men, probably commuters, have not the class of the older man, a "colonel-looking gentleman." Notice Maria imagines that the "gentleman" has traveled one of the few avenues of success available to Catholic Irish: the British Army. Maria feels herself part of his genteel class. She chats with the gentleman politely, bows on taking her leave, and reflects "how easy it was to know a gentleman even when he has a drop taken" (D, 103). The contrast between Mooney's "sup of porter" and the gentleman's "drop taken" is significant. Tellingly, when Maria herself drinks, she "takes a glass of wine" (D, 105), employing a polite euphemism incongruous with her economic station.

Lenehan and Corley, two unemployed young men in "Two Gallants," are conscious that they are slumming when they cultivate relationships with working girls. They discuss the virtues of dating workers, who are cheaper than middle-class "girls off the South Circular" and who are more likely to allow an indiscretion (D, 52–53). Lenehan considers a slavey's crass "Sunday finery" a mark of Corley's right to exploit her. The woman's showy blouse, "ragged black boa," and ostentatious "red flowers . . . pinned in her bosom" all reinforce Lenehan's sense of superiority, and thus makes him think Corley is entitled to her. Such a working girl, with "her stout short muscular body" and "unabashed blue eyes," is not bound by middle-class rules of sexual behavior, or so Lenehan imagines. She is beneath him and beneath middle-class girls, so she is fair game.

This snobbery creeps from his testicles to his stomach. Looking for a place to eat, Lenehan "paused at last before the window of a poor-looking shop over which the words *Refreshment Bar* were printed" (D, 57). He glances "warily up and down the street," as if he is afraid of being seen going into the lower-class restaurant, and, once inside, he is conscious that he is out of place. For the first time in *Dubliners,* we see someone eager to shed his superiority:

> He sat down opposite two work-girls and a mechanic. A slatternly girl waited on him. . . . He spoke roughly in order to belie his air of gentility for his entry had been followed by a pause of talk. . . . To appear natural he pushed his cap back on his head and planted his elbows on the table. (D, 57)

No doubt Joyce is satirizing Lenehan's "air of gentility," which is a foil to his vicious thoughts about women. But that air of gentility, his manners and his clothes, also makes Lenehan stick out in the only restaurant he can afford. This discrepancy between his manner and money frustrates him:

> He was tired of knocking about, of pulling the devil by the tail, of shifts and intrigues. He would be thirty-one in November. Would he never get a job? Would he never have a home of his own? He thought how pleasant it would be to have a warm fire to sit by and a good dinner to sit down to. (D, 57–58)

His "air of gentility" here is a foil to his pocketbook. Lenehan feels entitled to a middle-class life: a secure job, a nice house, a wife, home-cooked meals, and a hearth. The question "Would he never get a job?" should not be read, "Would he never take initiative?" but "Would he never have a decent opportunity?" As we have seen and as Joyce well knew, jobs that would satisfy Lenehan's expectations were few in Dublin. Joyce here links spiritual and moral paralysis to economic paralysis— purse and spirit go together. I am not suggesting that Joyce expects us to sympathize with Lenehan's predicament so much as understand it. Like Lenehan, most Dubliners in Joyce's book are frustrated by the gap between their expectations (raised by their education and the relative success of their parents) and the economic reality for middle-class Catholics in turn-of-the-century Dublin. Nearly all of the adult characters in

Dubliners feel that they are, by right of birth and education, members of the comfortable middle class, not of the lower class, and they are consumed by the conflict between their feelings of entitlement and their empty pockets.[116] Moral paralysis derives, then, from Ireland's economy: the failed promise of the middle class leads it to despise workers and insist on its connection to the Protestant gentry all the more violently.[117] *Dubliners* argues that these sympathies are misplaced.

The Socialist Alternative

Joyce made no bones about what he thought of capitalism. This new economic system, which had replaced an aristocratic society, was as oppressive as its predecessor. Even his earliest stories show this attitude. Drawing especially on the groundwork laid by David Ward's admirable study in *Eire-Ireland* and on two contemporary articles in *The Irish Times,* James Fairhall suggests that in "After the Race" Joyce "was reacting as both a socialist and an Irish nationalist" to "the contemporary national and international context" surrounding the story.[118] The *Irish Times* promoted the race on the grounds that it would bring tourists into the city and that it would spur local industry. Fairhall points out that the Irish public funds spent on the race exceeded the influx of money and that no Irish industry rose in consequence of it. In particular, he chastises the tendency of Dublin "merchant princes" to keep their money to themselves or invest it abroad. Citing the Doyles' indifference to Irish laborers and George Russell's complaint that Dublin's capitalists did not endow the city with museums, libraries, and the like, Fairhall implies that the moral of Joyce's story is that Irish capitalists ought to be more genuinely nationalist.[119]

Although Fairhall does concede that Joyce censures the Doyles' class "for taking for its model the capitalistic competition of the great powers," his emphasis is on the "competition of the great powers." Jimmy's attempt to play with the big boys, so to speak—to invest with the French, the English, and the Americans in the consummate capitalist venture of making cars—will end the way the card game ends. The game ends up between Routh and Segouin, the Englishman and the Frenchman, and Jimmy, the Irishman, realizes he "would lose, of course" (*D,* 48). Likewise, Fairhall predicts that Jimmy would lose his investment. Shifting from economics to politics, Fairhall suggests that "Joyce seems to be hinting" that "Irish involvement on any side in conflicts among the great powers" of England and France is foolish.[120] The Irish will always lose. Fairhall concludes that, "The need for Irish independence—political, economic, cultural—is the main theme" of the story.[121]

The theme of paralysis, according to Fairhall, is a private matter in "After the Race," tangential to the social and economic implications of the story: "paralysis [is] reflected in the protagonist's inability to make good this escape [from humdrum Dublin] and to live or act meaningfully".[122] In an otherwise well-documented and concrete discussion of the story, Fairhall seems satisfied with this vague interpretation of paralysis. What "to live or act meaningfully" means exactly is never defined, nor does it command Fairhall's attention. Despite his good insights, and despite his protestations of Joyce's socialism, Fairhall fails to interpret the story as a socialist's critique of capitalism. To a socialist, the problem with capitalism is not the lack of philanthropy practiced by the rich, nor is it the failure of capitalists to invest at home rather than abroad.

"After the Race" unequivocally rejects capitalism as a humane basis for social structure. The story begins with the "gratefully oppressed" poor watching "the Continent [speed] its wealth and industry" through the "channel of poverty and inaction" of Dublin's streets (D, 41). The oppression of Dubliners clearly is economic, not political. Their sympathy for the French (Ireland's traditional ally against English rule) suggests that the poor Dubliners perceive (and are not grateful for) England's political domination of Ireland, as Fairhall argues. What they do not perceive is that Continental wealth and industry—borne of capitalism—also oppresses them. Even capital invested in Ireland would not, in Joyce's view, relieve the suffering. And capitalism, even for its beneficiaries, would not lead to any liberation from paralysis. Indeed, the point of "After the Race" seems to be that paralysis is a necessary condition of capitalism, for the Doyles are successful capitalists, but they are just as paralyzed as any other Dubliners. They have merely made themselves into a new aristocracy of money (indicated by the epithet "merchant *prince*"), which in Joyce's view infects his class with a retrograde and paralyzing ideology.

In the years he wrote *Dubliners,* Joyce was looking beyond the revolution that accounted for the rise of the middle class; he was looking forward to the changes that James Connolly, founder of the Irish Socialist Republican party in 1896, was calling for in the *Workers' Republic.* As Lyons writes, Connolly professed a blend of nationalism and socialism that saw enemies in both the feudal, colonial structure of old Ireland and in the capitalism of new Ireland:

[Connolly's] aim was to demonstrate that the two currents of thought [socialism and nationalism] were not antagonistic but complementary. As he put it in a statement . . . "The struggle for Irish freedom has two aspects; it is national and it is social. The national ideal can never be realised until Ireland stands forth before the world as a nation, free and independent. It is social and economic because no matter what the form of government may be, as long as one class owns as private property the land and instruments of labour from which mankind derive their substance, that class will always have it in their power to plunder and enslave the remainder of their fellow creatures." From this it seems that although he might regard the two currents as complementary, he was quite clear that, as he phrased it in later years, "the Irish question was at bottom an economic question." [123]

Joyce's political philosophy was hardly different from Connolly's. In a letter to Stanislaus written in September 1906, shortly after he completed *Dubliners* (except "The Dead"), Joyce wrote, "if the Irish question exists, it exists for the Irish proletariat chiefly" (*Letters II*, 167). Manganiello also notes this letter and connects Joyce's socialism to Connolly: "political independence was not enough, and . . . Joyce desired socialism in an Irish context, the very thing James Connolly had been trying to initiate." [124] But Manganiello left it to Robert Scholes to recognize that "in *Dubliners* and probably in much of his other work, Joyce felt himself to be engaged in the bringing to consciousness the social problems that beset his nation." [125]

While a socialist critique of the middle class pervades the book, socialism itself only appears in two of the stories: "A Painful Case" and, naturally enough, the overtly political "Ivy Day in the Committee Room." In the first of these, James Duffy dabbled in the Irish Socialist Party,

> a unique figure amidst a score of sober workmen in a garret lit by an inefficient oil-lamp. When the party had divided into three sections, each under its own leader in its own garret, he had discontinued his attendances. The workmen's discussions, he said, were too timorous; the interest they took in the question of wages was inordinate. He felt that they were hard-featured realists and that they resented an exactitude which was the product of a leisure not within their reach. (*D*, 110–111)

This passage illustrates not only class snobbery, but also Joyce's socialist alternative to the middle-class nostalgia for a society organized by feudal class distinctions. Duffy certainly belongs to the narrow class I have identified as the subject of *Dubliners*. He is well-educated. His *Maynooth Catechism* indicates he was educated in Catholic, not public, schools. *Michael Kramer* indicates he knows German—a sign of a university education. He lives in the suburbs. He is employed as a cashier in a bank, but the job is, apparently, beneath him. Like Lenehan, who feels ill at ease in the poor restaurant, and Chandler, who is revolted by the slums, Duffy feels superior to the "sober workmen" who make up the Irish Socialist Party. His "leisure"—that is, his membership in the middle class—sets him above them because it purchases an exactitude they cannot afford.

Interestingly, Joyce's satire of Duffy parallels Connolly's complaint against the Socialist Labor Party of America for rejecting "the day-to-day industrial struggle for improved remuneration and conditions of labor." [126] Duffy treats socialism as a philosophical, romantic quest rather than a practical strategy for democratic and economic reform. Actually, Duffy is as undemocratic as Mr. Fulham, the rural burgher in *Stephen Hero* who saw the Church as a levee against the flood of democracy (*SH*, 241). Duffy's sense of superiority is so developed that he sets himself above his own middle class, which he describes as obtuse and philistine, even as, ironically, he proves himself entirely bourgeois by trying to live, like Mr. Fulham, in the manner of the gentry (*D*, 111). He makes "appointments" to "engage the lady's society"; he has "a distaste for the underhand ways" (*D*, 110); and, when he learns of Mrs. Sinico's death, its "commonplace" and "vulgar" character fill him with righteous indigestion (*D*, 115).

Joyce shared Duffy's dislike of middle-class ethics, but Joyce, as I have shown, deplored them precisely because of their petty insistence that the social hierarchies be maintained. Stanislaus reports that "Mr. Duffy's disillusionment with socialism . . . does not reflect my brother's ideas but mine. At Trieste," when he was composing *Dubliners*, Joyce "still called himself a socialist" (*MBK*, 170). Though Duffy does not realize it, the solution to his problems lies not only in rejecting capitalism but also in giving up the airs of gentility that so charm the middle class. The workmen in the socialist party offer him a tonic. Only their "hard-featured" realism can put to rest his struggle to maintain an anachronistic gentility, because it rejects class distinctions altogether. Throughout *Dubliners*, the working class figures as a foil to the postures struck by Joyce's own class, a source of hard-featured sober realism that exposes the false consciousness of the Catholic middle class. The laborers in "An Encounter" and Frank in "Eveline," for example, perform this function, as does Lily in "The Dead." Such realism would give Duffy the courage to ignore propriety and pursue his affair with Mrs. Sinico, who is his untrodden path to liberation.

The Irish Socialist Party that Joyce alludes to in "A Painful Case" is probably Connolly's Irish Socialist and Republican (I.S.R.) party. As Manganiello points out, Stanislaus remembered that his brother "had frequented meetings of socialist groups in back rooms in the manner ascribed to Mr. Duffy" (*MBK*, 170). We do not know if the meetings were of Connolly's party, but Joyce's intended readers, Dubliners, would naturally link Duffy's meetings to the I.S.R. party. The vitality of that party, especially after Connolly's removal to America in 1903, dissipated like the socialists in "A Painful Case."[127] Arthur Griffith of Sinn Fein supported Connolly in the 1902 municipal elections, and it has been well established by both Ellmann and Manganiello that Joyce followed Griffith's paper with great interest. As a matter of fact, Manganiello plausibly assumes that the election in "Ivy Day in the Committee Room" (which Joyce wrote in the summer of 1905) is based on the 1902 election and that Colgan in the story alludes to Connolly, who ran for municipal office against a nationalist candidate.[128]

Joe Hynes, a visitor to the committee room, supports the socialist candidate, Colgan, with a couple of short speeches:

What's the difference between a good honest bricklayer and a publican—eh? Hasn't the working-man as good a right to be in the Corporation as anyone else—ay, and a better right than those shoneens that are always hat in hand before any fellow with a handle to his name? . . .

One man is a plain honest man with no hunker-sliding about him. He goes to represent the labour classes. This fellow you're working for only wants to get some job or other. . . .

The working-man, said Mr. Hynes, gets all kicks and no half-pence. But it's labour produces everything. The working-man is not looking for fat jobs for his sons and nephews and cousins. The working-man is not going to drag the honour of Dublin in the mud to please a German monarch. (*D*, 121)

Hynes's attack on the Nationalist party in general parallels Joyce's own deploring of class elitism, and I suggest that his endorsement of Colgan is Joyce's endorsement of Connolly.

Later Hynes attacks the middle class's infatuation with the aristocracy. The "shoneens that are always hat in hand before any fellow with a handle to his name," the publicans and other Catholic middle class, had only recently been allowed to run in local elections—the result of the Local Government Act of 1898 discussed above. Dick Tierney, the Nationalist candidate, is one of the new class of "democratic" politicians described by Lyons. He is a publican. "He's a big ratepayer," as Mr. Henchy is quick to remind Conservative voters, and he "has extensive house property in the city and three places of business" (D, 131). According to Fairhall, Joyce felt that changes initiated by the Local Government Act hardly effected a revolution at all. The Catholic politicians did not reform the policies that made Dublin the worst slum in Europe. They presided over the slums themselves, becoming the landlords and benefiting from their cozy relationship with Dublin's capitalists.[129]

Manganiello connects "Ivy Day" to the 1902 municipal elections principally to extract a conventional anti-Church and anti-English interpretation:

> The "paralysis" in Irish political life arises out of the inability of the parliamentary party to wrench itself free from the hold of the church and the British State.[130]

But the story itself seems to locate paralysis in the Nationalist party's commitment to the interests of capitalists and in its failure, once it attains money and power, to resist the lure of class elitism.

The chief issue in the fictional election and the actual municipal election of 1902 was Edward VII's visit to Ireland, which forced the Irish into a difficult decision between snubbing or welcoming the imperial king. Tierney, as it becomes clear at least to Mr. O'Connor, will welcome the monarch. Henchy defends this betrayal of Dublin's honor on capitalist grounds:

> What we want in this country . . . is capital. The King's coming here will mean an influx of money into this country. The citizens of Dublin will benefit by it. Look at all the factories down by the quays there, idle! Look at all the money there is in the country if we only worked the old industries, the mills, the shipbuilding yards and factories. It's capital we want. (D, 131)

In Henchy's view, capital and the regeneration of the Irish economy is linked to the monarch. But Joyce already has established the bankruptcy of that connection in "After the Race." The king's visit, like the *gran prix,* would end up costing the citizens of Dublin considerably. The real paralysis, as Hynes diagnoses it, does not come from Edward VII or from England but from people like Tierney.

Even so, "Ivy Day" hardly resembles a manifesto for socialism in Ireland. But the relatively obscure view of socialism and of the working class in *Dubliners* does not necessarily reflect an insignificance in Joyce's mind. The stories are chiefly diagnostic in their intent, not prescriptive. And they describe Joyce's audience—his own class. According to Joyce, moral and spiritual paralysis descend from economic paralysis, as surely as middle-class, nationalist values followed on a UCD education. The revival offered only a regressive solution. If James Connolly's Irish Socialist and Republican party had not nearly dissolved when its chief left Ireland for America in 1903, Joyce's propagandism would be more obvious.

Joyce the Realist

But to accept that Joyce's main intention for *Dubliners* was so parochial, we have to change our understanding of his early period. We have to recognize that in Joyce's mind his commitment to recording the frank, honest experiences of the Catholic middle class constituted his contribution to Irish letters. We must recognize that, as a young writer, Joyce committed himself to demystifying the Catholic, imperial, and nationalist "truths." In a letter to Nora Barnacle, Joyce described himself and his work thus:

> Six years ago I left the Catholic Church, hating it most fervently. I found it impossible for me to remain in it on account of the impulses of my nature. I made secret war upon it when I was a student and declined to accept the positions it offered me. . . . Now I make open war upon it by what I write and say and do. (*Letters II,* 48)

The impulses of Joyce's "nature" led him to reject the Church, which, presumably, frustrated those impulses with unnatural dogma. And as early as August 1904, when he was beginning *Dubliners,* Joyce declared that he was making open war on the Church. His letters reveal that Joyce believed that realism was an important weapon in his war.

One letter to Stanislaus, written in November 1906, takes issue with Oliver Gogarty's articles in Sinn Fein's *United Irishmen* that attacked the English army for its "venereal excess." Gogarty intended to discredit the

English, and, by contrast, he intended to praise the Irish for their chastity. Joyce questioned this implied virtue:

> Why does nobody compile statistics of "venereal excess" from Dublin hospitals? . . . My opinion is that if I put down a bucket into my soul's well, sexual department, I draw up Griffith's and Ibsen's and Skeffington's and Bernard Vaughan's and St. Aloysius's and Shelley's and Renan's water along with my own. And I am going to do that in my novel (inter alia) and plank the bucket down before the shades and substances above mentioned to see how they like it: and if they don't like it I can't help them. I am nauseated by their lying drivel about pure men and pure women and spiritual love for ever: blatant lying in the face of truth. (*Letters II*, 191–192)

Like nineteenth-century realists, Joyce preferred observation and scientific investigation of the world to political and moral idealism. Rather than trust a nationalist posture that offered anecdotal evidence for Irish purity and English debauchery, he would "compile statistics from Dublin hospitals."

Joyce seems to have been particularly sensitive to lies about sex. He complained to Stanislaus that Seamus O'Kelly's *By the Stream of Killmeen* was full of "beautiful, pure faithful Connacht girls and lithe, broad-shouldered open-faced young Connacht men." While granting that "[m]aybe, begod, people like that are to be found by the Stream of Killmeen," Joyce insisted that "none of them has come under my observation" (*Letters II*, 196). Such characters at first "come as a relief, then they tire." "Nora," Joyce went on, "considers his [O'Kelly's] stories tiresome rubbish." The words "tiresome" and "tired" seem to be Joyce's epithet in these years for unrealistic, unbelievable prose, prose that contradicts plain observation. He faulted George Gissing and William Buckley for rendering nature tiresome; more specifically, they "write eloquently about nature" (*Letters II*, 196)—but "eloquence" here carries the negative, antirealist connotation. In this context he praised Tolstoy, whom he called "a magnificent writer," for being "never dull, never stupid, never tired, never pedantic, never theatrical!" (*Letters II*, 106).

Nora Barnacle seems to have been Joyce's touchstone. Not only did he rely on her unlettered, unsophisticated eye to detect O'Kelly's poetic, romantic, dishonest style, but she must have given the lie to his portrait of Connacht girls. As Brenda Maddox reconstructs it, Joyce's first date with the woman from Galway included her putting her hand down Joyce's pants and making "him a man."[131] After becoming a man Joyce refused to romanticize sex.[132] He grew dissatisfied with his own poetical lyrics in *Chamber Music*. As early as December 1904, he expressed to Stanislaus his disillusionment with poetry in general (*Letters II*, 75–76), and when *Chamber Music* eventually was published in 1907, Stanislaus reported that Joyce "wanted to wire the publisher [Elkin Mathews] to suspend the publication" because the love poems were "false." According to his brother, Joyce "always spoke disparagingly of himself as a 'pote' and of his lyrics as 'pomes', a joke. . . . In any case, he considered prose the higher literary form."[133] Joyce himself was actually more equivocal about the verses than Stanislaus implied. He wrote to his brother that he did not "like the book but wish[ed] it were published and be damned to it." He defended it on the grounds that "it is a young man's book. I felt like that" (*Letters II*, 219). The years 1903 and 1904, then, saw not only a shift from poetry to fiction, but a maturing of Joyce's aesthetics. He was done with the "lying drivel" and, instead, tried to put "the face of truth" into his work.

Joyce had been formulating this aesthetic at least as early as 1900. His two early essays, "Drama and Life" and "Ibsen's New Drama," embrace not only realism but also the political activism of that style. In these essays, written in 1900, Joyce proclaimed that the end of art is truth, not beauty; that "truth" in art is accomplished by making art a reflection of the real, ordinary world; that by reflecting the real world art discovers natural laws governing human behavior; that realism demystifies; and that realism is politically charged—that it can change society. He denies "that men and women [should] look to art as the glass wherein they may see themselves idealized," because "this doctrine of idealism in art . . . has in notable instances disfigured manful endeavor." And idealism, according to Joyce, "has also fostered a babyish instinct to dive under blankets at the mention of the bogey of realism" (*CW*, 44). Joyce insisted that the proper end of art is neither to instruct, to elevate, nor to amuse. Nor is it contemplation of the beautiful: "A yet more insidious claim is the claim for beauty. . . . Beauty is the swerga of the aesthete; but truth has a more ascertainable and more real dominion. Art is true to itself when it deals with truth" (*CW*, 43–44). Joyce actually relies on the word "truth" to define the category "drama": "By drama I understand the interplay of passions to portray truth" (*CW*, 41). And the truth consists in what we can observe: "Life we must accept as we see it before our eyes, men and women as we meet them in the real world, not as we apprehend them in the world of faery" (*CW*, 45).

This attitude is evident in Joyce's reviews of other writers, mostly written in 1903 and 1904, which consistently condemned eloquent stylists and consistently praised those who wrote frankly. One review expressed his disdain for Mallarmé, the symbolic poet, and for Lady Gregory, the revival's folklorist. Another dismissed Huysmans. But in October 1903, his review of Alfred Ainger's monograph, *George Crabbe,* found a rare occasion for praise:

> At a time when false sentiment and the "genteel" style were fashionable . . . Crabbe appeared as a champion for realism. . . . Crabbe . . . is an example of some judgement and sober skill, and . . . has set forth the lives of villagers with appreciation and fidelity, and with an occasional splendor. (*CW,* 129)

Fidelity to the "real" world appears to have been Joyce's main criterion for good writing. And Joyce's use of "fidelity" shows none of the subtlety with which Virginia Woolf, for example, later would use the concept to promote the modernists over the Edwardian realists. Joyce's understanding of verisimilitude seems no more complex in these reviews than the traditional realist impulse to avoid sentimentality and eloquence, to write with scientific precision. Thus, in November 1903 he praised T. Baron Russell for his "merit . . . of 'actuality'" (*CW,* 139). The author, Joyce wrote, drew

> very faithfully the picture of the smaller "emporium," with its sordid avarice, its underpaid labour, its intrigue, its "customs of trade." The suburban mind is not invariably beautiful, and its working is here delineated with unsentimental vigour. (*CW,* 139)

This is not to say that Joyce did not attack realists. In September 1905, he asked his brother to read the English realists and report back—Joyce did not have enough time to do it himself (*Letters II,* 111). But a year later, after finding time for a novel by George Gissing which he found "terribly boring," Joyce declared he had "little or nothing to learn from English novelists" because he felt that their work was unrealistic (*Letters II,* 186). He faulted a Hardy story for its implausible plot and unrealistic dialogue:

> Servant-wife blows her nose in the letter and lawyer confronts the mistress. She confesses. Then they talk a page or so of copybook talk

(as distinguished from the servant's ditto). She weeps but he is stern. Is this as near as T.H. can get to life, I wonder? (*Letters II,* 199)

Joyce criticized Moore, Hardy, and Gissing not for being realists, but for being bad realists, especially compared to himself: "O my poor fledglings, poor Corley, poor Ignatius Gallaher!" (*Letters II,* 199).

One of Joyce's greatest concerns was that his characters speak in their natural idioms and not in copybook talk. In the spring of 1906, Grant Richards objected to this passage in "The Boarding House": "The reunion had been almost broken up on account of Jack's violence. . . . Jack kept shouting . . . that if any fellow tried that sort of a game on with his sister he'd bloody well put his teeth down his throat, so he would" (*D,* 68). The problem was the word "bloody," but Joyce refused to omit it: "The word, the exact expression I have used, is in my opinion the one expression in the English language which can create on the reader the effect which I wish to create" (*Letters II,* 136). That "effect" could hardly be anything other than a revelation of Jack Mooney's temper, his proprietary feelings for his sister, and the influence of his threat on Bob Doran's decision to marry Polly. Joyce refused to submit to Richards because "bloody" was the exact idiomatic expression someone like Jack Mooney would have used. Any substitution would ring false and thus would have diminished the story's credibility. Furthermore, in Joyce's own mind the word "bloody" linked him to the nineteenth-century realists. Trying to mollify Richards, Joyce explained that "the worst that will happen, I suppose, is that some critic will allude to me as the 'Irish Zola!'" (*Letters II,* 137). When John Synge's *Playboy of the Western World* caused scandals in 1907, Joyce (wrongly) imagined that it offended Dublin sensibilities because he "uses the word 'bloody' frequently" (*Letters II,* 211). Joyce fancied that "[o]ne writer speaks of Synge and his master Zola (!) so I suppose when *Dubliners* appears they will speak of me and my master Synge" (*Letters II,* 211). The public's misconception, Joyce implied, would have been reasonable, and while he might not have savored the notion of being fathered by Synge (after all, Joyce had a legitimate claim to using vernacular before Synge), being the grandson of Zola seemed to suit him well enough. At any rate, he was willing to jeopardize the publication of *Dubliners* to rally around a flag of realism.

Never in the long negotiations with Grant Richards over what could and could not be omitted from the stories did Joyce indicate that he constructed the stories along a symbolic pattern. But he did imply the book was organized by the cumulative effect of its moral lessons:

The points on which I have not yielded are the points which rivet the book together. If I eliminate them what becomes of the chapter of the moral history of my country?

Joyce went on to insist,

I fight to retain [these points] because I believe that in composing my chapter of moral history in exactly the way I have composed it I have taken the first step toward the spiritual liberation of my country. (*Letters I*, 62–63)

Typically, critics have emphasized "spiritual" over "liberation" in this phrase, but the second word is much more important. The call for "liberation" implies that Irish society needed to progress. Joyce said as much to Stanislaus: "Of course I see that [Sinn Fein's] success would be to substitute Irish for English capital but no-one, I suppose, denies that capitalism is a stage of progress" (*Letters II*, 187)—progress, we must assume, that leads toward socialism. Joyce claimed for himself a role in this progress when he told Richards, "I seriously believe you will retard the course of civilization in Ireland by preventing the Irish people from having one good look at themselves in my nicely polished looking-glass" (*Letters I*, 64). Note Joyce's use of the conventional realist metaphor. According to the social project of realism, whether the realist is reactionary (like Balzac, for example) or progressive (like Zola and Ibsen), the first step toward liberation is a diagnosis of the ills of society, a frank look in the mirror.

After discussing Ibsen's scandalous use of Norwegian idioms and his own scandalous use of Irish idioms, Joyce remarked, "I fancy I[bsen]'s attitude toward litherathure and socialism somewhat resembled mine. . . . I doubt, however, that he ever fell so low as to chronicle the psychology of Lenehan and Farrington" (*Letters II*, 183). According to Joyce, "Counterparts" examined the causes of wife and child abuse in Dublin: "I am no friend of tyranny, as you know," Joyce wrote his brother, "but if many husbands are brutal the atmosphere in which they live (vide Counterparts) is brutal and few wives and homes can satisfy the desire for happiness" (*Letters II*, 192). Apparently, in Joyce's mind, one thing (inter alia) he was going to do with "Counterparts" was diagnose the social environment that creates tyrants like Farrington. Joyce subscribed to the connection between realism and social change, and, once again like Zola, he seems to have seen realism as a branch of the science of psychology.

It is in this context that Joyce called the style of his own stories scrupulously mean. Despite our various interpretations of that phrase, its most obvious meaning is what Joyce intended Grant Richards to understand: he wrote directly, in the exact, untheatrical style of realism.[134] Elaborating on his style, Joyce said that he wrote *Dubliners* "with the conviction that he is a very bold man who dares to alter in the presentment, still more to deform, whatever he has seen and heard" (*Letters II*, 134). "A style of scrupulous meanness," then, is nothing other than prose that perfectly reflects reality. There is no hint here of the complexities of point of view and expression that so characterized the modernists, or of the self-reflexivity that characterized their work. *Dubliners* simply reflects Ireland. But *Dubliners* never really had the chance to propagandize the way Joyce wanted it to, because its publication was delayed until 1914. By that time, Joyce's reputation had passed into the hands of Ezra Pound.

The Egoist's Joyce

2

Joyce had written all of *Dubliners* and most of *A Portrait of the Artist as a Young Man* by December 1913, but virtually no one outside of Dublin had heard of him. He could not get his stories into print. He was discouraged. But in that month he received a letter that would change his fortunes. It was from an American named Ezra Pound. On a recommendation from Yeats, Pound sent Joyce a letter introducing himself and offering to help get Joyce published in any of the four journals with which he was associated, admitting affably "don't in the least know if I can be of any use to you—or you to me." The tone of the letter differed remarkably from Joyce's correspondences with the reluctant publishers, Grant Richards and George Roberts. Pound promised "a place for markedly modern stuff" and the opportunity to "speak your mind on something The Spectator objects to." Joyce, who had faced enormous difficulties because of the frank themes and language of *Dubliners* (and who already had written more frankly, especially concerning sex, in *Portrait*), must have been heartened by Pound's candor. And to have his work solicited, after so many disappointments, must have been a tonic to Joyce's injured pride.[1]

This encounter was the most influential event in Joyce's literary career. Not only did Pound get Joyce published and into the hands of readers, but he also readdressed Joyce's early fiction to an audience vastly different from the Irish middle class. Pound de-Irished Joyce's reputation, and, in the process, stripped his early fiction of its po-

Save T's dignity, by making him understand that he is being used at the pint of a wedge. A new order; a totally different relation between the poet and the public.
—EZRA POUND

litical force. What originally had been intended to criticize middle-class, Dublin Catholic society became a general comment on the universal human condition in the modern age.

Pound's Half-Thousand

Ezra Pound's great influence on the modern movement in literature is well-established. He "discovered" Robert Frost, Marianne Moore, T. S. Eliot, James Joyce, Hilda Doolittle, and Wyndham Lewis, to name the more famous of his charges. Aside from any intellectual influence on modern writers, his material influence was indispensable: whether introducing unknown authors to sympathetic editors, finding sinecures, or lending clothes, Pound might justly be said to have gathered together, nurtured, and sustained the authors we now designate as modern. But his help came with obligations. As critics have pointed out, Pound made his "discoveries" promote his own literary program. To be discovered was to be admitted into this program. Pound helped unknown writers get their work published in a few avant-garde journals, reviewed them favorably, and, ultimately, matched them with a small group of intellectual, cosmopolitan readers. But this was a narrow context in which to be placed, and the yoke of discovery irritated most of his protégés at some time or another. Robert Frost and Amy Lowell are probably the most obvious examples.

Though he did not particularly mind, Joyce was one of those Pound put to use. Despite Pound's claim that "the Egoist may have a slight advertising value if you want to keep your name familiar," he did not offer Joyce a wide readership. Hugh Kenner claims that *The Egoist* "ended with 185 subscribers and *no* newsstand or store sales."[2] It was always on the verge of collapse. On 2 February 1914, the day *The Egoist* began running Joyce's *Portrait,* Pound predicted to Amy Lowell that the paper would last only another six months; three weeks later he informed Lowell that, under its present circumstances, *The Egoist* would not survive through June. A month later Harriet Shaw Weaver "chucked" £250 at the paper, which staved off its imminent decline and established a subsidy that would ameliorate its immediate dependence on subscriptions.[3] Even so, by October 1914, after the outbreak of war, the paper's lack of readers brought on another financial crisis.[4] Trying to sell *Portrait* to H. L. Mencken and *The Smart Set* in March 1915, Pound even admitted that

> *The Egoist* has so few readers that I don't think it would matter, and a lot of people (oh well, no, not a lot, I suppose, in the large

sense of lot but some) who want the whole story would buy the *S.S.* to get it.[5]

Apparently if *The Egoist* would keep Joyce's name familiar, it would be familiar only to a tiny group of people.

Who were those readers, and how did they regard literature? *The Egoist* began in 1913 as *The New Freewoman*, a revival of the feminist *Freewoman*, and its readership was defined by its politics. The first issues were taken up with women's concerns—not only the suffrage movement and its hunger strikes, but the wider women's movement, which Francis Grierson described in the first issue as one of five great movements in the preceding half-century. The "awakening of women after a slumber of three thousand years" was in the company of "the emancipation of slaves in America, the placing of the French Republic on a permanent basis, the military triumph of Japan, [and] the founding of the Chinese Republic."[6] Rebecca West's first contribution described England as a country in which "peace [is] maintained by the torture of women."[7] A regular column, "The Eclipse of Woman," began a historical consideration of "the whole subject of the relation between the sexes."[8] Theodore Schroedor wrote a defense of free love.[9] The first correspondence in the paper concerned the wrongful conviction of a woman for prostitution and her futile attempts to appeal to an indifferent justice system.[10] In the second issue, Godfrey Blount linked the democratic movement with the women's movement. When the paper advertised for the establishment of a "Thousand Club Membership" made up of £1 subscriptions to support the paper for eighteen months, it petitioned feminists.

Pound joined the paper in August 1913. Dora Marsden, the original editor of *The New Freewoman*, feared he would take over the paper. Her fears were well founded.[11] Pound put an end to activism. On 1 September the regular column, "The Eclipse of Woman," was suspended. The departure of Rebecca West as assistant editor (her regular contributions ended two months after Pound joined the staff) subordinated the literary parts of the journal to Pound's "complete domination."[12] By December the character of the paper had so changed that a number of its male contributors requested in a letter to the editor that the name of the paper be changed: its title had become a false advertisement. They wrote,

> We offer a commodity for sale under a description which is not only calculated to attract a section of the public for which in itself it can have no attraction [that is, feminists] but which would be an active deterrent to those who should compose its natural audience.[13]

Apparently, many of its feminist readers were upset by the individualist philosophy the paper had come to espouse. The last issue of *The New Freewoman* tried to set things right by changing its name to *The Egoist*, declaring what the paper stood for, and describing "who should compose its natural audience."

Although she apparently was not against the name change, just two months later Marsden would inform Pound she was "willing to quit" as editor.[14] She did stay on to write the opening articles for many issues, which, as Ellmann unkindly describes, "gradually and impenetrably fulfilled her intention 'to probe to the depths of human nature'" (*JJ*, 352). Her articles also pointedly interpreted political events and issues, which, juxtaposed with Pound's own apolitical contributions, gave the paper an almost schizophrenic character.[15] Nevertheless, Pound's personality was dominant.

Pound's article, "The Serious Artist," published over three late issues of *The New Freewoman*, articulated the attitude toward art that would dominate the new paper.[16] Pound did profess certain beliefs that seem to coincide with Joyce's own. For example, he declared that good art "bears true witness" and that the serious artist observes "the nature of man."[17] Art frankly records the psychology of individuals, and, extending the scientific metaphor, Pound held that art not only records data but diagnoses and cures.

But, significantly, Pound's emphasis on individualism alters these familiar metaphors of realism. Art does not diagnose society. Art does not cure anything by moving people to action against social injustice, because, in Pound's view, art has no exhortative power: "art never asks anybody to do anything, or to think anything, or to be anything." On the contrary, art cures individuals: "Beauty in art reminds one of what is worth while. . . . You don't argue about an April wind, you feel bucked up when you meet it. You feel bucked up when you come on a swift moving thought in Plato or on a fine line in a statue."[18] The vagueness of this curative power—the bucking up of the reader—does not so much reflect Pound's foggy thinking as it does his indifference to the social effect of art. Pound's enthusiasm flitted elsewhere.

Art for Pound did not really constitute a public act, because its audience is not the general public. Good poetry, for example, is "communication between intelligent men," by whom Pound meant men who have taken the pains to acquire culture, who know "half a dozen great literatures."[19] Brandishing a romantic metaphor, Pound reduced the number of readers further, actually to no readers at all. Art "exists as the trees exist": "You can admire, you can sit in the shade, you can pick bananas, you can cut firewood, you can do as you jolly well please."[20] But no matter what you (the reader) do with the tree, you have nothing to do with the its *raison d'être*. The tree's intention, if you will, has nothing to do with the people who put it to use. It grows limbs and sprouts leaves and bananas for its own devices, not to give anyone shade or fruit or firewood. Similarly, readers are merely observers who happen across a poem. What they do with the poem, according to Pound, has nothing to do with the poem's existence. Poems were not written for readers.

In Pound's view, then, art is not a communication even between the artist and intelligent men. The artistic impulse has nothing to do with communication. It is merely the desire "to effect . . . beautiful things."[21] And we know that standards of beauty are eternal, in Pound's view, because he constantly invokes recognized classics—Dante, Rembrandt, Velasquez—as touchstones of great art. For example, ignoring any exhortative, persuasive, or even communicative intentions, Pound attributes the existence of the Victory of Samothrace to the sculptor's impulse to create beauty. Not surprisingly, his description of a viewer's response corresponds to the experience of someone coming upon the statue in the Louvre, which completely removes the statue from its historical context. The viewer, according to Pound, tries to imagine a head as beautiful as the extant statue.[22] Pound does not discuss the occasion for the statue, Rhodes's naval victory over Syria in 190 B.C., nor its original location, the Sanctuary of the Great Gods in Samothrace.[23] Quite possibly the artistic impulse in this case was more complex than the desire to effect beauty, and, possibly, viewers participated in the statue more fully than they would participate in the existence of a tree. The title of the piece suggests what the statue might have communicated to its original viewers: probably it contributed to civic pride, to a conviction of the virtue and moral superiority of Rhodes, or, if nothing else, at least to a celebration of Rhodes's naval prowess.

In Pound's view, the production of great art is even further removed from viewers and readers than is mediocre art:

> Great art must be an exceptional thing. It cannot be the sort of thing anyone can do after a few hours' practice. It must be the result of some exceptional faculty, strength, or perception. It must almost be that strength of perception working with the connivance of fate, or chance, or whatever you choose to call it.[24]

Others have chosen to call it inspiration, even divine inspiration, or at least the inspiration of a muse, though Pound could hardly admit to more than the "fate" or "chance" of an innate faculty of perception. But whatever he calls it, Pound attributes great artistic production to an artist's exceptional receptive abilities. The artistic impulse of the great artist is passive (being moved by something) as opposed to active (the desire to move others). Readers are not considered; if they participate in art at all, it is merely as observers.

In light of this definition of art, it is not surprising that *The Egoist* declared that "[p]rimarily the paper is not written for [readers], it is written to please ourselves [the contributors]."²⁵ That declaration established an unusual rhetorical situation: readers would be mere eavesdroppers on a conversation among a small group of writers. When applied to artists, this philosophy translates into an exclusion of the readers, for whom *The Egoist* itself professed disregard.

We know from his letters that Pound did consider the practical need for readers, at least when it came to selling the paper. For example, he advised Amy Lowell that readers would not care for an American correspondent, since "you can interest London in the state of the American mind no more than you can interest Boston in the culture of Dawson or Butte, Montana"; that *The Egoist* would have been better off paying "an occasional 'selling' [i.e., popular] contributor" than relying on "voluntary work"; and that it should include "a column of fortnightly information for the provincial reader" to increase circulation beyond London.²⁶ But Pound hardly meant for *The Egoist* to become widely popular. *The Egoist* imagined that its readers were what it called individualists, so we should view these commercial sentiments as concessions Pound felt compelled to make in order to continue publishing.

Individualists, according to the last issue of *The New Freewoman,* are dedicated to nothing—no creed, belief, or custom—but "truth." On the surface, then, the journal seems to have devoted itself to realism. The journal appears to have taken as its mission the debunking of accepted beliefs that run counter to a modern, progressive understanding of reality. In declaring itself for "the self," the new paper declared itself against "the states, the churches, laws, moral codes, duties, conventions, public opinion," all the "variant forms which the efforts to put the self under restraint have taken." This self, by implication, is not socially constructed. It is an individual transcending social relations. Consequently, the journal ridiculed "Democracy, the Brotherhood of Man, the cult of Humanity and The Race—all holy entities requiring capital initial letters!" This declaration echoes Joyce's own ridicule of "those big words which make us so unhappy" in his review of William Rooney's patriotic verses, and the general thrust of this announcement for *The Egoist* seems to parallel Joyce's own ideas in "The Day of the Rabblement." The journal insisted that "the egoist stands for nothing: his affair is to see to it that he shall not be compelled to kneel." The egoist was committed to work that bore "the marks of first-hand vision, and the ring of honest and economised expression" rather than to work that served the cant of any creed.[27]

Even after he quit writing regularly for *The Egoist,* Pound carried on his campaign for this new breed of readers, which was distinguished most clearly by its cultural superiority over normal, fettered people. In other words, Pound not only promoted and nurtured a modern style, but he created a modern readership to go along with it. The creation of readers was perhaps the more important of the two achievements, because without this concept of readers, modern literature could not have taken the form it did.

Pound energetically schemed to bring such a readership into existence. According to one of his plans, a small number of contributors—twenty or thirty—would pay T. S. Eliot annual stipends, which would revolutionize literature by reversing the writer's traditional obligation to appeal to readers. The scheme was to initiate "a general movement, in which T. [Eliot] is merely the first man to bee [*sic*] freed." Later the arrangement, which was christened "Bel Esprit," was to incorporate more artists, so many, Pound thought, that he rashly promised Richard Aldington, "We are restarting civilization, and have devised a new modus of making art and literature possible."[28] Eliot balked at being patronized, so Pound added, "Save T's dignity, by making him understand that he is being used as the pint of a wedge. A new order; a totally different relation between the poet and the public." Aldington protested the indignity of the relationship, so Pound replied, "You persistently miss the whole point which IS that it is just as honourable to sell ones stuff, or to receive ones pay from thirty people as from thirty thousand, or from twenty intelligent people as from one newspaper owner."[29] Pound's twenty intelligent people were to be handpicked. He even instructed Aldington to keep stupid people (that is, people with different ideas about art) from joining, no matter what amount they wanted to contribute. The contributors, in essence, would have to subscribe not only to the fund but to the aesthetic views proclaimed in "The Serious Artist." The readers would have to appeal to the writers.

Honor was at stake for Eliot, who thought the idea smacked of "slightly undignified charity." He might have overcome this scruple had it not been for the insecurity of the arrangement. Pound imagined a stipend of £300 per year for five years. But Eliot insisted that he could not quit his job at Lloyds Bank until he had "such guarantees—for my life or for Vivien's life" of an income near £500 per year, which was beyond what Pound could arrange. Bel Esprit collapsed finally in December 1922 when its keystone removed himself from its structure. The *Liverpool Post,* by publicizing the scheme, jeopardized Eliot's position at Lloyds, and Eliot felt obliged to write a public letter disowning the whole thing.[30]

Pound, undaunted, expanded the number of patrons from twenty to five hundred in 1923. The character of his proposal remained the same: Pound opened his contribution to the January 1923 *Criterion,* an article "On Criticism in General," with the proclamation:

> The publication of a review is in itself an appeal to the populace, and as the populace has already shown thumbs down and repeatedly for everything of the slightest interest in literature and the fine arts, this appeal appears to me useless. . . . If there are three hundred people worth writing to, they would do better to organise in some stricter fashion. One would like a list of the resolute, of the half-thousand exiles and proscripts who are ready to risk the *coup.*[31]

Pound wanted a list of the resolute so he could more conveniently solicit their money. Their unwillingness to organize more strictly and pay their dues more regularly does not mean five hundred such people did not exist. Already they were subscribing to *The Egoist* and other avant-garde journals; they were buying the modern paintings Pound peddled; and they were contributing to the onetime stipends Pound solicited. Apparently, they just were not willing to pay more.

But these readers, a small group of intelligent, like-minded, wealthy, educated men and women, were crucial to Pound's literary movement, because, ultimately, it was to these people that writers in Pound's literary movement were supposed to be writing. By campaigning for their existence as a cohesive group, Pound promoted his concept of what the proper readership should be—observers and patrons, but not participators. The image of this readership and of the writer's relation (or lack of relation) to this readership came to dictate how the fiction and poetry discovered by Pound was read. Whether the five hundred readers really existed was not as important as the concept of their existence. This concept justified the attitude toward literature that Pound wanted others to adopt. So long as people believed that writers wrote with these elite readers in mind, they would try to read avant-garde literature as they imagined Pound's half-thousand read literature. In effect, the concept would create the readers.

Eliot's Geniuses

Though Eliot hesitated to accept patrons even on such favorable terms, he shared with Pound the conviction that artists ought to be free of the financial exigencies that bound them to broad readerships. They both labored, not only in such patronage schemes but also in their work for *The Egoist, Dial, The Little Review,* and *Criterion,* to develop a small body of readers that would support them and the literature they approved, which was literature that purported to ignore readers. As part of this program, they had to change Joyce's reputation.

For example, the attitude Eliot professes in the later issues of *The Egoist* supported the notion that Joyce was not writing to the general public. In the first issue for which Eliot was assistant editor, that of June 1917, the magazine included a series of short excerpts from reviews of *The Egoist*'s book edition of *Portrait.* Nearly all of the excerpts were hostile, but that very hostility gave the reviews their advertising value. Since it was Eliot and Pound's conviction that good writing will be scorned and misunderstood by the multitude, bad reviews indicated good literature, or at least good reviews indicated bad literature. In fact, the Egoist Press, which succeeded the journal, was predicated on the poor taste of the general public. The last issue of the magazine explained in a "Notice to Readers" that it would change its mission to book publications, because geniuses, who are neither commercial nor supported by special interest boosters, have trouble finding publishers.[32] The Egoist Press's mission was to provide a venue for great writing that, because it was great, would not be supported by the public.[33] Similarly, in the June–July 1918 issue, Eliot defended *Ulysses*'s lack of popular appeal as a virtue. Like all great art, *Ulysses* terrifies, and "this attractive terror repels the majority of men; they seek the sense of ease which the sensitive man avoids."[34] Eliot, as we might expect, counted himself and a few others among the sensitive men, and, because *The Egoist* was publishing *Ulysses* serially, the sensitive men naturally would presume Joyce was writing to them.

Eliot's concept of an elite readership eventually led to his special concept of artistic "genius," which, in turn, eventually disengaged literature from any necessary connection to a general readership, just as Pound's concept of great art eliminated public participation. The ordinary writer writes for the many, the genius for the few. And Eliot reduced the number of these elite readers, these sensitive men, to fewer than Pound's half-thousand. In his famous 1923 review in *The Dial*, "*Ulysses,* Order, and Myth," Eliot criticized Richard Aldington for censuring *Ulysses* on the grounds of its possible influence on normal people. He decried Aldington's "pathetic solicitude for the half-witted," disavowing any responsibility of the genius toward his readers: "a man of genius is responsible to his peers, not to a studio-full of uneducated and undisciplined coxcombs." [35] Eliot's implication is clear. Joyce did not write *Ulysses* for normal people. He wrote it for other geniuses; consequently, only those few geniuses could properly interpret it. Eliot was in a position to teach normal people how geniuses read books, and much of his criticism is written to this end. "Tradition and the Individual Talent," one such lesson published in *The Egoist* beginning in September 1919, instructed readers to place contemporary writers in the company of the great, dead writers:

> No poet, no artist of any art, has his complete meaning alone. His significance, his appreciation is the appreciation of his relation to the dead poets and artists. You cannot value him alone; you must set him, for contrast and comparison, among the dead. [36]

Eliot's famous and influential rubric oversimplifies: either you interpret a writer without regard to anything, or you interpret the writer with regard to the literary tradition. Not included among Eliot's alternatives is interpreting a writer with regard to a large contemporary public and with regard to the issues preoccupying that public.

A large space in Eliot's article describes what he takes to be the artistic process—in essence, his description of what an author does. His description allowed no place for the contemporary political, social, and religious issues surrounding the artist. Instead, Eliot dwelled on the artist's attitude to the tradition: "he can neither take the past as a lump, an indiscriminate bolus, nor can he form himself wholly upon one preferred period"; "the poet must procure the consciousness of the past." [37] The "consciousness" of which Eliot speaks is not really a description of a given society, nor is it even a class consciousness, because it is based largely on the evidence of the literary tradition. The "consciousness of the past" is a fiction convenient to Eliot's critical program. It had nothing to do with people in the past.

This type of criticism dissolves what Eliot called the artist's "personality": "the progress of an artist is a continual self-sacrifice, a continual extinction of personality."[38] Four months later, in December, Eliot wrote that literature is liberated from its author: "the poet has not a 'personality' to express, but a particular medium, which is only a medium and not a personality, in which impressions and experiences combine in peculiar and unexpected ways"; "the more perfect the artist, the more completely separate in him will be the man who suffers and the mind which creates."[39] Fittingly, Eliot compared the artistic process to a chemical reaction. The artist is the catalyst, which, it is important to point out, has no intention. Literature in this sense is not a social event. Eliot justifies his characterization by again offering oversimplified alternatives: either we regard art as personal expression, or we recognize that it is "an escape from personality."[40] A third possibility is not considered: that literature is a conversation between writers and readers. But, since Eliot cuts off both readers and writers from a work, art seems to function more as a physical science than as an utterance from one person to a group of people.

In Eliot's view, then, literature is liberated from the context of its production. It no longer says things to people. It happens autonomously, separate from the author and the readers, and its appreciation, its interpretation, becomes little more than a learned observation of its workings. Not surprisingly, Eliot, like Pound, portrayed readers as observers. What little interaction the reader does have with the work takes place in isolation from other readers.[41]

Eliot's treatise was published over the last two issues of *The Egoist*. A section of the "Hades" episode of Joyce's *Ulysses* immediately followed the first installment. On the page following the conclusion of the treatise, in the December 1919 issue, Joyce's "Wandering Rocks" episode appeared. That same issue of the paper announces the forthcoming Egoist Press edition of *Ulysses*, to be published despite its lack of commercial promise (that is, its lack of readers) and despite censorship by English printers. (In fact, it would not be published in England for over a decade.) Joyce's publication in *The Egoist,* and Eliot and Pound's general promotion of his work, made Joyce out to be precisely the type of artist Eliot described: an artist in conversation not with a broad readership but with his peers (other artistic and critical geniuses) or with the dead geniuses of the tradition or with no one at all. They made Joyce an egoist.

Joyce the Egoist

I need hardly point out that this version of Joyce opposes the version I offered in Chapter 1. Being an egoist has direct consequences for a writer's intention and, consequently, for the reception of a writer's work. Pound's "The Serious Artist," published in *The New Freewoman* just months before the serial publication of *Portrait* began in *The Egoist,* delineates the consequences:

> It is obvious that ethics are based on the nature of man, just as it is
> obvious that civics are based upon the nature of men when living
> together in groups. . . . We must know what sort of an animal man
> is, before we can contrive his maximum happiness. . . . The arts,
> literature, poesy, are a science, just as chemistry is a science. Their
> subject is man, mankind and the individual.[42]

Pound seems to have believed that literature is ethical and political—it examines the nature of man and the nature of men living together in groups. Later issues of *The Egoist,* including Pound's own literary commentaries, seem to connect literature with practical politics. In his announcement of the book publication of *Portrait,* Pound made the bold statement that

> It is very important that there should be clear, unexaggerated, realis-
> tic literature. It is very important that there should be good prose.
> The hell of contemporary Europe [that is, the First World War] is
> caused by the lack of representative government in Germany, *and* by
> the non-existence of decent prose in the German language.[43]

Legislators failed to represent the governed, and writers failed to honestly represent their subject. These two failures were related. Pound implied that if Germany had had a few Joyces writing a few books like *Portrait,* representative government would have flourished in that country, because the writers would have brought about clear thought, and, since "clear thought and sanity depend on clear prose . . . [a] nation that cannot write clearly cannot be trusted to govern, nor yet to think." Tongue-in-cheek, Pound attributed tyranny in Germany to the "mush[y]" practice of placing verbs at the end of sentences. But less comically he asserted that "only a nation accustomed to muzzy writing could have been lead by the nose and bamboozled as the Germans have been by their controllers." "[H]onest and economised expression," like the work Pound promoted in *The Egoist,* would buck up citizens against tyranny. Good government requires good prose. *The Egoist,* then, linked literature to politics. But the link was tenuous and vague. The paper studiously avoided advocating any particular public policy, since the role of literature merely was to debunk creeds, which invariably cloud "thinking." It performs an ethical, not a civic, function.

The Egoist first mentioned Joyce in its second issue. Titling the article "A Curious History," Pound replaced his usual column with Joyce's open letter to the "press of the United Kingdom" deploring the censorship that *Dubliners* had encountered in London and Dublin. Pound made little comment, except that Joyce was "an author of known and notable talent." (*The Egoist's* readers neither knew nor had noted Joyce's talent, but he was fairly known and noted by London's publishers, like Elkin Matthews and Joseph Hone.) This same letter had already been published in Dublin by Arthur Griffith's *Sinn Fein,* and its different effects in these different journals illustrates the difference between a civic or political and an ethical writer. In *Sinn Fein* the letter remonstrated with Dublin publishers for kowtowing to imperial interests by sparing Edward VII's virtue from a few unsavory allusions. In *The Egoist* the letter remonstrated with London publishers for refusing to treat "the nature of man" frankly and honestly. (Pound probably also meant to titillate readers with a promise of Joyce's iconoclasm, since he began serial publication of *Portrait* in the next issue.) So in Dublin Joyce spoke in a political dialogue, while in London he did not.

Pound published *Portrait* without any comment on Joyce until 15 July 1914, when he reviewed *Dubliners,* which finally had been brought out by Grant Richards. That review claimed Joyce belonged to Pound's "own generation, that is, to the 'nineteen tens,' not to the decade between the 'nineties' and today."[44] Pound's generation had gone beyond impressionism, which Pound regarded sympathetically, and it was characterized by a commitment to realism. Joyce "is a realist," Pound declared, and he put Joyce at the end of a line descending from Stendhal and Flaubert. But the realism that Pound advocated is not the sort of realism that agitates for social change, the sort Joyce tried to establish in Ireland. While distinguishing Joyce from the Celtic revival, Pound insisted that Joyce "is not an institution for the promotion of Irish peasant industries,"[45] and, by implication, neither is he an advocate of any political party or policy in Ireland. Instead, according to Pound, Joyce "accepts an international standard of prose writing and lives up to it."[46] In other words, he should not be read in the context of Irish politics the way writers in the Celtic revival are read. Pound actually insists that, though Joyce "gives Dublin as it presumably is," *Dubliners* is not about Ireland:

> He gives us things as they are, not only for Dublin, but for every city. Erase the local names and a few specifically local allusions, and a few historic events of the past, and substitute a few different local names, allusions and events, and these stories could be retold of any town.[47]

But Joyce, we know, already had refused to erase local names, local allusions, and historic events from the Maunsel edition of his stories. Presumably, they were important to him, and to Irish readers (if not to Pound) they were more than incidental. They made *Dubliners* criticize Irish life, not human life, so that a Dubliner might claim that Maria in "Clay" and Duffy in "A Painful Case" were "present types of [Irish] celibates."[48] Stanislaus Joyce did just that, interpreting the stories as a criticism of the Irish Church and Ireland's economy, which caused such celibacy. But Pound universalizes the stories: "Mr. Joyce does not present 'types' but individuals. I mean he deals with common emotions which run through all races. He does not bank on 'Irish character.'"[49] Joyce's letters and critical writings contemporary with *Dubliners* indicate that Joyce did bank on an "Irish" character, though he bases it not on race but on the influence of Ireland's unique conditions and institutions. Pound's disavowal of the word "types" is misleading, because what Pound is really saying is that Joyce presents types even broader than those Stanislaus identified. His characters are universal types. Either they are not in the least determined by their environment, or all environments are identical. If this is realism, it bears little resemblance to the Continental tradition in which Joyce puts himself.

Pound's fullest assessment of *Portrait*, published three years later, continued to universalize Joyce's work. Occasionally he did make a concession to Joyce's original intent:

> Flaubert pointed out that if France had studied his work they might have been saved a good deal in 1870. If more people had read *The Portrait* and certain stories in Mr. Joyce's *Dubliners* there might have been less recent trouble in Ireland. A clear diagnosis is never without its value.[50]

But Pound was not much interested in the diagnostic force of Joyce's fiction, and that force remained as shadowy as Pound's attribution of German tyranny to sloppy German prose. Instead, Pound spent most of his energy trying to define Joyce by comparing him to other great writers. If Flaubert figures most prominently in those comparisons, it is not because of the political aspects of his work. It is because Flaubert's style was so precise. Ultimately, Pound argued that Joyce belongs in the company of Wyndham Lewis and T. S. Eliot, the writers of Pound's own generation to whom he alluded in 1914. The effect of all of Pound's commentaries on Joyce's reputation was to place Joyce in this small coterie of artists. He made Joyce one of the chief parts of his cosmopolitan, international literary machinery. The success of such a project required the destruction of Joyce's reputation as an *Irish* writer, and so Pound ignored Ireland.

Pound's de-Irishing of *Dubliners* and *Portrait* is all the more striking when we consider that Dora Marsden's political articles in *The Egoist* discussed not only Irish politics in great detail but even the relation of Irish literature to Irish politics. For example, James Larkin and the general strike in Dublin dominated the "Views and Comments" in the first issue of *The Egoist*, just two weeks before publication of "A Curious History" and a month before the first installment of *Portrait*. In the latter half of 1913, labor and management waged a virtual civil war in Ireland. After a series of successful strikes, Larkin faced off against William Martin Murphy's United Dublin Tramways Company by calling a strike during Horse Show week in late August. Murphy, who led the Employers' Federation in Dublin, organized a citywide lockout of union workers in response to Larkin's sympathetic strikers. The strikes became violent when Larkin was arrested for making seditious speeches. Riots broke out in protest. Two people were killed, and hundreds, including police, were wounded. Late in the year Larkin, released from jail, traveled to England to garner support for his strike from British trade unions, which already had given much relief to the Irish workers. Larkin sought sympathetic strikes and increased militancy from the English, but the English labor leaders, who disliked Larkin's brand of unionism, withdrew nearly all support, so that British relief contributions "dwindled to a trickle in the New Year of 1914." [51]

The first issue of *The Egoist*, published New Year's Day, 1914, came on the heels of Larkin's failed trip to England. In her column, "Views and Comments," Marsden discussed Larkin's visit and denounced British labor's rejection of militancy. Praising Larkin as the sort of individualist that *The Egoist* wanted to promote, Marsden likened the English labor delegates to "happy domesticated [barnyard] brethren." She unequivocally approved of Larkin's militancy, asserting that "the poor will cease to be poor when they refuse to be: the down-trodden will disappear when they decide to stand up: the hungry will have bread when they take it." She nearly endorsed open rebellion:

It is *inaction* which has killed the recent "strike" efforts. What form the requisite definite action should take the strikers must judge for themselves. They know best what they stand in need of to make their defiance effectual.

She went on to discuss the arming of James Connolly's new, socialist Citizen Army, which finally precipitated the government's ban on importing firearms to Ireland, long after Edmund Carson's unionist volunteers had fully armed themselves in Ulster.[52]

Marsden also commented on the Easter Rising of 1916. This discussion proposed a role for literature similar to Pound's own. Marsden blamed the republican revolution on the Celtic revival's clouding of Ireland's thinking. Ireland's religion, literature, and art, according to Marsden, were "a menagerie of exquisite spooks" that flattered Ireland "into permitting herself the extravagance of a 'temperament.'" Like Pound, Marsden contended that "plain speaking is a cheap remedy, but it happens to be the one which would meet the situation in Ireland." But unlike Pound, she connects literature to specific political goals. "Plain speaking," in Marsden's view, would convince Ireland of England's resolve to deny home rule, and, consequently, the Irish would "appreciate that wisdom lies in acquiescence and in turning their minds and energies to more profitable things" than rebellion. Perhaps she was driven to a small degree of patriotism by the First World War, for she refused to condone any extraconstitutional action by the Irish—an about-face from her earlier endorsements of union militancy.[53]

The readers of *The Egoist* were fully aware of the situation in Ireland, by which I mean not only the volatile nationalist politics but also the economic class conflicts. As I have argued in my previous chapter, both of these issues are central in *Dubliners*. Yet, in Ezra Pound's presentation of Joyce's fiction, these issues are hardly mentioned. Their omission amounts to a rejection of the political force of *Dubliners* in favor of its ethical force. If Pound admitted that Joyce's fiction could have done much to clear up the clouded "thinking" of the Irish, he purposely neglected to discuss the fiction in relation to any specific Irish political policy. The neglect is all the more significant since Joyce's hopes for Ireland were identical to Marsden's endorsement of socialism in 1913 and nearly opposite her advocacy of imperialism in 1916. It was hardly likely that readers of *The Egoist* would recognize these positions, since Pound insisted that Joyce did not write about Ireland.

Apparently Pound's concluding remarks in his first letter to Joyce— "don't in the least know if I can be of any use to you—or you to me"— were not pro forma. They frankly suggest the reciprocal nature of their relationship. Joyce could use Pound to advertise his name. Pound could use Joyce in his literary movement. Pound required not only that Joyce's reputation grow larger, but also that Joyce's reputation change. Pound had no use for Joyce so long as he was an Irish writer presenting a chapter in the moral history of his country to general readers in Ireland and abroad.

In reality, Pound changed Joyce's readership from the very limited group of Irish who had read his work in manuscripts to the larger (though still small) readership of *The Egoist*. The first readers of *Portrait* and *Ulysses*, of course, were *The Egoist*'s subscribers. Most of the people who bought Grant Richards's edition of *Dubliners* were probably also Pound's own readers. Printings did not go much beyond a half-thousand until the 1926 Modern Library edition in New York, which printed 5,000 copies.[54] And the relationship between *Dubliners* and patrons of *The Egoist* was officially confirmed on 31 December 1921, when the Egoist Press acquired rights to the book from Grant Richards for fifty pounds.[55] This authority over Joyce's work cemented Pound's influence on his reputation.[56] Before Pound, Joyce had the reputation of an Irish writer bitterly attacking certain institutions in Dublin with the weapons of realism and satire. But under Pound's influence, he took on the reputation of an international writer exploring the human psyche for the benefit of a tiny number of like-minded literati. Joyce seemed to be another of Pound's authors writing to select readers.

The Modern Classic

This reputation was adopted by Ben Huebsch and Bennett Cerf, who expanded Joyce's market to America, but hobbled his books by wrapping them in Pound's terms. They were marketed as modern classics, which by definition have a limited appeal and no bearing on contemporary history. B. W. Huebsch published Joyce in 1916, when he came out with the first American editions of *Dubliners* and *Portrait*. *Dubliners* must have sold moderately well, because he issued a reprint in 1922 and then again in 1925, just before he was bought out by Harold Guinzburg and George

Oppenheimer of the newly founded Viking Press. *Portrait* sold considerably better, requiring reprints in 1917, 1918, 1921, and 1922 under Huebsch, and in 1925 and 1927 under Viking.[57]

Before he merged with Viking, Huebsch was "in the forefront of a small group of new publishers who brought new European writers to America."[58] In his memoirs, Huebsch avowed his political intentions as a publisher:

> I was always more likely to succumb to the persuasion of authors who wanted to make the world over than to those who celebrated the world as it is. Unable myself to create "the Federation of the World" or to emancipate the victims of a clumsy social system, I sank into vicarious saviorship.[59]

He helped found the American Civil Liberties Union. He published such works as *The Truth About Socialism* by Allen Benson, who ran for president as a socialist candidate in 1916.[60] His book list was notoriously controversial and put Joyce in the company of writers who were considered political radicals.[61] But he never expected Joyce to have a popular appeal, and so he marketed him primarily as a serious artist rather than as a thinker. Though he did advertise *Dubliners* and *Portrait* in *Publishers' Weekly,* his ad on the back cover of *The Little Review* indicated that his real target audience was *The Egoist*'s American counterparts. As Ann McCullough has noted, he believed Joyce's "success would be artistic rather than popular."[62]

Huebsch promoted recent fiction writers like Joyce and D. H. Lawrence as if they were established "classics," giving them the stamp of approval typically reserved for long dead writers already studied in the academy, and he brought this attitude with him to Viking, where he served as vice president until 1956. Both *Dubliners* and *Portrait* were issued by Bennett Cerf's The Modern Library imprint—*Dubliners* for the first time in 1926 and *Portrait* in 1928.[63] These Modern Library editions had been reprinted twenty-seven and thirty-seven times by 1950, so they seem to have been the dominant form in which Americans read Joyce's first two books. But these popular editions went even further than Huebsch did to promote modern works as classics. The Modern Library was founded in 1917 by Albert Boni and Horace Liveright in order to issue cheap "reprints of English and European classics, including contemporary works otherwise unavailable in the United States."[64] The first list included Oscar Wilde, Nietzsche, Kipling, Stevenson, Dostoevski, and

Ibsen, and each book sold for sixty cents. Grant Richards had actually shipped 500 sets of sheets for *Dubliners* to Boni in 1915, presumably for a Modern Library edition, but they went to the bottom of the sea on the torpedoed SS *Arabic*.[65] Bennett Cerf bought The Modern Library in 1925, and though in two years he expanded it into Random House, Cerf kept The Modern Library as an imprint. Discussing Random House's publication of *Ulysses,* Cerf indicated the amicable relations between himself and Viking:

> [Joyce's] *Portrait of the Artist as a Young Man* and *Dubliners* were also selling well for Viking Press. Harold Guinzburg, the founder of Viking, was one of my best friends, and I didn't want to harm that relationship. There are some publishers who respect the rights of others. Viking and Random House would never dream of doing anything to hurt each other.

Cerf and Viking had similar sentiments. In 1925 Cerf declared in his preface to his first catalogue for the newly acquired publishing house that "The Modern Library is a collection of the most significant, interesting, and thought provoking books in modern literature, hand bound, fully limp, and designed to sell at ninety-five cents a copy." The editors, he assured potential buyers, for eight years had been judiciously selecting, in "strict adherence to a definite policy," one title a month. The catalogue did not define the editors' policy, but clearly Cerf meant to imply that his list was comprised by modern classics. The list of titles in The Modern Library series, appended to the end of The Modern Library *Dubliners* (which was published one year after Cerf acquired the press) and *Portrait* (which was published two years later), confirms this impression. The writers we today recognize as the moderns—Conrad Aiken, Sherwood Anderson, Joseph Conrad, e. e. cummings, John Dos Passos, William Faulkner, E. M. Forster, etc.—mingle with cheap reprints of established classics like Balzac, Chaucer, Dante, Dickens, Milton. The list might serve to define "the tradition" as Eliot described it fifteen years earlier in "Tradition and the Individual Talent." The effect was to raise the status of the contemporary authors so judiciously selected by Cerf and Boni, which must have been Cerf's goal. It also encouraged readers to read the moderns like they read classics—as if the authors were geniuses writing for no particular audience or at least for a vague posterity. I do not mean to suggest that Balzac, Dickens, and Dante really wrote with no particular audience in mind, but to market these books to a twentieth-century audience that was not likely to know the historical context of their original publication presupposes that these books are valuable for some "time-less" quality.

While Padraic Colum's introduction to The Modern Library *Dubliners* does not promote the "classic" Joyce, Herbert Gorman's introduction to The Modern Library *Portrait* does. The contrast between these two introductions—the first by one of Joyce's Irish schoolmates, someone who knew the man personally, and the other by an American critic introduced to Joyce only after publication of *Ulysses*—is instructive. Colum, mainly recounting his version of the book's suppression in Dublin, avoids hagiography. Gorman's Joyce is heroic:

> To this effort Mr. Joyce brought an astonishing and awe-inspiring array of talents. He brought independence and arrogance, psychological acumen and dialectical skill, vividness of conception and treatment, moral freedom and human passion, sensitivity and intuition, and, above all, a literary courage that was undisputed.[66]

This is the type of inflated praise that can come only from someone who knows the egoist, not the man. Joyce, in Gorman's portrait, comes off as something of a modern Byronic hero, and *Portrait* is the "painful autobiography of a sensitive soul, lonely and proud."[67] This version of Joyce goes a long way to justifying Gorman's claim that *Portrait* is the precursor to "that new literature, new both in form and content, that will be the classics of tomorrow."[68] The main theme of Gorman's essay is that *Portrait* is a prelude to *Ulysses*, that Joyce's career displays the kind of continuity that (as I will discuss in Chapter 5) is a characteristic of the New Criticism's artists. All in all, in the spirit of The Modern Library, Gorman further establishes Joyce as a classic.

Eliot's defense of *The Little Review* against charges of obscenity drive this point home: good literature has no effect on society at large. In 1918 *The Little Review* was seized in the mail for including "Cattleman's Spring Mate," a short story regarded by the U.S. Post Office as lewd and indecent. As Eliot points out, the court justified confiscating the material because it had a "tendency to excite lust."[69] Classics that contained explicit sexual material sometimes were exempted, not because of the intent of their authors, but because of the attitude of their readers. Eliot, claiming that the cat "was let out of the bag with really injudicious candour," quotes Judge Hand's rationale for the exemption:

I have little doubt [said he] that numerous really great writings would come under the ban if tests [of obscenity] that are frequently current were applied, and these approved publications doubtless escape only because they come within the term "classics," which means for the purpose of the application of the statute, that they are ordinarily immune from interference, because they have the sanction of age and fame, and usually appeal to a comparatively limited number of readers.[70]

Classics are safe, because they are read only by the highly educated, who, because of their unusual reading practices, tended not to be aroused by such material. Eliot implies that the same exception should be granted anything published in *The Little Review,* because *The Little Review* publishes works written for a select, elite readership. Works in *The Little Review* may not have been sanctioned by age or fame, but they had been sanctioned by the smallness of the magazine's circulation.

Eliot's defense of *The Little Review* rests squarely on the exclusivity of this small group of readers, whose distinction from the general public he continually emphasizes. For example, Eliot believes the "Cattleman's" case will be of interest "to the small public which cares for literature." He insists that *The Little Review* is a small periodical, "struggling quite alone in America to obtain and publish only contemporary work of the finest quality." He concludes, "In America the small number of people who are sensitive to good literature are now forbidden to read one of the finest pieces of prose in the language."[71] His rationale is quite clear. Literature in *The Little Review* should be exempt from obscenity law because it is high art written not for the public but for a small number of people, literary people, who have learned to read literature without being aroused. Eliot cares not at all for the large number of people, the general public, who are susceptible to arousal or, by implication, who are susceptible to exhortation or persuasion.

These issues applied directly to Joyce, for his *Ulysses* was seized and destroyed just like "The Cattleman's Spring." The celebrated entry of *Ulysses* into America after John Woolsey's decision in December 1933 ensured that Pound and Eliot's version of Joyce would dominate his reputation in America. Joyce gained and lost with Woolsey's decision. He gained the right to be published and distributed. But that right was predicated on his failure to move people. Woolsey's decision marked a capitulation to "the literary world," which produced guides to help readers interpret *Ulysses* in the detached method Eliot and Pound approved. For if *Ulysses* would not sexually arouse, nor would it politically arouse. If a book is "literature" it can talk frankly about sex, because it will not have the direct and exhortative effect on people that "obscene" literature does. The *Ulysses* trial would convince readers that Joyce did not intend to arouse them. In fact, readers would learn that to be aroused would be an admission of their own stupidity.

Ernst's Joyce   3

The Erotic Joyce

On 4 October 1920 John Sumner swore out a warrant against the proprietors of the Washington Square Bookshop for selling the July–August issue of *The Little Review,* which published the "Nausicaa" episode of *Ulysses.* Included in the warrant were Margaret Anderson and Jane Heap, editors of the avant-garde magazine, which kept its offices above the bookshop. The women were not taken into custody—a benevolent concession by Sumner, who, by Heap's own account, was "a decent enough chap" though "serious and colorless and worn." [1] Thus began *Ulysses*'s long career in American courts. It had had brushes with the law before. In January 1919, under the authority of what were known as the Comstock Laws, the issue of *The Little Review* carrying "Lestrygonians" was banned from the mails. In May the post office seized "Scylla and Charybdis." [2] But by seizing "Nausicaa" from a bookshop, Sumner enforced a New York state law (Penal Code 1141) rather than a federal postal law and brought into a New York court Margaret Anderson and Jane Heap.

Anderson and Sumner might be taken as representatives of opposing ideologies, liberal and conservative, and so their battle and the subsequent legal battles over *Ulysses* illustrate the gradual liberalizing of American literary culture. Sumner was the Secretary of the New York Society for the Suppression of Vice. Anderson found him "charming," and she warmed to his shyness, his sensitivity, and the intensity with which he

There isn't a chance in a million that any point will be raised as to the facts.
—ALEXANDER LINDEY,
ATTORNEY FOR RANDOM HOUSE

believed in his ideas, even those she disliked. She once met him on the street, and their cordial argument brought them into the Washington Square Bookshop, where Anderson felt "embarrassed by the antipathy with which everyone in the bookshop regarded him." Sumner, she observed sympathetically, was "probably hurt by [their dislike] and used to this hurt."[3] By most accounts, Sumner had softened the ham-fisted methods that the Vice Society had used in the Victorian era. He succeeded Anthony Comstock, founder of the society and general bully, in 1915. When Sumner suppressed books, arrested booksellers and publishers, and threatened authors, he did so with an air of literary sensitivity and with a genial, if insincere, smile.[4] But he could be cruel, and he abused his powers nearly as often as he exercised them.[5]

Anderson and Heap had begun *The Little Review* in Chicago but had moved to New York, and, even in the cosmopolitan metropolis, they must have made quite a stir by living openly as lesbians and providing a place—in *The Little Review* and in their offices, which they painted black and purple—for the lively and often eccentric conversation of the modern set. Their magazine, which consistently attacked censorship of sex, stirred up the Vice Society like a stick poked at a hive.[6]

The case against *The Little Review* proceeded like a farce. Offstage, animated press conferences starring Anderson and Heap competed with the trial, which exasperated their lawyer, John Quinn, who, enjoying his center stage performances in court, practiced a nonconfrontational brand of good-old-boy politics.[7] Quinn relished his role as patron and guardian of the arts. He was an "irascible" Irish American who made a fortune as a clever Tammany Hall lawyer and spent it on modern art—manuscripts, painting, sculpture—which densely packed his Central Park West apartment.[8] Quinn did not like Heap and Anderson, and they never took to him. But Ezra Pound, who was acting as *The Little Review*'s European agent, lectured the editors on Quinn's value:

> Quinn made me mad the first time I saw him (1910). I came back on him four years later, and since then I have spent a good deal of his money. . . . I don't know if his talk about art is like all American talk about art, but his *act* about art is a damn sight different.[9]

Quinn bankrolled not only Pound: he and his friends endowed *The Little Review* with enough money to publish *Ulysses*. So naturally, despite their personal feelings, Anderson and Heap turned to their benefactor for help against Sumner. He blustered about their stupidity, but when Anderson suggested they look for someone else to take the case, he snatched it up.

"No power on earth," Anderson later wrote, "could have wrested that privilege from him."[10]

Quinn telephoned John Sumner to talk him out of the suit, but that did not work because Sumner was not at liberty to cut a deal. He had been pushed to issue the warrant by the district attorney, who had been pushed by a prominent stock broker, who had found his unmarried and impressionable daughter reading "Nausicaa." So the case went to court, where Quinn attempted to present Joyce as a serious artist of high renown. Under the court's indulgence, he brought three experts to testify to the seriousness of the book. But this plan did not work either: "one of the judges protested that he wasn't interested in hearing anything about James Joyce, that he merely wanted to discuss the obscene writing in question."[11] Precedent in obscenity cases, as I will explain below, gave judges the prerogative to focus exclusively on the offending passages taken out of context. Such a focus was dangerous to Quinn's case, for under such a narrow test the book was sure to be adjudged obscene. So Quinn quickly retreated.[12] He conceded that *Ulysses* was an experiment carried too far and that it was disgusting and repulsive. But, he insisted, it was not lascivious.

The retreat did not work. The women were fined, although the judges spared them from prison. Irving Younger, a celebrated teacher and historian of the New York legal scene, suggests Quinn would have won the case had Anderson and Heap not so loudly protested their prosecution. Younger faults their press conferences and their published tirades for destroying Quinn's chance of bringing out *Ulysses* as a book, which, since the mails would not have been involved, might have escaped the censors.[13] It is true that Sumner was attracted by the type of notoriety that Anderson and Heap accrued when they publicized each burning of their magazine, and it is also true that the standards the post office imposed on magazines were generally higher than those Sumner imposed on the book industry. But still Sumner seized books pretty vigorously, and his subsequent attitude toward *Ulysses* indicates that Younger and Quinn were wrong.

Anderson and Heap, who despaired of defending art in a court of law, felt their battle should be fought in the court of public opinion.[14] Even as they planned their legal strategy with Quinn, Anderson "began to speak of broadening the public." Quinn predicted acerbically, "You'll be broadening the matron at Blackwell's Island," the women's prison in New York.[15] His warning was not idle. Other women, most notably Ira Craddock, had been imprisoned for publishing obscenity before. Even so, Anderson thought that by acquiescing in court Quinn "let his opportunity [for edifying the public] slip entirely." Describing her frustration with the trial, Anderson wrote, "I nearly rose from my seat to cry out that the only issue under consideration was the kind of person James Joyce was. . . . But, having promised [Quinn], I sat still."[16]

It is a good thing she did. Had she delivered her speech, one judge (who had indicated an indifference to Joyce already) would have told her to sit down, explaining that the author's character was irrelevant. And then he might have sent her to prison, for the judges, in a patronizing show of chivalry, insisted that since Anderson was a woman she could not have understood what she had printed. This supposed ignorance mitigated her guilt. A spirited defense on her part would have emancipated the judges from their gallant illusions about female editors. Quinn astutely never undertook to emancipate them himself. So in the courtroom he made Anderson swallow her urge to defend *Ulysses*'s beauty and its singular (if frank) artistic merit. She was reduced to *post camera* sour grapes: "the question which should [have been] up for discussion in court," she insisted, was the issue the court, following precedent, refused to consider: "the relation of the artist—the great writer—to the public."[17]

But Anderson did as poorly in the court of public opinion as Quinn did in the Court of Special Sessions. Even before the trial, "complaints about 'Ulysses' . . . pour[ed]" into *The Little Review*, so many that Anderson felt herself "becoming inured to the most insulting, the most offensive, the most vulgar letters telling us exactly what the public thought of James Joyce."[18] In her memoir, written in 1930, Anderson claims that she answered only one, particularly angry letter, though in 1953 she said "we answered them all."[19] Perhaps she meant the letters were answered by *The Little Review*, which spent many pages trying "to make *Ulysses* intelligible to certain of its readers" and to explain Joyce's experiment "to people who understand nothing."[20] Anderson asked her readers, "Do you think the public will ever be ready for such a book as *Ulysses*?"[21] Her question assumed a difference of opinion between her readers and "the public," though it was her readers, America's *literati*, not the general public, who were vilifying Joyce.[22] Nevertheless, Anderson preached *Ulysses* with the fervor and self-sacrifice of John the Baptist. Before the trial, Anderson "tried to prepare the public for the coming debate by writing . . . that [she] would disagree with nearly everything that would be said in court, both by the prosecution and by the defense."[23] In retrospect, she agreed with Otto Kahn, who told her,

[Y]our "Ulysses" affair was badly managed. John Quinn is rather old-fashioned, I'm afraid. I should have given you Morris Gest as a publicity agent and had the case on all the front pages. That would have helped you.[24]

No doubt a press agent might have sped Anderson's readers down the road to acceptance. But in 1921, despite Anderson's efforts, Americans were convinced that Joyce was a dirty writer. The *New York Times,* for example, applauded Sumner's victory, stating that "Mr. Joyce and the editors of *The Little Review* probably would defend [the offending passages] as 'realistic,' but that does not make them the more tolerable in print, and certainly does not make them either artistic or literary." The paper was happy that Anderson and Heap did not go to jail, but only because "to make . . . pseudo-martyrs . . . is not wise."[25] Anderson recognized how effective martyrdom might have been to the prophet's mission. She wrote that it was a mistake to "allow the persuasions of [her] friends or [her] lawyer to keep [her] out of jail." Denied the satisfaction of having her head served on a platter, Anderson survived to complain that "not one New York newspaper came to our defense, not one spoke out for Joyce, not one cared to be identified with the 'Ulysses' scandal."[26]

The result of the case was that both arenas—the judicial and the public—considered *Ulysses* erotica. No reputable publisher, including Ben Huebsch (who had published *Dubliners* and *Portrait*) at Viking, would take on the unexpurgated book, and Joyce would not publish it any other way. Joyce finally turned to Sylvia Beach, proprietor of the Shakespeare and Company bookshop in Paris, to bring out the book in 1922. Beach tried to export it to America but failed, and the book (which was produced in a rather expensive ten-dollar edition) had to be smuggled into the country by tourists. Ernest Hemingway helped Beach smuggle copies to her American subscribers via Canada.[27] We might expect that the general public's notion of Joyce's decadence increased: *Ulysses* was published only in Paris, it remained official contraband, and its readers were the urbane sophisticates of New York and Chicago who traveled to France. Sylvia Beach acknowledged that *Ulysses* brought her bookstore an unwelcome notoriety: "After the success of *Ulysses,* writers flocked to Shakespeare and Company on the assumption that I was going to specialize in erotica."[28] Such a reputation would have been confirmed by the book's next publication in America, the bootleg publication in 1926 by Samuel Roth, which occasioned the famous petition against piracy signed by 167 notables, including Albert Einstein.[29] Roth specialized in cheap publications of erotica, and, though he used *Ulysses* to try to raise the respectability of his magazine (*Two Worlds Monthly*), the subtlety of the gesture was probably lost on most of the reading public. Roth probably sullied *Ulysses* more than *Ulysses* ennobled him.

The Second Round: A Test of Beach's *Ulysses*

Empowered by the conviction of Anderson and Heap in 1921, U.S. customs officials seized and destroyed five hundred copies of Shakespeare and Company's "second" edition in the fall of 1922, which indicated definitively that the book was contraband.[30] But *Ulysses* did not find itself in court again until the summer of 1928. On August 1, the customs court in Minneapolis included seven copies of *Ulysses* in a general condemnation of eleven separate titles that were seized from A. Heymoolen, a bookseller (*M*, 18, 142–144). *Ulysses* was found in the company of *Crossways of Sex, The Law concerning Draped Virginity, The Strangest Voluptuousness, The Vice of Women, The Physiology of Vice,* and *Aphrodite.* The justices held that even "a casual glance through the books in evidence is sufficient to satisfy us that they are filled with obscenity of the rottenest and vilest character" (*M*, 144). This was the first court test of the Shakespeare and Company edition, but it would later prove inconclusive because it was not clear if the justices examined and commented on *Ulysses* in particular. Apparently *Ulysses* was guilty by association, since a casual glance would not reveal its dirty parts.

Nevertheless, in a subsequent sweep of New York City, Sumner rounded up five different booksellers for distributing obscenity.[31] At least two of them—David Moss, the husband of Frances Steloff and co-owner of Gotham Book and Art, and the ubiquitous Samuel Roth—were found in possession of *Ulysses,* as well as hundreds of other volumes Sumner considered to be obscene, up to $3,500 worth of books from Gotham alone. Moss engaged the firm of Greenbaum, Ernst, and Wolff to defend him. Though Morris Ernst already had shown a keen interest in censorship, for some reason Eddie Greenbaum, Ernst's old schoolmate from Williams College, handled the case, with the help of his assistant, Norman Levy.

Moss presented Greenbaum with a difficult case, for he was guilty. He had been clandestinely selling marginal books and even some books that previously had been judged to be well beyond the margin, like Frank Harris's *My Life.* Steloff, whom her biographer describes as something of a prude, had "pleaded with Moss not to handle actionable books," but he had protested, "'What shall we do with our good customers? Send them to a rival shop?' They deserved the same service on marginal items as on others, [Moss] believed." [32] In exchange for a guilty plea, Greenbaum got the prosecutor to leave most of the titles out of the suit and enter into evidence only the most offensive. *Ulysses* was not among those in court. At sentencing, Justice Healy said,

> Moss . . . [w]e have letters here from a great many persons, substantial citizens, who seem to feel that you are all right, but we have to teach you a lesson to be careful in the future. This time we are going to impose a fine [of $250] instead of a jail sentence.[33]

Shortly thereafter Greenbaum began the always difficult task of getting Sumner to return the books that had not been condemned by the court. He sent a list to Sumner, which included *Ulysses* and Paul Jordan Smith's *Key to "Ulysses,"* which quoted liberally from its subject. Sumner would not give up any of the books, and he and Greenbaum began a protracted negotiation over what Sumner, to avoid a lawsuit, would release. They drew up lists. Sumner wrote down the titles he felt were absolutely obscene, while Greenbaum wrote down the titles he felt any court would pass on. *Ulysses* was on both lists. Greenbaum suggested they submit the disputed books to the district attorney for arbitration, presumably to get his opinion on which books he would consent to prosecute, and Sumner agreed, though he refused to submit *Ulysses* on the grounds that it had already been condemned by the special sessions court in *The Little Review* case.[34] It didn't matter, because the district attorney declined the office, preferring to act as a prosecutor after publication rather than as a censor before. A New York public librarian and two professors were approached, but they declined to be arbiters as well.

Sumner decided to read each of the books himself, and by March 1929 he informed Greenbaum that he had gotten around to *The Key to "Ulysses"*:

> Of the books I took to read [on vacation], I have read the Key to Ulysses which contains rather specifically the matter which was condemned by the Court of Special Sessions [in *The Little Review* case]; also various other passages which are objectionable.

But he was not intransigent, for he added, "We can take this matter up together." [35] Over the next year Sumner's list encroached further on Greenbaum's.

In the meantime, Roth's case came to trial. Already under a suspended sentence for selling other obscenity, Roth was not as lucky as Moss. In

January 1930 he was sent to prison. His trial gave Sumner more ammunition against *Ulysses,* for, "although it was not the subject of a prosecution," the book "was condemned by Judge Knox of the U.S. District Court," as Sumner informed Greenbaum.[36] Actually, since the copies of *Ulysses* seized from Roth most probably were his own two-volume pirated and expurgated edition, it might have survived a direct prosecution. Knox probably condemned it without reading it.[37] At any rate, Sumner reminded Greenbaum that *Ulysses* "has also been condemned by the federal customs officials and is not allowed for importation if discovered."[38] Finally, on 23 May 1930, the titles in question were settled. Apparently *Ulysses* was not among those condemned, for when Greenbaum sent Sumner a final list of books to which he relinquished all claims, he pointed out, "I have not included the *Ulysses,* which is to be disposed of as we agreed."[39] I have not found any evidence about that agreement, but Sumner probably released the book because he had seized only one copy from Moss, a first edition, valued at fifty dollars. The other titles, each of multiple copies, were of more obvious commercial purpose. I imagine that Sumner stipulated that the *Ulysses* would not be offered for sale. Whatever their agreement, *Ulysses*'s second round in the courts ended inconclusively. It was condemned, ignorantly and gratuitously, by one judge, and Sumner, in a gesture that obviously had no consequences for the policies of the Society for the Suppression of Vice, U.S. customs, or the post office, had relaxed his vigilance over at least one copy of the book.

So matters stood in 1931, when a personal financial crisis prompted Joyce to explore an American and an English edition of the book. His agent, Pinker, put out feelers to the major publishing firms, but most of the offers that came back were from publishers of erotica. Ben Huebsch put in a bid, but he still insisted that parts of the book be cut out.[40] Joyce's reputation for obscenity attracted the wrong publishers and scared off the right ones.

Morris Ernst and the Obscenity Laws

Despite the unpromising court proceedings, Morris Ernst, Greenbaum's partner, thought the time was ripe to test the book definitively. Ernst was particularly well-suited to taking on unpopular causes, especially obscenity cases. He was born in 1888 in Uniontown, Alabama, the son of a Bohemian immigrant who had nurtured a general store into a real estate fortune. The family was among the only Jews in town, and, when Morris was two years old, his mother insisted that they move back to

New York. His father was rich then—he left the South with a fortune of $200,000—and grew richer yet through real estate speculations in New York. Morris spent a solitary and unpopular childhood, punctuated by utilitarian lessons (insisted upon by his father), such as how to play piano and cello, and by demeaning jokes (delivered by uncles) about his ugly nose. He went to an exclusive, progressive prep school established by Horace Mann, and one summer he attended a camp called Camp Marienfeld, at which, Ernst recalled, the boys spent a great deal of time naked. He probably inherited a literary sense from his mother, who not only "had read all the classics" but was also "very modern in her reading."[41] Rejected by Harvard, Ernst went to Williams College, where he achieved a degree of popularity by playing school songs on the piano (his lessons had a practical application after all) and joining a fraternity. Later he would despise the fraternities, which had given him for the first time a feeling of belonging to something, but only at the price of excluding others. Eventually his own fraternity would draft rules against admitting Jews, except the sons of members.

In college Ernst was not particularly rich. His father had lost most of his money in the depression of 1907, and Ernst was obliged to pay for his first trip to Europe by working on a cattle ship. He paid for law school by selling men's shirts, and after he graduated, since he was unable to get a job as a lawyer, he kept on selling. But his life changed when Eddie Greenbaum invited him to join a partnership with Herbert Wolff. Ernst and the firm prospered so much that, by the 1930s, as Julia Blanchard described him, Ernst hardly fit the mold of "the usual crusader." He must have seemed a New York aristocrat in his expensive, custom-made suits. He had an abiding interest in leisure sports, including sailing, and was a patron of the theater.[42] He had the deserved reputation of a devoted family man, though he was known throughout the smart set as "the wittiest conversationalist in New York." He had a good sense of humor and his "charmingly simple, natural and direct manner" assured him a memorable place in the New York legal establishment.[43] But given his youthful experience, Ernst was always attracted to the underdog, especially to those bullied by government and big business. He might be described as a civil liberties lawyer, and by 1931 his firm had already made a name for itself by participating in "virtually every major lawsuit challenging censorship on the grounds of obscenity."[44]

His commitment to free speech was piqued by a case he lost. Defending an "innocuous" book called *What Happens* against a charge of obscenity, Ernst noticed that on breaks the jurors relaxed by reading the tabloids, which were full of tawdry stories less decent than the book they were judging. Ernst thought this fact indicated that his case was won, so he was stunned when the jury found the book obscene. After the verdict, one juror told Ernst that the jury had been offended by the word "masturbation." The juror suggested that if the publisher had substituted the word "self-abuse" they would have acquitted. "This so offended what little I have of rational thought," Ernst later said, "that I immediately started to write articles on the subject of obscenity."[45] Ernst wrote so many articles and books that he seems to have written the prevailing history of obscenity law. His books on obscenity and his briefs in the many obscenity cases he argued echo in all the standard texts today.[46]

Obscenity law, like the blue laws, crossed over from ecclesiastical to secular jurisdiction as the power of the Church waned in eighteenth-century England and America. The first American laws were judge-made—that is, they were judges' interpretations of common law. The first successful prosecution in America was in 1815: the Commonwealth of Pennsylvania convicted Jesse Sharpless and his buddies for charging people to ogle "a certain lewd, wicked, scandalous, infamous, and obscene painting, representing a man in an obscene, impudent, and indecent posture with a woman, to the manifest corruption and subversion of youth, and other citizens of the Commonwealth."[47] Five years later, in 1821, Massachusetts successfully prosecuted Peter Holmes for publishing *Memoirs of a Woman of Pleasure* (better known as John Cleland's *Fanny Hill*), the first book banned in the United States on the grounds of obscenity. These prosecutions instituted a couple of difficulties that have plagued obscenity law ever since: the difficulty in defining the term (hence the foliation of adjectives in the indictments), the problem of describing to the court the indecent material (without further publishing the alleged obscenity), and the issue of audience (and its relative susceptibility to corruption). These ambiguities were perpetuated by obscenity law well into the 1920s and '30s. Indeed, unlike most criminal offenses, obscenity seemed to necessitate ambiguity. Charges of obscenity could be (and in practice were) vague in order to avoid the unpleasant consequence of having obscene material entered into the public record or shown to a jury. Neither the lewd painting (in the Sharpless case) nor the lewd book (in the *Fanny Hill* case) were put in evidence, so the defense had no opportunity to argue that the material was not obscene. "Obscenity" was something considered to be self-evident, and the "self" to whom it was evident theoretically would be society, represented by the jury, but in practice it was the prosecutor, since the jury never saw the offending material. Essentially, trials began with a presumption of guilt rather than innocence, and defendants were hamstrung in their efforts to demonstrate otherwise.

Statutes banning obscenity began appearing in 1821, but they did little to clarify the vagaries that characterized common law. One of the earliest tests of obscenity emerged from an 1857 British parliamentary debate over Lord Campbell's Act, which outlawed the sale of obscenity in England. In an effort to exempt from the ban "celebrated pictures" (such as prints of paintings in the British Museum) and also such celebrated authors as Rochester, "Wycherley, Congreve, and the rest of them," Lord Campbell insisted the act applied only to works intended by their authors to corrupt youth. Thus the first exemptions for what later would be called "classics" were established, and the importance of authorial intention—at least the intentions of long-dead authors—was confirmed.

But Lord Campbell's new touchstone of obscenity, "the common feelings of decency in any well regulated mind," was as vague a standard as any, so in practice the act depended on the same self-evidency of the earlier statutes.[48] A decade later, in 1868, another test was established by Lord Chief Justice Cockburn, who wrote,

> I think the test of obscenity is this, whether the tendency of the matter charged as obscenity is to deprave and corrupt those whose minds are open to such immoral influences and into whose hands a publication of this sort may fall.

This inelegant statement came to be known as the "Hicklin rule," and, though it was a definition of sorts, it hardly clarified matters.

But the Hicklin rule was a solid club that was wielded with a vengeance. In 1872 an unlikely shop clerk named Anthony Comstock, backed by J. P. Morgan and the YMCA, organized the New York Society for the Suppression of Vice with himself as secretary and thereby institutionalized the Victorian rage against smut. The next year Comstock successfully lobbied the U.S. Congress to outlaw sending obscenity (and materials related to contraception and abortion) through the mails. The torrents of local statutes that sprung from this act of Congress became known as the "Comstock Laws." Comstock was able to secure for himself a special appointment from the post office, and so his society became a quasigovernment agency with the power to raid and seize property, which he did with great relish.[49]

The vagueness of the Hicklin rule gave Comstock his best weapon. What was depraved, what was corrupt, and which texts were likely to fall into the hands of youth or women (for they, so Comstock thought, had minds that were open to immoral influences) were determined by the Society for the Suppression of Vice. Any publisher who was afraid of losing an investment to seizure would seek approval from Comstock before setting type. As Morris Ernst observes, even H. L. Mencken found himself obliged to traipse "over to the Vice Society office with the manuscript of a book by Theodore Dreiser to beg absolution." [50]

Vague as the Hicklin rule was, it was a departure point for the courts. The late nineteenth and early twentieth centuries saw a number of attempts to refine this definition. In 1893 Judge O'Brien of the New York Supreme Court allowed the sale of a bundle of expensive volumes, including *Tom Jones,* Ovid's *The Art of Love,* and Rousseau's *Confessions.* This case established a number of important precedents for opponents to the obscenity laws: the "very artistic character [and] the high quality of style" of the books, which were products of "the greatest literary genius," mitigated the obscenity; their renown as established, "standard literary work[s] . . . [that] rank with the higher literature" prevented their seizure; and, due to the high cost of the editions, the unlikelihood that they would "be bought or appreciated by the class of people from whom unclean publications ought to be withheld" weighed in their favor. Two years later, in 1895, scatological words—the cloacal terms of which Joyce was so fond—were exempt on the grounds that obscenity laws applied only to sexual material. In 1915 Judge Learned Hand, one of three judges later deciding the appeal of the *Ulysses* case, introduced the idea that obscenity ought to be defined by a community standard, which could change from place to place and from year to year. This precedent gave defendants a powerful strategy: if they could prove a community had already accepted a work, the courts were likely to accept it as well. In 1922 Raymond Halsey, who had been acquitted of selling obscene material, turned the tables on the New York Society for the Suppression of Vice by suing it for false arrest and malicious prosecution (members had had him arrested for selling *Mademoiselle de Maupin* by Theophile Gautier). The case is particularly important because it considered evidence of the author's high reputation, furnished by critics (though not yet by living critics), and even entered into evidence that greatest certificate of literary merit, the test of time. Most importantly it established the possibility that a book could be considered in its entirety. Until *Halsey,* prosecutors excerpted the offensive passages, even if the book ultimately condemned the lewd behavior described in those excerpts.

In 1929 Ernst started winning his own exceptions to the obscenity law. He defended Radclyffe Hall's *The Well of Loneliness,* a novel that must have been particularly loathsome to the society, for it traced the series of events that lead a young woman to lesbianism. In his brief Ernst portrayed the book as a valuable social document. Though it was clearly a work of imaginative fiction, the novel boasted an introduction by Havelock Ellis, the psychologist, declaring its importance as a record of deviant sexual psychology.[51] Ernst's brief exploited this assessment, contending that *The Well of Loneliness* was "a distinguished novel of social value and significance":

> It does honestly attempt to present a social problem, predicating such presentation on the assumption that social problems can be solved only by deliberation and discussion and the free interchange of ideas.[52]

The brief included "Statements from Eminent Doctors, Clergy & Critics" supporting the need to treat such topics openly. And the seriousness with which Hall treated her subject, Ernst argued, made it unlikely that it would weaken the heterosexuality of young women:

> By its very nature, [the novel] is not likely to be read by any but those who can fully grasps [*sic*] its full import, and who—far from being corrupted by it—will be quickened to sympathy and understanding: the two human qualities without which no social perplexity can be overcome.[53]

This delicate statement allowed the judges to think Ernst was defining the "social perplexity" as lesbianism, when he really meant the problem was *intolerance* of lesbianism. The judges were convinced: Ernst won the case on appeal, establishing that no theme—not even homosexuality—could be banned from literature.

In 1930 Ernst again used both of these tactics. In his defense of *Pay Day,* a novel by Nathan Asch, Ernst called attention to the "scientific value" of the book: it was "acknowledged to be a valuable psychological record."[54] That same year, Mary Ware Dennett was hauled into court for writing and selling a sex-education pamphlet. She wrote the tract to supply her teenaged sons with a sensitive and truthful account they could not get anywhere else. Through word of mouth the demand grew large enough for her to print and sell the pamphlet, though at a price so modest that the publication was not considered commercial. Among her customers were ministers and both the YMCA and YWCA. Ernst successfully defended her, and in deciding not to seize the pamphlets the court considered new circumstances: the truth of the material and the sincerity of the motives with which it was written. In 1931 Ernst twice defended Dr. Marie Stopes, once for her book *Married Love* and again for her book *Contraception*. In both cases Ernst relied on the scientific merit of the books and the unlikelihood that they would be used by unmarried young women, and in both cases Judge John Woolsey ruled in his favor.[55]

But since none of these cases—neither Ernst's cases nor those preceding him—came before the U.S. Supreme Court, the growing exceptions to obscenity laws were not universally adopted. Until the Supreme Court began a series of rulings with *Roth* in 1957, conservative and liberal judges alike found precedents for their personal convictions.[56] For example, in a significant dissent from *Halsey,* Judge Crane argued that literary merit does not exempt a book from obscenity law and "genius" does not excuse a writer's prurient preoccupations. Likewise, in 1924 Robert Wagner held in *People v. Seltzer* that "Charm of language, subtlety of thought, faultless style, even distinction of authorship, may all have their lure for the literary critic, yet these qualities may all be present and the book be unfit for dissemination to the reading public." He once again invoked the Hicklin rule, insisting that obscenity laws are meant to protect "the young and immature, the ignorant and sensually inclined." In a similar vein, the dissenter in the appeal of the *Ulysses* trial, Judge Martin T. Manton, said,

> If we disregard the protection of the morals of the susceptible, are we to consider merely the benefits and pleasures derived from letters by those who pose as the more highly developed and intelligent? (M, 460–461)

In other words, Manton argued that the testimony of literary experts should not take the place of the Hicklin rule: "To do so would show an utter disregard for the standards of literary decency of the community as a whole and an utter disregard for the effect of a book upon the average, less sophisticated member of society. . . . notwithstanding the deprivation of benefits to a few" *littérateurs* (M, 461). Wagner and Manton both feared that the privileges of an unpopular audience (urban literati) were considered more important than the danger to a corruptible audience (young women, degenerates, etc.).

Class Conflict

Ironically, Manton voiced an insight already well-articulated by Ernst in his 1928 book, *To the Pure*: that the growing exceptions to the obscenity law were based on class prejudice. Ernst begins that book with the question: "What is obscenity? Is it more than an empty word?" Early statutes, like the New York law under which Anderson and Heap were prosecuted in 1920, strung the words "lewd," "lascivious," "indecent," "disgusting," and "filthy" together with "obscene." One lawyer in 1928 tried to get his client off the hook because the indictment failed to accuse him of being disgusting. He argued that a book broke no law if it was only lewd, lascivious, indecent, filthy, and obscene. His argument, though manifestly stupid, is countered only by the equally stupid alternative notion that books prosecuted in New York were charged with six different crimes, one designated by each synonym. More likely, as Ernst points out, the New York legislators strung the words together because they did not know themselves how to define what they banned, so they cast their net widely. The courts were obliged to turn to the dictionary to decide just what the legislators meant. But in the pages of the dictionaries, judges discovered that "lewd" was defined as "lascivious," and "lascivious" was "lewd," while "indecent" was "obscene," and "obscene" was "indecent." In *Contraception,* Judge Woolsey himself felt this uneasiness when he struggled to understand the meanings of "obscene" and "immoral." Woolsey ruled in favor of Dr. Marie Stopes, but only after using a dictionary to define "obscene" as indecent, lustful, impure, and lewd; and "immoral" as the "opposite of moral; not moral . . . non-moral." Woolsey did not seem to recognize the tautologies. Ernst, who argued the case, must have been delighted with the outcome, if not with Woolsey's reasoning.[57] "The multiplication of adjectives," Ernst noted wryly, "is often a sign of uneasiness."[58] Uneasily, legislators tried to justify the self-evidency rule of prosecutors, which in turn allowed the government to execute and the courts to interpret the laws arbitrarily.

The laws were executed arbitrarily because they were not meant to limit the freedoms of wealthy and educated audiences, who, presumably, were well equipped to resist corruption. The laws were meant to protect the susceptible—"those whose minds are open to such immoral influences and into whose hands a publication of this sort may fall," in the words of the Hicklin rule. Ostensibly, the susceptible minds belonged to the ubiquitous "school girl" of so many oral arguments in obscenity cases. In reality, the minds belonged to the lower classes. That is why, Ernst wrote,

[t]here are a great many people who would grow apoplectic if a censorship of the theatre were suggested but who are ready to find all

sorts of justifications for a censorship of the movies. . . . The censorship is based rather upon the assumed low character of the masses of
movie patrons than upon the greater capacity for demoralization
which is inherent in the movie as an art form.[59]

In other words, obscenity resided in the audience, not in the text. Ernst
points out that "[w]hen a Latin classic, for instance, is translated into English, it is the custom to permit the most obscene passages to remain in
the original Latin. This ingenious device keeps the obscenity from the
eyes of the vulgar," while allowing educated men and women to read as
much as they want. "Obscenity," Ernst writes, "is a class concept," and
obscenity laws were decidedly undemocratic.[60]

A work need not be written in Latin to prove itself inaccessible to the
uneducated masses. High prices, for example, regulated distribution. The
general history of censorship bears this out. Censorship of books, for example, really began only after printing presses began to distribute books
cheaply in the market place.[61] In England, the royal licensing of plays in
the early twentieth century was an anachronism left from the seventeenth
century, when theater was a popular art form. The American theater,
which, because of its cost and relative sophistication, was patronized
mainly by the middle and upper classes, did not need to be controlled.
But movies, whose theaters were filled with the poor, were strictly cen-
sored in the 1920s. Indeed, according to Ernst, the belief that high "art"
should be afforded a special status above the reach of the censors is based
on prejudices about audiences:

> It is not surprising to find that the same literary critics who as a class
> grow terribly indignant when a literary magazine is barred from the
> mails or a book is attacked by the Vice Society, often show them-
> selves quite apathetic to movie censorship, and regard the vagaries
> of Will Hays and the minions of censorship under him as so many
> harmless jocosities. They are more than inclined to agree with the
> Supreme Court of the United States that the movies are indeed not
> an art but an industry.[62]

What makes one thing art and another a mere industrial product is its
audience. If a work is intended for everyone, rich and poor, if it is consumed by the millions, rather than by the hundreds, if it can be compre-
hended by the uneducated, then it is not art. It is industry and thus susceptible to government regulation and unprotected by civil liberties. No
doubt the higher status of films today derives at least in part from all the

incomprehensible, decidedly uncommercial, highbrow movies—movies that the unwashed masses would not pay to see—that have been produced since 1928. Thus we call "art" theaters those movie houses that cater to the well-educated.

This distinction was no less true of books, and, despite the fact that giving "literature"—Shakespeare, Rabelais, the Bible, etc.—some special consideration was a wedge in the obscenity law, and despite the fact that Ernst would willingly and skillfully use that wedge, he recognized and deplored the undemocratic sentiment responsible for it. The trick was to broaden what was allowed under the exception. What, after all, made a book "literature"? Or, in the more precise term, what made a book a "classic" and thus worthy of special consideration?[63] Ernst, ironically, recognized two illogical criteria—the tests of time and unpopularity:

> Must a period of five, ten, twenty-five, fifty, or seventy-five years first elapse? . . . Perhaps, however, the secretaries of the vice societies are cynics, and believe that the very definition of a classic is a book that is no longer read.[64]

Though tongue-in-cheek, Ernst's point is hardly facetious, for the vice societies and the courts recognized that books that are no longer read— or, rather, books that are not read by the masses—did not need to be regulated. To be a classic, a book had to be very old and its author long dead.

The case of the Bible is a bit more puzzling, since it is the most widely distributed book in the English-speaking world. But, even though the poor read the Bible, its special status also derived from the definition of its audience. Ernst hit on the important distinction in its case: "Does the Bible owe its immunity to the greater reverence with which it is supposed to be approached?" The answer of the courts and vice societies would most certainly have been "yes," although usually they did not entertain the question, even though it was put to them often. Ernst ridiculed the notion that the Bible was read reverently, but he recognized the principle that exempted it: the environment in which an audience reads a book does much to constitute that audience, and so the context in which a book is read is more important to classifying it than the words in the book itself. Admittedly, sometimes a text alone might establish the attitude of an audience. A gang of debauching high schoolers out on Saturday night will be moved to sobriety if they stumble unexpectedly into Speilberg's *Schindler's List*. But more often than not, the audience's attitude is defined by things external to the text—for example, the place where it is read. And something read with great ceremony in church is hardly going to be obscene, even if it is the Song of Solomon.

So the exceptions to obscenity law derived not just from the belief that the educated are less susceptible to corruption than the uneducated, but also from the comforting knowledge that the educated reader will take up a leatherbound, gilded *Art of Love* in the sanctity of his personal library (which also stores Horace in the original and the ethical writings of Quintillian), slouching in his familiar wingback chair, pipe in hand and a halo of smoke reverently (I might add academically) swirling above his head. The uneducated reader, presumably, would thumb through the public library's already well-thumbed copy (which seems to open automatically to the dirty parts) in his bathroom, with its water-stained tub and leaky faucet the super has not yet fixed. In the first case the book is not obscene, while in the second it is. This reasoning is still based on a class prejudice, which holds that expensive furniture and the richness of the book itself, its vellum and gold, protect against prurience as much as education.[65]

Edward Bishop admirably demonstrates this point in his recent article about the covers of various editions of *Ulysses*. Bishop begins with Jerome McGann's axiom that literary meaning is produced not only by the words in a book, but by "the price of a book, its place of publication, even its physical form and the institutional structures by which it is distributed and received."[66] By examining the covers and the accompanying advertisements for many editions of the book, Bishop convincingly argues that the literary meaning of *Ulysses* has changed through the years. Unfortunately, he did not analyze Roth's edition, but undoubtedly he would have concluded that that cheap edition was more nearly obscene, even though expurgated, than Beach's blue and white covered, unexpurgated, limited, expensive edition.

So Manton, the dissenting judge, and Ernst, the defense attorney, both agreed that the adjudication of obscenity was based on class prejudice. The difference between them was this: Manton held that the wealthy and educated should not have the privilege of reading *Ulysses,* while Ernst held that the lower classes were no more susceptible to corruption and so should not be barred from it. But Ernst was a practical man. He saw that the argument for a more democratic society would not influence the courts. So he used the wedge at hand, even if that wedge was fear of the poor.

The object of both the prosecution and the defense, then, in obscenity cases, was to define the literary meaning of a book. In other words, both sides tried to produce literary meaning by packaging the book in their own way. Ernst understood this principle well, for he often argued that the vice society's successful prosecution of one edition of a book should not apply to other editions that are packaged differently. Each package changed the meaning of the book. For the defense, the package involved all the items Jerome McGann lists—price, place of publication, physical form, method of distribution—and some he did not, such as the seriousness of the author's intention, which Ernst used in the Hall, Dennett, and Stopes trials. The records of the *Ulysses* trial provide us with a telling view into the first extensive American packaging of Joyce, and Ernst constructed that package according to the demands of his ongoing war with the vice society.

The Third Round

By the summer of 1931 Ernst and his assistant, Alexander Lindey, had the vice society on the ropes. The Stopes cases were particularly significant, because, as Ernst noted, ten years earlier "quite a number of printers and booksellers went to jail" for publishing and selling Stopes's books.[67] His ability to get previously condemned books passed by the courts encouraged his ambitions. Just three weeks after the second Stopes trial, Ernst and Lindey began plotting for *Ulysses,* whose possible celebrity was irresistible to Lindey. On 6 August 1931 Lindey wrote to Ernst in a memo, "I still feel very keenly that this would be the grandest obscenity case in the history of law and literature, and I am ready to do anything in the world to get it started" (*M,* 77). The first thing to do was "line up some American publisher." Ben Huebsch, who had published Joyce's *Dubliners* and *Portrait,* and who had contracted for *Work in Progress,* was the obvious front-runner. Even so, apparently Ernst did not want to go with Viking, the company that bought Huebsch out. Lindey's 6 August memo to Ernst acknowledged that "[b]y reason of the connection of Guinzberg and Schwabacher with the Viking Press I realize that you would not be very anxious to see *Ulysses* sponsored by them" (*M,* 77).[68] But if Viking got the contract, Ernst was ready to put his feelings aside, and by October he was discussing legal strategy with Huebsch. The day after their meeting, Ernst wrote a long letter detailing possible costs, proposing that he forgo the normal legal fees and instead take a 4 percent royalty (*M,* 100).

But Viking was having trouble securing a contract with Joyce. The problem was Sylvia Beach. As Lindey had discovered through Beach's sister, Shakespeare and Company had "sole and exclusive world rights" to

Ulysses, and so Viking had to go through the book's first publisher (*M*, 100). Apparently she had already vetoed an advance offer of £850 on the 15 percent royalty that Viking had tendered to Joyce in July 1931.[69]

It is not entirely clear why Joyce had relinquished his American and British rights to Beach. It was not until 1930, eight years and numerous reprints after Beach's first edition of *Ulysses,* that Joyce insisted on drawing up a contract. He gave Beach exclusive rights for publishing *Ulysses* worldwide, while she gave him a guarantee of 25 percent royalty—10 percent higher than the American industry standard.[70] Beach suggests that the legal contract helped Joyce in his fight against Roth's pirated edition of *Ulysses.*[71] Stuart Gilbert speculated that Joyce rashly signed the contract "at the time of his son's marriage, wishing to have some dowry for that penniless youth."[72] I suspect that by abandoning all rights to Beach, Joyce felt he was protecting himself against any litigation that might result from publication in England and America. The most benevolent interpretation would be that Joyce wanted to make sure Beach would profit from any American and English editions—the contract did stipulate that other publishers had to purchase the rights to the book from Beach, which was an unusual stipulation.

Whatever his aim, Joyce missed his mark, because within a year the contract proved to be an impediment to bringing the book out in America. Beach was angry that Joyce and his agent, Pinker, were treating her "as if they were proposing to publish a manuscript, not to take over a book that had been published by somebody else for almost ten years."[73] So she demanded the ridiculously high sum of $25,000, which chased away all interested parties except Viking. Huebsch offered her a royalty on the book, but, since this would have come out of Joyce's royalty, both Beach and Joyce refused.

It seems fairly clear that relations between Joyce and Beach were strained in the fall of 1931 and winter of 1932. Already Joyce had been diminishing his dependence on her by relying more and more often on Paul Leon. Through the fall of 1931, Huebsch was caught in the cross fire. He was never able to change Beach's mind, and by 17 December 1931 he relinquished the fight to Bennett Cerf, who had recently bought The Modern Library:

Pinker writes from London that he thinks it's hopeless to try to wrench *Ulysses* away from Miss Beach. She refuses even to consider our offer, although, as I need not tell you, I tried to make the offer attractive. Under the circumstances I think that we [Viking] will have to retire. . . . You graciously stood aside for us, and naturally we cannot object if you should now determine to try to get the book. (*M*, 100)

Huebsch also wrote to Ernst, who immediately contacted Cerf: "Ben Huebsch has written to me that he has already notified you that Viking Press is not interested at present in the American publication of ULYSSES. The only thing to do is for you and I to hop a boat and spend a weekend with Miss Beach in Paris." [74] Apparently, despite his work for Viking in October, Ernst had been talking about the project with Cerf.

In the early months of 1932, Cerf, without Ernst, went to Paris to meet with Beach and Joyce. [75] Cerf makes no mention of it, but the breakthrough came when Joyce (through one of his spokesmen) accused Beach, with justice I think, of obstructing his interests. [76] The remark "floored" Beach. Immediately she phoned up Joyce and "told him that he was now free to dispose of *Ulysses* in any way that suited him and that [she] would make no further claims on it." [77]

The popular understanding of this story, based largely on Cerf's account in *At Random* and Ellmann's account in *James Joyce,* which is based on an article Cerf wrote in 1934, is that Cerf went to Ernst with the idea of getting *Ulysses* into America. [78] According to Cerf, sometime in December Robert Kastor, a New York stockbroker and the brother of Joyce's daughter-in-law, called Cerf into his office to see if he wanted help getting *Ulysses.* Kastor was going to Europe in a few weeks and offered to put in a word for Random House with Joyce. According to Cerf, "I tore uptown, talked the matter over with Donald Klopfer, my partner, and before five that evening we were closeted with Morris Ernst, the lawyer, outlining a contract to offer Mr. Joyce, and laying the plans for the legal battle before us." [79]

Cerf's memoirs aim for the fine effect of the anecdote rather than for accuracy. As Lindey's memo of August 1931 suggests, Random House was brought into the project by Ernst at least four months after Ernst had begun work on it. No doubt there was a good bit of talk about *Ulysses* among publishers in the summer of 1931, for that was when Pinker started soliciting again. Perhaps this talk generated the idea between Ernst and Lindey in the first place. But in any event, the whole thing was really initiated by the lawyers. This point is not trivial. For the first time in their fight against Sumner and obscenity laws, Ernst and Lindey went on the offensive. They initiated a case on their own terms (rather than on Sumner's), in the venue of their choice. Before Cerf was even let in on the conversations, Lindey and Ernst were deciding how to best present *Ulysses* to the courts. That presentation, the fabulous package that accompanied *Ulysses*'s first legal entry into America, was determined by the demands of Ernst's larger battle against obscenity law. The first publication in America was not really by Random House. It was by Greenbaum, Wolff, and Ernst, and their plan was to make their edition of *Ulysses* conform to the exceptions to the obscenity restrictions that they had already established. If Cerf tore uptown to plot strategy with Ernst in December, Ernst, who had had the plans drawn up since August, must have done all the talking.[80]

The Preparation

Armed with his successful defenses of *The Well of Loneliness, The Sex Side of Life, Contraception,* and *Married Love,* Ernst and Lindey met for lunch with Cerf and Klopfer on 22 March 1932. Cerf had returned from Europe with the go-ahead from Joyce, so their first order of business was to settle his contract. Joyce would get advances amounting to $2,500—a thousand of which he could keep even if Ernst lost the case—on royalties of 15 percent for the first 25,000 copies, 20 percent on further sales, and 10 percent of a popular edition that would come out two years after the trade edition.[81] Cerf and Ernst also settled their arrangement, which was similar to the terms Ernst had suggested to Huebsch in October: in addition to a $500 retainer and money for expenses and court appearances, Ernst would get 5 percent royalty on the trade and deluxe editions of the book and 2 percent on cheap reprints (*M*, 108–109).

They also plotted their method of attack. Ernst preferred to test the book in a federal court, because a victory there would carry considerable weight with postal authorities and the various state courts, each of which had their own obscenity policies (*M*, 99).[82] So they would import one copy of the book and have it seized by customs, which, according to procedure, would forward it to the U.S. Attorney, who in turn would initiate a libel suit against the book. This venue—the United States District Court for the Southern District of New York—had a number of other advantages as well. The defendant would be the book itself, so if they lost the trial Cerf could neither be fined nor jailed. Also, the book could be tested without Cerf going through the expense of publishing it first.[83] It would be fairly easy to dispense with a jury in this venue, which, as I will discuss below, was extremely important to Ernst. And finally, Section 305 of the Tariff Act of 1922, the statute under which the book would be prosecuted, banned only *obscene* matter. Ernst would not have to bother proving that the book was not indecent nor lewd nor lascivious nor disgusting nor filthy, which he might have had to prove in a New York state court.

Within a week they had already begun constructing evidence that *Ulysses* was not pornography. Lindey told Cerf exactly what to procure: first, "testimonials" from "prominent critics, librarians, authors, physicians, psychologists, psychoanalysts, welfare workers" about the book's "literary, scientific, or sociological value"; second, a bibliography from Edmund Wilson, who had published a long article on Joyce in the *New Republic*; third, a bibliography of "essays, articles and criticisms" from Joyce; and fourth, statistics gathered from "one hundred or more colleges and universities" concerning whether "Joyce is considered in any course given by the institution on contemporary literature . . . [and] whether *Ulysses* is used as collateral or prescribed reading" (*M*, 111–112). Lindey and Ernst were relatively sure they would be allowed to use such expert testimony, but just in case they landed in a conservative court, they had Cerf instruct Paul Leon to paste articles into the copy of the book to be imported, so at least a few critical opinions would be entered into evidence.

Even though the Dennett and Stopes trials were about technical books—sex education for minors and married couples—his success with Radclyffe Hall's *The Well of Loneliness* demonstrated to Ernst that the techniques used in defending those scientific and educational books could apply to works of imaginative fiction. So Ernst had to demonstrate the sincerity of Joyce's motives, the truth of the work, and the uncommercial nature of its publication, just as he had in the other cases. Most importantly, he had to demonstrate the social utility of the novel.

One way of demonstrating that utility was by selecting the proper recipient for the copy that was to be seized by customs. Ernst realized that by selecting a famous recipient he could enter into evidence another endorsement. It is not surprising, then, that on 24 March 1932, Lindey wrote to Cerf that

> Mr. Ernst and I have given some time to choice of a sendee. In our opinion, the head of a public or university library would be most desirable, especially if he happens to be a person of national repute. The president of a medical or scientific society would be a good second choice. (*M*, 109)

The endorsement of such an upstanding citizen would help establish from the start the kind of audience that *Ulysses* had. Far from the school girl into whose hands fell a copy of *The Little Review,* a librarian of national repute would give the book an apparent authorization from an official bound by a public trust to edify society. Such a person would have been the perfect mix of literary sophistication and government conservatism.

In addition, Ernst and Lindey were trying to align the Joyce case more closely with the Dennett and Stopes cases. If the book's recipient were a scientist or doctor, that would seem to attest to the truthfulness of its portrait of human psychology. It would testify to the novel's social utility, which was a central part of the defense in the Stopes and Dennett cases as well as in Ernst's successful defense of birth control clinics. Ernst and Cerf further pursued this line of defense with *Ulysses* by asking sociologists, psychologists, psychiatrists, and social workers, among others, to write opinions of the book. In his solicitation, Cerf wrote, "What we should like to have is not so much a strict literary appraisal, *as an estimate of the novel as a social document*" [emphasis added] (M, 122). Apparently, Ernst meant to present *Ulysses* in terms not inconsistent with the way I presented *Dubliners* in Chapter 1—in the tradition of Zola and the experimental novel. But only a few sociologists, psychologists, and anthropologists replied to the solicitation, and the plan to send the copy of *Ulysses* to a scientist or college president or librarian fell through as well.[84] Very early on, it became clear that the "social utility" defense would not sustain the case, for they garnered practically no estimates of the novel as a social document.

Within a week of their lunch meeting, Cerf and Lindey agreed on the best possible sendee: Justice Oliver Wendell Holmes. It was a masterful decision. If Holmes were to agree to receive the book, that would render other strategies obsolete. Hardly anyone in the lower echelons of the justice system could resist such an endorsement. Unfortunately, Holmes declined to help (M, 115). By mid-April they were leaning toward soliciting a critic of repute. Cerf suggested that they try H. L. Mencken (the editor of the *American Mercury*) or Henry Seidel Canby (the editor of *The Saturday Review of Literature*). Lindey settled on Canby, possibly because of the relative conservatism of his review, but Canby either declined or Lindey and Cerf decided to abandon entirely the idea of a famous recipient, because on 19 April Cerf told Paul Leon to simply address the book to Random House.

Leon cabled Cerf when he sent the book, telling him that it left Europe on 28 April and was scheduled to arrive in New York on the *Bremen* on 3 May (M, 133). Lindey called up the customs house to make sure they would not miss it, then wrote them a letter explaining that he did not "wish the book to slip through without official scrutiny." But, despite these precautions, the seizure did not go according to plan. Cerf told a colorful anecdote about the proceedings, and, though he is typically unreliable, his is the only account that remains. The day the boat arrived was one of the hottest ever in New York, and the customs officials were stamping everything without inspecting anything. Cerf's agent had to insist that his bag be inspected, and, when the reluctant official found the copy of *Ulysses,* he cried, "Oh for God's sake, everybody brings that in. We don't pay attention to it." Cerf's agent insisted. The custom's official called over his superior, who thought the agent's persistence ridiculous. But finally they relented. *Ulysses* was seized and launched on its final voyage through American courts.[85]

It was a slow cruise. Customs took almost three weeks to send the book to the U.S. Attorney of the Southern District of New York, who would decide whether or not to bring a libel proceeding. By mid-June, Assistant U.S. Attorney Samuel Coleman, who had read 300 pages of the book, declined Lindey's offer to send "several books . . . which were bound to be helpful in the first reading of [*Ulysses*]." Coleman must have subscribed to the typical prosecutorial assumption that obscenity is self-evident, because he saw no need to consult the critics. But things seemed fairly promising anyway. "Coleman," Lindey reported to Ernst, "made a special effort to be cordial and cooperative. . . . He made a special point of wanting to be remembered to you" (*M,* 154).

Coleman finished the book by the end of July and declared that it was a "literary masterpiece." But he also thought it was "obscene within the meaning of the law," and so he sent it to his superior, George Medalie, an old opponent of Ernst, who spent the next two weeks reading it. By 12 August Medalie somewhat reluctantly was leaning toward prosecution. By the end of September, after "a long talk" with Ernst, Medalie still had not decided. He asked Ernst for more of the evidence they were gathering, particularly from colleges and libraries (*M,* 160). At a luncheon meeting on 11 November 1932, a full seven months after the book had been seized, Medalie finally announced that he had decided to proceed with the libel (*M,* 164).

As early as 17 November 1932, just a week after Medalie decided to prosecute *Ulysses,* the U.S. Attorney's office was trying to get the trial a preference, which would have moved it up on the waiting list, in order to get the case into court while either Woolsey or Judge Knox, another judge likely to be interested in the case, was sitting (*M,* 165). The libel was filed on 9 December 1932, and Ernst's countermotion to dismiss the libel was filed a week later. In early January 1933 Lindey met with Coleman, who was handling the case for Medalie, to work out the coming schedule. Both sides—Coleman and Lindey—wanted to get a sympathetic judge, preferably Judge Woolsey. Coleman suggested to Lindey that they delay the trial to get past Judges Coleman and Coxe, neither of whom were "suitable for our purposes" (*M*, 172). But as late as 20 March 1933 Ernst informed Lindey that both Woolsey and Knox were still "out of the question for months" (*M*, 175). Through April Coleman tried to contact Woolsey, presumably to offer him the case, but without success (*M*, 176). Lindey and Ernst decided not to wait. On 5 May they filed a motion to dismiss the libel, even though Coxe, who was likely to be hostile to the book, was sitting "the latter part" of May (*M*, 177). But by 17 May, with Woolsey still unavailable, motions were set for hearing on the 23rd before Judge Coxe. On 23 May Coxe declined the case "for technical reasons." Probably he did not want to read the book, but whatever his reason, the motion was adjourned until 16 June, Bloomsday, 1933. Despite the propitiousness of that date, Lindey and Coleman's assistant, Nicolas Atlas, conspired to delay the trial once more when they discovered that Judge Coleman—the other judge they wanted to avoid—would get the case (*M*, 185). Just three days before the 16th Nicholas Atlas, who handled the government's case while Coleman was on vacation, was able to get the case delayed again, this time until 11 July (*M*, 202). Nicolas Atlas was a great asset to Lindey and Ernst. A well-read and articulate judge of literature, apparently he felt (like his superior) that *Ulysses* was a masterpiece, but (unlike his superior) he felt it should be published in the United States. When Coleman returned from vacation, *he* mysteriously delayed the trial further, beyond even Lindey's patience with the matter. When pressed for a reason, Coleman admitted that he was again thinking about dropping the suit. That reconsideration was the result of a secret strategy Lindey and Ernst had set in motion more than a year earlier.

The Modern Classic and the Secretary of the Treasury

Before the book ever arrived in Woolsey's court, it took a side trip through the Treasury Department. That story begins back on 9 November 1931, two months before Cerf began negotiations with Joyce and just a month after Ernst first plotted strategy with Ben Huebsch. John Sumner had seized two books from Frances Steloff at the Gotham Book Mart, *Hsi Men Ching* and *From a Turkish Bath,* both very old Eastern texts, the former a book established in the Chinese literary tradition and sanctioned (in an introduction) by Arthur Waley of the British Museum, and the latter a series of tales likened to *Arabian Nights*. Frances Steloff engaged Ernst to represent her before Judge C. M. Brodsky, who, following the lead of Ernst's brief, found that the "connotation" of lewd, lascivious, obscene, and the rest was "elastic." Giving due consideration to good judgment, common sense, current opinion, and moral standards, all supported by the testimony in Ernst's brief attesting to the literary importance of the works, Brodsky held that the books did not break the law.[86] Ernst had been able to provide enough evidence—including the opinions of living experts—to persuade the court that the books were classics.

The case provided Ernst with another strategy for the *Ulysses* case, a strategy that in some ways contradicted the demands of a social utility defense. If he could demonstrate the high literary merit of *Ulysses,* he might be able to get it approved as a classic. The problem was that the exemption was not available for works by living authors. *Hsi Men Ching* and *From a Turkish Bath* were both very old and very obscure. Just as Judge O'Brien had reasoned about the expensive editions of *Tom Jones* and *The Art of Love* back in 1893, Brodsky probably believed these old Chinese books were more likely to fall into the hands of the highly educated than into the hands of impressionable young women. The special consideration for classics, which dates back to the Lord Campbell Act of 1857, had never been applied to a contemporary work.

Ernst decided to try the strategy out before he committed himself to it in the *Ulysses* case. At about the same time that Paul Leon sent *Ulysses* to New York, Ernst and Lindey, at the request of the National Council on Freedom from Censorship, took on the defense of George Moore's *The Story-Teller's Holiday.* They succeeded in lining up a recipient for this book, a biologist named Ernest Bates, and the book was sent to him in early May. Unfortunately, it got through Customs, and Lindey was obliged to spend most of the summer getting it seized. Finally, on 12 September 1932, Bates was informed by H. C. Stuart, the customs collector, that the book had been impounded.[87]

Ernst chose to use Customs proceedings in this case, because a provision written into the Tariff Act in 1931 expressly allowed the secretary of the Treasury to exempt classics from seizure at his own discretion. The provision was meant to allow rich collectors to import for their personal libraries established classics, such as *Hsi Men Ching* and Boccaccio's *Decameron,* that were sometimes considered obscene. Though the exemption was not meant to apply to commercial importations, Ernst and Lindey felt that if they could secure the exception for a book once, surely they would be able to apply it generally, which would effectively open America to the obscene books. They chose to use Moore's book as a test case, I imagine, because of its relative obscurity. And it nearly worked. The Treasury Department did not figure out what they were up to until it was nearly too late.

On 14 September Lindey informed the customs collector that Bates wanted to contest the seizure of *The Story-Teller's Holiday,* and a month later, on 18 October, the assistant customs collector explained the requirements of petitioning the secretary of the Treasury. Whenever importers want to contest a seizure "on the ground that the book is a classic, or of recognized and established literary or scientific merit," he wrote, they must "establish their claims by satisfactory evidence. Mere unsupported statements or allegations will not be considered." [88] In other words, the petition required what was so often impossible to get into court: expert testimony.

Ernst found plenty of critics to explain Moore's importance to Irish and English literature, and, though many were not so impressed with *The Story-Teller's Holiday,* they allowed that it was an important work. Ernst and Lindey argued that

> Authorities could be marshaled *ad infinitum* showing that George Moore's works in general deserve to be called modern classics. . . . I believe that we long ago left behind us the fatuous and unwarranted and destructive theory that a literary work must be hundreds or thousands of years old in order to be a classic. Our truly perspicacious critics have given homage to the living great where homage has been due. We have come to realize more and more that there can be *modern* classics, as well as ancient ones.[89]

The brief attempted to apply the test of time prematurely by calling on the testimony of Mr. Macrae, the president of an old publishing house, E. P. Dutton, who opined that "George Moore in fifty years will be looked upon in his way as, as much a classic as Socrates is." [90] On December 7 they filed the petition, and before the year was out Frank Dow, Acting Commissioner of Customs, held that the "evidence [in the petition] satisfies the bureau that the book is of recognized and established merit." [91] Lindey immediately wrote to the National Council that, "Since we have now secured the very admission that we have been after . . . we are now ready to stage the second part of our fight." [92] In this second stage they had to establish that since the book was a classic it could be imported freely into the United States. If they could import it in large numbers on the authority of the secretary of the Treasury they probably would be able to publish it in the United States without opposition.

Unfortunately, someone at Treasury must have figured out what they were up to, because on 31 January 1933 Lindey was informed by the acting assistant collector that every new instance of importation would require a new petition.[93] The government was forced into an illogical position, as Lindey pointed out:

> We necessarily assumed that the decision of the Customs Bureau definitely established the book as a work of recognized literary merit. . . . [A]ny other assumption would have been absurd. . . . The only conceivable justification which we can see for the Bureau's position is that, between the time of one application and another, a book previously ruled to have been a classic might cease to be one.[94]

Despite the obvious absurdity, the government was intransigent. Customs refused to let Lindey and Ernst expand a provision, intended to allow private, noncommercial importation by rich people, into a giant loophole in the obscenity law. (Ironically, the Moore case, which was meant to pave the way for *Ulysses,* would not be settled until after the *Ulysses* case was decided by the appeals court. In September 1934 a Mr. Ennis in the U.S. Attorney's office phoned Lindey to inform him that no action would be taken on *The Story-Teller's Holiday* until the *Ulysses* decision could direct their policy.)[95]

Though they failed to secure a general approval for *The Story-Teller's Holiday,* Lindey and Ernst did establish the category of the "modern classic" in the eyes of the Department of the Treasury. And their petition provided a model for how to successfully argue that a book was a modern classic. Getting the Customs Bureau of the Treasury Department to recognize that even one copy of *Ulysses* was a classic could lend weight to their ultimate fight in the federal court. Accordingly, they set about securing such status in May 1933—a year after they first got *Ulysses* seized by Customs—by importing a second copy. Rather than allowing this copy to be sent to the U.S. Attorney's office (which was still deliberating on the copy that had been imported the previous year), they petitioned the secretary of the Treasury that it be admitted on the grounds that it was a classic. Their petition followed the lead of *The Story-Teller's Art:*

> In introducing the stream-of-consciousness method and developing it to a high degree of perfection Joyce has, in ULYSSES, made an epochal contribution to letters. There can be no doubt that his work is a modern classic in every sense of the word. It has endured the test of time. After almost a decade of arduous and monastic labor, it was completed in 1914 and during the last two decades it has steadily grown in stature. . . . If there is any book in any language today genuinely entitled to be a "modern classic" it is ULYSSES. (*M, 189*)

The test of time that *Ulysses* had endured by 1933 was barely ten years, let alone the two decades they claimed. And the petition begged the question when it declared: "It is axiomatic that only a man of genius challenges serious attention and critical treatment. . . . One persuasive proof of ULYSSES may be found in the fact that important men have written important books and articles about it and its author" (*M, 188*).[96] Even if we accept the importance of the men or the importance of their books—a concession that need hardly be made—the fact remains that many of the articles Lindey and Ernst cited actually criticize *Ulysses*. For example, they included Michael J. Lennon's vicious and inaccurate attack on Joyce that appeared in *Catholic World* in 1931, which must have prejudiced many potential American Catholic readers against Joyce. But Ernst and Lindey knew that bureaucrats would be impressed by the length of their bibliography and that they could be relied upon not to go to the trouble of finding any of the articles and reading them. The strategy worked: on Bloomsday, 1933, the Customs Bureau of the Treasury Department admitted one copy of *Ulysses* into the country as a "modern" classic.

When Coleman in the U.S. Attorney's office got wind of the Treasury ruling, he was upset. He phoned Lindey to tell him that Ernst had "put a fast one over on [him]." Even so, he

> intimated that since the government has committed itself to the position that *Ulysses* is a classic, and what with the new administration, new Secretary of Treasury and new Postmaster [following Roosevelt's election], that the libel proceedings will be dropped and *Ulysses* cleared through Customs without a court fight.

Coleman asked for an adjournment of the case so he could consider the Treasury decision and review the "complete file" (*M, 207*). Despite this apparent setback, the U.S. Attorney's office decided to go ahead with the prosecution: the process finally started moving in the fall of 1933. After some late maneuvering by Coleman and Atlas, Lindey was surprised and delighted to report to Ernst that the case was scheduled for "August 22, at which time—believe it or not—Woolsey will be sitting" (M, 213). The case was delayed further, but neither Woolsey nor Ernst would let it get away. Woolsey, according to Ernst, wanted the case, and Ernst wanted Woolsey (M, 217).

The Briefs

The briefs Lindey and Ernst submitted to Woolsey—actually printed pamphlets—were more impressive and lengthier than those in any of their other obscenity cases. On 12 September 1933 Lindey sent a "Preliminary Memorandum" to Woolsey, which opened with a short statement arguing that "the test of obscenity is a living standard," and that therefore "public opinion furnishes the only true test of obscenity." The rest of the memo was taken up with nine exhibits, many of which had been included in the petition to the secretary of the Treasury, which were meant to demonstrate Joyce's high literary reputation and the literary merit of *Ulysses*.[97] In addition, Lindey sent Paul Jordan Smith's *The Key to "Ulysses,"* Stuart Gilbert's *James Joyce's "Ulysses,"* and Herbert Gorman's *James Joyce: His First Forty Years* (M, 226). Arguments were set for 2 October, but they were delayed, and on the 14th Lindey sent Woolsey their Claimant's Memorandum in Support of Motion to Dismiss Libel. This massive document included a short biography of Joyce, a description of the book itself, a description of Random House, a narrative of recent cases (including Woolsey's own decisions in the Stopes trials), Ernst's interpretation of the law, and his arguments for dismissing the libel.[98] Woolsey heard oral arguments on 25 November, and in response to Coleman's case, Ernst and Lindey sent a "Supplementary Memorandum" to Woolsey on the 27th.[99]

The briefs pull in two contradictory directions: on one hand, they claim that *Ulysses,* like the Hall, Dennett, and Stopes books, is a serious and useful social document; on the other hand, they argue that the book is a modern classic. Ultimately, the weight of the latter argument overwhelms the former, and the consequences for *Ulysses* are serious. For a book to be a classic, according to the tests developed in the obscenity cases, it cannot be socially useful. Indeed, it will be read only by a narrow audience in a rarefied atmosphere. Ernst and Lindey gave the book a designation that both dignified and debilitated *Ulysses,* and in the process they gave Joyce a corresponding reputation from which he has yet to escape. I cannot overemphasize the importance of Ernst's and Lindey's work to this definition. Taken together, their briefs constitute the first American publication of *Ulysses*. Before the trial, *Ulysses* was not a modern classic. After the trial, after Lindey and Ernst manufactured and published their package, it was. The trial constructed Joyce's reputation and defined his readership in America for the next two generations.

Both the social utility defense and the modern classic defense rely on a certain presentation of the author's motives. If the writer wrote for ends other than commercial and if the writer honestly attempted to reproduce the world faithfully, then he or she could not produce obscenity. The short biography included in the Claimant's Memorandum indicates that Joyce, "born of Roman Catholic parents," was "steeped in an atmosphere of ritual and theology" (*M*, 239). Treating *Portrait* as autobiography and failing to mention either Stephen's or Joyce's debauches and apostasies, the brief describes the novel's "vivid picture of . . . a sensitive, brooding child, reared amid incense and colored images and mystical teachings, and torn between religious obsession and doubt" (*M*, 239). So much for sincerity and seriousness of purpose.

Joyce studied medicine in Paris, the brief explains, before he "devoted himself to Latin, German, Norwegian and the Romance languages" and "became a linguist and a teacher." These points are accurate enough, but the portrait continues in a vein hardly credible today. "Unlike [George Bernard] Shaw and others of his countrymen," it reads, "Joyce has steadfastly scorned ballyhoo and self-exploitation. He has led a monastic existence, and has made no attempt to benefit by the furor created by ULYSSES" (*M*, 239). Though this monk might have scorned the grosser forms of commercialism, his refusals heaped up his store of cultural capital—a store upon which he drew generously throughout his life. Hindsight and a keener understanding of bohemia expose this subtlety to us today. Whether or not Lindey and Ernst believed this portrait of Joyce, it is clear why they presented it. They had to convince the court that Joyce wrote scurrilous passages not for commercial gain but to hold an undistorting mirror up to the human psyche.

But the main thrust of the biography does not so much demonstrate the motives of sincerity and truth as profess Joyce's uniqueness as a writer. "Nearly as blind as the Greek master from whose epic he borrowed the name of his novel," the brief reads, "[Joyce] has lived apart, an austere Olympian" (*M*, 239). Quite possibly Lindey and Ernst believed this portrait. After all, it corresponds to the image Joyce liked to present to the world in the 1930s, well after he wrote *Ulysses,* and to a large extent it corresponds to the image Herbert Gorman, acting for

Joyce, presented in *James Joyce: His First Forty Years,* a book which Lindey quotes liberally. The image is the product of Joyce's brand of ballyhoo and self-promotion, subtler than Shaw's, but self-promotion nonetheless. I need hardly point out that it was false, that Joyce did not live "apart," that he surrounded himself with sycophants, that for years he enjoyed the cafés of Paris, and that, while he was writing *Ulysses,* he surged with everyone else in the tides of human events.

Again, given the context of previous obscenity cases, it is clear why Lindey made the statement. If the court knew how Joyce conducted himself in Paris, it would be less inclined to think him a genius and more inclined to think him capable of obscenity; and this, really, was the purpose of the biography: to convince Woolsey that Joyce was "a genius of the first rank." Despite the implications of chastity attached to the monkish writer (which for obvious reasons were important to a defense against obscenity), the biography emphasizes Joyce's stature as an "Olympian." In the realms of gold, among the goodly states and kingdoms, Joyce ruled a demesne vast and unequaled but by those of Homer and Shakespeare. Again, I need hardly point out that in 1933 few people shared this opinion, even few critics. But Lindey skillfully strings together quotations, taken out of context, from Rebecca West, Arnold Bennett, Shane Leslie of the *London Quarterly,* and Ernest Boyd of the *New York Herald Tribune,* among others, that make it seem as though Joyce had been crowned emperor of letters ten years earlier. Even his critics, Lindey exclaims, have come to concede his genius. The point led to the summary conclusion: because he is "a genius of the first rank . . . [i]t is monstrous to suppose that . . . Joyce would or could produce a work of obscenity" (*M,* 240–241).

Genius requires elite readers, and elitism was crucial to the obscenity exemptions. The better educated and richer its audience, the less likely a book would be considered obscene. Naturally, then, Ernst feared juries in all obscenity cases. Because "persons belonging to the book-buying public usually possess sufficient wealth or political influence to keep their names off jury panels," juries are usually drawn from the lower and middle classes. And these classes, ironically, were disposed to a hypocritical, undemocratic puritanism. The man who reads no further than the tabloid press, Ernst wrote, "knows his obscenity, and is the acme of righteousness when considering the welfare of others." [100] Proponents of censorship also recognized this tendency of juries. In 1923 the Clean Books League promoted the Jesse-Cotillo amendment to the New York Penal Code 1141 (the law under which Anderson and Heap had been prosecuted a few years earlier), which tried to beef up the law by requiring that obscenity trials be heard by juries. Luckily for Ernst and other censorship lawyers, the bill was defeated.[101] Ernst preferred to leave the matter to judges, who, because they are "somewhat immunized against public flattery or condemnation, are more tolerant or brave than jurors."[102] More importantly, though Ernst never made this argument, judges are less likely to unseat an Olympian because judges themselves are more likely to read "classics." Clearly this was not the case in the New York special sessions court that convicted Anderson and Heap, but Ernst chose to fight his case in a federal court, where he could count on a higher degree of sophistication among the jurists. In effect, Ernst tried to define Joyce's audience as people like the federal justices themselves: the intellectual elite. Even so, Ernst knew that some federal judges would be hostile. But in this case the government wanted a literary judge also, so on 29 August 1933 *Ulysses* was submitted to an audience of one: Judge John Woolsey.

Woolsey, like Ernst, came from the South. His father, once a civil engineer, turned to cotton farming, so Woolsey grew up in South Carolina. But unlike Ernst, his family belonged to patrician New York. He could trace his roots back to the mid-seventeenth century, when George Woolsey stepped off a sailing ship onto the streets of New Amsterdam. He and his descendants did well. Woolsey's "grandfather was president of the Merchants' Exchange of New York, and a great-uncle . . . was president of Yale." Woolsey himself studied at Yale as an undergraduate, went to Columbia law school, and then established a successful practice in New York. He argued "several cases before the Supreme Court," before he was appointed by Herbert Hoover to the U.S. District Court for the Southern District of New York in 1929. He was a learned jurist (he was an editor of the French *Revue de Droit Maritime Comparé*) and a member of the upper class. His dislike of obscenity law did not come, apparently, from a liberal background, but from a conservative "belief in the virtue of unfettered competition in the realm of ideas as in the marketplace."[103]

The best thing in *Ulysses*'s favor was that Woolsey (quite rightly) considered himself a learned, even a literary jurist. The more literary the judge, the less likely he would take passages out of context; the more likely he would entertain expert opinion about the book and the author. When Woolsey took on the case, he already had a copy of Stuart Gilbert's *James Joyce's "Ulysses."* Judging from the opinion he eventually wrote, Woolsey read Gilbert carefully, and he must have read the copies of Paul Jordan Smith's *The Key to "Ulysses"* and Herbert Gorman's *James Joyce* that Lindey sent him in September. Also in September, in the Preliminary Memorandum, Lindey sent nine exhibits of expert testimony, the last of which contained "Testimonials of Distinguished Persons in Various Walks of Life, Relative to *Ulysses*" (M, 229). The goal was to make the judge believe that people like himself—distinguished citizens—were Joyce's proper audience and that they already had endorsed the book.

Woolsey fell for it. Or, perhaps more accurately, he subscribed to the prejudice that Ernst was exploiting. Unwilling to be the sole arbiter in the case, Woolsey recruited two readers of his own. These friends, he wrote in his decision, were people with "average sex instincts—what the French call *l'homme moyen sensuel.*" They would be able to serve the same role as "the 'reasonable man' in the law of torts and 'the man learned in the art' on questions of invention in patent law." In other words, they would serve as indicators of how people into whose hands the book was likely to fall would react to it.

The two readers were Henry Seidel Canby and Charles E. Merrill, Jr.[104] Charles Merrill was probably the Merrill who, with Edmund Lynch, founded Merrill Lynch, the famous securities company. He went to a prep school attached to Stetson University and later to Amherst College. An innovative stockbroker, Merrill also launched the *Family Circle* magazine, the first magazine distributed through grocery stores, so he was acquainted with the publishing industry. He was a member of the same patrician society that claimed Woolsey himself.

Canby, too, was well-educated, even if he was not a millionaire. Woolsey probably knew him from Yale because their attendance at the college overlapped. From 1911 to 1920, Canby was assistant editor of the *Yale Review,* and, after a brief stint as a teacher at Yale, he became editor of the *Literary Supplement* to the *New York Evening Post.* In 1924 he left the *Post* to found the *Saturday Review of Literature,* which "became America's most influential journal of liberal criticism . . . [by reaffirming] supposedly timeless aesthetic standards while responding to the needs of a middle class eager to acquire culture along with consumer goods."[105] Such a publication might seem hesitant to endorse *Ulysses,* but it must be remembered that in early 1933 Lindey and Cerf wanted Canby to receive the copy of *Ulysses* that was on trial. For some reason that plan fell through, but still Canby provided them with a testimonial supporting *Ulysses.* Woolsey drew this man of "average sex instincts" from Ernst's ranks. His name was fifth on the list of *Ulysses*'s supporters that Lindey and Ernst sent to Woolsey in September. Describing himself as "one of the first Americans . . . to read *Ulysses*," Canby called it "one of the books of the last twenty years which however so we may doubt its absolute excellence and permanence in literature is certainly a milestone in literary history." Lest anyone mistake how narrowly Canby defined Joyce's audience, he added, "I cannot conceive of morals being damaged by a work of this kind which is much too erudite and too psychological to attract the prurient seeker after erotica" (*M*, 431). Such an opinion perfectly coincided with Ernst's strategy, for Canby's argument suggests that so far as the masses are concerned, the dirty parts of *Ulysses* are entirely inaccessible.

Merrill and Canby may or may not have had average sex instincts. There is no way to tell today. But as these short biographical sketches indicate, they were not average readers. As Ernst pointed out, the obscenity laws were really meant to keep certain books out of the hands of the lower classes and the uneducated. Woolsey did not gauge the effect of *Ulysses* on them. His method of testing the book—showing it to men like himself—merely confirmed the elitism inherent in Ernst's defense. By consulting Canby (and, for all practical purposes, Merrill), Woolsey declared that the average reader of *Ulysses* or the reader into whose hands *Ulysses* was likely to fall was equivalent to the class of experts Ernst had mobilized on Joyce's behalf. Despite his earlier cynicism regarding such snobbish attitudes, Ernst tried to convince Woolsey that *Ulysses* was not obscene because only those at the top of the social ladder read it. And Woolsey conceded the point. According to both Ernst and Woolsey, Joyce wrote for the educated and rich.

Some of the testimonials included in the briefs take this point for granted. For example, Ellis Meyers, the executive secretary of the American Booksellers Association, wrote, "[T]o withhold [*Ulysses*] from free circulation among *intelligent people,* is to commit a crime against letters" [emphasis added]. W. A. Neilson, the president of Smith College, wrote, "It seems preposterous to attempt to prevent the *intelligent public* from getting access to a book of such international importance" [emphasis added]. Robert Morss Lovett (an English professor at the University of Chicago) felt the book addressed "the thinking person," and the author John Cowper Powys made definite allusions to levels of education when he compared *Ulysses*'s "intelligent readers" (the kind of man who also reads Aristophanes, Petronius, Rabelais, Swift, and Cervantes) to "fastidious and thin-skinned readers." F. Scott Fitzgerald offered a parallel commentary, though Ernst did not quote it for the judge: "[P]eople who have the patience to read *Ulysses* are not the kind who will slobber over a few Rabelaisian passages" (*M*, 128). People with such patience, he seems to imply, are sophisticates. Perhaps the most telling and most elitist comment was Robert Briffault's. The anthropologist, in a curious and quaint phrase, insisted that *Ulysses* was not written for "persons of imperfect culture," though its prosecution, ironically, may have alerted imperfectly cultured people to it (*M*, 431–434).

The evidence suggests that the audience of *Ulysses* was not even as broad as "the thinking [i.e., intellectual] public." In both the Preliminary Memorandum and the Claimant's Memorandum to Woolsey and in the Petition to the Secretary of the Treasury, Ernst called the writers of the testimonials a cross section of society: journalists, professors, critics, educators, authors, librarians, clergymen, and publishers (*M*, 264). In another place he added psychologists (*M*, 190). Forty-nine men and women comprise the list. Of these, three were educators. One was a psychologist, one a sociologist, another an attorney. Thirty-nine could be described as editors, writers, or publishers. Ernst drew up his list of prominent citizens almost entirely from the literary professions. He was not able to garner much support from outside the industry because, apparently, in 1932 *Ulysses*'s audience did not extend beyond a relatively small class of literati. Joyce appears to have been something of a coterie writer. Malcolm Cowley implied as much in his letter of support: "[p]reventing American *authors* from reading [Joyce] is about as stupid as it would be to place an embargo on the theory of relativity" [emphasis added] (*M*, 434). Canby wrote that those "who like myself are interested in literature should most certainly have free access" to *Ulysses* (*M*, 431). Among Ernst's expert witnesses the issue was never one of general access. Only John Dos Passos suggested that the general public could have any use for *Ulysses* as a picture "of the internal struggle [of] the dying middle class." But even Dos Passos believed that the book was not a "social document" so much as "a piece of imaginative virtuosity, a poem" (*M*, 126). (In light of these testimonials, it is not surprising that Ernst and Lindey gave up espousing the social utility of *Ulysses* and pursued more vigilantly the "classic" defense.)

They listed in the Claimant's Memorandum many of the "intrinsic features" of *Ulysses* that indicate the loftiness of Joyce's target audience. The book does not include pictures. It is a long "prodigious work of 732 closely-printed pages." "It is far too tedious and labyrinthine and bewildering for the untutored and the impressionable," who "would not get beyond the first dozen pages." Since "the first passage dealing with sex occurs deep in the book," the court could be assured that no poorly educated reader would have the opportunity to be corrupted. The most persuasive arguments concerned the book's style. "It is axiomatic," the memorandum began, "that only what is understandable can corrupt." If a work is "incomprehensible to all but a comparatively few," the intellectual elite who "are immune to what the censor calls the suggestive power of words"—for example, if it is written in Chinese or Latin—it is innocuous. The brief uses six pages to demonstrate that *Ulysses* might as well have been written in Chinese (*M,* 256–261). Ernst and Lindey argued that, because the structure of the book was based on the Linati scheme rather than on any comprehensible novelistic plot conventions, its structure was "unbelievably involved" and "baffling." [106] Furthermore,

> ULYSSES taxes a reader's intellectual resources more severely than any other book in English literature. To comprehend it, one must have encyclopedic knowledge.

Add to this the "polysyllabic barriers" of all the long words and also the words that are just plain difficult, like "whelks" and "epicene." The brief supplies a list of thirty-two of these words with their corresponding page numbers, pointing out that they "are not egregious examples; there are thousands of others as difficult in the book." "The book is a treasure trove," Ernst asserts,

> but its riches are so well hid in grottoes of recondite learning, of classical allusions, of literary and scientific profundities, that the average seeker—blindly groping about in the surrounding maze—soon tires of the venture and turns back.

To read *Ulysses,* then, you must have the scholarly discipline to suffer tedium, you must be tutored, you must be unimpressionable, you must be inured to the emotional effects of words, you must have access to the Linati scheme and the wherewithal to use it, you must have had an encyclopedic education and a long memory or a set of reference books at your elbow, along with a good dictionary. Otherwise, you might as well be reading Chinese. Only those who can read books the way scholars read books have any business reading *Ulysses.* Despite the democratic principles Ernst avowed in *To the Pure,* he skillfully exploited the court's class prejudice.

But if demonstrating its obscurity helps prove that a book is a classic, it simultaneously undermines the argument that the book has been approved by a community standard. During oral arguments Woolsey asked Ernst if he had been able to read the book cover to cover. The ever vigilant Ernst detected the reasoning behind Woolsey's question: "nothing much will be lost if an unreadable volume is prevented entrance to our shores." So, paradoxically, Ernst had to demonstrate that despite its remoteness from the common man, all of America accepted *Ulysses:* hence the ridiculous claim that *Ulysses* "has been generally accepted by the community," which required Ernst to argue that society's elite—newspaper editors, college professors, critics, educators, authors, librarians, clergymen, and publishers—"furnish an accurate social mirror." Only through such elites, according to the memorandum, do the people who as a mass are "inarticulate" register their "moral reactions and . . . judgments" (*M,* 264). Ernst's fear of juries belies this claim: all too often "the people" and the elites disagree. Besides, I have already pointed out that, despite his claims to the contrary, Ernst's testifiers nearly all came from the literary community, which could hardly be trusted to accurately represent the public's view of literature. In fact, Ernst and Lindey manufactured the idea that the American community had accepted *Ulysses,* and they doctored the evidence to prove it.

Nowhere is this point more evident than in their treatment of the data they collected concerning libraries. In April 1932 Cerf sent out nearly eight hundred letters to librarians across the country polling them on the demand for *Ulysses.* The questionnaire asked if the libraries had *Ulysses* in the stacks, what the librarians' opinion of the book was, whether they would order it if it were available in a reasonably priced American edition, and other such questions. The answers provided Ernst with some of his most compelling data supporting the notion that the community had already accepted *Ulysses* and that the "community" was the reading public of the whole country, not just a coterie in "ultrasophisticated metropolitan centers" (*M,* 188). William S. Brockman explains in his interesting study of this questionnaire that librarians both reflected and originated public taste, and so they were in a unique position to demonstrate the public's attitude toward *Ulysses.*[107] Petitioning the secretary of the Treasury, Lindey wrote,

The librarians were requested to give their opinion of [*Ulysses*]. With scarcely a dissenting voice they conceded its greatness. A few of their comments culled at random from hundreds appear in Exhibit 'C'. (*M,* 188)

Exhibit C, which does indeed include glowing praise of *Ulysses*, was sent to Woolsey in the Preliminary Memorandum on 12 September 1933, and in the main Claimant's Memorandum, Woolsey was reminded that "*Ulysses* has been placed on the shelves of many of our leading libraries" (*M*, 264). To illustrate the point, Ernst sent Woolsey Exhibit F, a "Map of the United States, Showing the Location of Libraries that Have Expressed a Desire to Secure and Circulate *Ulysses*" (*M*, 229).[108] Earlier, in August 1933, trying to get the U.S. Attorney to drop the suit, Lindey had sent this map to Nicholas Atlas. He told Atlas that "the purpose of the map," on which Lindey drew a dot for each approving library, "is to show that ULYSSES has won countrywide recognition, and that it is not being championed only by ultraradical literary cliques located in large metropolitan centres" (*M*, 216). The map is fairly compelling. The Northeast has the densest concentration of dots, but the Midwest is full of them also, and the South has more than a dozen, while a half-dozen are scattered in California, and a few others appear in the West—two each in Montana and Utah. The map suggests a grassroots demand for *Ulysses* across most of the country.

But the survey was a sham. Ernst translated his data into the map because presenting it any other way would damage his case. The evidence indicates there was little or no demand for *Ulysses* outside "ultrasophisticated" circles. Many librarians did dissent from the accolades, and the praise other librarians volunteered was highly suspect. Lindey came up with the idea for soliciting libraries as early as August 1931, just a week after Ernst and Lindey first broached the idea of defending *Ulysses*. Lindey came across a reference to Joyce in *Censorship and Other Papers* "by Bowerman, the librarian" of the Public Library of Washington, D.C. (*M*, 78). Nothing was done, of course, until March 1932, after Joyce committed to Random House. Then Lindey told Cerf to begin collecting testimonials (*M*, 112). On 21 April Cerf sent Ernst a draft of a letter to librarians, and Lindey promptly revised it and added the questionnaire:

> With respect to the librarians we have borne in mind the important element of inertia, and we have therefore obviated the necessity of placing upon each librarian the onus of sitting down and composing a letter. It is much easier to fill in blanks. (*M*, 121)

Included in the cover letter for the questionnaire was an apparent endorsement from Bowerman, who, the letter claimed, "pointed out that the unrestricted circulation of *Ulysses* in this country was merely a matter of time" (*M*, 123). When the questionnaire arrived at the Public

Library of Washington, D.C., Bowerman was surprised to see himself quoted in the cover letter.

By 10 May 1932 the replies began to arrive, and Cerf forwarded the "first batch" to Lindey (*M*, 139). Among them was an angry letter from Bowerman. He denied that he ever claimed it was only a matter of time "before *Ulysses* will circulate without restriction." He actually said that *Ulysses* "will be a candidate to be considered by public librarians."[109] Emphasizing that he did not endorse *Ulysses,* Bowerman went on to say, "We have at present no copy of the book in our library and the demand for it has been so slight as to make its purchase no issue." Cerf was unsettled by the letter and asked Lindey what he should do about it. Lindey, either disingenuously or obtusely, told Cerf that "the point [Bowerman] makes is somewhat silly, and is in the nature of splitting hairs." He insisted that no one reading the cover letter would think that Bowerman claimed *Ulysses* "would be circulated without restriction *by librarians.*"[110] It seems to me that every recipient of the letter would read it that way. In the context, "free circulation" naturally would mean circulation by libraries. Nevertheless, Lindey drafted a brilliant apology to Bowerman, which was rounded out by the statement,

> It may interest you to know, incidentally, that we have received hundreds of replies from librarians throughout the country in response to our questionnaire, and the overwhelming majority agree as to the profound literary significance of ULYSSES, and indicate that if the book were legalized they would put it on their shelves.[111]

This claim cowed Bowerman, who accepted Cerf's apology a week later. He obviously was surprised, and it seems that peer pressure softened his disapprobation. Chastened, he replied,

> I am interested to learn of the replies from librarians. . . . I should like to see some such letters, particularly from the larger and stronger municipal libraries. As I said in my earlier letter, the demand for Ulysses here is negligible. Perhaps the situation is different elsewhere.[112]

Bowerman seems afraid that he has betrayed himself to be hopelessly behind the times. If other librarians are praising the book so highly, maybe he should concede its greatness too.

But the situation was not different elsewhere. Reading through the questionnaires gives the decided impression that most librarians were like Bowerman and that most libraries were like the D.C. public library.[113] Obviously, very few of the respondents had read the book, and of those who did, many disliked it intensely. Otto Kinkeldey wrote, "The Cornell University Library is particularly anxious not to have its name associated in any way with Joyce's Ulysses in the form of a public comment." Julian Fowler at Oberlin said the book "has very doubtful literary merit." The librarian at St. Louis University said it "is literary 'jazz,' intriguing for sophisticated half-morons." The public libraries at Durham, Belmont Abbey, Troy, Omaha, Winston-Salem, Wilmington, Chicago, and St. Paul, and the libraries at Hunter College, Colgate University, Barnard College, Brigham Young University, Rice University, the University of Texas at Austin, the University of South Carolina, the University of Nevada, Kent State, Radcliffe College, the University of Mississippi, John Hopkins University, and the University of Detroit, among others, had experienced no demand for the book. Indeed, many of the librarians fended off the questionnaire as if it were an advertisement.

According to Cerf's own tabulations, 87 libraries recorded no demand for the book, while 124 said they had some demand. It is probably safe to assume that the bulk of questionnaires that went unanswered would have received negative responses. But leaving such speculations aside, still only 36 of the 211 said they had "much demand" for *Ulysses*. The questionnaire asked those librarians who experienced any demand to indicate who was asking for the book. I presume most of the responses came from the college libraries, because 44 said faculty had asked for the book, while 79 said students had. Only 34 said members of the general public had asked for it. If the data indicate anything, it is that in 1932 America neither demanded to read nor had accepted *Ulysses*. America had not heard of it.

That conclusion is borne out by the other tabulations. Two hundred forty librarians said they did not have *Ulysses* on their shelves, while only twenty-four said they did. One hundred sixty-six said they had made no attempts to get a copy, while only fifteen said they had. What, then, accounts for the map Ernst sent to Woolsey? It was based on responses to the sixth question, which asked "Do you believe that an American publication [of *Ulysses*] at a reasonable price will be of value?" One hundred forty-four librarians said it would, while only twenty-two said it would not. But this statistic does not indicate a general endorsement of the book. For example, Merrit Moore at the University of Chicago wrote, "Probably such an edition as you speak of would be worthwhile but on the other hand I can't believe its not being republished would be a great loss." It is not hard to imagine that the general acquisitiveness of librarians, no matter what their indifference to *Ulysses,* accounts for their saying a cheap edition would be of some value.

From the start, Lindey's goal was to "have the data furnished in the answers so concentrated as to make the data easy of presentation to the court" (*M,* 141). But in 1832 he probably did not suspect how much he would have to leave out. Translating the statistical data into the map was a brilliant strategy, because Lindey could honestly claim that the map represented "libraries that have expressed a desire to secure and circulate *Ulysses,*" even if the impression it gave—that *Ulysses* had a wide and general audience in America—contradicted the full evidence.

Questions 7–9 in the questionnaire called for substantive answers that were not amenable to graphic presentation. The most important, question 7, asked, "What is your impression of the literary significance of the book?" It was from the answers to this question that Lindey drew most of the testimonials in Exhibit C. But these testimonials leave an impression as false as that left by the map. The brief claims the comments were "culled at random" (*M,* 188, 421). This was a lie. There is no more delicate way to put it. None of the negative comments, some of which I quoted above, found their way into any of the briefs. And most of the comments that were included are unreliable, because the opinions offered by the librarians are lifted, sometimes verbatim, from the cover letter that accompanied the questionnaire. The cover letter reads in part:

> [*Ulysses*] is generally conceded to be a literary work of the first magnitude. It was the first novel to make use of the so-called stream-of-consciousness method, and it still stands in the forefront of psychological narratives. So profound has been its influence on letters during the past two decades, that it has been acclaimed by many critics as a modern classic: perhaps the most important literary work of the twentieth century. (*M,* 123)

This letter applied something like the peer pressure Lindey applied to Bowerman. Only the most assured respondent would contradict general concessions and the acclaim of critics. Those who were timid or ignorant might borrow their opinions from the cover letter. A. B. Metcalf from Massachusetts wrote in his testimony, "As the first English novel to use the stream-of-consciousness method, [*Ulysses*] has had a very considerable influence." Annie Craig of Granville, Ohio, wrote, "Apparently a stupendous piece of work." From Omaha, Nebraska, Catherine Beal wrote, "I think its influence has been tremendous." M. E. McClain in Eugene, Oregon, said, "It will always be of significance as literary history." Fred Bestow in New Jersey followed the same lead: "Certainly no other 20th century book has exerted so great an influence." Nearly all of the comments included in the brief echo the cover letter to the questionnaire. The cover letter was not included in the briefs.

Lindey offered to provide the raw data to the judges. In the memorandum filed on appeal, for example, he wrote, "The claimant herein will be glad to place at the disposal of the Court the original answers to the questionnaires, if the Court so desire" (M, 421). If the court had examined these questionnaires, it would have been obliged to discard one of the pillars of Random House's case. But Lindey was confident that offering to provide the original questionnaires would satisfy the judges that his presentation was accurate. In a statement of amazing candor, Lindey boasted, "There isn't a chance in a million that any point will be raised as to the facts." [114]

Ulysses in School

That frank admission was occasioned by Lindey's attempt to prove that *Ulysses* had been accepted by American colleges and universities. Given the isolation of the ivory tower, this was not, perhaps, the best way to demonstrate that Joyce was embraced by community standards, but it would have been a convincing way to demonstrate that the book was a classic. From the very start, Lindey and Ernst planned to use college and university curricula to demonstrate the high literary merit of the novel. On 29 March 1933 Lindey wrote to Cerf that statistics demonstrating that "educational institutions" use the book would help their case. He suggested that Cerf

> prepare and send out a circular letter to one hundred or more colleges and universities, requesting information as to whether (a) Joyce is considered in any course given by the institution on contemporary literature; and (b) whether *Ulysses* is used as collateral or prescribed reading. (M, 112)

Cerf probably never sent out the circular letter, because nowhere in the Ernst collection have I found any indication of further action. Neither Ernst's memo to Lindey (dated 20 April 1932) nor another letter from Lindey to Cerf (dated 25 April 1932), both of which discuss the drafts of the library survey and the survey of "eminent people," mention the plan to poll universities (M, 120–121). Something happened in the intervening six weeks that persuaded them to drop the plan.

Whatever it was, it must have convinced them the survey would yield absolutely no positive evidence. Otherwise they would have gone ahead, if not in the spring of 1932 then certainly in the fall. As I mentioned above, sometime in September 1932, when he was considering whether or not to proceed with the libel, George Medalie, the supervising U.S. Attorney, had "a long talk" with Ernst and asked to see "everything that comes from libraries and particularly from colleges" (*M*, 160). So Lindey and Ernst knew that any indication that *Ulysses* was taught in the colleges would have helped persuade Medalie to drop the suit. They must have been desperate to get evidence that *Ulysses* had entered college curricula.

But not until July 1933, nearly a year later and long after Medalie decided to prosecute, did any evidence come their way. Peter Pertzoff, a graduate student at Harvard, happened to read about the *Ulysses* case. Having recently finished a master's thesis on Joyce, he wrote to Bennett Cerf on the 4th of July to offer his sympathy and help. Cerf forwarded the letter to Lindey, who must have been delighted with the prospect of adding Harvard to his list of endorsers. Pertzoff sent his thesis to Lindey, who, finding it "a scholarly and thorough piece of work," asked if he could use it in the "fight for the legalization of the book" (*M*, 211).[115] Pertzoff was happy to oblige, and he sent Lindey an account of a class he took at Harvard, English 26, which included *Ulysses* on its reading list. Lindey put English 26 into the Claimant's Memorandum to Woolsey:

> It would be absurd to assume that an obscene work would appear as assigned reading in our leading institutions of learning. Yet no course dealing with twentieth century English letters, given at any of our colleges and universities, fails to include Joyce and ULYSSES. For instance, the book has been on the reading list at Harvard in connection with English 26, given last year by T. S. Eliot, the distinguished poet (then occupying the Charles Eliot Norton Chair of Poetry), and three years ago by I. A. Richards, Professor at Cambridge and Peking. (M, 262–263)

The brief goes on to quote Richards's lectures, relying on Pertzoff's account of the class. In October, when Pertzoff saw a copy of the memorandum, he was afraid that he had given Lindey the wrong impression of English 26. *Ulysses* was on a reading list, but the list consisted of fifty to seventy books. It was not, Pertzoff was at pains to point out, assigned reading: "No one was obliged to read *Ulysses* or any other book."[116]

Lindey, no doubt, felt Pertzoff was splitting hairs as finely as Bowerman had earlier. "At any rate," he wrote back to Pertzoff, the facts are "substantially correct."[117] But they were not correct. Lindey clearly wanted to imply that *Ulysses* had been embraced by the English department at Harvard, and clearly it had not. But leaving the English 26 issue aside, there remains his claim that "no course dealing with twentieth century English letters, given at any of our colleges and universities, fails to include Joyce and ULYSSES." If they never sent out a survey of colleges and universities, how did Lindey know this was true? The Petition for Release of *Ulysses* filed with the Department of the Treasury in June 1933, a month before Lindey found Pertzoff, does not mention colleges and universities at all. Apparently, Lindey had no evidence in June about courses in twentieth-century literature, and so the entire argument concerning colleges stood on the strength of Pertzoff's ambivalent letter. Lindey, emboldened by his belief that there was not "a chance in a million that any point will be raised as to the facts," made up the claim from whole cloth.

No one did challenge the facts. Nicolas Atlas, the one person in the U.S. Attorney's office who had enough literary sophistication to recognize distortions of Joyce's reputation, wanted Random House to win the case. And the government, following tradition in obscenity cases, argued that all this "expert" testimony was beside the point. For example, on appeal, Martin Conboy, who took over the case from Coleman and Atlas, relied on the self-evidency of the old Hicklin test, which meant that "no argument may be based upon the purpose of the author, his literary importance or unimportance or psychological truthfulness or falsity." "The statute," Conboy insisted, "does not make intent an essential element of its violation" (*M*, 375). In other words, the government did not waste time examining the facts presented by Lindey and Ernst because it held those facts to be irrelevant. The only "evidence" required by the case was the book itself, or, rather, certain pages of the book itself, which Conboy conveniently listed for the appeal judges. This strategy left Lindey free to claim anything he wanted, so long as it was not so outrageous that the judges themselves would challenge it. Woolsey, being a sympathetic judge, was prepared to believe much. And the appeal judges were more concerned with points of law than the facts of the case.

Manipulations are evident in the other exhibits as well. For instance, the experts whom Ernst and Lindey consulted were "prominent individuals" whom they had "used in past cases"—people who already had demonstrated their antipathy to the obscenity laws (*M*, 121). The letter soliciting their help spelled out exactly what they were expected to say:

We are addressing this letter to you in the hope that you will give us your frank opinion of *Ulysses*. . . . We intend to offer your opinion, together with those of other prominent persons, to the authorities as indicative of the preposterousness of the ban which now exists. (*M*, 122)

It seems fairly clear what opinion Lindey and Ernst expected to hear. As I indicated above, the response to this letter must have been disappointing, for practically no one outside the publishing industry wrote back. Some testimonials, those "obviously of no help," were ignored (*M*, 148). And at least one of the positive testimonials was actively coached. John Dos Passos originally wrote, "I think if you try to get [*Ulysses*] by as an Elsie book, even the dumbest judge will smell a rat" (*M*, 126). Lindey suggested to Cerf that "it would not be politic to submit [such a letter] to a judge." But he was not willing to leave out such a famous author: "Dos Passos' name is valuable and you ought to get in touch with him and secure a revised opinion, with no animadversions on our courts" (*M*, 148). The testimonials presented to Woolsey, then, were clearly manufactured. The respondents were solicited selectively; the responses were scripted; and any response that did not follow the script was rejected.

"The Salutary Forward March"

Woolsey handed down his decision on 6 December 1933. At 10:15 that morning, Donald Klopfer called up Random House's printer, Ernest Reichl, and "five minutes later" they started the race to get the book out. Reichl was ready. He had a system of relays set up to expedite the process, and by 17 January the book was done.[118] Cerf released it for sale on 25 January at $3.50 a copy, one dollar more than he had thought he would be able to charge back in 1932. In the meantime, the government was deciding whether or not to appeal. Since Woolsey's judgment was not filed until 19 December, the U.S. Attorney's office had until 19 March 1934 to decide. Samuel Coleman, who reportedly was happy with the decision, advised against it (*M*, 359). On 8 February Coleman made that recommendation to the U.S. Attorney (*M*, 358). But George Medalie, Coleman's boss, was replaced by Martin Conboy, who shared none of his employee's admiration for the book and none of his predecessor's ambivalence. He filed his appeal on 16 March, just days before the term would have expired. Ernst filed his reply to the appeal, which, other than disputing points of law raised by Conboy, was generally the same as the briefs he gave Woolsey—except that reviews of the new Random House edition and editorials concerning Woolsey's decision were included. Justices Augustus Hand, Learned Hand, and Martin Manton heard arguments on 16 May 1934, and the press generally made Conboy, who stammered red-faced as he read the dirty parts aloud, out to be a fool. On 7 August the appeals court ruled in favor of *Ulysses*, with Justice Manton dissenting. After a protracted but successful attempt to retrieve the battered and well-thumbed copy of *Ulysses* sent across the Atlantic on the *Bremen* back in 1932, Lindey was able to report to Cerf, "the famous case of *United States* v. *Ulysses* is finally, definitely and conclusively closed. And I may say, happily" (*M*, 475).

Exactly what was the legal significance of the *Ulysses* trial is difficult to say.[119] Morris Ernst himself insisted that its importance was not in "any new principle laid down by the Court," but that "it represented a psychological breakthrough in the censorship field": public standards of smut "became just a little more sophisticated."[120] Nevertheless, its place in judicial history seems to be cemented. Jay Daily credits Woolsey's decision in the *Ulysses* trial with revising the Hicklin rule, "making the 'person with average sex instincts' the test of whether the book would 'stir the sex impulses.'"[121] Frederick Shauer suggests the *Ulysses* decision (not the Halsey case) established the rule that a book must be considered in its entirety rather than in excerpts.[122] Kenneth Stevens, in his excellent article summarizing the trial, writes that the "widespread publicity attending the case" gave new importance to the guidelines used by Woolsey, even if those guidelines had been established previously.[123] Edward de Grazia's reprints of the judicial opinions on obscenity law in America include all three opinions in the *Ulysses* case. His *Girls Lean Back Everywhere: The Law of Obscenity and the Assault on Genius*, published in 1992, takes its title from Margaret Anderson's commentary on the *Ulysses* trial. The recent attorney general's report on obscenity commissioned by the Reagan administration cites the case (along with *Lady Chatterly's Lover* and *An American Tragedy*) as among the notorious prosecutions of literature under obscenity laws. And, whether or not the case established any matters of law, it changed the policy of the Customs Bureau of the Treasury Department and the U.S. Attorney's office in New York, two of the main agencies charged with rooting out smut in America. Only after the *Ulysses* appeal was decided did the U.S. Attorney's office release George Moore's *The Story-Teller's Holiday*, signaling that henceforth modern classics would not be seized by Customs nor prosecuted for libel by the U.S. Attorney's office.[124] In the Claimant's Memorandum, Ernst asked the court to use *Ulysses* to vindicate "the salutary forward march of our courts" and to continue "to liberalize the law of obscenity and to thrust back the narrow frontiers fixed by prudery" (*M*, 239). The *Ulysses* trial was one of the cases that liberalized the law—perhaps the best publicized and celebrated among them. In his press release following Woolsey's decision, flush with success, Ernst quoted these lines from the brief and added, "The *Ulysses* case is the culmination of a long and determined struggle against the literary censor." He might have overstated its importance, but Ernst had won a stunning battle in his war against John Sumner.

The consequences for Ernst, Cerf, Joyce, and *Ulysses* were equally dramatic. Before the book even appeared in January 1934, Cerf had sold twelve thousand copies, a figure he had not expected "to reach for months" (*M*, 357). Joyce made $6,300 in the month between Woolsey's judgment and publication of the book. More money would come later, enough to make everyone rich. Cerf would later declare that *Ulysses* was Random House's "first really important trade publication . . . a big commercial book—with front-page stories to help launch it—and it did a lot for Random House."[125] As late as 1977, thousands of copies were still being sold every year.[126] And, because of his unique contract, Ernst made money off every one.

This point should not be taken lightly. Ernst was always happy in the limelight, and he promoted his own celebrity throughout his career. And because his fee was tied to sales of the book, he had as keen an interest in publicizing this case as Cerf did. The library surveys and the surveys of bookstores had the secondary purpose of advertising *Ulysses* should it ever be published. When Woolsey's decision came down, newspaper editors editorialized the decision, reporters reported it, *Time* magazine carried a three-column article with a photograph of Woolsey, radio station WABC in New York re-enacted the oral arguments and read from Woolsey's decision on its "March of Time" program. Lindey and Ernst orchestrated this publicity. In October Lindey had printed two hundred copies of the Claimant's Memorandum and sent them to Cerf for distribution to "prominent men throughout the country" and, we should presume, the press (*M*, 234, 274). On 6 December Lindey had Woolsey's opinion mimeographed and distributed, and Ernst published his own statement to the press. Lindey took care of the morning papers; Cerf canvassed the afternoon papers (*M*, 315). Less than a week after the decision, Cerf wrote to Joyce,

[Woolsey's] decision has resulted in a tremendous amount of favorable publicity, and we have high hopes that the book will get off to
a magnificent start. It would have been marvelous, of course, if we
could have had books ready to deliver the moment the decision was
rendered so that we could have taken full advantage of the publicity.
Naturally, this was impossible. We are rushing production of the
book with all possible speed. (*M*, 338)

No opportunity for exploiting the trial was overlooked. Even the trial
copy of *Ulysses*, the one sent over by Paul Leon in 1932, was enlisted in
the campaign. When he finally got it back from the government, Cerf,
amid some fanfare, donated it to the Columbia University Library.
Lindey observed, "You ought to get swell publicity on the presentation"
(*M*, 475).

But to say that this was exploiting the trial is misleading, because the
trial itself forged more than reflected public opinion of *Ulysses*. As I indicated above, America—even the intellectual elite of America—had little
or no opinion about the book prior to the case. Ernst supplied Woolsey
with his opinion and Woolsey supplied the newspapers, magazines, and
radio stations with theirs. And, perhaps most significantly, all of this supplied Cerf with his package for *Ulysses*.

Besides all the publicity that attended the trial, the Random House
edition incorporated into its pages Woolsey's decision and a foreword by
Ernst based on his press statement of 6 December. Ira Nadel was, I believe, the first person since Joyce to question the advisability of this preface, implying that Woolsey's "presuppositions" were faulty.[127] It is true
that Cerf incorporated Woolsey's decision so that any future prosecutions of the book would automatically include the judge's opinion as part
of the evidence and because the decision's presence would itself likely dissuade many local authorities from challenging the book. But these two
documents—Woolsey's decision and Ernst's foreword—indicate the degree to which the trial provided the publishing context for Joyce's text. In
his briefs Ernst had argued, if tepidly, that *Ulysses* is a truthful psychological portrait. Woolsey recognized "Joyce's sincerity and his honest effort to show exactly how the minds of his characters operate." Ernst had
argued with more vigor that Joyce was a serious artist dedicated to his
craft at the expense of money, companionship, and the other comforts
and distractions of normal men. Woolsey agreed that "Joyce has been
loyal to his technique and has not funked its necessary implications,"
and that this loyalty was what got his book in trouble. Ernst had argued

that the book was so complex and the language so difficult that it was nearly incomprehensible. Woolsey held that it was "brilliant and dull, intelligible and obscure by turns." Joyce was a mosaic worker painstakingly piecing together "the picture which . . . he is seeking to construct for his readers." Though he refers to those readers as "the American public," Woolsey, again following the lead of Ernst's arguments, implies that only intellectuals will read the book, for "in order to properly approach the consideration of [Ulysses], it is advisable to read a number of other books which have now become its satellites." In 1934 these books, of course, were Gorman's biography, and Gilbert's and Smith's guidebooks, which Woolsey himself read alongside Ulysses. By implication, many of the items listed in Ernst's bibliographies orbited Ulysses as well, and with each passing year the list of these satellites grew longer.

The result was that Ulysses was officially published as a "classic," for only classics require the gentle influence of satellites. Cerf was perfectly amenable to such a designation. As Ernst had pointed out in the Claimant's Memorandum, Random House had made its reputation by publishing the classics: Chaucer's *Troilus and Cressida*, Coleridge's *Complete Works, Wuthering Heights, Candide, Tom Sawyer, The Scarlet Letter*. Adding Joyce to his list was like adding Joyce to the canon of recognized great literature. Woolsey's opinion assured his place among these others and justified Cerf's decision to place him there.

The only problem was that Joyce himself was not so amenable. While he might have relished the company of famous dead authors, he did not relish the consequences. Joyce did not want anyone to rely on the "satellites" to read Ulysses. The trial and Cerf's subsequent publication of Ulysses marked the moment when the novel began to pass out of Joyce's authority. This point is made clear in the dispute between Joyce and Cerf over the Linati scheme—one of the items Ernst had cited in his brief as evidence that Ulysses was a classic. On 13 October 1933 Cerf, sanguine about the progress of the trial, conveyed his publishing plans to Paul Leon. In particular, he asked for permission to publish the scheme for the book that Joyce had supplied to Herbert Gorman (M, 234). Leon both cabled and posted his reply emphatically denying permission. He reported that Joyce felt that "an American reader seeing the chart [might conclude] that since he has to study it before reading it is not worthwhile reading the book" (M, 278). He does go on to claim that since the book is "a classic," "if it needs explanations these belong to the class of critical and historical writings, not to the book itself." But Joyce's opinion seems to be that Ulysses should not require explanations. Presumably, an

American reader put off by a chart would be more put off by Gilbert's or Smith's guidebooks. Cerf, afraid of losing sales, countered, "Without some guide for their enlightenment, you must know as well as I do that *Ulysses* is not for the general public" (*M,* 279). Leon's reply was more emphatic yet: "Mr. Joyce's decision is absolutely definite. *Ulysses'* text must stand on its own feet without any explanation" (*M,* 280). Mr. Joyce, Leon continued, felt that the chart might help sales at first, but within a year his decision would be vindicated. Apparently Joyce was afraid that the presence of the chart would indicate to potential buyers that *Ulysses* was a certain type of book—the type normal people do not buy. Cerf must have felt his possible windfall had melted away, for, making "no effort to conceal our disappointment in this decision," he was driven to wondering intemperately why Joyce "ever signed a contract with us" if he had "so little faith in our judgment" (*M,* 281). Leon and Joyce succeeded in keeping the chart out of the book, but they could not succeed in their final goal, to let *Ulysses* stand on its own feet. So long as it was prefaced by Woolsey's decision, which declared that you must read the guidebooks to understand the novel, it would limp on crutches. Authority over *Ulysses* was slipping out of Joyce's hands.

It would be impossible to measure with any precision the effects of this transfer of authority. *Ulysses* became a "modern classic"—officially recognized by the U.S. government and so advertised by his publisher. Though the trial put *Ulysses* under the authority of the "experts," it would be another generation before it fully passed into academe. What is clear is that before the trial Joyce was considered neither a genius nor the author of classics, and after the trial he was. This reputation got *Ulysses* into America, but it circumscribed his audience.

Nevertheless, a certain class of readers would find the book useful. In the statement he issued to the press on 6 December, Ernst compared the victory in Woolsey's court to the ratification of the Twenty-first Amendment to the Constitution:

The first week of December 1933 will go down in history for two repeals, that of Prohibition and that of squeamishness in literature. We may now imbibe freely of the contents of bottles and forthright books. It may well be that in the future the repeal of the sex taboo in letters . . . will prove to be of the greater importance. Perhaps the intolerance which closed our breweries was the intolerance which decreed that basic human functions had to be treated in books in a furtive, leering, hypocritical manner. (*M,* 318)

The comparison was repeated in the revised document that became Ernst's foreword to the Random House *Ulysses,* and, while to our eyes today it might seem to be a comical inflation of the importance of the case, it is based on a truth: the intolerance that banned *Ulysses* was closely related to the intolerance that banned liquor. The battle over the suppression of books in the 1920s and early 1930s was part of larger ideological conflicts within the nation. As Paul Boyer demonstrates in his admirable history of the vice-society "movement," Sumner and the New York Society for the Suppression of Vice were one regiment in an army of reformers who, having just made the world safe for democracy, meant to continue their work by making the nation safe for morality. Their goal, like the realists' and like Joyce's, was to perfect or at least improve society. But their greatest achievement was Prohibition, instituted by the Eighteenth Amendment in 1919. The censorship of books was a hotly debated issue in the 1920s, and, though of less consequence and lower volume than the temperance debate, the opposing camps were the same in each.

These camps were divided along ideological lines that we might vaguely but perhaps not inappropriately call liberal and conservative. I hesitate to use those terms because of negative connotations associated with liberalism today, but even today's senses of these words—and certainly the political connotations they carried in the 1920s and '30s—do apply. One side was given voice by a young generation of American writers like Theodore Dreiser, F. Scott Fitzgerald, Ernest Hemingway, and Sherwood Anderson, and by writers imported from Europe like D. H. Lawrence and Joyce. In the wake of the war these writers flooded bookstores with novels that refused to pander to what they saw as a pious, untruthful, platitudinous, and (most importantly) debilitating view of sex. The established American publishing industry—publishers, authors, and booksellers alike—viewed them as an upstart generation aiming to upset the foundations of morality, which had just been reset by the war. The writers were able to get into print only because an upstart generation of publishers rose to challenge the large, venerable houses. Small publishers like Seltzer, Huebsch, Boni, Liveright, Covici, and Friede might be called modernist publishers, for their goals (besides, of course, the goal of making money) were sympathetic to the goals voiced in the manifestos of the modernist writers and the editors of the little reviews. This camp relied on the support of the liberal magazines like *The Nation* and the *The New Republic* and, perhaps more significantly, some New York lawyers who thought censorship threatened civil liberties and thus threatened democracy. Ernst, Lindey, and Greenbaum were in company that included a significant number of prominent lawyers around town, like Harlan Fiske Stone, dean of the Columbia Law School. (John Quinn, who never treated censorship from a civil liberties position, belonged to the pre-war generation of lawyers.)[128] Though the American Civil Liberties Union, which was founded to defend conscientious objectors in World War I, avoided the controversy, lawyers like Ernst were active both in the ACLU and the anticensorship campaign.

Marshaled against them was an impressive phalanx that drew its ranks from older publishers (represented by *Publishers Weekly* and the National Association of Book Publishers), established authors (like the members of the prestigious Authors Club of New York), conservative lawyers (like Judge John Ford, who organized the Clean Books League), church leaders and their various publications, public librarians (as represented by the *Library Journal*), and, before his death in 1923, the republican president Warren G. Harding. The pronouncements of these various groups consistently treated the new wave of postwar writers as a disease that corrupted the nation's moral constitution. For example, in 1923 the septuagenarian poet Edwin Markham, speaking in what Paul Boyer calls the "familiar vice-society rhetoric," asked "Why this recrudescence of sex-excesses when we have so much progress in other directions? . . . These young radicals in fiction . . . are spreading a contagion that will tend to corrupt youth and to engender an enervating cynicism in all minds." The nativism that swept so many Americans after the war strengthened this view, for if these "young radicals" spread a contagion, the contagion was communicated by European intellectual decadents. Often the procensorship camp resorted to deplorable chauvinism, as when Stuart Pratt Sherman attributed the problem to "writers whose blood and breeding are as hostile to the English strain as a cat to water." Or when novelist Mary Austin wrote, "Neither the Russian or the Jew has ever been able to understand . . . that not to have had any seriously upsetting sex adventures may be the end of an intelligently achieved life standard." Or when Hamlin Garland, as Boyer explains, "declared that the collapse of literary standards reflected the baleful influences of Manhattan, 'a city of aliens, with a vast and growing colony of European peasants, merchants, and newly rich, who know little and care less for American tradition.'"[129]

Such attacks were based on the perception—not altogether incorrect—that the new publishers and writers were of recent immigrant stock, and that they wanted to infuse American society with principles of

European pedigree. Though equating the literary revolution with Bolshevism, which the American Booksellers Association did at its convention in 1923, took things too far, these conservative groups were right to recognize that writers like Joyce and publishers like Cerf meant to challenge their influence on society. Ten years later, after the Soviets declared themselves against modernism, such an equation would require greater mathematical gymnastics. But during the censorship debates of the 1920s, sexual frankness in literature was considered one feature of a dangerous realist tendency.

That the conservatives expressed their opposition to the liberal sentiments of these writers through a forthright anti-Semitism is not surprising either. As de Grazia points out, Ben Huebsch was

> the first Jew in the twentieth century to enter general publishing in the United States. His entry cracked the solidly Gentile facade of the book publishing business and rebuked the unacknowledged anti-Semitism. . . . Between the world wars a significant number of publishing houses headed by Jews was founded.[130]

Greenbaum and Ernst were united to this group not only by their shared liberalism but by the prejudices of their opponents. It is not surprising that Joyce, who frankly discussed sex and who held up a Jew as a modern hero, would be vilified by conservatives and championed by American supporters of civil liberties. The *Ulysses* trial, then, was one engagement between opposing ideological forces trying to press their particular agenda on America.

To those New York readers who picked up their newspapers on December 8th, 1933, Ernst's linking of the repeal of prohibition to the *Ulysses* victory would not have been entirely facetious. It is ironic that Martin Conboy was the man who insisted on carrying the case to the New York Court of Appeals, since he was installed as U.S. Attorney as a result of Roosevelt's election in 1932. It is equally ironic that Woolsey, who was appointed by Herbert Hoover, should have been the one who approved *Ulysses*. In the larger drama, these two characters are anomalies. Morris Ernst, who went on to battle big business, support the labor movement, and write a controversial, celebrated apology for Roosevelt's attempt to stack the Supreme Court, acted in character through the whole *Ulysses* affair. The triumph of *Ulysses* was one fairly substantial contribution to the cause of liberalism in America.

But the victory was pyrrhic, since it depended so heavily on establishing that the book was a classic. The "classic" argument maintains that

Ulysses cannot corrupt society (as conservatives feared it would) because it cannot influence society. Paul Vanderham has made this very point:

> Morris Ernst [argued that] insofar as [*Ulysses*] was a genuine work of art, [it] could not influence readers morally, let alone influence them for ill. . . . This sort of esthetic defense of freedom of speech in literature may seem expedient in the short term, but it will not serve in the long run.[131]

Taking a controversial (and eventually censured) stance at the 1923 convention of the American Booksellers Association, Arthur Proctor, owner of a Detroit bookstore, said,

> We don't want wholesome books . . . but we do want books . . . that will portray life as it really is. . . . The younger people of today are demanding books that may seem to some of you who are over thirty years of age as revolutionary. . . . [They] are demanding those books not from any motive of immorality, but from what they can learn about life.[132]

This claim sounds exactly like the realist agenda Joyce proposed for *Dubliners* before the war. It was echoed by an anonymous author complaining in *The Nation* about the insidious effects of sex censorship on the writer:

> I write a passage that I believe to be as true as it is important. . . . But between it and myself has fallen the shadow of Comstockery, of my publisher's mingled bravado and desire to avoid trouble. . . . We must destroy the censorship not because it forbids books, but because it corrupts souls.[133]

Again, we hear echoes of Joyce's own complaints about the English "realists," the writers in the Celtic revival, and all those who objected to *Dubliners*. But Ernst's victory undermined the possible salutary effect of *Ulysses* because it was predicated on the axiom that the book is inaccessible to all but the learned and scholarly. Academe was the only arena of influence allowed by Ernst's *Ulysses*.

Ellmann's Joyce   4

Edmund Wilson's 1929 article on Joyce in *The New Republic,* which helped spark Ernst's and Lindey's interest in 1931 and which they included among the materials they sent to Judge Woolsey, probably kept Americans from dismissing Joyce as a bourgeois decadent. Wilson enlisted Joyce in the cause of American liberalism. Jeffrey Segall, in his intelligent book, *Joyce in America: Cultural Politics and the Trials of "Ulysses,"* argues that

> In the trajectory of Joyce criticism beyond the 1930s, Wilson's contribution was most important, for it established Joyce . . . as a liberal who advanced progressive human values. . . . Wilson was the catalyst in the launching of Joyce's reputation as what we might call a "good" liberal, a characterization that would be reinforced and amplified by James T. Farrell, Trilling, Howe, Harry Levin, Delmore Schwartz, and most exhaustively, by Richard Ellmann.[1]

But if the "good" liberal advances the progress of human values, we must conclude that the liberal adoption of Joyce was "bad," because it debilitated rather than enhanced his practical effect on the public. Just as Ernst's defense stripped *Ulysses* of any real power, the version of Joyce advanced by liberal critics, ironically, further rarefied his work.

Wilson, for example, emphasized the Odyssean parallels in the book, even going so far as to claim that the "narrative cannot be properly un-

I hereby predict that your errors about Joyce will be the last to depart from this earth.
—ELLSWORTH MASON TO
    RICHARD ELLMANN,
    20 MARCH 1955

derstood without reference to the Homeric original." Cribbing from the Linati scheme that Joyce would later refuse to publish, he dismissed early reviewers who "could not even discover a pattern" in the novel, and he claimed that "*Ulysses* suffers from an excess of design rather than from a lack of it." The Joyce Wilson gives his readers is a genius, "the great man of letters."[2] And his genius derives from the universality of Joyce's book:

> [I]t is proof of Joyce's greatness that, though we recognize Bloom's perfect truth and typical character, we cannot pigeonhole him in any familiar category, racial, social, moral, literary or even—because he does really have, after all, a good deal in common with the Greek Ulysses—historical.[3]

When Wilson's article was published as a chapter of *Axel's Castle* in 1931, it helped define modernism as the literary successor to classicism, romanticism, and naturalism. I do not need to review here the praise-worthy influence Wilson had on the following generation of academics: *Axel's Castle* helped make modernism a legitimate field of study, and it helped canonize Joyce in the process. But the stream of criticism sprung from Wilson continued to dehistoricize, and thus depoliticize, Joyce's work. Charting the currents of liberalism that Segall sketches, though certainly important, is beyond the scope of my study. But I do want to examine one source of that liberalism—Richard Ellmann's Joyce—to demonstrate how that critic manipulated Joyce's reputation.

Stanislaus Joyce v. the Critics

In 1956 Marvin Magalaner and Richard Kain, two young American crit-ics, published their influential *Joyce: The Man, the Work, the Reputation.* As their concern with Joyce's reputation suggests, they recognized that the main problem confronting their brand of criticism was the lack of a proper biography:

> No biographer has yet dealt satisfactorily with the shaping forces of this formative stage [Joyce's Dublin years]. Perhaps Richard Ell-mann's projected biography of Joyce, based on exhaustive researches in Ireland and elsewhere, will supply the background for further study. At the moment, however, Joyce's biography is very much a problem—in fact, *the* problem of Joyce scholarship.[4]

Magalaner and Kain (and American critics in general) needed a biogra-phy that would demonstrate that Joyce was uninterested (or at least not primarily interested) in the social issues of his day. Such an image of the author would justify their method, which tended to treat texts as autonomous artifacts.[5] Richard Ellmann's biography eventually would satisfy Magalaner and Kain, and it is a tribute to Ellmann's skill to recognize how he was able to reverse the image in the earlier, unsatisfactory biographical sketches of Joyce.

Before 1959 Joyce biography was confusing. Herbert Gorman's authorized biography was distrusted if not discredited, and most of Joyce's acquaintances, from his sisters to his childhood teachers to his literary rivals, had something to say, and usually they contradicted each other. Stanislaus Joyce was only one among these commentators, though he did have, perhaps, the most to say, since he had been in close contact with his brother during the composition of *Chamber Music, Dubliners,* and *Portrait,* and during the planning of *Ulysses.* Even so, few critics in the 1940s and early 1950s gave Stanislaus any more credibility than they gave other acquaintances of Joyce. He managed to publish a couple of articles here and there, the most substantial of which was a memoir called *Recollections,* translated from Italian in 1950 by Felix Giovanelli (for *The Hudson Review*) and Ellsworth Mason (for a pamphlet published by the James Joyce Society of New York).[6] For the first time Stanislaus's view of his brother was available to a general American audience. But these publications failed to establish Stanislaus as a reliable authority on his brother's life, because the editors of *The Hudson Review* expressed their disagreement "with many of the author's individual opinions and judgments";[7] and the James Joyce Society called the piece a "controversial portrait" and recognized that it was only a provisional "source of biographical material concerning the early and obscure period of James Joyce's life," which must serve "until the passage of time permits the full telling" of Joyce's family life in Dublin.[8] American critics regarded Stanislaus's contributions skeptically.

But in 1952 Stanislaus began corresponding with Ellsworth Mason. Encouraged by John Slocum, Stanislaus enlisted Mason's help in publishing an attack on Oliver Gogarty, whose unflattering portrait of Joyce had appeared in *The Saturday Review of Literature.*[9] Eventually, Mason was able to publish Stanislaus's "Open Letter to Dr. Oliver Gogarty" only in the obscure journal, *Interim.* But the "Open Letter" instituted a profitable association between Mason and Stanislaus, and it began a warm friendship that would last until Stanislaus's death in 1955. Stanislaus provided Mason with a neglected store of Joyceana—Joyce's book reviews and his articles for the Italian paper *Piccolo della Sera.* Eventually, Mason would publish a number of articles and two books derived from these materials and from his association with Stanislaus.[10] Meanwhile, Mason tirelessly represented Stanislaus before the American scholarly community, increasing both his circulation and his credibility. For example, in a letter on 2 June 1953, Mason asked Stanislaus for permission to respond to an article by John H. Raleigh, which used *The Hudson Review* version of Stanislaus's memoir to portray him in a poor light.[11] Stanislaus granted Mason permission on 8 June 1953, characterizing Mason as his "champion against what seems to be almost deliberate misunderstanding" by the critics.[12] Mason published his response in March 1955, which begins by asserting forthrightly that "John H. Raleigh's portrait of Stanislaus Joyce as his brother's keeper is drawn from the wrong model and painted in the wrong colors, as anyone who knows Mr. Joyce will testify."[13] Mason faults Felix Giovanelli's translation of Stanislaus's memoirs (from which Raleigh drew his evidence) for failing "to preserve the personality of Stanislaus Joyce." Mason, speaking as one of only three or four critics "who knows Mr. Joyce," tells readers that the original Italian *Recollections,*

> reflect[s] Stanislaus's feeling of personal hurt at Joyce's leaving him, which is expressed with great dignity and moderation, and against this plays an affectionate pride and delight in his brother as an artist and a personality. . . . Stanislaus emerges as a man and a mind of considerable stature.[14]

Trying to get Stanislaus's "Open Letter" published, Mason wrote to one editor explaining that Stanislaus was a more reliable source of biography than Gorman.[15] Mason also offered to help Stanislaus edit Joyce's book reviews and translate the *Piccolo* articles, which Stanislaus had saved from oblivion.[16] When Stanislaus told him that the Italian articles were already translated into English by his own pupil, Mason disappointedly and unselfishly instructed him to send the translation so Mason could get it into print.[17] When, against Stanislaus's wishes, John Slocum and Herbert Cahoon published a bibliography of these items, Mason asked the Yale Library to "hold anyone who would have access to them [the *Piccolo* articles]" until Stanislaus had a chance to bring them out in print himself.[18] The library did not reserve the articles for Mason, but it did tell him that Richard Kain and Joseph Prescott both had begun work on them; Mason then undertook the task of getting those scholars to recognize Stanislaus's prior claim to the material.[19] Kain graciously stopped his project. Mason advised Stanislaus about the possibility of libel in America.[20] He helped Stanislaus prepare Joyce's book reviews for the

American scholarly audience, querying him for annotations where he felt they would be useful to scholars who were ignorant of matters that would be taken for granted by the native Irish.[21] On the day Stanislaus died, Mason wrote that he was trying to get Stanislaus a foundation grant to give him the leisure to finish *My Brother's Keeper*.[22]

Mason also helped Stanislaus situate himself in the American critical terrain, which was foreign to the Triestine. In June 1953 Mason informed Stanislaus of what he considered excesses in Marvin Magalaner's interpretation of "Clay," a polemical defense of symbolic explication which cast Maria in the roles of the Blessed Virgin Mary and a witch.[23] Mason used the article to indicate how Stanislaus's memories of his brother could temper the extravagances of American criticism.

Stanislaus attempted to do just that in "The Background to *Dubliners*," which was published by *The Listener* in 1954. Claiming that he was "in a position to state definitely that my brother had no such subtleties in mind when he wrote ['Clay']," Stanislaus dismissed Magalaner's claims. He insisted that Joyce had very different intentions for *Dubliners* than he did for *Ulysses*. The only underlying plan Joyce had for "Clay," according to Stanislaus, was its thematic link to "A Painful Case": both stories were about "present types of celibates, male and female."[24] In other words, the story should be read as a realistic example of the Dublin female celibate *circa* 1904. The short stories were not composed according to an elaborate symbolic plan; in Stanislaus's description, they are much closer to the realism of Zola and Balzac, who used character "types." In short, Stanislaus portrays Joyce not as a symbolist but as a realist.

Stanislaus's publications consistently promoted Joyce's early, realistic fiction (*Dubliners* and *Portrait*) at the expense of the later, more difficult work (*Ulysses* and *Finnegans Wake*). In one article he put Joyce in the company of Dickens and Balzac, and calls his brother an "uncompromising realist."[25] In fact, Stanislaus suggested that Joyce would never have abandoned his realist intention and would never have written *Finnegans Wake* had Stanislaus "still been at his elbow" in the '20s and '30s. He also claimed to have convinced Joyce to succeed *Finnegans Wake* with a new, "more intelligible" (i.e., realistic) novel.[26] Stanislaus's commentaries emphasized his brother's criticism of both the Catholic Church and the Irish nationalists who, in Stanislaus's view, paralyzed Dublin. For example, he remembered that "Joyce's intention [in 'Aeolus' was] to illustrate the influence of political rhetoric on the little man in the street," and that "Joyce meant [one scene in 'The Sisters'] as a symbol of Irish life, dominated by priests, and half paralyzed."[27] Stanislaus's portrait of Joyce reflects his own political concerns and his own tendency to read his brother's fiction as a criticism of Dublin society.

This portrait, which stressed Joyce's realist intentions, ensured that Stanislaus's view would not be accepted by American critics, who perceived Joyce as a different type of artist. The most scathing attack on Stanislaus came from Magalaner and Kain:

> This type of personal-acquaintance criticism is understandable but dangerous. What family of a deceased writer has not felt that blood relationship and lifelong closeness afforded deeper insight into the writer's work than detached criticism? This is a natural and healthy family tendency; yet the results . . . are generally regarded with amusement or dismay by today's scholars. One should respect such prime sources of biographical information, but, at the same time, one may suspect critical judgments enunciated by such sources as the last word on, say, literary symbolism.[28]

Instead of "personal-acquaintance criticism," Magalaner and Kain promoted a detached interpretive method which does not seem to take into account authorial intention—that is, which does not seem to depend on a portrait of the author. Yet, despite their amusement with Stanislaus's unsophisticated critical method, they themselves had to promote their own portrait of Joyce to sustain their claim about the presence of symbolism in "Clay." Magalaner's original interpretation of "Clay" illustrates this necessity. Defending his detached method, Magalaner asserted,

> [T]here is a greater danger, it seems to me, in stopping short of *what the author is trying to say*. To the reader who refuses to admit the possibility of multiple symbolism, "Clay" is a drab recital of an old woman's night out, of an unsuccessful party.[29] [emphasis added]

Magalaner's criticism requires the belief that "the author is trying to say" something through a complex web of symbols. Magalaner believed that Joyce intentionally constructed a symbolic structure and that he was not writing with the literalness with which realists like Zola wrote. But the dismissal of Stanislaus's version of Joyce's intentions was not based on biographical evidence. Magalaner and Kain do not offer any evidence outside Joyce's texts to disprove Stanislaus. They dismissed him because his testimony did not suit their own critical practice, and Magalaner justified his methods only by the richness of his interpretation: "how much more effective and rich the story becomes if the reader will admit the applicability of merely half of the observations on witches and the Virgin made in this article." [30]

The problem that confronted critics was that biographical sketches of Joyce—mostly penned by "acquaintances" like Stanislaus—tended to portray him as a writer trying to do something about Ireland. So long as Stanislaus insisted that Joyce intended to affect Irish society and politics, his version of Joyce would remain unsatisfactory.

Mason, who himself insisted on a strict separation between Joyce's life and fiction, was the first to modify Stanislaus's version of Joyce. Mason's main concern was to prove that Joyce was not an autobiographical writer, that "Joyce is not Stephen." [31] Thus, Mason's chief use for Stanislaus's testimony was to invalidate biographical criticism. His letters to Stanislaus reflect this aim. [32] Only Stanislaus knew how little of Stephen is James, Mason assured Joyce's brother, so only he could stop the "misreading of Stephen's character that goes on, and [the] major misreading of Joyce as a person." [33] Neither critics who based assertions about Joyce on his fiction nor critics who based interpretations of his fiction on what they thought they knew about Joyce practiced the type of criticism of which Mason approved. Mason essentially was a New Critic, and, despite his censure of Magalaner, he also treated Joyce's fiction as autonomous artifacts. Mason did admit that Stanislaus would provide much outside historical material that would be useful to critics, but only because Americans in the 1950s did not know what was common knowledge in Dublin pubs in 1904. [34] Stanislaus could provide details about Dublin life, idioms, and landmarks, but his knowledge of his brother's life, Mason hoped, would not be used to interpret the fiction historically. He attacked John Henry Raleigh for following "a well-established, and completely invalid, tradition . . . [of reading] a knotty section of the *Wake* as biography, *as though the greatest novelist of the century were an historian*" [emphasis added]. [35] Mason's method of teaching *Ulysses* illustrates the autonomous method:

> It is fairly easy to show that intensive reading of the text and not outside information resolves most of the novel's obscurity. . . . We first concentrate on subtlety and complexity of statement, then on chapter structure, then on complexity of tone, and finally on the characterization of Bloom and the development of the Father-Son theme. [36]

And Mason's interpretation of Bloom illustrates the tendency of detached criticism to universalize rather than historicize. After directing readers to the broadest concern ("What then, according to Joyce, is the nature of man?"), Mason answers: fallibility, frustration, confusion, yet "generosity of heart." "Bloom . . . *is* the hero of the modern world, and he carries the spark of divinity as surely as did Odysseus."[37] Bloom is not, as Stanislaus might have argued, the hero merely of modern Ireland or even of modern Europe.

Unlike Mason, Stanislaus never wanted to separate Joyce's real life from his fiction. If anything, Stanislaus had been trying to restore considerations of Joyce's real life. For example, in 1949, before he became acquainted with Mason, Stanislaus pointed out that the "unwilling and unhappy believer in substantive realities, Daedalus [*sic*], is partly a reminiscent self-portrait. . . . The original of the portrait [Joyce himself] found his vocation as a creative artist."[38] In fact, Stanislaus tended to treat Joyce's fiction as autobiographical so he could link it to the issues that concerned Joyce in Ireland. If we read *Portrait* the way Stanislaus would have us, as referring to things outside the text, Catholicism and nationalism would not figure merely as metaphorical snares trapping the human soul's freedom; they would be indicted as real, regressive institutions in the lives of the Irish. Stanislaus tended to view his brother almost as a historian; he read his books in a specific historical context and uncovered his brother's social intent. In contrast, Mason wanted readers to confine themselves to the texts alone, with as little reference as possible to the historical (including the biographical) context of their composition.

Apparently neither Mason nor Stanislaus realized they were at cross purposes. Mason's letters indicate that he had a sincere desire to advance Stanislaus's authority. With that goal in mind, Mason introduced Stanislaus to another American critic, Richard Ellmann, the young accomplished biographer of Yeats, on 23 August 1953. Mason told Stanislaus not to speak to other biographers. Richard Ellmann, Mason assured Stanislaus, was the only biographer worth his time.[39] That introduction would prove to be the most significant event in Joyce biography, though neither Ellmann nor Mason suspected it.

Mason and Ellmann

By the time Mason told Stanislaus about Ellmann, he and Ellmann had already been consulting on the biography for over a year. The two critics had been friends at Yale before World War II, served together for part of the war, and corresponded while they were separated. In 1945 Mason discovered Joyce by reading *Portrait, Stephen Hero* (which was published in 1944), and the Modern Library *Ulysses*. Ellmann, not yet interested, actually tried to dissuade Mason from working on Joyce, insisting in 1946 that the basic, necessary biographical and exegetical work had not yet been done. Ellmann was aware of the authority Joyce's friends still had over Joyce's texts: "You can't work on a man so recently dead without being a constant prey of his friends' misconceptions," Ellmann wrote to Mason on 11 November 1946.[40] Ellmann himself had other concerns on his mind: his biography of Yeats, which would be based on the exclusive access he had won from Mrs. Yeats to her dead husband's letters and diaries—a "gold mine" into which he had fallen, in the words of Mason. After he was discharged in 1946, Ellmann went to Ireland with a Rockefeller Foundation fellowship and finished his research for *Yeats, The Man and the Masks*. He submitted the book as his dissertation in 1947, and it was accepted as the first allowed by Yale on a twentieth-century author. Ellmann told Mason that his biography would be "the definitive book on Yeats for many years to come."[41]

In 1947 Mason was back at Yale in Cleanth Brooks's seminar on twentieth-century literature (the first offered at Yale), and in 1948 he submitted his dissertation on Joyce—the second Yale dissertation on a twentieth-century author.[42] He sent it to Richard Kain, who viewed the dissertation favorably.[43] Mason was on close terms with many other Joyceans, including John Slocum, Herbert Cahoon, Frances Steloff, and James Spoerri. He was a young insider in the nascent Joyce studies. Naturally, when Ellmann's attention finally turned to Joyce in 1952, he sought out Mason's direction. Mason told Ellmann, "I very actively urge you to do the Joyce biography, and I'll give you all the help I can."[44] Help fell into two categories. Mason told Ellmann whom to talk to and how to win confidences, and he counseled Ellmann about the uncertainty of evidence about Joyce's life. Ellmann accepted the first advice but rejected the second.

By the end of 1952, Mason had led Ellmann to most of the collectors of the available Joyceana—Slocum, Cahoon, Spoerri, Frank Budgen, Herbert Gorman, Stuart Gilbert, Padraic and Mary Colum, and the Yale and New York Public libraries.[45] But securing access to Stanislaus proved to be delicate business. Mason advised Ellmann not to appear as a competitor, because Stanislaus, who was writing his own book, was wary and reticent:

> Stan, as he wrote me, is writing a book about Joyce based on his personal knowledge of him and unpublished material which he has on

hand. . . . I had thought about mentioning your project to him, but did not for the same reason. If he thinks you are trying to beat him to his book, he will not tell you anything.[46]

Ellmann did visit Stanislaus twice, and he agreed that Stanislaus had "a lot of the necessary keys" to Joyce's Dublin period.[47] But Ellmann's visits met with only moderate success. He complained that Stanislaus,

> showed me not his diary, but some vignettes of people like Byrne and Curran which Joyce wrote up early in his stay in Trieste—but I only had 45 seconds to look at them. . . . Stan answered a number of specific questions, but he is obviously taken up with his own book—for which I don't blame him. He was very kind to me and I appreciated it. I found him crotchety but intelligent. He is about through with the 4th of nine chapters. I'm sure it's hard for him to write, and he has an enormous amount of material, I should guess. He said he would try to finish soon, but will he? His book will be enormously interesting, and I'd be much happier about my own if I could see his first.[48]

Stanislaus never did publish his book. He died on Bloomsday in 1955 with only four chapters completed—the Dublin years. Mason wrote Ellmann, "There is an important part of the information on Joyce's life that will never be told. This will make your biography easier, but will certainly cut back the total picture considerably."[49] Ellmann's job was made easier because Stanislaus was no longer a competitor. And if Ellmann could win exclusive access to Stanislaus's materials, he even could enlist Stanislaus's support for his own portrait of Joyce.

If Stanislaus never fully accepted Ellmann, his widow Nelly did.[50] Apparently, Stanislaus had instructed Nelly, in the event of his death, to trust only Mason to advise her on James's and Stanislaus's papers.[51] Knowing this, Ellmann wrote to Mason on 6 March 1956, the eve of another trip abroad:

> I . . . should be grateful if you will pave the way with Mrs. S[tanislaus] Joyce. I don't know exactly what approach to recommend—you will know better than I—but I suppose the main thing is to give her confidence, in so far as you feel you can without excessively perjuring yourself.[52]

Mason wrote to Nelly that Richard Ellmann would be stopping in Trieste to pay Mason's respects for her dead husband and to help her assess the papers.[53] Ellmann expressed his thanks, remarking, "If anything can dislodge her, that [letter] will."[54] Nelly did welcome Ellmann, and, as Ellmann discovered that spring, she had a remarkable collection— Stanislaus's unfinished memoirs, his diaries, and a horde of Joyce's letters, notebooks, and essays. "With this rich material," Brenda Maddox wrote in her biography of Nora Barnacle, Ellmann "was assured that his biography of Joyce would be extraordinary. It would totally eclipse Gorman's."[55] It would also totally eclipse anything anyone else could produce, and, as his letters to Mason indicate, as late as 1958 Ellmann was concerned about his competitors.[56] The collection was Ellmann's second gold mine, and it would enable him to write his second "definitive" biography.

Mason's Objections to James Joyce

Mason's second category of advice regarded the difficulties concerning the evidence of Joyce's life. Mason himself had once contemplated writing a biography, but he had despaired of completing it in less than ten years because of the problem of documenting Joyce's life.[57] Mindful of a lack of evidence, Mason early and often cautioned Ellmann against presenting Joyce's life in definitive terms. He warned Ellmann in July of 1952:

> Right now I don't know what kind of book you could complete, because there are yawning gaps in the available information which cannot be closed quickly.[58]

Six months later he advised Ellmann to distrust the information that *was* available:

> You must learn to disbelieve and follow up, everything that you hear about Joyce. There is more disinformation about Joyce than about most anyone. Many people "knew" him, but very very few got to know him. . . . You weave your way through confusion and darkness. . . . It is my opinion that the life of Joyce will never be fully documented, *always remain hinged on conjecture,* and that what tangible evidence there is is in a few solid correspondences with people, and Joyce never fully revealed himself in any letters that I've seen. He is no Yeats. [emphasis added][59]

And two years later Mason voiced a related concern:

> In history, or biography, the events can be deduced with a great degree of certainty if there is enough evidence around to rub against

each other, counterchecks; if there is only a thin line of evidence, and you [Ellmann] are working in that shadowy realm, it is a hell of a job. *The most difficult thing for a man bent on finding out something is to admit that he can't, but such an admission is centrally important in the soundness of results.* [emphasis added][60]

The thin line of evidence available to Ellmann, in Mason's view, was unsound, because it was not confirmed by counterchecks. Clearly Mason was apprehensive about any biography of Joyce that would claim to be definitive and that would substitute conjecture for an admission of ignorance.

As the biography got underway, Mason's initial confidence in Ellmann's judgment began to diminish. Just five months after Mason's first encouragements, he wrote Ellmann, "You could do a hell of a [full] biography, but you can't do it in your present rush state of mind. . . . You could probably do it in five [years], but not sooner."[61] (This prediction proved to be accurate: Ellmann finished the book about five years later.) By the fall of 1954, Mason got his first look at Ellmann's production in the *Kenyon Review,* and what he saw troubled him.[62] He was so concerned that he jeopardized the biographer's standing with Stanislaus. He told Stanislaus in a letter that Ellmann confused biography with criticism.[63] A day later he wrote to Ellmann, "You have a certain tendency to identify the plausible with the actual."[64] Five months later, in March 1955, he sent Ellmann a long critique of particular points, arguing for more rigor and accuracy in Ellmann's assertions.

The chief problem was that Ellmann had adopted the strategy of supplementing his thin line of real evidence with events in Joyce's fiction. Mason criticized Ellmann for making simplistic correspondences between *Ulysses* and Joyce's real life. This familiar mistake of Joyce biography was especially dangerous, Mason insisted, because of the elegance of Ellmann's prose:

> The trouble with your performances is that they have a kind of self-contained beauty of their own, and even in deepest error you have an intelligence of expression that is rare in Joyce criticism. I hereby predict that your errors about Joyce will be the last to depart from this earth.[65]

Admittedly, this concern was voiced before Stanislaus died and before Ellmann won access to his memoirs and to hundreds of Joyce's letters. After Ellmann discovered those materials in 1956, Mason expected

Joyce's life to be accurately documented, presumably because the new materials would close the gaps in the evidence and supply Ellmann with counterchecks.[66] Nevertheless, as Mason would discover, Ellmann's use of Stanislaus's material would not eliminate his reliance on Joyce's fiction.

Mason and Ellmann had a serious falling out in the fall of 1956 over the sale of Nelly Joyce's collection, and that seems to have disrupted their close association. A flurry of letters between Mason and Ellmann in December 1956 argue over the negotiations between American libraries and Nelly Joyce.[67] Ellmann had secured for Nelly the services of Ottocaro Weiss. Mason felt Weiss had acted dishonorably with James Spoerri and a Mr. Vosper, who had been trying to purchase the collection for the University of Kansas library and who had successively bid five, ten, fifteen, and then twenty thousand dollars. Mason believed that Nelly had accepted and then rejected each bid on the advice of Weiss. Mason wrote Nelly telling her what he thought of Weiss, and he went so far as to warn Stephen McCarthy at Cornell against dealing with Weiss. Ellmann was infuriated, demanded a retraction from Mason, and warned him that he was hurting everyone, including their own collaboration on Joyce's *Critical Writings*. Shortly after Christmas Mason backed down, cabling Ellmann: "No need to phone will keep quiet."[68]

In 1958 Ellmann mailed Mason a draft of *James Joyce*, soliciting his comments. Mason's letters clearly demonstrate that, despite Ellmann's discovery of Stanislaus's papers, he continued to be troubled by Ellmann's method:

> If I intuit rightly, and if you are weaving both the works and the non-works [i.e., Joyce's real life] into a single, supposedly factual, fabric, it is a serious flaw in the work. We simply must have a biography that will tell us what can and what cannot be determined as actually having existed outside Joyce's works.[69]

Apparently Ellmann continued to use Joyce's fiction to speculate about Joyce's life. Quite reasonably, Mason did not accept Joyce's fiction as any part of Ellmann's line of evidence. The frankness of Mason's objection may have been influenced by the cooling of his relation to Ellmann in 1956. But even so, this objection is profound; it amounts to a rejection of the biography's historical accuracy—a rejection leveled by someone who had been a part of the project from its earliest stages. Ellmann defended himself perfunctorily:

I have been making up footnotes for the book, and these will at least indicate whether there's any source for a given fact beyond James Joyce's books. I'm not sure that this will meet your objections.[70]

The Ellmann collection at Tulsa does not preserve Mason's response, but I suspect that Ellmann's footnotes would not have satisfied Mason. What became clear by 1958, after six years of close association on matters of Joyce's life, was that Mason and Ellmann had very different views of literary biography. Ellmann, apparently, was troubled neither by a thin line of evidence, which necessitated conjecture, nor by using Joyce's fiction to form conjectures.

Conjecture: Theory and Practice

Despite Mason's objections, Ellmann purposely drew connections between Joyce's life and his fiction. Ellmann believed that the proper domain of modern biography is the subject's inner life. This focus, he held, is especially true of literary biography, which tries to capture not only the artist's psyche or "inner compulsions," but his or her creative process.[71] Ellmann wrote to Mason that, although New Critics would not agree, "methods of composition" are revealing—they reveal Joyce's personality, his inner life.[72] Ellmann seems to have been advocating a study of the fiction to understand the life, and in *James Joyce* he adopted such a method. "This book," he divulges in his introduction to *James Joyce,* "enters Joyce's life to reflect his complex, incessant joining of event and composition."[73]

According to Ellmann, the biographer who traces the creative process—the joining of real-life event and composition—must imagine him or herself "not as outside but as inside the subject's mind, not as observing but as ferreting." The "counterchecks" that Mason exhorted Ellmann to use do not exist for someone's inner life. Despite diaries and personal letters, a subject's inner life is impossible to document with anything near the authority that one might document public life. But the lack of confirming evidence did not trouble Ellmann as much as it did Mason. "Biographers," he held, "have never felt so free of the necessity of distinguishing fact from fancy." While he warned against taking speculation to an extreme and sympathized with biographers who were hesitant to take on "the responsibilities of this kind of subtle and devious interpretation," Ellmann thought speculation was a potential strength of modern biography: "The unknown need not be the unknowable. To paraphrase Freud, where obscurity was, hypothesis shall be. In this sense, paucity of information may even be an advantage, as freeing the mind for conjecture."[74] A biography of inner life, then, requires something much different of the biographer than public events require of the historian—it requires psychological conjecture rather than confirming evidence. Phillip Herring's assessment of Ellmann's theory of biography comes to the same conclusion: "Speculation, even in the absence of factual support, he deems indispensable."[75]

Giving such weight to the biographer's speculation would lead, presumably, to a subjective biography. Ellmann agreed, though not in so many words. He wrote that the biographer "introduces an alien point of view, [one] necessarily different from the mixture of self-recrimination and self-justification which the great writer . . . has made the subject of his lifelong conversation with himself."[76] In a letter to Mason in 1953, at the beginning of his project, Ellmann used nearly the same phrase: "My notion of biography is that it should be *a portrait of the writer* [biographer] as well as the subject" [emphasis added].[77] In a letter turning down Richard Kain's offer to collaborate on the biography, Ellmann elaborated:

I realize that this is a dangerous theory, and that what people want is a portrait of Joyce *rather than of any biographer.* But the slow germination of a certain image in the mind—which any biographer would aim at—is something, I think, that one can only go at alone.[78] [emphasis added]

This description—the germination of an idea, the organic growth of an image in the writer's mind, the writer's self-expression—seems more appropriate to fiction writing than to historical research. Ellmann implies that the biographer imagines the subject and creates a character, and he insists that such a biographical technique, though "dangerous," is no defect.[79]

No biography, then, could claim definitiveness. Even the most revered biographies would be limited by the prejudices of the biographer's point of view. Ellmann himself conceded that

Whatever the [biographer's] method, it can give only incomplete satisfaction. . . . Biographical possibilities cannot be exhausted; we cannot know completely the intricacies with which any mind negotiates with its surroundings to produce literature.[80]

The biographer is at least bound by the point of view—the ideology, if you will—of his or her circumstances. Brenda Maddox's account of Ellmann's support for her biography of Nora Barnacle bears this concession out. Ellmann at first balked, but then he agreed that a "feminist treatise" was "waiting to be done," apparently implying that his own version of Nora, and thus his own point of view, was limited.[81]

Ellmann seems to have frankly admitted what I have taken as my own premise. Put into my terms, the literary biography will be a portrait of the *biographer* insomuch as it reflects the biographer's critical prejudices. The biographer's attitude to a writer's fiction will dictate the biographer's portrait of the writer. As I hope to demonstrate, Ellmann's speculations about Joyce ultimately derived from his reading of Joyce's fiction, and he would draw on the historical evidence, especially the evidence provided by Stanislaus, only when it supported those speculations. Ellmann could not extricate his portrait of Joyce from Joyce's fiction because his portrait originated in the fiction.

We should not be surprised, then, that Ellmann's biography would be composed without counterchecks. After all, its subject, the artist's inner life, is not amenable to such confirmation, and the portrait is dependent, Ellmann conceded, on the biographer's own conjecture. Neither of these observations would invalidate Ellmann's biography, and both might be made of most literary biographies. But an examination of exactly what these observations mean in the case of *James Joyce* should demonstrate that Mason's fears about historical accuracy were valid.

Ellmann's line of outside evidence, at least for the Dublin years and for certain key episodes during the Trieste years, was comprised almost wholly of Stanislaus Joyce's testimony. To a lesser extent, Ellmann re-ferred to Joyce's own letters. The testimony of other friends and relatives was either ignored or incorporated into the general picture established by Stanislaus—fleshing out the skeleton, so to speak. The debt to Stanislaus Joyce in chapters II through X, the Dublin years, is undeniable. Of the 622 citations in those chapters, attributions to Stanislaus total 134, more than one in five. No other friend or relative comes close. Eugene Sheehy is cited nineteen times; Gogarty, Byrne, Curran, and Colum each receive a similar handful of citations. The only other substantial source is Joyce himself in his letters. Furthermore, if we were to separate the citations that substantially contribute to the themes of the biography (those which support Ellmann's characterization of the author Joyce) from those that are incidentals (sources of street addresses and the like), the percentage attributed to Stanislaus would rise considerably.

For example, borrowing from *Finnegans Wake*, Ellmann compared Stanislaus's relationship with James to the fabled ant and grasshopper.[82]

As early as 1903 "Stanislaus had . . . begun," Ellmann writes, "on the long course of humiliation from which his brother rarely allowed him to play truant." While Stanislaus admired James, James was bored by Stanislaus. Stanislaus had literary aspirations that James ridiculed; yet James borrowed incessantly from Stanislaus's diary, both for material and for stylistic experiments. "At his warmest he treated Stanislaus with chaffing affection, at his coldest with impatient scorn" (*JJ*, 132–134). "James spent . . . ten years getting into scrapes and . . . Stanislaus spent the ten years getting him out of them." [83] And Stanislaus got him out of the scrapes, which were usually financial, without any thanks. Ellmann narrates at least four fights between the brothers in which James repays Stanislaus's selfless generosity with scorn (*JJ*, 270, 300, 311–312, 339).

Ellmann supports these characterizations with Stanislaus's *My Brother's Keeper* and a letter Stanislaus wrote (but never sent) to his father. In one place Ellmann does seem to confirm the evidence with a second witness:

The pressure upon the young man [Stanislaus] was very great, but he won support from the Francinis who told him . . . that they always felt he was mistreated in the house. (*JJ*, 312)

But, as Ellmann's endnote reveals, the Francinis' corroboration was penned by Stanislaus himself. Ellmann's counterchecking seems to have broken down. It continually breaks down regarding Stanislaus's character. Ellmann's entire confirmation of the ant-and-grasshopper relationship comes from Stanislaus.

But Stanislaus's perceptions were not objective, no matter what his privileged information. They were colored by his personality, which was as eccentric as his brother's, perhaps more so. Today, even the most casual reader of Stanislaus's diaries, letters, and memoirs would identify his sense of responsibility as abnormally developed. Stanislaus seems to have learned the role of the keeper in Dublin and to have transported it with him to Trieste. He abandoned his role as provider for his drunk father's household only to assume the same role in his brother's household, because a keeper needs a charge. Francini-Bruni provides at least some evidence to suggest that James began drinking heavily *after* Stanislaus arrived in Trieste.[84] And in Eileen Joyce's version of life in Trieste, Joyce was "like a father" to her and her sister Poppie, certainly a more responsible person than Stanislaus suggests.[85] If in his life James escaped his keeper by moving to Zurich, he could not escape him after death. As Ira Nadel has asserted, "Joyce as the feckless, sponging, egotistical man who constantly mistreated his brother was an idea originated by Stanislaus."[86] After James died Stanislaus projected unreliability onto him at will, and projected reliability onto himself. And in at least two significant cases, Stanislaus seems to have projected the role of betrayer onto Joyce's old friends. Ellmann swallowed this portrait uncritically because it served his own version of Joyce.

The Gay Betrayers

In some cases it can be demonstrated that Ellmann did have access to counterchecks for Stanislaus's line of evidence. For example, the testimony of John Francis Byrne, Joyce's cohort at the university who was the origin of Cranly, supplied one countercheck. But Ellmann tended to suppress him rather than to use him. Byrne's *The Silent Years,* published in 1953, narrates a number of incidents that seem to have clear analogs in *Ulysses.* Richard Ellmann reviewed the book favorably and wrote to Byrne late in 1953, and the two began exchanging cordial letters. They met in Chicago in the spring of 1954, when Ellmann interviewed him. Byrne continued to advise Ellmann on the biography, especially portions of it that were published in various journals, until 1958—one year before the book came before the public. But his letters to Ellmann reveal a gradual souring of his esteem, mostly over Ellmann's portrayal of Vincent Cosgrave.

Cosgrave is maligned in *James Joyce,* and the most damning accusations appear without cross-examination. The condemnation refers to Joyce's 1909 visit to Dublin, during which he met with his old friend (back in 1904, Cosgrave had introduced Joyce to Nora Barnacle). Ellmann prepares readers for Cosgrave's betrayal by reporting that, in 1909, Cosgrave "bore several grudges against" Joyce: "Joyce had succeeded with Nora when Cosgrave had failed"; Joyce had put Cosgrave into *Portrait* with the "unsavory name of Lynch"; Joyce had landed on his feet in Trieste, while Cosgrave was still a failure in Dublin; and "Joyce's manner . . . probably irritated" Cosgrave (*JJ,* 279). Ellmann offers evidence for only one of these four grievances: that Cosgrave hated the name "Lynch." The evidence (actually presented at another place in the biography) is a letter Cosgrave wrote to Joyce in 1905, when they were on good terms, when Joyce was sending him the draft of *Portrait* and soliciting his comments. The evidential passage reads,

> I am unable to say anything about your novel as I have lost the continuity. Please send some more soon to Charlie [Joyce's brother]

and I will do my best to help you with criticism. Meanwhile why in the name of J[esus]—Lynch? Anything but that. (*JJ*, 205)

The tone of the letter is very cordial, and Ellmann seems wrong to construe Cosgrave's protest as a grievance. Ellmann justifies his interpretation of the letter by referring to a conversation between Cosgrave and Stanislaus, during which Cosgrave supposedly expressed his relief that Joyce was not attacking him in the novel the way Joyce was going to attack Gogarty (*JJ*, 207). Stanislaus's recollection of a conversation nearly fifty years after the fact seems a dubious basis for an interpretation clearly at odds with Cosgrave's letter. But it is the only evidence that supports Ellmann's belief that Cosgrave bore grudges.

Ellmann's narration of the 1909 reunion is also one-sided. Apparently, Cosgrave told Joyce that he had gone out with Nora on alternate nights when Joyce first started his courtship. That Cosgrave said as much seems indisputably true, since it appears in a letter Joyce wrote to Nora shortly afterward.[87] What is not so clear is whether Cosgrave was lying or telling the truth, and what motivated him to tell Joyce the story. Ellmann reduces Cosgrave's claim to a vindictive lie designed to break Joyce down. As evidence, he paraphrases an interview with Stanislaus that confirms such a characterization of the event:

In 1904 he [Stanislaus] had seen Cosgrave one night in a public house looking morose, and had asked him what the trouble was. Cosgrave swore him to secrecy, then said he had been trying to "get inside" Joyce with Nora, and had just been rebuffed. Over several years Stanislaus had darkly hinted to James *that Cosgrave made one among his betrayers,* but kept his word and never said anything explicit. Now he felt free to write him the truth, and he did so in his downright, unimpeachable way. (*JJ*, 281–282) [emphasis added]

Ellmann bases his claim about Cosgrave's character wholly on Stanislaus's condemnation. Ellmann told Phillip Herring (in another context) that he confirmed Stanislaus's testimony with "a complicated system of crosschecking."[88] Ellmann's crosscheck for the Cosgrave affair was John Francis Byrne, to whom Joyce poured out his soul after Cosgrave's assertion. Ellmann reports in *James Joyce*:

Byrne, a great discoverer too of conspiracies, rendered an unhesitating verdict. Cosgrave's brag was "a blasted lie." It was probably the second stage in a joint plot of Cosgrave and Gogarty to wreck Joyce's life, he said; Gogarty having failed at cajolery, the pair had decided to try slander. (*JJ*, 281)

But Ellmann knew that Byrne thought no such thing. Byrne denied having rendered such a verdict and would not join Stanislaus's attack on Cosgrave's character. Ellmann's endnotes reveal that this evidence, apparently supplied by Byrne, was Joyce's version of his interview with Byrne in a letter to Stanislaus. Byrne himself had refused to mention Cosgrave's name in his account of the incident in *The Silent Years*. Indeed, that version focuses on Joyce's exaggerated sorrow and leaves us with the impression that if Byrne did hint that Cosgrave and Gogarty conspired against Joyce, he probably would have hinted at anything to calm Joyce and assure him of Nora's fidelity.

Actually Byrne thought that Cosgrave was not lying to Joyce—something he certainly would not have told Joyce in 1909 but something he did strongly hint to Ellmann twice. In an interview in Chicago on 22 March 1954, Byrne first elaborated to Ellmann his version of the story. Ellmann's notes of the interview read,

> He [Cosgrave] had a great way with women, and seduced several young women at the University. . . . Cosgrave picked up Nora on the street—she was a slavey at Finn's—she'd come to Dublin in 1903; it was through Cosgrave. In 1909 Joyce was in Dublin, and he said to Byrne that he thought he would call on Cosgrave on Synett Place. Byrne said, What's the point? After all, you've not come to Dublin to see him. Joyce seemed convinced, but went out, was in the neighborhood of Cosgrave, and did go to see him. They went to a pub to drink, and Cosgrave told him he had slept with Nora before Joyce did. This put him in the state of agitation described in Byrne's book. When Byrne went to visit the Joyce's in 1927, he spoke with Joyce briefly about Cosgrave's death and said good riddance. At the moment of saying this he happened to look at Nora's face, the expression of which seemed very revealing.[89]

Byrne, always circumlocutious, does not tell what was revealed to him by Nora's expression, but we might safely assume that it was not a confirmation of Stanislaus's version of events. Byrne seems to have been hinting to Ellmann that Cosgrave did go out with Nora.[90]

In 1957 Byrne voiced a less equivocal protest against Ellmann's treatment of Cosgrave. Byrne wrote Ellmann insisting that Joyce should not have felt cuckolded, because whatever happened between Nora and Cosgrave happened before she committed herself to Joyce. He defended Nora, but not on the grounds of chaste behavior with Cosgrave: "Nora was a splendid, outstanding helpmate for James Joyce. She was a great girl and woman. This is what everyone ought to know now; this is all they need to know."[91] His refusal to deny that Nora slept with Cosgrave amounts to a request that Ellmann—on the grounds of its irrelevancy— suppress what Nora may have done before she eloped with Joyce to the Continent. And finally, Byrne explicitly disputed Stanislaus's honesty in recording Cosgrave's secret confession:

> I shall say no more than that this [Stanislaus's claim] does not have any valid bearing, particularly for those who recall that in 1904 Cosgrave was a mature man of the world, approximately thirty while Stan was a mere unsophisticated stripling not yet nineteen years of age.[92]

Ellmann wrote back,

> I'll of course reconsider the events of 1909 in the light of what you tell me. . . . The incident is of course—as you pointed out to me in Chicago—of crucial importance in Joyce's life, and in any effort to fathom his character. . . . The disparity of their ages [Stanislaus's and Cosgrave's], which you point out, was certainly great, but I suppose Stan's story not unfounded.[93]

In February 1958, Byrne questioned Stanislaus's general reliability, claiming, "He is *so* wrong in some things he wrote. And, perhaps so right in some other things he wrote" [Byrne's emphasis].[94] Three months later, after he apparently had completed reading Gilbert's edition of Joyce's letters and Ellmann's edition of Stanislaus's *My Brother's Keeper,* both sent him by Ellmann and both of which disturbed him greatly, Byrne grew more insistent in his censure: Stanislaus was "a bitter, frustrated, confused and inaccurate man."[95] Ellmann may have reconsidered the events, but in the end he chose Stanislaus's version over Byrne's, and he neglected to mention Byrne's dispute.

Ellmann neglects to mention anything in Cosgrave's favor in *James Joyce,* and Byrne's final assessment of that book reveals his dissatisfaction with Ellmann's portrayal. That dissatisfaction is all the more significant because Byrne was disposed to trust Ellmann earlier in his project. In 1959, when *James Joyce* was published, Byrne wrote a "rather cranky early review of Ellmann's book."[96] He took Ellmann to task for a number of factual errors which seem innocuous—the type of errors that are bound to crop up here and there in a book so large. But the bulk of Byrne's complaint is over Ellmann's treatment of Vincent Cosgrave. The review disputes only Ellmann's assertion "that Cosgrave drowned himself in the Thames" (whether it was suicide is in question), but clearly Byrne would have had more to dispute about Ellmann's treatment of Cosgrave were he one to speak of such things in print. He concludes with serious reservations: "This [*James Joyce*] is not the definitive biography of Joyce. I doubt that one can ever be written."[97]

Byrne apparently believed that the reader who looks to *James Joyce* for the origin of Lynch finds a character already fictionalized by Ellmann and Stanislaus, and that other versions, including his own, are completely effaced. Not that Cosgrave comes off very well in Byrne's version—to sleep with Nora so casually and use that coupling later to hurt Joyce is certainly, in Byrne's view, contemptible behavior. But Cosgrave does come off differently in Byrne's version. He is not a vindictive liar plotting with Gogarty to bring Joyce down by cajolery and slander. He is no betrayer.

Whatever led Ellmann to trust Stanislaus, it is certainly true that Stanislaus's version of the Cosgrave episode fit one of the major themes Ellmann was developing in his biography, and it is true also that Byrne's version would have diminished that theme. Betrayal is construed by Ellmann as central to Joyce's fiction and thus as crucial to his life. But it is a theme that was more important to Stanislaus than it was to James, so Ellmann found in Stanislaus great evidence to support such speculation. Stanislaus eventually saw betrayal in many of Joyce's friends and relations, including his father, John Francis Byrne, George Russell, and especially Oliver Gogarty.

The case of Gogarty, the original of Buck Mulligan (who usurps the Martello Tower from Stephen Dedalus), is more famous than Cosgrave's, and his indictment by Ellmann was more thorough. But it was just as dependent on Stanislaus. In fact, it was Stanislaus who first convinced Joyce that Gogarty was not a true friend. Discussing Gogarty's attempts to reconcile with Joyce, Stanislaus admits:

> He [Joyce] was at first inclined to entertain the suggestion, but I opposed it as forcibly as I could. I was Pretty Sure I Knew Gogarty— burly, bustling Gogarty, the Hyperborean, careless of temporalities, hail-fellow-well-met with everybody, the perfect fount of randy rhymes, honest Iago.[98]

With the notable exception of *Recollections,* Stanislaus's publications consistently vilified Gogarty. He attacked Gogarty in particular as an unreliable source of biography. He disputed Gogarty's "wrong account" of Joyce's meeting with Yeats; he disputed Gogarty's "misleading assurance" that Joyce took notes on his friends' manners and speeches; he accused Gogarty of attributing to James or inventing for James "many wild escapades," some of which Gorman ignorantly believed;[99] he accused Gogarty (and Colum, Byrne, and Cousins) of being "good liars";[100] he disputed Gogarty's anecdote about the naming of *Chamber Music;*[101] and in "Open Letter" he enumerated a number of Gogarty's "lies" in no uncertain terms. Altogether, Stanislaus established Gogarty as his brother's betrayer, and Ellmann was inclined to believe him. Citing Stanislaus, Ellmann reports in *James Joyce* that

> Gogarty said to Elwood, in a sudden burst of malice, that he would "make Joyce drink to break his spirit," and when Elwood told Joyce and his brother, they both accepted it as evidence of Gogarty's permanent ill intentions. (131)[102]

To confirm Stanislaus's testimony, Ellmann used the crosscheck of Joyce's letters.

But the letters themselves are demonstrably unreliable. For example, Ellmann quotes one of Joyce's letters to establish Gogarty as a betrayer:

> As for O.G. [Oliver Gogarty] I am waiting for the S.F. [Sinn Fein] policy to make headway in the hope that he will join it for no doubt whatever exists in my mind but that, if he gets the chance and the moment comes, he will play the part of MacNally & Reynolds. I do not say this out of spleen. It is my final view of his character: a very native Irish growth, and if I begin to write my novel again it is in this way I shall treat them. (*JJ,* 237–238)

Ellmann glosses the letter thus:

> Leonard MacNally (1752–1820) and Thomas Reynolds (1771–1832) were informers, notorious for having betrayed the United Irishmen. MacNally also betrayed Robert Emmet. In *Ulysses* (14 [15]), *Stephen refers to Mulligan, modeled mostly on Gogarty, as Ireland's "gay betrayer."* (*JJ,* 238n) [emphasis added]

It is unclear whether Ellmann first regarded Gogarty as a betrayer because Stephen so regards Mulligan, or whether Ellmann merely invokes

Ulysses to support Joyce's letter. Either method is questionable. Ellmann fails to point out that Gogarty served Arthur Griffith, the founder of Sinn Fein, loyally; that he stuck to Griffith to the end, attending him at his deathbed; that he was a senator in the Irish Free State; and that he was nearly murdered by De Valera's Irish Republican Army, which fought a civil war against Griffith's faction. Indeed, after Griffith's acceptance of the treaty partitioning Ireland, followers had to choose between the founder of Sinn Fein and Sinn Fein itself, which rejected the treaty and adopted a nationalist stance more intransigent than the policy Joyce here approves. In a sense, Gogarty, like all Irish, would become a betrayer to whomever he chose to follow. In any event, Gogarty followed the policy that Joyce, in my view, would have followed himself: he chose Griffith and peace.

The failure to mention these things diminishes confidence in Ellmann's method, which relies on Joyce's letters inordinately. The letters have at least three strikes against them. Firstly, the letters possibly were screened and selected by Stanislaus to support his version of Joyce's life. For decades Stanislaus was the sole proprietor of many of the letters. Brenda Maddox has suggested that "Stanislaus had ample time to censor the papers to his own advantage," and she notes "one striking feature of the Trieste collection . . . is that there is nothing in it that shows Stanislaus in a bad light." [103] Secondly, the letters themselves are unreliable because of the influence exerted on their composition by their recipients. As Ellmann himself warned readers in his introduction to the letters, perhaps more than in any other genre the expectations and prejudices of the reader guide the letter-writer's pen (*Letters II,* xxxv). Nevertheless, Ellmann gleans a cohesive portrait of Joyce from what Joyce said to a range of correspondents without taking into account Joyce's possible guises. The correspondent of the letter accusing Gogarty of betrayal is, not surprisingly, Stanislaus. Ellmann makes nothing of that fact, but the context is worth noting.

The letter was written in 1906. James was nearly destitute in Rome— an unsuccessful writer working in a bank. Stanislaus was nearly destitute in Trieste—a young, poor teacher of English far from home. The two, somewhat jealously, had been observing from afar the successes of their old friends in Dublin (*Letters II,* 153–154). And Stanislaus had insisted to Joyce already that his friend Gogarty was duplicitous. In other words, if Joyce called Gogarty a betrayer of Sinn Fein in a correspondence with Stanislaus in 1906, it might have been because Stanislaus, out of spleen, demanded the label. Imagined political betrayal is a small extension from imagined personal betrayal in a letter to one's brother. In a biography it is too large an accusation to make lightly, and it should not have been Ellmann's final view of Gogarty's character.

The letters have a third defect—especially when we turn to Ellmann's editions of them. Scholarship is only recently becoming sensitive to the influence editorial apparatuses have on our reading of a text. How a text is introduced, what is glossed, what is not glossed, all editorial decisions contribute to our interpretation of the writer's work.[104] Such a situation is unavoidable if we are to benefit at all from scholarly editions. But we ought to keep in mind the editor's prejudices, and Ellmann's apparatus displays a prejudice against Gogarty. For example, Ellmann writes in his introduction to the second volume of *Letters of James Joyce:*

> Joyce does not condescend to argue the case for socialism on an abstract level, but he names rich and church-married Oliver Gogarty as his epitome of the "stupid, dishonest, tyrannical and cowardly burgher class." Gogarty appears in these letters as a kind of mythical adversary. (xl)

Ellmann makes a number of interpretations here. He trivializes Joyce's engagement with socialism—an interpretation that recently has been called into serious question.[105] He also asserts that Gogarty figures as a "mythical adversary" in the letters. Such an interpretation seems to me unsupported extrapolation from the evidence. Nothing in the letters ennoble the dispute between Gogarty and Joyce to the level of myth. Joyce may raise the adversarial relationship to the level of myth in *Ulysses,* where Stephen figures as Telemachus and Mulligan as Antinoos. But if that is the evidence for his assertion about the letters, Ellmann seems to be following a questionable method of biography. His interpretation of *Ulysses* lends weight to his interpretation of the letters which lends the weight back to his interpretation of *Ulysses.* Ira Nadel (like Mason) has identified this backward motion as Ellmann's method in *James Joyce:* "for all its basis in fact, [Ellmann's] biography is written from the novels outward towards the life. . . . [Joyce's] literary works narrate [his] life."[106] Ellmann's insights into Joyce's relationship to Gogarty derive from his interpretation of Stephen's relationship to Mulligan.

At the heart of the passage in question is Ellmann's assertion that Joyce considered Gogarty to be the epitome of the cowardly burgher class. Joyce may have thought that Gogarty capitulated to the bourgeoisie, but he did not call Gogarty stupid, dishonest, tyrannical, or cowardly. Actually the letter from which Ellmann takes these adjectives has nothing to do with Gogarty. Joyce was condemning his coworkers at his bank in Rome (*Letters II*, 231). Ellmann dubiously projects Joyce's opinion of Roman clerks onto his opinion of Gogarty. All in all, Joyce's characterization of Gogarty in the letters is more equivocal than Ellmann asserts.

In *James Joyce*, Ellmann prepares readers for Gogarty's betrayal the way he prepared them for Cosgrave's: by building up, over the course of a few pages, Gogarty's increasing hostility for Joyce. He makes out that Gogarty was insulted by Joyce's poem, "The Holy Office," which disparaged nearly all the literary figures of Dublin, Gogarty included. Gogarty "was accustomed to wound," Ellmann writes, "rather than to be wounded" (*JJ*, 167). The notion that Gogarty feared the lancet of Joyce's art derives ultimately from Stephen's characterization of Mulligan, which Ellmann cites later in the biography. But it was not true. Gogarty often found himself in others' fiction—he once even sued successfully for libel. He never sued Joyce. On the contrary, he wrote, "when [Joyce] paid me the only kind of compliment he ever paid, and that is to mention a person in his writings, he described me shaving on the top of the tower. In fact, I am the only character in all his works who washes, shaves, and swims." Nor did Gogarty mind the name Malachi Mulligan, since Joyce gave himself the nickname "Kinch." [107] Gogarty was accustomed to being wounded and could take his wounds equably.

Ellmann's confirmation of Gogarty's piqued pride over "The Holy Office" is a letter from Gogarty to G. K. A. Bell written shortly after his falling out with Joyce (27 August 1904). Actually Gogarty expressed no anger at Joyce's treatment of himself. Gogarty was angered by Joyce's treatment of "Yeats, AE, Colum, and others to whom he [Joyce] was indebted." He wrote that Joyce's "lack of generosity became to me inexcusable. . . . A desert was revealed which I did not think existed amid the seeming luxuriance of his soul." [108] According to Gogarty, his growing coolness was due to Joyce's lack of the high virtue of generosity. Ulick O'Connor, Gogarty's biographer, offers a third motive: Gogarty "began to notice also that his friend was adopting a conscious, artistic pose." [109] The truth is elusive, contested, and perhaps indiscernible.

Ellmann does not present readers with Gogarty's version of the tower episode, nor with the darkness surrounding the events. Instead, he quotes Stanislaus's *Dublin Diary*:

At present [Joyce] is staying on sufferance with Gogarty in the Tower at Sandycove. Gogarty wants to put Jim out, but he is afraid that if Jim made a name someday it would be remembered against him

(Gogarty) that though he pretended to be a bohemian friend of Jim's, he put him out. Besides, Gogarty does not wish to forfeit the chance of shining with a reflected light. Jim is scarcely any expense to Gogarty. He costs him, perhaps, a few shillings in the week and a roof, and Gogarty has money. Jim is determined that if Gogarty is to put him out it will be done publicly.[110]

But the *Dublin Diary,* which Ellmann treats as contemporary to the events it recounts, was not contemporary at all. It did not even faithfully record Stanislaus's youthful version of events. As Arnold Goldman points out, Stanislaus performed "deletion, alteration, [and] addition" to the original 1903–1904 text.[111] George Healey, editor of the *Dublin Diary,* explains that the text we have was "copied from a draft of some kind" and that the dates assigned to certain passages "refer not to the time of the writing but rather to the time of the incident itself."[112] Ellmann himself once even admitted to George Healey that Stanislaus "touched up in style and perhaps even in detail" events in his diary.[113] Quite possibly, the diary reflects Stanislaus's late assessment of Gogarty's character, formed in the 1940s and 1950s. C. P. Curran, another Dublin contemporary, has suggested that Stanislaus's views were "coloured not only by his own strong prejudices, but more reasonably, by Oliver Gogarty's [unflattering] writings *after* Joyce's death" [emphasis added].[114] Stanislaus's 1941 portrait of Gogarty in *Recollections* is considerably kinder than *Dublin Diary, My Brother's Keeper,* or "Open Letter," suggesting that the diary may have been altered in the late 1940s.[115] At any rate, the diary would seem to be the least reliable source of the tower incident, since it records Stanislaus's retrospective, perhaps even touched-up, version, which was hearsay anyway.

Only three people were witness to the events in the tower. One (Trench) killed himself five years later. Another (Joyce) gave his version in fiction: Stephen Dedalus abandons his home in the Martello Tower the morning after one of his two roommates (Haines, not Mulligan), rants and raves in the middle of the night about a black panther. The only other account that is not hearsay is Gogarty's, and his version, though less sinister than Stanislaus's, is more critical of himself than Joyce's. The roommate, Trench, actually shot his pistol into the grate at the imagined panther. Later that night, when Trench screamed about the panther again, Gogarty "shot down all the tin cans on top of Joyce," who rose and "in silence left the tower forever." Gogarty added: "To this day [in 1947] I am sorry for that thoughtless horseplay on such a hypersensitive and difficult friend."[116] Apparently Gogarty regarded the incident as a practical joke. He seemed to be motivated neither by malice nor jealousy nor fear of public opinion nor frugality, as Ellmann, relying on Stanislaus, implied. And he was sorry. Little corroborating evidence exists to suggest that Gogarty was an insincere friend, and much evidence suggests he remained loyal to Joyce. But Ellmann, citing Stanislaus's retrospective, secondhand evidence, leads us to believe that Gogarty ruthlessly and conspiratorially drove Joyce from the tower. To borrow Mason's phrase, Ellmann wove together Joyce's fiction and Stanislaus's testimony—two unreliable lines of evidence—"into a single, supposedly factual, fabric." Gogarty comes off unfairly as a malicious friend, a traitor to his country, a liar, a panderer to the middle class, a bad poet, a bad surgeon, and a fat false genius.

It may be contended that, since Ellmann's subject was Joyce's inner life and since Joyce thought Gogarty was a betrayer, Ellmann is justified presenting Gogarty so. I have two objections to this contention. First, Ellmann does not qualify his condemnation of Gogarty by admitting that, in reality, he was not a betrayer. And second, we do not really know what Joyce thought of Gogarty. If we do not admit the evidence of *Ulysses,* the burden of proof falls mainly on Stanislaus, whose testimony is unreliable.

Ellmann's James Joyce

More important than Ellmann's portrait of Cosgrave or Gogarty is his portrait of James Joyce. Ellmann's Joyce conceives of art in highly personal terms, and, thus, his artistic intentions are private. Indeed, as I have already noted, Ellmann regarded a writer's fiction as "a lifelong conversation with himself," not as a conversation with readers. Chapter XV of *James Joyce,* "The Backgrounds of 'The Dead,'" illustrates how this critical bias influenced Ellmann's portrait of Joyce. The first half of the chapter details Ellmann's surmises about the origins of Joyce's characters (*JJ,* 243–248). The space Ellmann devoted to his speculations about origins reflect his axiom, asserted in the introduction to *James Joyce,* that the transformation of personal life into art is the proper subject of literary biography. This axiom leads Ellmann to treat Joyce's personal life as if it were a draft of his fiction. Meaning is discovered in the changes made to that draft. For example, Ellmann explains that Michael Furey, Gretta Conroy's melancholy lover in "The Dead," originally was Sonny or Michael Bodkin, a young paramour who apparently died for Nora Barnacle's sake. Ellmann suggests that Joyce changed "Bodkin" to "Furey" to indicate the dormancy of Gretta's passion: "the new name implies . . . that violent passion is in [Gretta's] Galway past, not in her Dublin present" (*JJ*, 248).

Ellmann spends much effort speculating, with varying degrees of evidence, about Joyce's motivations for many such transformations. Nora was the origin of Gretta; Mrs. Callanan and Mrs. Lyons were the original Misses Morkan; Mary Ellen Callanan was the original Mary Jane; Freddy Malins was based on Freddy Lyons; Bartell D'Arcy was based on Barton M'Guckin; Miss Ivors was originally Mary Sheehy Kettle; Gabriel was based on Joyce himself, Constantine Curran, and Joyce's father John. Ellmann's scrutiny of the artistic process is little more than speculation about Joyce's motives for modifying or choosing these real life originals. For example, Barton M'Guckin was chosen instead of John McCormack to be the model for Bartell D'Arcy because Joyce "needed [a tenor] who was unsuccessful and uneasy about himself; and his father's often-told anecdote about M'Guckin's lack of confidence furnished him with just such a singer" (*JJ*, 246). Ellmann only discusses the artistic process in relation to this type of choice. The result of such an attitude is that Joyce's intentions in "The Dead" become largely personal: he wanted to pay tribute to Nora's "artless integrity"; he wanted to begin "the task of making amends" with Ireland; he was "dwelling upon the horrors of middle age"; and he was singing "his first song of exile" (*JJ*, 245, 249, 253). Ellmann reduces Joyce's intentions to a private matter—either the working out of his own feelings for his native country or his expression of his own feelings for his wife. In Ellmann's view, Joyce's intentions did not consider his readers.

Other than this one interest in origins and prototypes, Ellmann displays the traits of Magalaner's detached criticism: he tends to treat texts as self-contained artifacts. Where Ellmann does allow that Joyce's artistic decisions might have had broader concerns, it is only within the boundaries of an autonomous view of literature, and so the second half of the chapter is taken up with detached methods of analysis (249–253). Ellmann puts "The Dead" in the context of the literary tradition—specifically, George Moore's *Vain Fortune* and Thoreau's translation of Homer's *Iliad*—and he explicates the symbolic meanings of the snow. According to these treatments, "The Dead" communicates something about the universal human condition: "the mutuality . . . that all men feel and lose feeling, all interact, all warrant . . . sympathy" (*JJ*, 252).[117] In other words, Ellmann's Joyce intended his work to be explicated in a literary tradition, by symbolic analysis, and as applying universally to humankind. He did not intend his work to be read in the limiting historical context of Dublin *circa* 1907—that is, he did not specifically mean it to be read by the Irish. This view contradicts my argument in Chapter 1, which draws on Joyce's letters to Grant Richards to demonstrate that Joyce conceived of the Irish as his primary readers for *Dubliners*.

It also contradicts Stanislaus. The difference between what Stanislaus thought were Joyce's intentions and what Ellmann thought were Joyce's intentions is illustrated by a letter Ellmann wrote to Stanislaus in 1954. In praise of Stanislaus's "The Background to *Dubliners*," Ellmann wrote, "It is customary to deal with [*Dubliners*] too much in the terms your brother used in his letters to Richards, about corruption and paralysis and the nicely polished looking glass. To see the stories merely as an excoriation of Dublin is to miss most of their point and beauty."[118] Ellmann here has stated succinctly what is at stake in his portrait of Joyce. Did Joyce intend *Dubliners* to be an excoriation of contemporary society or an aesthetic object autonomous from history? Ellmann seems not to have understood that Stanislaus *did* think the point of *Dubliners* was to excoriate Dublin. Or, if Ellmann did understand, he seems to have been trying to nudge Stanislaus out of that view.

I do not mean to imply that Ellmann's way of reading "The Dead" is wrong, nor do I mean to imply that his identifications of the origins of characters are inaccurate. The origins he identifies may or may not be correct; some seem more plausible than others (the amalgamation of Constantine Curran, James Joyce, and John Joyce into Gabriel Conroy seems particularly tenuous). I have already discussed his inaccurate portrayal (though his accurate identification) of two of those origins—Cosgrave and Gogarty. Peter Costello's new biography takes Ellmann to task for misidentifying (though accurately portraying) the original Emma Clery. But their degree of probability concerns me less than the preeminence origins have in Ellmann's attention. Ellmann's treatment of Joyce's artistic process implies that the transformations of these originals into fictional characters are the most significant intentions to gauge. Other artistic decisions, especially those that might be motivated by a desire to affect his readers politically, are either ignored or acknowledged only in passing.

For example, the issue of nationalism in Ireland, according to Ellmann, only "finds small echoes in ['The Dead']" (*JJ*, 245). Ellmann holds that even these small echoes were motivated not by Joyce's politics but by his recoiling from Yeats's suggestion that he, like Synge, "find inspiration in the Irish folk" (*JJ*, 245). Miss Ivors's proposal that Gabriel go to the Aran Islands, in Ellmann's view, echoes Yeats's suggestion to Joyce. This discussion of artistic motivations reduces a matter of political significance—a Dubliner's conversion to nationalism—to a matter of Joyce's personal artistic integrity. For Ellmann, the presence of Miss Ivors says nothing about Irish nationalism itself, and so Ellmann precludes the possibility that Joyce meant for "The Dead" to participate in the lively politics of Ireland. *James Joyce* does not entertain the possibility that fiction might participate the same way theater obviously participated in Irish politics. But to a reader like Stanislaus, Miss Ivors would introduce much more than "small echoes" of Yeats's suggestion; and the artistic process that composed her must have been more involved than a transformation of Mary Sheehy Kettle. In the same year that Joyce wrote "The Dead" he wrote three articles for *Piccolo della Sera* and three lectures for the Università Popolare, and all discussed Irish nationalism. One, his lecture on James Clarence Mangan, discussed the relation between poetry and Mangan's "hysterical nationalism" (*CW*, 186). In 1907 Joyce was fairly obsessed with political events in Dublin. It would be surprising if he did not intend "The Dead" to contribute to the Irish political debates. Likewise, if we admit the possibility that Joyce had political intentions throughout his life, Buck Mulligan indicates more than a personal attack on Gogarty; he comprises Joyce's critique of "hellenising" Ireland.

But Ellmann's portrait of intentions supplanted Stanislaus's. Even the leftist critic William Empson was, to some degree, won over by Ellmann. In his review of *James Joyce*, in which Empson takes Ellmann to task for laughing away Joyce's socialism, he admits that the biography changed his own reading of "The Dead." At first Empson had believed that Gabriel's famous fatuous toast was an "undeserved bit of satire by Joyce on his homeland."[119] After discovering in Ellmann's biography that Joyce's loneliness in Rome compelled him to pay tribute to Ireland's hospitality, Empson modified his interpretation. In Empson's eyes, Ellmann's biography proved "The Dead" was Joyce's personal tribute to rather than his political satire on Ireland. A powerful social criticism was reduced to a matter of the artist's loneliness. For example, Gabriel's toast begins with his belittling of the "new generation . . . growing up in our midst . . . actuated by new ideas and new principles" (*D*, 203). Clearly Gabriel refers to the enthusiasms, like Miss Ivors's, for nationalism, and Gabriel's eventual recognition that he ought to travel west indicates a conversion potentially as compelling to Irish readers as Michael Gillane's conversion in Yeats's nationalist play, *Cathleen ni Houlihan*. But Empson failed to see it. That Ellmann's portrait could so monopolize Empson's attention attests to the power of literary biography.

Canonization and Dissent

After the publication of *James Joyce* in 1959, Joyce's biography was no longer confusing. In the words of Frank Kermode, Ellmann's biography "fixes Joyce's image for a generation." [120] Despite Ellmann's heavy reliance on Stanislaus, which was recognized by a number of reviewers, *James Joyce* was almost universally hailed as the definitive biography of Joyce. Nearly all the reviewers, from Kermode to Robert Martin Adams to Stephen Spender to the jurors of the National Book Award, hailed the biography for its objective voice and wealth of documented fact—two criteria important to Mason but secondary to Ellmann himself. [121]

Why was Ellmann's biography revered for an objectivity that its author did not profess? And why would so many critics overlook its reliance on Stanislaus, whom they distrusted five years earlier, for its documented facts? Because the Joyce that emerges in Ellmann's biography is not the realist writer that emerges in Stanislaus's memoirs. Indeed, despite Mason's complaints about mixing up Joyce's life with his fiction, Ellmann presented an author who intended his work to be autonomous of the limiting context of contemporary Irish history. Certainly Magalaner and Kain were satisfied with his portrait. In 1962, when their *The Man, the Work, the Reputation* was republished as a Collier paperback, those critics asserted that Ellmann (and Stanislaus) had "supplied many of the answers to Joyce's life." [122] The publication of *James Joyce* had eliminated *the* problem for criticism. The Joyce in Ellmann's biography was quite capable of intending Maria to figure as a witch and the Virgin Mary, and he was incapable of seriously practicing politics.

So Ellmann was hailed as "the ultimate authority on Joyce's life," which cemented his version of the author. [123] Ellmann's work was canonized alongside Joyce's, so that today it is nearly impossible to read Joyce's fiction outside the context of Ellmann's biography. Ellmann's "The Backgrounds of 'The Dead'" is published in the Viking Critical Edition of *Dubliners*. Another section of the biography, "The Growth of Imagination," is incorporated into the Viking Critical Edition of *Portrait*. Thomas Jackson Rice identifies nine places in which extracts were reprinted, including *Joyce: A Collection of Critical Essays; James Joyce: The Critical Heritage;* Morris Beja's *Casebook to "Dubliners" and "Portrait"; Joyce's "Portrait": Criticism and Critiques;* William Morris's *Casebook to "Por-*

trait"; and *Twentieth Century Interpretations of "A Portrait of the Artist as a Young Man.*"[124] The *James Joyce Quarterly* directs contributors to cite *James Joyce* parenthetically, the way it directs them to cite *Dubliners, A Portrait of the Artist as a Young Man, Exiles, Ulysses, Finnegans Wake,* the four volumes of Joyce's letters, and his poems. Of the seventeen books (not counting the many volumes of the *James Joyce Archive*) cited in the *James Joyce Quarterly* in this abbreviated form, Ellmann's biographies, the 1959 and 1982 editions of *James Joyce,* are the *only* items not written by Joyce himself. *Joyce Studies Annual* also follows this practice. That may seem like a little thing, but such little things reveal what critics take for granted: that they should refer generously to Ellmann in their discussions of Joyce's fiction. *James Joyce* was even selected for a 1986 Quality Paper Back Book of the Month Club package that included *Dubliners, Portrait,* and Gabler's edition of *Ulysses,* but excluded *Finnegans Wake.*

And Ellmann's presence in the canon extends beyond the two editions of *James Joyce.* His reputation as a biographer won for Ellmann the custodianship of Joyce's own work.[125] Of those fifteen volumes listed by the *James Joyce Quarterly* and written by Joyce, Ellmann governed the preparation of seven, consulted on the preparation of another, and supplied an introduction to a ninth; he had a hand in the editions of *The Critical Writings, Dubliners, Giacomo Joyce, Letters (I, II, III,* and *Selected), Portrait,* and the Gabler *Ulysses. James Joyce* secured for Ellmann not only the highest authority to speak of Joyce's life but the authority to edit his fiction.

Ironically, Stanislaus's *My Brother's Keeper* today enjoys credibility through its association with Ellmann, who edited it and wrote in the introduction that Stanislaus was "incapable of anything but honesty" (*MBK,* xxii). Much of the shift in the critical attitude toward Stanislaus was orchestrated by Ellmann, who, as editor of Stanislaus's memoirs, mitigated Stanislaus's anticlericalism and exaggerated his critical acumen. The reservations voiced by The James Joyce Society in 1952 were largely forgotten. Though they ridiculed Stanislaus in 1956, in 1962 Magalaner and Kain praised *My Brother's Keeper.*[126] So this line of evidence, on which Ellmann relied to confirm his speculations, is accepted largely because of Ellmann's own reputation.

The extent of Ellmann's influence on our understanding of Joyce's fiction would be nearly impossible to gauge. What T. S. Eliot wrote about *My Brother's Keeper* might be applied to the critical community's attitude about Ellmann's work as well: it is "worthy to occupy a permanent place on the bookshelf beside the works of [James Joyce]."[127] No doubt *Dubliners, Portrait, Ulysses,* and *Finnegans Wake* lean on *James Joyce,* which in turn leans on *My Brother's Keeper* and *Dublin Diary,* which lean on the *Letters* and *The Critical Writings,* all of which, we presume, lean on the bookend of Joyce's real life. But is the bookend there?

A few American critics have separately disputed elements of Ellmann's biography.[128] A few early reviewers noted distortions in Ellmann's point of view. William Noon, the Jesuit priest, and William Empson each recognized a bias—Noon because Ellmann reduced the importance of Catholicism in Joyce's life and Empson because he trivialized Joyce's socialism.[129] Both biases were shared by Stanislaus. Byrne, as I mentioned, took issue with the treatment of Cosgrave. More recently, Hugh Kenner questioned Ellmann's use of crosschecks, claiming that, "Ellmann's handling of [testimony] obeys certain imperatives, as that no good story should be rejected."[130] Ellmann told stories like the betrayals by Cosgrave and Gogarty, Kenner would seem to suggest, because they were too good to leave out. Byrne, Noon, and Kenner understood what most reviewers did not and what a generation of Joyce critics have refused to recognize: that Ellmann's biography, even granting its merits, does not sift through the available testimony and discover a plausible truth. It relies on Stanislaus to support its assertions.[131] More recently, Ira Nadel has made this same complaint.[132] (To avoid obscuring controversy myself, I should point out that Phillip Herring puts Kenner's comments in a mitigating context: between Ellmann and Kenner there was "disagreement, even hostility" stemming perhaps from 1975, when Ellmann published in *TLS* a "mean-spirited book review" of *James Joyce's* Ulysses: *Critical Essays,* in which Kenner "perhaps received more than his share of criticism.")[133]

Nevertheless, even those who have dissented from the hagiographic view of Ellmann have been reluctant to challenge the overall image of Joyce in Ellmann's biography. Even Phillip Herring concludes his critical essay with a strong qualification:

> Criticizing Ellmann's biography of Joyce, as some of us have done, can hardly dent its greatness, for we are like a few small mice nibbling around a royal wedding cake. . . . We will probably never be able to replace any major element of the portrait with a competing image.[134]

I disagree. Though "replacing" Ellmann's book may be impossible or inadvisable, competing images of the author can be presented. Nadel has suggested a number of possible images that might compete with Ellmann's, including "a proper contextual life of Joyce . . . that recognizes that he lived during one of the most unsettling periods of European history, from agitation by the Irish Land League to the rise of Hitler." [135] I might add that Joyce's relationship to those he perceived to be his readers has yet to be explored, though it is, perhaps, the most accurate way to gauge Joyce's intentions.

For a generation critics have based their work, either explicitly or implicitly, on the author Ellmann presented. Yet, while criticism has moved past the detached method, our image of Joyce has not changed accordingly. I hope to have demonstrated that, to some degree, Ellmann's presentation is derived from his tendency to view fiction as a manifestation of the artist's psyche, and that, consequently, Ellmann's biography ended up succumbing to many of the inaccuracies Mason feared. It supplied critics with a version of the origins of Joyce's fiction that claims authority but which in certain important places is inaccurate speculation. But more important than the questionable accuracy of these "origins" is how such concerns affect our reading of Joyce's fiction.

Mason, who fought against the biographical fallacy, wanted to paint Joyce as a nonautobiographical writer. He wanted Joyce's work to be interpreted outside the context—personal and historical—of its composition. Stanislaus had other ideas. He even claimed that Stephen Dedalus was the young James Joyce. By grounding Joyce's work in real people, real places—in short, by grounding Joyce's work in Dublin—Stanislaus promoted the political aspects of the fiction, treating it as a diagnosis of the ills of Ireland. Ellmann adopted yet a third position. Like Stanislaus, he was interested in the "origins" of Joyce's fiction, but not to historicize Joyce's work. He wanted to examine Joyce's compositional process, his inner life. Methods of composition may be revealing, but Ellmann's treatment of them reveals mostly Ellmann's own speculations about the writer's "inner self." Ellmann was interested in what *Ulysses* revealed about Joyce, not what Joyce revealed about Dublin. As a consequence, Joyce appears as an autonomous artist, and his fiction has not excoriated Dublin since 1959.

Revisionist Views of Joyce

Linking Joyce's fiction to "liberalism" is relatively new. In the years following Ellmann's biography, Joyce's politics were either ignored or considered adolescent, naive, and inconsequential. But they have enjoyed more attention recently.[136] Not the least of the revisionist views was penned by Ellmann himself in 1977. His *The Consciousness of Joyce* does allow for Joyce's politics, cursorily discussing Joyce's work in the context of Arthur Griffith's Sinn Fein movement:

> Although he [Joyce] refused to endorse the revival of the Irish language, Joyce was in other ways on the side of the separatist movement, and particularly for Griffith's programme. He thought that the time for parliamentary action, of the sort espoused by Parnell, was over, and that an economic boycott would have more hope of succeeding.[137]

He admits, though only in passing, that *Dubliners* was, in some way, a diagnosis of life in Dublin: "it exposed the shortcomings of Irish life under British rule." Ellmann observes that *Ulysses,* too, explored the problems in life under an English king and the Catholic pope. But Ellmann is careful to avoid saying that Joyce's fiction agitated for separation: "*Dubliners* was not a summons to action." This insistence denies the persuasive force of Joyce's fiction. For Ellmann, exposing problems is not linked to doing something about them, so Joyce's work is political only in "the oblique fashion that Joyce used to express himself."[138]

Ellmann elaborates what he meant by "oblique": *Ulysses* "summons into being a society capable of reading and enjoying it [*Ulysses*] because [it is] capable of as frank and open an outlook on life as the book manifests. *Ulysses* creates new Irishmen to live in Arthur Griffith's new state."[139] This claim is quite provocative, and I believe is at the heart of the claim American liberals have made on Joyce. Jeffrey Segall, for example, praises Joyce in nearly the same language:

> Joyce's liberal sensibility and espousal of essentially progressive values won him favor from like-minded critics—critics who defended him the more ardently from the crassness, the extremism, and the intolerance demonstrated by ideologies from the right and left. Joyce, like Wilson, Trilling, and Farrell, moved against the illiberal spirit of his time. He eschewed tragic and heroic themes and celebrated what Irving Howe has called the "public virtues" of liberalism: "doubt, hesitation, and irony."[140]

Ulysses helped train people, so to speak, to live as free and responsible citizens in a democratic country. Ellmann's enthusiasm for the liberties of those new Irishmen living in Arthur Griffith's new Irish Free State is today undercut by the work of Irish scholars like Seamus Deane and Declan Kiberd.

Joyce is prized by Deane precisely because of his rejection of the yokes with which nationalism burdens individual souls. Deane, like Ellmann, emphasizes Joyce's nonpartisanship: "Yeats and Joyce repudiate the more pronounced forms of political nationalism—those associated with Pearse and with the journalism of newspapers like D. P. Moran's *The Leader.*" Those partisan nationalists, Deane points out, were engaged in propaganda, not art, because they summoned people to action. Deane purports to demolish the myth that Joyce "turned away from his early commitment to socialism, and devoted himself instead to a highly apolitical and wonderfully arcane practice of writing." But in Deane's revision, Joyce remains aloof from public politics: "The relationship between literature and politics was not, for Joyce, mediated through a movement, a party, a combination or a sect. For him, the act of writing became an act of rebellion; rebellion was the act of writing." In other words, according to Deane, Joyce's fiction is political not because it participates in the politics of its day, but because Joyce "discovered the fictive nature of politics." Joyce's work, Deane concludes, is "an examination of the nature of the fictive."[141] That type of politics is at least as oblique as the type Ellmann describes, and the revision it proposes is too subtle to change Joyce's reputation very much. It might be taken as typical of the "revisions" of Joyce's politics, which, reiterating Pound's distinction between the ethical and civil, locate the politics of Joyce's fiction in the reading experience of individuals rather than in public debate.

Colin MacCabe, whose *Revolution of the Word* may be said to have excited new political readings of Joyce's fiction, focuses on the individual reader. The revolution he purports to examine takes place in readers who, confronted with Joyce's unconventional texts, are liberated from the oppressive constraints of conventional narrative. "Joyce's texts disrupt the normal position assigned to a reader in a text and thus alter the reader's relation to his or her discourses." *Dubliners,* MacCabe writes, allows the reader "no purchase on the text. . . . These stories function as collections of stereotypes without any discourse that will contain or resolve them. The narrative, in its refusal of a discourse which will explain everything, resists the reduction of the various discourses to one discourse shared by author and reader." *Dubliners,* according to MacCabe, resists the authority of any reader who declares unequivocally, *This is what Joyce meant when he wrote the book.* A multiplicity of discourses must be admitted in any interpretation; *Dubliners* is a rich, symbolic text. Thus, according to MacCabe's theory, *Dubliners* remains aloof from Irish politics, even from Irish society at the time of its publication, because such a context would constitute a single discourse of containment or resolution, which would claim to interpret "a single message inscribed in the code." [142] Liberation, according to MacCabe, takes place only in the individual, who learns to be liberal by reading Joyce's texts. People are liberated in their reading chairs, not in the thoroughfares. Margot Norris argues the same thing about *Finnegans Wake,* which, in her estimation, liberates readers from the patriarchal "law of man" through the experience of reading Joyce's text, which violates the "law of language." [143]

Dominic Manganiello discovers politics in Joyce's supposed refusal to participate: "Joyce's declarations of artistic independence contained unmistakable political overtones. . . . Joyce's refusal to accept political shibboleths constituted a political act." [144] Manganiello defines that political act as the promotion of individualism above any creed, political or religious:

> For Joyce, then, the emancipation made possible through literature transcended those notions of freedom embraced by nationalists and socialists. Literature operated as an instrument for altering men's minds. The transformation of institutions does not depend on force, lobbying for peace, or pleading for social justice, but can only follow upon this unsuspected process of changing basic attitudes and prejudices. [145]

While Manganiello does admit the ideological force of literature ("this unsuspecting process of changing basic attitudes"), he retains the strict demarcation between literature and political discourse. Art "transcends" the lower sort of summons to action made by nationalists and socialists. Again, Joyce's politics are made oblique. Manganiello echoes the liberationist tone of Ellmann and the rest: "Joyce set out to embody and ensoul Ireland in his works by giving birth to the individual, alerting him to those secular and spiritual snares which aborted that growth, and preparing for his release." [146] Ellmann also held that the act of reading Joyce's work is an act of liberation: he claimed that the pun, as exercised in *Finnegans Wake,* is the "agent of democracy and collectivist ideas." [147]

In sum, recent critics have argued for Joyce's politics on the grounds that he transcended politics, claiming that Joyce tried to liberate individual readers from whatever fettered their individual souls. One of the chief defects of this revision is that it fails under historical scrutiny. Ellmann neglects to point to any of the citizens of Griffith's Free State who were newly created by *Ulysses;* MacCabe neglects to point to any person who was liberated by Joyce's revolution of the word; and Manganiello neglects to point to any individual who was mothered, embodied, and ensouled by Joyce's fiction. If we are to examine Joyce's politics and the politics of his writing, we should turn away from this transcendent politics of "liberating" individuals, and turn toward much more conventional and historically verifiable politics. We should look at Joyce's work as public utterances in an already well-defined public discourse. We must ask the historical question, Who reads Joyce? And in what context? In the 1960s the work wrought by Pound, Eliot, Cerf, Wilson, Ernst, and Ellmann finally came to fruition: Joyce entered academe.

5 Our Joyce

If by Industry, we mean a system that cranks out dissertations, articles, and books in great numbers, I suppose we had one. . . . [But] [o]n the whole, the "custodianship" [of Joyce] was a good one since there was a healthy sense of humor and a general openness to ideas, even a nice sense of internal feuding pretty early on.

—DAVID HAYMAN

Late in 1921, Sylvia Beach organized a literary evening in Adrienne Monnier's Paris bookshop to advertise *Ulysses*.[1] Jacques Benoîst-Méchin, who was translating the "Penelope" episode into French to read aloud, asked Joyce for the now famous scheme to the book. According to Benoîst-Méchin, Joyce at first refused, protesting "humorously" (as Richard Ellmann notes), "If I gave it all up immediately, I'd lose my immortality. I've put in so many enigmas and puzzles that it will keep the professors busy for centuries arguing over what I meant, and that's the only way of insuring one's immortality" (*JJ*, 521). We are all familiar with this anecdote. A lot of our articles begin by reciting it; we quote it so often that it seems to betray an anxiety that we have to justify what we do with Joyce's texts. The anecdote sanctions our proceedings because it declares that Joyce intended us to do what we do.

But Benoîst-Méchin probably made up the story. It more accurately reflects the academic situation in 1956, the year Ellmann interviewed the Frenchman, than in 1921, the year Joyce supposedly made the remark. Very little in 1921 would have suggested to Joyce that the academy would end up his primary audience. Not until 1932, when Joyce learned that *Ulysses* had been adopted by New York University (which, he expected, would increase the demand for the book tremendously), was there much evidence that the professors would ever bother to read his work.[2] Very likely Benoîst-Méchin invented or altered Joyce's joke, or, at the very least, we have for years misinterpreted it. Perhaps the "enigmas and puzzles" to which he refers are merely the literary allusions to Homer—the tracing of sources and allusions had been, after all, the work of professors since the late nineteenth century. But if we take "enigmas and puzzles" to mean the symbolic coherence of the novel, including the organs and symbols and narrative techniques and arts assigned by the Linati scheme to each episode, then the comment is certainly an anachronism, because professors did not bother themselves with such riddles in 1921, nor did they bother much with contemporary literature.[3] The academy incorporated modern literature into the canon only after professors changed their method of criticism in the 1940s. Joyce could not have anticipated that change, because it grew out of the politics of the 1930s and 1940s and was the result of the purposeful efforts of a few critics not yet professing literature in 1921. Insightful as he was, Joyce could hardly have known that the professors, especially American professors, would be busy for centuries explicating *Ulysses*.

The story of Joyce's canonization, then, is the story of secondary textual moments, because canonization moved Joyce's texts entirely beyond his purposive control and into the control of the academy. These secondary moments are not necessarily any less valid or less important than the texts' originary textual moments. But they are different. As I discussed in the previous chapter, Ellmann's biography, deriving from the liberal ideology of critics like Edmund Wilson, holds central importance in this process of canonization. In this chapter I will put Joyce's evolving reputation into the context of the academy at large. My specific purpose is to demonstrate how we in the academy have fashioned Joyce's reputation to promote our own authority over his texts. The Joyce we know, Joyce the Genius, the omniscient, omnipotent grand artificer, derives from the evolving structures and practices of English departments between the early 1940s and 1970.

Criticism, Inc.

English departments in the 1940s and 1950s were torn by conflict between "scholars," who practiced the largely historical methods of philology that had been established sixty years earlier, and "critics," who favored an ahistorical, interpretive method that treated literature as a unique type of discourse. The battle was older than any of its participants. As Gerald Graff explains at length in *Professing Literature,* it began in the conflicts surrounding the founding of American graduate studies in the 1870s. Since the establishment of Johns Hopkins University on the German model of scientific, independent, often esoteric inquiry, every generation of academics has staged some sort of debate between specialized research and broader humanist studies. Often the sides were drawn between proponents of the teaching mission of the college and advocates of the research function of the university. Always the debate participated in larger arguments about the common weal: during World War I, for example, the specialists were international in their outlook while the generalists were easily enlisted in the cause of nationalist and anti-German propaganda. Typically, generalists, like Irving Babbitt at Harvard, were driven by a moral agenda, and the highly specialized professionals were driven by what they considered to be disinterested, scientific curiosity.

The first generation of New Critics—John Crowe Ransom, Robert Penn Warren, Allen Tate, René Wellek, Cleanth Brooks, et al.—belonged to the generalist category, for they tried to recuperate for literature its "moral and social function."[4] Today it might seem a great irony that the champions of the autonomous text should have been the highly politicized Agrarians in the 1930s. Jeffrey Segall believes that their "crudely reactionary social perspective" was "at odds with their aesthetic values," and he is right to note that the exacting and scientific method of later New Critics distanced them from politics, even, perhaps, aligning them with the scholars.[5] But Graff more accurately recognizes that the New Critical pseudoscience of aesthetics did not "crudely purg[e] moral and social significance from literature":

> Emphasizing the aesthetic over the directly social was a way of
> counteracting what the New Critics saw as the overtly acquisitive
> and practical tenor of modern urban society.[6]

The close attention to aesthetic form was, paradoxically, part of an ethical program not unlike the New Humanist and Great Books programs a generation earlier. But the New Humanists failed to advance themselves in the universities because they failed to impress the scholars, who held the power in English departments. Wellek attributes the vagueness of "appreciation" criticism in the English (and, therefore, Arnoldian) mode as the cause of its failure. The failures of the Marxist and sociological revolts against antiquarian scholarship also involved an inability to adapt to the standards of the academy.[7]

The New Critics flourished in the academy because they adapted their programs to the expectations of the scholars. More than anything else, the scholars expected English to be hard, which means they expected research. This demand for rigor had been the classicist's original objection to the study of modern philology in the late 1800s. Quoting Francis A. March's 1892 MLA paper, Graff points out that English was able to establish itself as a discipline in the universities only after the professors figured out how to "make English as hard as Greek."[8] As soon as publishing about English literature was as hard as publishing about Greek and Latin literature, English quickly eclipsed classics and became the entrenched defender of academic standards. If the New Critics could similarly demonstrate that they were engaged in a discipline, they would be able to join the ranks of tenured professors. But traditional scholars were hardly impressed with the first New Critics, a few of whom had no advanced degrees (like Allen Tate and R. P. Blackmur) and all of whom seemed amateurish, as evidenced by the fact that they wrote or wrote about modern literature.[9]

It is not surprising that critics had an affinity for modern literature. T. S. Eliot was, as Wellek puts it, "the great initiator" of New Criticism.[10] While Eliot's own criticism hardly looks like what we call New Criticism today, he did toil to distinguish literary discourse from other types of discourse. Many of the early New Critics were creative writers—Delmore Schwartz, Allen Tate, and Robert Penn Warren, for example—who conceived of themselves as inheriting the obsession with style bequeathed not only by Eliot, but by Henry James, Joseph Conrad, Joyce, Virginia Woolf, et al. Graff goes so far as to suggest that critics could not have gotten their feet into the academic door but for the merits of their poetry.[11] So, though they had made it into some universities, their association with modern literature kept their positions tenuous, not only because the moderns were perceived as daring, anti-establishment, and iconoclastic but also because modern literature was not yet amenable to scholarship. Writers were hardly cold, if dead at all; manuscripts were not collected and catalogued; letters had not been retrieved. As Ransom puts it, "Contemporary literature" was "almost obliged to receive critical [as opposed to scholarly] study . . . since it is hardly capable of the usual historical commentary."[12] Modern literature was still living. It had not yet settled into the coffins and crypts that scholars were accustomed to haunt.

By the late 1930s, then, the New Critics were under considerable "pressure to measure up to the institutional criteria set by its scholarly opposition, which was still in control of literature departments."[13] To this end, John Crowe Ransom, the father of New Criticism, published his

"Criticism, Inc." in the *Virginia Quarterly Review* in 1937. Going on the offensive, he boldly declared that traditional scholarship was not the proper business of English departments:

> It is as if, with conscious or unconscious cunning, [professors] had appropriated every avenue of escape from their responsibility which was decent and official; so that it is easy for one of them without public reproach to spend a lifetime in compiling the data of literature and yet rarely or never commit himself to a literary judgment.[14]

The problem with the academy, according to Ransom, was that it pursued scholarship (the compiling of data) as an end in itself, neglecting aesthetics in favor of "historical scholarship," "personal registrations," "synopsis and paraphrase," "linguistic studies," "moral studies," and "any other studies which deal with some abstract or prose content taken out of the work." Yet he recognized that criticism would ascend the academic ladder only if the "professionals" (by whom he meant professors) would begin practicing it. And so he admitted, "Perhaps I use a distasteful figure, but I have the idea that what we [i.e., critics with a foothold in academe] need is Criticism, Inc., or Criticism, Ltd."[15]

Its distastefulness aside, Ransom's comparison of English studies to business was particularly keen: they both are collective enterprises that manufacture products, and they both are subject to what we might call institutional forces. Like businesses, English departments are driven by self-interest:

> [I]n a department of English, as in any other going business, the proprietary interest becomes invested, and in old and reputable departments the vestees have uniformly been gentlemen who have gone through the historical mill. Their laborious Ph.D.'s and historical publications are their patents. Naturally, quite spontaneously, they would tend to perpetuate a system in which the power and glory belonged to them.[16]

For criticism to rival scholarship, critics would have to invent their own patents: it "must become more scientific, or precise and systematic, and this means that it must" stop looking subjective and start looking like it was "developed by the collective and sustained effort of learned persons."[17]

In the late '30s and '40s criticism demonstrated just how systematic it could be. Cleanth Brooks and Robert Penn Warren's *Understanding Po-*

etry, a textbook which detailed their exacting method of reading, came out in 1935. Brooks's *Modern Poetry and the Tradition* came out in 1939. Ransom's book on I. A. Richards, T. S. Eliot, and Ivor Winters that coined the term "New Criticism" came out in 1941.[18] Wellek and Warren's *Theory of Literature* appeared in 1949. These and other theoretical works laid out the diligent and rigorous method of New Criticism. In the meantime, these same critics founded reviews to publish the results of their method: *The Southern Review* in 1935, *The Kenyon Review* in 1939, *The Explicator* in 1942. New Criticism, by the 1950s, was established as a rigorous discipline, and its products had begun to be distributed quite effectively.

In the '40s and '50s New Criticism must have seemed like a refreshing reform of English departments. But after the reformation its own vested interests and patents found themselves in charge. Graff suggests that "criticism was open to the same abuses that the old scholarship had been. It was not immune to becoming an industry in which the routines of production obscured the humanistic ends production presumably served."[19] Drawing on the complaints of a number of original New Critics, Graff describes the tendencies of what he calls "the guild mentality" of critics: attitudes and beliefs about literature that derive from the method—not the theory—of criticism. First, criticism required professors to promote "their" writers, because "the very stockpiling of competing explications came to seem a prima facie proof of a work's complexity and therefore its value," and therefore confirmed the critics' own prestige.[20] Traditional scholarship, the fruit of years of careful research, tended to narrow the range of interpretation. But the critical belief that "literary meanings were in and of themselves aesthetically desirable" meant that the critic's job was to increase the range of interpretations.[21] Thus critics produced more books and articles than scholars ever had. These tendencies derive from the New Critical criterion of value: good literature is structurally coherent, so close reading always increases our sense of order. Incoherent work, works with unreconcilable anomalies, are judged to be bad literature. But once a writer has been canonized, critics take for granted that each of his or her works are perfectly, if mysteriously, ordered, and that assumption leads critics to find order. In other words, if you come to a text believing it is coherent, New Critical methods of scrutiny will always confirm your belief.[22]

Such methods seem to invalidate a consideration of authorial intention. Wimsatt and Beardsley's influential article, "The Intentional Fallacy," published in *The Sewanee Review* in 1946, set down for New Critics the doctrine forbidding the use of evidence outside the text to construe authorial intention. That article exhorted critics not to identify the speaker in lyric poems and the narrator in novels with the author (it also sought to invalidate evaluations of how well or poorly a work measures up to what the author intended to achieve).[23] "The poem itself shows what [the author] was trying to do," they declared, and what authors try to do, they imply, is handle a "complex of meaning . . . all at once." Implicit in their discussion is a fundamental assumption of New Critics: literature differs from referential language (like the language of newspapers) because literature, unfettered by authorial intention, can (and should) mean many things, while referential language, which is successful "if and only if we correctly infer the [author's or speaker's] intention," means one thing. This notion of being tied to an originating author or of being cut away from the author was all-important to the New Critics' assessment of texts. Treating a text as literature meant ignoring the author; treating a text as rhetoric meant including your perception of the author's intention in your interpretation. These categories of language, literary and rhetorical, were held by New Critics, but more often under the terms "poetry" and "propaganda," as I discussed in Chapter 1. According to this view, literature, in the words of Wimsatt and Beardsley's "The Intentional Fallacy," is an orphaned utterance: "it is detached from the author at birth and goes about the world beyond his power to intend about it or control it." [24]

Despite what they claimed, critics did not really treat texts as if they were orphaned. Their method required the belief that authors toil away constructing symbolic works of art open to a multiplicity of interpretations. Indeed, the division of "literary" language from referential language posits a bunch of authors conscious that they are creating "art" as opposed to, say, journalism or history. The best justification New Critics could offer for ignoring authorial intention was that authors intended us to ignore authorial intention. According to New Critics, literature, unlike ordinary language, was meant to be read outside the immediate context of its production.

But, as I discussed in the Introduction, an image of the author is never far from the interpretive process and is usually a projection of the reader's interpretive method. Take, for example, a passage from T. S. Eliot's essay on Ben Jonson which attempts to place Jonson in the pantheon of geniuses. Note particularly how Eliot's argument turns on denying that the playwright referred to contemporary society:

Jonson's drama is only incidentally satire, because it is only incidentally a criticism upon the actual world. It is not satire in the way in which the work of Swift or the work of Moliere may be called satire: that is, it does not find its source in any precise emotional attitude or precise intellectual criticism of the actual world. It is satire perhaps as the work of Rabelais is satire; certainly not more so. The important thing is that if fiction can be divided into creative fiction and critical fiction, Jonson's is creative. That he was a great critic, our first great critic, does not affect this assertion. Every creator is also a critic; Jonson was a conscious critic, but he was also conscious in his creations.[25]

For Eliot's argument to work, he must adjust his readers' perceptions that Jonson was primarily a critic of Stuart England. Eliot sets up those familiar categories of poetry and propaganda, only his terms are "creative" and "critical." He needs to assert that Jonson was "conscious in his creations" to justify treating Jonson's drama as "creative" rather than "critical" fiction. And by treating Jonson's drama as creative, Eliot opens it up to a multiplicity of interpretations, which is a method of reading incompatible with discerning in the drama a "precise intellectual criticism of the actual world." If Jonson's plays had been "precise criticism of the actual world" (like Swift's works), then Jonson would have intended to say a particular thing to a particular group of people, and his plays would not be open to many interpretations. Eliot's version of Jonson implies that he intended his work to drift free of intention. And we might assume, following Foucault, that Eliot's portrait of Jonson is less the fruit of careful biographical study of Jonson's expressed intentions and more the projection of Eliot's own critical principles. Eliot's failure to cite *any* biographical evidence to support his version of Jonson's intentions bears out that assumption. Eliot's intention for *Volpone* replaced Jonson's.

The metaphors used by critics in the 1950s and '60s betray this fiction. Only in a second or third or umpteenth reading do we begin to "uncover" a work's "richness"—only by "digging" below "the surface" can we fully appreciate a work. The assumption of coherence—that lodes of wealth form a network below the surface—leads to the belief that authors always know what they are doing, either through a superhuman consciousness or through a natural artistic genius. Critical practice in the 1950s and 1960s demanded that we regard authors as geniuses, for if we are going to dig up treasures we must first believe treasures have been buried.

Critics and teachers of literature have a lot vested in this belief. General readers and students suspect texts are much simpler and more direct than we do. How many times have we heard the question, "Did the author really mean all that?" And how many times have we heard the story of some author, giving a lecture at a college, delighting students by admitting that he or she did not put in all those symbols? After the lecture in the auditorium, back at the classroom we patiently explain to students that once texts have been launched into the sea of public discourse authors are not allowed to captain them. Amy Tan told a recent and amusing version of this familiar story in *Harper's Magazine.* She read a master's thesis about her novel, *The Joy Luck Club,* that analyzed Tan's use of the number four, which appears in the novel "something on the order of thirty-two or thirty-six times." The analysis, Tan goes on to explain, led the student critic to conclude that four was a "symbol for the four stages of psychological development, which corresponded in uncanny ways to the four stages of some type of Buddhist philosophy I never heard of before." Tan attributes the symbolic plan to the student's, not her own, ingenuity. "In fact," she adds, "now that it's been pointed out to me in rather astonishing ways, I consider my overuse of the number to be a flaw." I admit, Joyce probably would not consider it a flaw, and certainly he possessed some of the "good organizations skills, and a prescient understanding of the story" that Tan says is required "to plant symbols like that." [26] But his prescient understanding cannot account for all we have attributed to it.

This trust in the super abilities of authors was not entirely new, of course. As early as 1915, George Kittredge declared his "rule of judgment that is of some value . . . in interpreting Chaucer's final masterpiece." The rule was as simple as it was incredible: "Chaucer always knew what he was about." [27] By the 1950s, after criticism had fixed its influence on the academy, this convenient fiction, what I call the "fallacy of genius," was fully established.

The "Scholarly Critic" of *Modern Fiction Studies*

Critics never replaced scholars. They established themselves in the academy through a sort of *rapprochement* with traditional scholarship. Writing as early as 1953, René Wellek reported approvingly that "the younger men in the universities are becoming critics and interested in criticism without having lost the advantages of historical learning and training."

He insisted that

> Our graduate schools, if reformed, must face the problem that we
> need not less scholarship, but better, more intelligent, more relevant,
> and more *critical* scholarship.[28]

The future, he predicted, belonged to such critical scholars. He was right.
By the late fifties, the conflicts between criticism and scholarship had
been put aside without being settled. As Gerald Graff describes it, "a
practical resolution was quietly achieved after the war by a new professional generation that had no vested interest in the earlier quarrels and
was eager to merge history and criticism in its own work."[29] Critics
adopted many of the research imperatives established long before by
scholars. In his plenary address before the South Central MLA meeting
in 1989, Thomas Staley described how institutional forces—like library
acquisitions and the post–World War II expansion of universities—contributed to this merging of criticism and scholarship:

> The availability of [twentieth-century] manuscripts and related mate-
> rials coincided with the increasing interest in contemporary literature
> in English departments in the United States. The pressure was on
> librarians to acquire materials from the period where the younger
> professors were teaching and writing. And with the [postwar] expan-
> sion of American universities there was an insatiable demand for
> research materials. And with this demand came keen competition
> among university libraries—expanding university libraries that could
> only build strength in twentieth-century materials [because earlier
> materials had already been collected].[30]

The increased prestige of criticism raised the value of modern literature,
which increased the demand for twentieth-century research materials,
which, coupled with the scarcity of older materials, encouraged libraries
to acquire modern collections, which supplied young critics with the
means of scholarship. The very supply of these materials precipitated
their use by critics, who were trying to look more legitimate to the traditional scholars. If English departments did not begin to look like Ransom's Criticism, Inc., they did resemble the Scholarship & Criticism Co.

Maurice Beebe founded *Modern Fiction Studies* in the spirit of the
postwar professors. In the second issue of the first volume (May 1955),
he paradoxically described *MFS* as a "critical-scholarly journal."[31] His
publication existed somewhere between the critical reviews, like *Kenyon*

and *Sewanee*, and "the staid academic quarterlies," like *Philological Quarterly* and *Studies in Philology*.[32] In the fourth issue of *MFS*'s first year, Beebe wrote,

> Anything which helps us to understand and appreciate a work of literature is, for our purposes, "criticism," let that "anything" come in the form of scholarship, explication, interpretation, a comparative study of sources or parallels, a study guide, a calendar, or a map. Thus we cannot get very excited about debates between New Critics and Old Scholars, Chicagoans and Kenyonites, Conservatives and Liberals, Freudians and Jungians; and we are annoyed by those who write of critical method as if there were only one good way to look at a novel or short story. We think that the more lights there are, the greater the illumination.[33]

This dismissal of the real and substantive differences between criticism and scholarship led to strange bedfellows. But the soft pillows of tenure can mollify old grievances, and the issue of this union was a new type of professional: a critic who does scholarship.

Scholarship distinguished *Modern Fiction Studies* from the reviews like *Sewanee*. What distinguished it from the journals like *Philological Quarterly* was that people read it. The first issue was modest, mimeographed rather than printed, but it sold well. Subscribers numbered more than four hundred by the second issue, and only forty of them, Beebe noted, were libraries. (Libraries were the main subscribers to prestigious scholarly journals, because, while contributors would pull those journals out of the stacks to research a particular article, they did not put their feet up on their desks and read each new issue the way they did read the reviews.) So *MFS* became a forum for discussion, especially with its semiannual newsletter, and it was more genuinely co-operative than traditional scholarship ever was. In fact, the "patterned isolation" of traditional, specialized research had fostered what Graff terms a "positive need [among scholars] to fail to communicate."[34] But criticism necessitated collaboration, for if critics were charged with uncovering the hidden structures of a work, each excavation aided the next. Perhaps the best example of this process is Clive Hart and Fritz Senn's *Wake Newslitter*, which provided an informal, often decidedly unscholarly forum for readers to exchange explications of *Finnegans Wake*. Each critical article excavated a little more; thus, knowing the criticism surrounding a text became more important than knowing the history surrounding it, and bibliographies like those published by *MFS*, which organized the burgeoning volume of critical publications, were great tools for anyone who wanted to join the conversation.

Modern Fiction Studies's initial of run of 500 disappeared in two weeks, and subsequent copies were distributed until the stencils faded beyond use. By the second year the journal was printed in typical academic format, and by the fifth year circulation had risen to 1,800. By the standards of academic publishing, these figures indicate great success, and that success reflects the importance of the new scholarly critic and of modern literature. By 1961 the readers of *Modern Fiction Studies* were so firmly entrenched in English departments that Beebe reported a backlash against them. Quoting Clarence Gohdes, Beebe addressed three reasons for the backlash. Two were arguments resuscitated from the battlegrounds of the 1930s and 1940s—that the "quality of training" of critics was deficient and that modern literature was "not conducive to disciplined study." With a thorough body of critical theory already published and with libraries in the midst of acquiring modern material, Beebe was able to dismiss both of those arguments. Beebe discredited the third reason as "so ignoble that it might better be ignored than attacked": it was, in Gohdes's words, jealousy among older professors of "the fabulous increase in the number of graduate students writing theses on recent authors."[35]

"Fabulous" must be qualified as a subjective impression. Certainly the number of Ph.D. candidates writing dissertations on modern authors increased through the 1950s, but that increase hardly encroached on established territories. If we define modern literature pretty broadly, in 1952 7 or 8 of the 98 dissertations in literature listed by *Dissertation Abstracts* were on modern writers.[36] Yeats, James, and Shaw each had a couple. In 1953 a dozen of 145 dissertations were on modern literature, while in 1954 fewer than 20 of approximately 270 dissertations were on the modernists. Though the number of graduate students exploded in this decade and the next, advances in the modern period, despite the impressions of contemporaries, were quite modest. By the early 1960s dissertations on modernists were roughly equivalent to the number of dissertations on Shakespeare. What looked like a "fabulous" number of students to Gohdes and Beebe really amounted to little more than the establishment of an accepted subdivision within departments. Modern literature became a period to be covered like any other and was not disproportionately populated by graduate students, or at least it was not disproportionately populated by graduating Ph.D.'s.[37] Criticism had accommodated the academy, and the academy reciprocated.

Acquiescing to the prejudices of criticism, scholarship surrendered its emphasis on historical context. The biographical, intentional, and affective fallacies ostensibly invalidated most historical scholarship, so, if professors wanted to research anything besides the recent critical readings of a work, they had to accommodate their findings to criticism. They examined manuscripts, biographical data, or history, not to reconstruct the genuine intentions of authors and the historical context of a work but to promote the image of genius that criticism used to justify its productions.

The first issue of *Modern Fiction Studies* entirely devoted to Joyce, published in the spring of 1958, demonstrates such scholarly criticism at work. At least four of the six articles are mainly critical explications, with little bits of outside research thrown in. One, a genetic study of *Ulysses* by A. Walton Litz, depends on research. But all of the articles require and most of them promote the image of Joyce the Genius. In one article that consciously invokes both "the 'old' method of critical comparison (the relationship to things 'outside' the book)" and "the 'new' criticism of internal evidence," Robert Bierman writes, "Whether or not Joyce intended ["Oxen of the Sun" to prefigure *Finnegans Wake*], he *should* have; to paraphrase Stephen Dedalus: 'A man of genius does nothing unconsciously. His accidents are volitional and are portals of discovery.'"[38] Bierman sanctions the implausibility of his explication by projecting onto Joyce an intention he could never have had, which is sustained by the connivance of "genius." Bierman's method was not unusual, though Bierman was exceptionally frank in declaring that he made up Joyce's intention.

Litz's discussion of the note sheets for "Penelope" is more scholarly and more impressive. He uses the note sheets to reconstruct Joyce's method of composition, because, he claims, "a number [of the notes] have an important bearing on the construction and meaning" of *Ulysses*:

> Joyce labored to a pattern already laid out and fixed in his mind.
> Each fragment of material he gathered was marked for a specific
> place in the novel's general design. The entire novel, with all its com-
> plex internal allusions, seems to have been constantly present for him
> as an "image."[39]

I do not bring this up to say that Litz's analysis of the note sheets is wrong, just that his decision to focus on them derives from the need to present Joyce as a coherent writer. The historical scholar would find the whole discussion trivial, if not irrelevant, and certainly not worthy of the twenty pages Litz devotes to it. Choosing to focus on them and choosing not to focus on other types of scholarship reinforce our notion that Joyce was the consummate modern author, piecing together with superhuman patience and industry a vast mosaic, intending above all else to make his book structurally coherent and self-referential. Litz is quite certain that his picture invalidates the view that Joyce was a realist: "Joyce's exactitude in the use of concrete details and his dependence upon actual data" was intended "not so much for verisimilitude as for the satisfaction of his own scrupulous sense of artistic integrity."[40] Litz uses his research to demonstrate that Joyce, even when he was most realistic, did not intend to refer to any specific place, time, or society.

As Litz points out, this "mosaic worker" version of Joyce can be traced all the way back to Valery Larbaud's "The *Ulysses* of James Joyce," which was written before Joyce had even published the novel. The "mosaic worker" image entered American criticism through the more popular venue of Frank Budgen's *James Joyce and the Making of "Ulysses,"* which Litz quoted liberally. Budgen's is an interesting case. He published his book in 1934, the year Random House brought out its *Ulysses* in America. Eventually it passed out of print, only to be resuscitated by academe—Hugh Kenner and the Indiana University Press—in 1960. Not surprisingly, Kenner's introduction touts the high authority of Budgen's story:

> Thousands of readers every year make the acquaintance of the Bloomsday chronicle, a book no one, least of all the author, expected us to absorb casually. A mentor is adviseable: not an unreasonable prerequisite for one of the key books of the space-time age.[41]

Kenner implies that Joyce meant us to read *Ulysses* with Budgen at our elbow, and he sanctions Budgen's version of the author, which, of course, serves academe. Every article in that 1958 special issue of *Modern Fiction Studies* either invokes or implicitly refers to Budgen's image of Joyce, whether the subject is *Finnegans Wake, Ulysses, Exiles,* or *Dubliners.*

Budgen's Joyce and similar portraits from the 1930s, like the Joyce in Gilbert's *James Joyce's "Ulysses,"* exaggerate Joyce's artistry to counter accusations of *Ulysses*'s formlessness and immorality. Patrick McCarthy, for example, argues convincingly that Gilbert stresses "the conservative, orderly qualities of the book—its completeness, accuracy, and static beauty" to counter the charges of chaos leveled by hostile reviewers like Richard Aldington. "Indeed," McCarthy continues, "much of [Gilbert's] analysis is an attempt to demonstrate that the apparently disparate elements of which *Ulysses* is composed actually form a coherent whole."[42]

Critics have repeated such images of the omniscient artist again and again to justify intentions that are patently false (as in Bierman's case) or merely improbable (as in Litz's).

Transition: New York's Joyce

Despite journals like *MFS* the academy did not control Joyce's image until the 1960s. In the 1940s, Frances Steloff's Gotham Book Mart was the unofficial center of Joyce activity in America. According to her biographer, W. G. Rogers, Steloff "did more than anyone else in the this country to get [Joyce's] writing into circulation" in America.[43] Her catalogue was called "We Moderns," and Joyce sales were second only to sales of D. H. Lawrence's work. While "the demand for Lawrence always existed," Steloff maintained that she "had to build up the Joyce interest," to which end, for example, she threw a party to celebrate Viking's publication of *Finnegans Wake*.[44] She pushed the literary magazines that published Joyce, actually becoming the American agent for *transition,* until the Gotham Book Mart built a reputation as an avant-garde bookstore, a place, like Shakespeare and Company in Paris, where "the author and his public . . . became acquainted."[45]

Though Joyce never met his readers there, the Gotham Book Mart became an informal clearinghouse for inquiries about him. William York Tindall, a professor at Columbia, sent his students to Gotham to buy their Joyce books, and, naturally enough, they and other curious readers bombarded Steloff with questions. Not able to supply the answers, Steloff asked first Tindall, then John Slocum, and then others to lead an informal reading group. With the help of her friend Maurice Speiser, a lawyer, the New York James Joyce Society was organized in the back room of the Book Mart on 3 February 1947. John Slocum was selected president, and he served "until he entered the diplomatic service and went to live in Washington" in 1949. Padraic Colum, Joyce's Dublin friend and a professor at Columbia University, took Slocum's place and served as president for over twenty years. The society gathered at least four times a year, often sponsoring lectures and presentations from writers, like Thornton Wilder; academics, like Tindall and Joseph Campbell; and Joyce's family and friends, like his sister May, daughter-in-law Helen, and Maria Jolas and Sylvia Beach.[46] It also occasionally published materials concerning Joyce, like the *James Joyce Miscellany,* Leon Edel's *James Joyce: The Last January,* and Ellsworth Mason's translation of Stanislaus Joyce's memoir.

To some extent, the society can be viewed as a mingling of Joyce's academic and nonacademic audiences in America, since its members came as much from outside the walls of academe as from within. It brought together independent publishers, like Ben Huebsch of Viking, intellectuals, writers, and Joyce acquaintances. In the late '40s and the early '50s, the society provided a place—literally and metaphorically—for these various groups to share authority over Joyce's texts. Joyce's family and friends contributed their own pictures of the author, Viking launched and promoted their Joyce books, while "distinguished scholars addressed the Society" in formal lectures.[47] The society in its early years seems to have been a remarkably congenial mixture of these different readers.

But by the late '50s the academics began to dominate. Those years saw a transfer of power from what Bruce Arnold calls the *belles-lettres* crowd of writers (mostly Irish writers) to the academy.[48] The academy took an important step toward dominion on Joyce's birthday in 1957, when the first issue of the *James Joyce Review* was published. Theoretically, the *Review* was meant to serve the various readers represented by the New York Joyce Society. Its masthead named Morris Ernst as "legal advisor," its advisory board included William Carlos Williams, Stuart Gilbert, Maria Jolas, Helen Joyce, and William York Tindall, so it reflected the heterogeneity of the society itself. In his foreword the managing editor, Edmund Epstein, acknowledged that the review would mix the professionals with the nonprofessionals:

> Serious and responsible criticism of the works of James Joyce, coupled with remembrances of his personality and his *milieu*, helps to enlarge the Free Reader's sensibilities to this latest partnership of high and low.[49]

Epstein did not name who the "Free Reader" was, but his statement indicates that, at least as late as 1957, academics felt they were partners with some general readers, even if they themselves were the senior partners.

The *Review,* Epstein held, was "evidence of the adaptability of the structure of scholarship and criticism of our time."[50] This sentiment is nearly identical to that expressed by Maurice Beebe a year earlier in *Modern Fiction Studies.* Like Beebe's journal, the second issue of the *Review* included a 250-item bibliography, collected by William White and meant to supplement his 1949 bibliography published in the scholarly *Publications of the Bibliographic Society of America.* In his review of Patricia Hutchinson's *James Joyce's World,* Marvin Magalaner complained that that book would not be of much value to "the specialist" and that the "serious reader" would be discouraged by "adoration of things which were once physically close to the Master." Epstein reviewed William M. Schutte's *Joyce and Shakespeare,* which, along with William Noon's *Joyce and Aquinas,* was published as a part of the Yale Studies series. Epstein praised Schutte's book as "an example of the best sort of scholarly writing in the field of modern literature."[51] The general tone of the *Review* seems to favor the professionals over everyone else. Joyce was well on the way toward canonization, and the *Review* approved and aided his progress. The first book-length study of Joyce was Harry Levin's 1941 *James Joyce: A Critical Introduction,* published by a non-academic press, New Directions. But by the late '50s, university presses were flooding the market, and the type of celebratory promotion of an author required by criticism had begun to turn Joyce into a mysterious, holy figure. (I should point out that even as Magalaner advanced the authority of the "serious reader" and "the specialist," he criticized the hagiographic tendencies these readers produced. Indeed, nearly every problem with criticism that I point out was first recognized and voiced by those early critics themselves. Reading the early Joyce critics leaves the impression that they sometimes felt they were riding a tide, which, despite doing some damage, was on the whole beneficial and unstoppable.) In the fourth issue of the *Review,* published in December 1957, William Noon, Richard Kain, and Maurice Beebe himself contributed to White's bibliography. By the next issue, Alan Cohn began his many contributions to Joyce bibliography. Erwin Steinberg joined the list of academic contributors. So rather than an equal partnership with the previous custodians of Joyce—people like Ernst and Jolas—the *James Joyce Review* was an early step in the transfer of authority to the universities. But the *Review* faltered. Though the first issue was printed handsomely and ran to an impressive forty-eight pages, the *Review* came out infrequently, and Epstein was obliged to suspend publication indefinitely within a few years.

The *James Joyce Quarterly*

When Thomas Staley, a young assistant professor at the University of Tulsa, decided to publish a James Joyce newsletter in late 1962, he was conscious that, to some degree, he would be inheriting the niche once occupied by the old *James Joyce Review.*[52] Practicing the fine diplomacy that would later serve him so well, Staley wrote to Edmund Epstein in January 1963, asking him to join the new project. On 4 February Epstein gave his blessing and accepted the role of advisor. Staley wrote his old professor from the University of Pittsburgh, Herbert Howarth, about his plans and invited him to act as advisory editor. Howarth wrote back on 9 February enthusiastically supporting the proposal, but he suggested that Staley broaden the scope so as to "avert any feeling on the part of the *JJReview* editors that their field has been overrun." [53] Fred Higginson suggested that Staley follow the *JJR*'s "proper blend of scholarly, bibliographical, personal, review, and polemic." [54]

Staley's initial plans for the *Quarterly* had been modest. In an undated form letter—probably circulated in January 1963—he made the first announcement of his intentions. The text of the circular, printed under the title *"A JAMES JOYCE QUARTERLY,"* seems, in retrospect, to have been amazingly unambitious:

> Professor Thomas F. Staley, of the University of Tulsa, is planning the publication of a general Joyce Newsletter, to appear quarterly. The main aim of the Quarterly would be to publish short notes and to keep readers in touch with the general progress of scholarship in the Joycean field.
>
> Professor Staley would appreciate comments and suggestions from interested persons.

The address that concludes the note was Staley's home in Tulsa, which indicates the almost naive simplicity with which he undertook the project. Originally he conceived it as a hobby, which he pursued for the enjoyment of the work and of the people he met, and the first issues, published out of Staley's garage, were (despite their high quality) the product of a cottage industry.[55]

No one familiar with the dissolution of the *James Joyce Review* could have predicted the enthusiasm and support that greeted Staley's circular. All through the spring and summer of 1963 he received suggestions and subscription orders. Early in 1963 he lined up an old friend from graduate school, Frew Waidner, as associate editor. Clive Hart, editor of the *Wake Newslitter,* wrote from Australia in January to say that he was "very interested indeed" in the *Quarterly,* that "there's certainly a need for one," that it would not conflict with the aims of the *Newslitter,* and that he was "very keen to help." [56] Three weeks later Hart wrote that he was "increasingly enthusiastic about the projected quarterly" and that he accepted Staley's offer to be an advisory editor. He also offered practical advice about how to publish a journal.[57] In February, David Hayman responded "to hazard a few tentative suggestions and indicate [his] willingness to help out in case of need." He hoped the *Quarterly* would serve as an informal forum, publishing "anything and everything of interest to Joyce people"—bibliographies, booksellers' lists, footnotes, information on manuscripts, even "random attacks on people publishing JJ criticism."[58] Staley wrote back, "I think you have hit the proper tone we should assume," and he asked Hayman to join the editorial board, which Hayman did.[59] Also in February Herbert Howarth signed on as advisory editor.[60] By late spring of 1963 five advisory editors had been lined up: Hart, Hayman, Howarth, Epstein, and Bernard Fleischman. Richard Kain would join shortly, and on 25 July Joseph Prescott became the seventh.[61]

In his first letter to his new editorial board (every member of which was an academic), which probably was written in April 1963, Staley imagined that each issue would include "an article length work . . . of about 1000 words (should have said very short article). This along with many short notes and bibliography items."[62] In his second memo, the *Quarterly* was still expected to be quite short; Staley happily reported to the editors that "a six page issue will be possible," because "the Dean here [at the University of Tulsa] said that he would bail me out if things got tough."[63] But by late spring it was clear that the market demanded something much more weighty. Because of the advance subscriptions and submissions, Staley was able to print a handsome circular, which promised that "Volume 1, No. 1" of the *James Joyce Quarterly* would arrive in October 1963. The flier announced that

> The *JJQ* will present critical, biographical, bibliographical material.
> All areas of James Joyce studies and his milieu will be covered. Special features of the *JJQ* will include notes, comments, letters, manuscript details, library holdings, collector's items, reviews.[64]

This flier, along with announcements in some academic journals, advertised the *Quarterly* through the summer. Hart suggested that they mail 60 copies of the circular to Fritz Senn for circulation in Europe, and he offered to send out 450 copies with the July *Newslitter*.[65] Fritz Senn, who had already been contacted by Staley, wrote on 9 June that he was "most eager to help." He offered to take "over the European distribution" and promote the new journal among Joyceans overseas.[66] Within a month Staley and Senn were working out the details of European subscriptions. Staley announced to his editors that Harvard University was the first library and Joseph Prescott was the first individual to subscribe to the journal. By 27 July the subscribers numbered 58. With an order for 100 from the Gotham Book Mart and "several other scattered orders" the total distribution came to 165.[67] Soon that number would increase, and it became clear from the deluge of hopeful contributors that the *Quarterly* would be far healthier than the *James Joyce Review*.

Harry Levin declined an invitation to contribute, stating that "when I completed the revision of my little book [*James Joyce: A Critical Introduction*] three years ago, I swore an oath that I would never hold forth in public on Joyce again," but he offered his best wishes for success and assured Staley that he would read the journal with interest.[68] Other than Levin, Richard Ellmann proved to be Staley's only major disappointment. On 6 March 1964, with two issues under his belt, Staley wrote Ellmann thanking him for his subscription and asking for a contribution to the first Bloomsday issue. Ellmann offered a review of a book by Oliver Gogarty, but, in the end, he published it elsewhere first.[69] Nearly everyone else who had anything to do with Joyce studies offered advice and moral and material support. Fred Higginson told Staley "it's a fine thing you're doing, and you have all my support." He offered to do reviews.[70] Warren Frend at Kansas State (where Alan Cohn was soon to move), editor of *Twentieth Century Literature*, offered the services of his bibliographic staff.[71] Philip Lyman at the Gotham Book Mart declined to send his mailing list, but offered to circulate Staley's formal announcement of the *JJQ* in his "next mailing to members."[72] He also offered to take subscriptions for the *JJQ*. Staley worked out a deal to exchange ads with *Criticism*.[73] After an announcement of the first issue in the *PMLA*, presses began seeking reviews of their books. As early as 15 July 1963, months before the first issue, the University of Minnesota Press wrote asking if Staley's publication would take on any of its Joyce books.[74]

J. S. Atherton, who was told of the *Quarterly* by Hart, wrote Staley, "If I can help in any way I will gladly do so." Offering advice from an English scholar's perspective, he suggested that Staley adopt a professional air:

> I think it was a mistake to give the Hart-Senn publication [the *Wake Newslitter*] so seemingly frivolous a title. Many British academicals still have doubts as to the real value of Joycean studies, and it is very doubtful if they would accept as useful contributions to learning papers which appeared in a periodical called "Newslitter."[75]

More to the point, he complained that "there have been too many unsupported statements about Joyce's work; failure to weigh articles with regard to the supporting evidence behind them has involved the 'Newslitter' in several acrimonious debates which bring discredit to Joycean studies in general." Atherton's comments reflect not a debate but certainly a discussion about the direction that the new periodical should take. Would it be a respectable academic journal, submitting to the scholarly requirements by which such respect was won and providing academics with a credible venue for advancing their careers? Or would it ignore the rigorous demands of literary studies to secure a less specialized audience?

In May Bernard Fleischman advised Staley to form a bibliographic committee,[76] but Hart suggested they sign on Alan Cohn to continue the bibliography of criticism that he had begun in the *James Joyce Review.*[77] Staley contacted Cohn, who, reassured by Epstein's presence on the board of advisory editors, jumped at the chance to publish more Joyce bibliography. In fact, he already had plenty of material on hand, as he told Staley on 27 June 1963:

> Bibliographic compilation, I have discovered, is like the weed—you don't kick the habit easily. Consequently I've kept up my note-taking since the last JJR listing in 1959 until now I have 2 great shoeboxes full of 3 X 5's, running, I would conservatively estimate, to some 1200 entries for the period 1950 to date. . . . I figure it would then take at least 2 whole issues of JJQ to empty my shoeboxes.

Cohn underestimated the success of the *Quarterly,* which eventually would dwarf the infrequent *Review*—Staley was able to accommodate Cohn's addiction, publishing his bibliographies as fast as he could prepare them, over 120 pages through the first seven numbers.

In September Vivien Mercier, the Irish scholar at City College in New York, wrote that he was "very pleased to hear of the establishment" of the *Quarterly,* but he expressed some concern at the absence of Irish scholars among the editors. "The situation" of publishing a Joyce quarterly in Tulsa, he wrote, "is rather as if I were to set up an *Oil Quarterly* in Dublin":

> Having said this much, I can hardly offer myself as an advisory editor without further immodesty, but why not invite John Kelleher of Harvard, David H. Greene of NYU, or Denis Johnston of Smith or Tom Flanagan of Berkeley to serve?[78]

Staley had already contacted Kelleher, who sent his "best wishes" for success but only ambivalent promises of contributions.[79] Mercier's modesty notwithstanding, Staley prevailed upon him to join the board as the eighth advisory editor well before the first issue went to press. So by late summer in 1963, well before the first issue was published, Staley had tapped into a market eager to coalesce, and it was a market of scholars. Publishing the *Quarterly* from Tulsa might have discredited it in some eyes, but removing Joyce from New York transferred authority from the *belles-lettres* community to academe.

The first issue of the *James Joyce Quarterly,* which came out in the fall of 1963, ran to forty pages and hardly resembled the informal pamphlet Staley had imagined just ten months earlier. It did retain the idea of a forum: Staley announced in his first "Notes and Comments" that he intended to "draw Joyceans together and publish provocative essays dealing with Joyce's life, work, and milieu."[80] But, as Atherton had hoped, the degree of professionalism would be high, because Staley also promised "serious and responsible scholarship." On the main, its contributors and primary readers were always academics. The voluminous correspondences in the *Quarterly* archives from these years demonstrate that "serious and responsible scholarship" was indeed the criterion for deciding the fate of submissions. To borrow a phrase that Adeline Glasheen applied to Clive Hart's *A Concordance to "Finnegans Wake"* in the first issue, the *JJQ* belonged "on the reference shelf of the college library and at the elbow of the working Joyce scholar."[81] The first issue under their belts, the editors met at the 1963 MLA convention in New York to confirm their policies. Primarily (and quite successfully), the *JJQ* was a forum for the "working Joyce scholar." By combining letters, comments, and reviews with bibliographies, manuscript details, and library holdings, it promised to be a journal in the scholarly-critical tradition of *Modern Fiction Studies.*

The similarity of these two journals was no coincidence. Staley was aware that he was trespassing on Beebe's territory and from the first sought to establish connections with him, inviting him to submit his own work to *JJQ.* As Beebe insisted and soon proved, the supply of Joyce articles was so large that the two journals would benefit each other rather than compete for contributors. Beebe promised to "do what I can to promote and support the journal," and he was able to do a great deal.[82] He announced in his "Modern Fiction Newsletter," "Welcome news is the founding of *The James Joyce Quarterly*" and told contributors and subscribers to contact Staley.[83] After the first issue, he wrote that he "was much impressed" with *JJQ,* so impressed, in fact, that he told Staley,

> During the past few months I have suggested the *Quarterly* as a possible outlet for perhaps as many as twelve of the Joyce mss submitted

to MFS. . . . Some of the more highly specialized pieces I have not read carefully, and others may be genuine duds. But obviously there is no shortage of material on Joyce.[84]

Beebe went so far as to offer Staley two essays he had already accepted for publication, provided the authors agreed to switch to *JJQ*, which would speed up their publication dates.[85] Staley wrote back immediately, asking for one of the articles for his *Dubliners* issue, stating, "I am sure if you accepted it, it is worthy of publication in the JJQ."[86] In April of 1964 Beebe accepted an article on Fitzgerald that Staley had submitted to *MFS*, and by 1965 Beebe was reviewing books for the *JJQ*. In the summer of 1964, Beebe wrote to Staley asking to supplement his *MFS* subscription to *JJQ* with a personal subscription because, he predicted, *JJQ* "is bound to become a collector's item."[87] The similarities between the journals was so striking that in 1968, when Maurice Beebe was leaving Purdue, Russell Cosper, head of the department of English, wrote to Staley to see if he was interested in taking over *MFS*.[88]

Clearly both editors imagined they were fellows laboring with the same goals. The *James Joyce Quarterly* was, in a sense, a specialized version of Beebe's journal. As David Hayman has noted, in an age when only a few universities deemed it "appropriate to teach a seminar on Joyce . . . [t]he Quarterly helped establish a base upon which to build a body of critical opinion and research."[89] It inherited the *rapprochement* between scholars and critics, and so it inherited the vested interests of the scholarly critic, which included presenting Joyce as the mosaic-worker. The first *Dubliners* issue, for example, published in the second volume of *JJQ*, included an article by Fritz Senn that argued that Joyce's style in *Dubliners* is nearly as allusive as it is in *Ulysses* and *Finnegans Wake*; another by Florence Walzl that uncovered the symbolism in "Two Gallants"; and a third by Sidney Feshbach that held that the old man in "An Encounter" is an allegory of Death. Like *Modern Fiction Studies*, the *James Joyce Quarterly* presented the New Critical version of Joyce.

It also shared *MFS*'s success. Seven hundred copies of the first issue were sold, cleaning out Staley's supply. He sold 850 copies of the second issue. In the *Quarterly*'s third year Staley reported that by August 1965 fifty-one articles had been submitted for publication.[90] Between September 1965 and August 1966 he received eighty-six manuscripts. By early 1966 subscriptions had risen to nearly six hundred.[91] The academic community never failed to support the journal.

Even so, Staley never wanted the *Quarterly* to be entirely academic.[92]

He was at pains to cement relations with the amateur Joyceans in New York, and the early volumes do reflect his attempts. He cultivated relations with Padraic Colum, president of the New York Joyce Society, who invited Staley to speak at official meetings in the Gotham Book Mart on a number of occasions, and he consistently reported on the New York James Joyce Society in *JJQ*. Some of the first subscribers to the journal were nonacademics: lawyers, psychologists, and other amateur Joyceans, like the Beatle John Lennon.[93] Staley's plans for the first Bloomsday issue included not only five or six "provocative essays on *Ulysses*" but also "an article or two which affords the 'general' reader an appreciative view of *Ulysses*."[94] His "Notes and Comments" throughout the early years of the journal demonstrate his sincere desire to serve those general readers (notice that as early as 1964 Staley was obliged to put that term in quotation marks). Nevertheless, six months after the first issue appeared and after he had sold out his own copies, Staley reported that the Gotham Book Mart still had some copies left, which might indicate a certain lack of interest among non-academics. Members of the society, perhaps, felt the journal was not directed primarily at them.

Academic Joyceans, a self-reflexive lot, have never been blind to this condition and have always been wary of its effects. Joyce critics have always seemed uncomfortable with some of the consequences of their authority. Reporting on the first James Joyce Symposium, held in Dublin in 1967, W. L. Webb observed that Joyceans, confronting hundreds of articles and books, "tend to stand back rather appalled at what they and their fellows have wrought." Richard Kain asked publicly, "Can 'Ulysses' (and the other works) survive this heavy freight, and if so, what does it contribute to our understanding?"[95] Bernard Benstock recalled that the first symposium included "a panel discussion on the state of Joyce scholarship at the time," adding that "we were BIG on that topic at the time."[96] In 1966 Benstock published a review of Joyce criticism with the ironic title, "The James Joyce Industry." And in his 1976 bibliography of Joyce, Thomas Staley wrote, "Because of the sheer mass of material, Joyce scholarship has acquired the epithet, whether pejorative or simply amazed, the 'Joyce Industry.'"[97]

The Joyce Industry

As I discussed above, as early as 1941 John Crowe Ransom compared the work of critics to business. Magalaner and Kain were the first critics to apply the analogy to Joyce criticism. In their 1956 edition of *Joyce: The Man, the Work, the Reputation*, they wrote, "If symbolism be a leg pull, then the entire Joyce industry is threatened," which, as we might expect from these early promoters of Joyce criticism, is hardly negative.[98] Hugh Kenner and Vivien Mercier, both critics themselves, began to use the term ironically, perhaps even censoriously, in the late '50s and early '60s.[99] In the hands of Anthony Burgess in 1964, the term was entirely pejorative. In a review of recent Joyce criticism, Burgess wrote:

> The four books I have in front of me are all American and all recent. They confirm my belief that American English departments have two main activities that amount to industries: one is the plucking of the Joyce-bird, now down to the more microscopic feathers; the other is the amassing of European literary holographs, drafts, toilet-paper jottings against the coming of Cisatlantic Doomsday. These pre-occupations are, of course, cognate: they both need time and money, of which (and American business has told us they are the same thing) American universities must possess a great deal.[100]

Burgess's complaints are worth a close look because they represent one protest against the academy's assumption of authority over Joyce and his work. While Burgess's book reviews were typically combative, here his tone reflects a genuine struggle. Burgess felt he was fighting to keep Joyce from being "crowned by the scholars and shut up in the throne-room . . . without being given a chance to rule in the hearts of ordinary decent people who love books." [101] Burgess's offer to speak for ordinary people might be refused by many decent book lovers, but his chief insight is valid: the canonization of Joyce narrowed the scope of his work.

Some readers complained vaguely that academic readings denied the spirit of Joyce's work. Often nonacademic readers regarded American scholars as laboratory scientists reading texts with such specialized equipment that they murdered to dissect, so to speak, and so missed the jokes. Bruce Arnold recounts the complaints of Irish writers—including Sean O'Faolain, Niall Montgomery, and Patrick Kavanagh—that "Joyce was being engulfed by the academics." But if Joyce was drowning, they were not equal to the task of rescuing him:

> [I]t was good hearted badinage for the most part, and totally insufficient to combat the wealth, seriousness and sense of purpose of the academic system which was turning itself into an industry.[102]

Denis Johnston, writing in *Envoy*, a Dublin magazine, "painted a light-hearted picture of obsessive American college students of Joyce, unable to read him for amusement because of the burden of having to write about him to qualify academically." [103] Arthur Power, one of Joyce's Dublin friends, claimed that Joyce himself once complained, "*Ulysses* is fundamentally a humorous work, and when all this present critical confusion about it has died down, people will see it for what it is." [104] I am as skeptical of the provenance of this quotation as I am of Benoîst-Méchin's. But it suggests at least that Arthur Power in 1974 was concerned about how the academy had marred Joyce's work. Burgess also noted the academy's tendency to mute Joyce's humor: "I feel the time has come for Joyce . . . to be released from the Babylonish captivity of the professors and presented to the people as one of the great comic writers of all time." [105]

This view was not without its sympathizers within the Joyce Industry itself. Most notably, Robert Martin Adams swam against the tide. In his 1962 assessment of Joyce studies, Adams argued that Joyce "is the only great modern humorist." [106] Not many Joyceans would have denied that Joyce is funny. But Adams sets Joyce the Humorist in opposition to Joyce the Ironist, arguing that he cannot be both and that the academy is wrong to portray him as the latter. Adams was unusual among Joyce critics in the 1950s and '60s. His 1962 book, *Surface and Symbol,* won the annual prize given by *The Explicator,* a heady approval from the New Critics. Yet he was perhaps the only academic to insist that Joyce was not always conscious of his art.

Both Adams and Burgess understood that the heart of the matter is what we think were Joyce's intentions, and Burgess drew on his own experience as a writer to deflate the academy's portrait of Joyce:

> Even minor novelists like myself have known the clumsy jabs of the American exegetists. I wrote a light-hearted book called *A Clockwork Orange* to which a certain amount of misguided semantic speculation has been applied. "Why does Mr. Burgess use this particular image at this particular point in the narrative? Can it possibly be because . . . ?" I am here; I am only too ready to be asked, though I may not know the answer. But some scholars don't like going to authoritative sources. "To hell with your theory," said one Harvard man to another; "I've got data." "Data shmata," was the reply; "I *like* my theory." Just so. All the Joyce scholars of America must thank God that Joyce is dead. [107]

They would thank God, of course, because a dead Joyce cannot contradict their claims about his intentions, and, most especially, because he is not around to admit that he did not put in this or that symbol: to borrow Kittredge's phrase, a dead Joyce cannot remind us that he is human, that he did not always know what he was about.

"The Joyce we have had up to now," Adams wrote, "was Daedalian—that is he exercised over many minds the authority of a puzzle, which has to be solved on its own given terms and which promises, tacitly but nonetheless distinctly, that it has a final solution." According to the academicians, Joyce is coherent and consistent: coherent in his form and symbolic structure, and consistent throughout his career. The Daedalian is omnipotent, omniscient, and purposeful in his creations; therefore, "every element in Joyce's entire canon is part of a single controlled composition." Adams and Burgess disputed each of these assumptions. Adams claimed that Joyce was neither coherent nor consistent. Rather than discovering synthesizing patterns, "the more rigorously you read [Joyce], the more loose ends you uncover."[108] And Burgess claimed that Joyce was not the same type of artist in his early and late careers.

Burgess's complaints were noted by the *James Joyce Quarterly*. In the spring of 1966, William Noon attacked Burgess for attacking professors. Noon conceded that the *JJQ* had become "something of a professor's preserve," citing its twelve "urbane scholars": Adeline Glasheen, Ruth von Phul, Clive Hart, Richard Ellmann, Fritz Senn, Matthew Hodgart, A. Walton Litz, James Atherton, Hugh Kenner, Fred Higginson, William York Tindall, and David Hayman.[109] It might be protested that Glasheen, von Phul, and Senn were not academics. But they cannot be labeled amateurs either. They were professionals in their treatment of Joyce, and the accident that they did not hold positions in colleges did not separate them from the Joyceans who did. They were nonprofessionals only in the strictest sense—they did not get paid for being Joyceans—and Noon was right to call them scholars. At any rate, to be a professor's preserve was not something bad, in Noon's view. And if Noon displayed some ambivalence, however small, about the influence of scholars, Bernard Benstock had no doubts. In the winter issue of 1967, Benstock, while reviewing Burgess's abridged *Finnegans Wake,* addressed the supposed conflict between scholars and general readers by suggesting that nonacademic readers of *Finnegans Wake* simply did not exist.[110]

I bring all of this up not because I think Burgess was truly defending the interests of ordinary decent readers against the academy. Even if Benstock exaggerated the case, "ordinary" readers were more than likely not reading Joyce in great numbers. But there is something to the notion that our exercise of authority over Joyce, which so often is wielded through our unconscious representations of his reputation, limits nonacademic readers as well as ourselves. While to be included in the canon guarantees a certain readership, it also excludes a writer from others. Entering the ivory tower means leaving the public square. Nowhere has this been more apparent than in the Joyce symposia, where, from the first meeting held in Dublin in 1967, the American academics and the bewildered public have crossed lances.

The International James Joyce Symposia

In the early 1960s the annual conferences of the American Committee for Irish Studies and the Modern Language Association provided Joyceans with their main venues for public meetings. With the first issue of the *JJQ* under their belts, a number of the editors got together at the 1963 MLA conference, many meeting Staley for the first time. James Spoerri and Alan Cohn hosted a dinner for Joyceans at the 1965 MLA conference,[111] the first in a tradition of popular and notoriously convivial annual meetings. In 1966 the dinner was hosted by Cohn, Chester Anderson, and Epstein; Staley comically referred to it as the "Joyce underground" of the MLA. Richard Kain advised Staley in 1963 to send announcements of the forthcoming journal to the members of the American Committee for Irish Studies.[112] Staley's "Notes and Comments" in the spring 1965 *JJQ* reminded readers of the upcoming ACIS conference, and by the spring of 1966 Joyceans had established a presence there, as Staley informed readers that Vivien Mercier and Kain would give speeches at the annual conference and that "several other papers of special interest to Joyceans" were on the program. But these venues were too narrow to keep up with the ever growing supply of Joyce scholars.

In November 1966, while Staley was in Trieste on a Fulbright fellowship, he visited Fritz Senn in Zurich. Together they decided to pursue their idea of a Joyce conference, which they had been kicking around with Bernard Benstock since he had joined the editorial staff of *JJQ* the previous year. Plans coalesced quickly. By 21 November Staley wrote to Maralee Frampton (who was running the *JJQ* back in Tulsa), "We hope to have a large crowd from all over the world." Senn already promised five or six Belgians and a comparable number of French Joyceans.[113] By December Dubliners were promising local support. Rivers Carew at *The Dublin Magazine* offered to sponsor and advertise the conference,[114] and, more importantly, the Bord Failte or Irish Tourist Board signed on later.[115] Before Christmas Senn had official stationery printed with himself, Staley, and Benstock on the letterhead.[116] Briefly, at the end of the year, Staley had doubts about the success of the conference on account of the short notice. But Senn suggested they go ahead, even at the risk of failure, so they would "be so much wiser for a perhaps bigger event a year later." [117] Senn's advice was well-founded, for in the end "over seventy-five paid registrants attended." [118]

The first conference became a battleground for authority over Joyce. Three factions fought two battles. The American academics found themselves confounded by their reluctant counterparts in Ireland. To a large degree, personality differences can account for this dispute. Roger McHugh, departmental chair of UCD, seems to have matched a personal lack of enthusiasm with a lack of energy. Benstock recalled the "foot dragging from Dublin academics." After the conference, the "Irish non-hosts" invited the organizers to a lunch at the Royal Hibernian, at which Fritz Senn, in a "thanking speech," cut the Irish "into small pieces without them ever being sure that he was being nasty. A great performance," Benstock remembered. "Roger McHugh came in his jodhpurs and riding boots and had to leave early (his horses were calling), but he was there long enough to hear Fritz's acknowledgment of Dublin hospitality and kindness." [119]

But some differences must be attributed to rifts deeper than those dug by personalities. Probably, an Irish suspicion of American academic methods—the scholarly critical method described above—and an American condescension for a perceived amateurishness in Irish scholarship added to the dislike. To Americans, the Irish academy's general neglect of Joyce must have seemed provincial and their institutional practices outdated. To the Irish, the American tendency toward hagiography must have seemed unfounded and their institutional practices superficial. Whatever its cause, this conflict lasted a long time. Of the 1973 Dublin Symposium Benstock wrote,

> Tom [Staley] and I had visited Dublin in September of '72 to lay the groundwork, including a bizarre morning with [Irish professor] Eileen MacCarvill (we offered Bloomsday for all-Irish program, but she interpreted that as the Americans making a week's worth of mistakes that the Irish would have to correct on the last day!). So we gave them the first day, which they "packed" with *two* lectures. Garvin read from a published piece and Montgomery talked in French. As chair I thanked him for addressing us in Gaelic, so Quidnunc the next day had a wonderful time explaining to the Irish that there were American professors who thought French was Gaelic.[120]

The distrust still exists. What is expressed by both sides as uninformed scholarship is really a debate over who gets authority over Joyce. The debate continues in the recent Irish editions of all of Joyce's works. These editions, edited by Declan Kiberd, Seamus Deane, Terence Brown, and J. C. C. Mays, were touted "as an Irish recuperation of Joyce, a rescuing from the alleged annexation and depredations of (mostly) U.S. critics." Terence Killeen's review of these editions, published in the *James Joyce Literary Supplement,* takes issue with the historicizing project of the Irish.[121] Interestingly, Bruce Arnold, a Dubliner himself, vilifies these editions in his review in *JJQ* for a number of reasons, not the least of which is that the "main objective of the 'Irish' scholars" is to present "Joyce as social commentator on Ireland's oppression by the British." Arnold, it seems, would have preferred a less nationalist but more socialist Joyce.[122]

The conference's academics also found themselves in conflict with nonacademics, chiefly represented by the media, waiters, and taxi drivers. While I hesitate to project such attitudes onto the whole population of "ordinary decent people who love books," I think these problems probably reflect ideological differences at least as great as the conflicts between American and Irish scholars. While Staley retained his typical high regard for nonacademics, the first symposium was organized from the beginning as an academic affair. Despite the banquets, the drinking, and the bus trips to Howth and to the headwaters of the Liffey, the supremacy of the scholarly paper was never in doubt. Reporting on the first Symposium in *Books Abroad,* Hayman wrote, "The business of the conference is not dinners, after-dinners, tours, but papers and dialogue. It is to the quality of these that the Seminar owes its success or failure."[123] The symposium gathered academics together to do in person what the *JJQ* had been doing for four years.

Part of the conflict recalled Joyce's own difficulties in Ireland. The scandalous nature of the material, or, from another perspective, the prudish nature of the public sparked the battle. Margaret Solomon's paper on *Finnegans Wake* caused one flare up. According to Benstock,

> Solomon decide[d] to check with me if the explicit language on the Phallic Tree in FW [was] permissible: I gave her the academic carte blanche. In front of 75 participants and a bunch of hangers-on she used her explicit language. THAT made the symposium memorable. I heard an aged gent walking out, saying, "Those words have NEVER been uttered in UCD before, and certainly not by a lady!"[124]

Hayman described the controversy euphemistically: Solomon's paper "seemed calculated to amuse the audience by the very incongruity of its presentation by a decorous lady before so decorous a gathering in so decorous a place." [125] More scandalous to the Irish in 1967 was Harry Pollock's theatrical production, "Yes I Will Yes." Hayman reported,

> Included in the entertainment was a dramatic reading by three buxom Mollys in light attire (light night attire in fact) of the "Penelope" sequence of *Ulysses,* an event calculated to amaze the attentive Irish waiters and to interest if not to amuse the after-dinner Joyceans. [126]

Hayman regretted Pollock's production, preferring "to hear a more dramatic episode, one that is less obviously a . . . shocker."

But the negative Irish reaction was not entirely due to their sexual delicacies. The Irish also suspected American scholars of hero worship. As Morris Beja notes in his "Informal History" of the symposia,

> The uncertain attitude of some Dubliners to the Symposium (and, for that matter, to James Joyce) was also reflected in the reports of the conference within the Irish press, which immediately set the tone that such coverage was to have for years to come: a bemused but impatient mockery over the fascinated care with which scholars and critics seemed to pore over the minutest facets of the life and career of a man of whom many Irish were still not sure they fully approved. [127]

The London press took a similar view. W. L. Webb, writing in *The Guardian,* described the conference as two skirmishes between various factions, each with their own vested interest in Joyce. The first encounter was between Giorgio Joyce, who, returning to Ireland after forty-five years (his last visit had been as a child, during the Civil War, when Nora took him to Galway), received "a bronze cast of his father's death mask," presented by Padraic Colum "on behalf of the Irish Academy of Letters." [128] Colum's speech interpreted the event as a sort of reconciliation between James Joyce and Ireland, an interpretation that, according to Webb, Giorgio accepted warily. It was, perhaps, an initial step in Ireland's reclamation project.

The other encounter was "between the gossips who at least are not in danger of forgetting that those words [Joyce's books] were written by a man, and the pedants who, unlike Irish writers can flourish in the huge shade of his art." [129] The gossips, presumably, were the Dubliners and Irish writers, who read Joyce in a straightforward manner, confident that they understood what he referred to. The pedants, of course, were the American professors, who continued to churn out "their ever more minutely detailed scrutinies." This was a continuation of the 1950s conflict that Arnold described between Irish writers and the Americans.

By October of 1967, Benstock already was proposing changes for the second Symposium:

> How about labeling the events under "general" and "scholarly" categories, having one or two general meetings of Joyce papers addressed to the public at large (but solidly intelligent . . .) and several scholarly meetings where the papers can be longer and discussion can follow each paper—the public invited but warned in advance that it is geared to the specialist.[130]

Staley responded with a complementary proposal:

> I suggest that we establish a host committee and that host committee be headed by Prof. Roger McHugh, the Chairman of English at University College. It strikes me that things from the Dublin area must be handled more formally. I suggest that we add Rivers Carew [of *The Dublin Magazine*] and the man with Bord Failte [Tourist Board]. We simply must establish a more viable relationship with the Dublin community.[131]

Benstock and Staley were trying to resolve both rifts—between American and Irish academics, and between academics and the general public. Staley must have anticipated this problem, because even before the first conference he published a sort of apology for American criticism in *The Dublin Magazine,* in which he attributes the "seemingly unrelenting outpouring of [Joyce] criticism" in America to Joyce's reputation as "a pioneer, a rebel, a solitary figure, even a man without a country"; to the influence of Edmund Wilson, Thornton Wilder, and Harry Levin; to the "large number of colleges and universities with their huge faculties and countless number of students" in America; to the academic "'bugaboo' of 'publish or perish'"; and to the availability of Joyceana in American libraries.[132]

At the first symposium Staley, Senn, Benstock, and others organized the International James Joyce Foundation. Nine months later, on St. Patrick's Day in 1968, David Ward, the secretary of this new Joyce society, circulated a letter soliciting members. "The Foundation," he wrote, "was conceived out of a desire to set up a loosely knit organization that would be international in scope and which could function to bring Joyceans all over the world into closer communication." He listed the four goals of the foundation as established in its charter: to sponsor the bi-annual symposia; to establish a permanent research library of Joyce studies;[133] to provide scholarships to Joyce students; and to publish a newsletter. The foundation was decidedly different from the James Joyce Society of New York. Ward's peroration rang the death knell for amateur Joyceans: "We . . . hope that we will, through this organization, be able to better pursue the study of that which was once a cult and which has now become a community."[134] Joyce, now the object of study for a community of scholars, had been entirely professionalized.

The Critical Editions

As I indicated in Chapters 2 and 3, the aims of Ben Huebsch's and Bennett Cerf's editions of Joyce were not antithetical to the purposes of the academy. Nevertheless, perhaps inevitably, the academy extended its authority over Joyce by taking over the publication of his works. T. S. Eliot's *Introducing James Joyce: A Selection of Joyce's Prose,* published by Faber and Faber in England in 1942, was an interim step in this transfer of power. Eliot, of course, was not an academic, but his close association with the American academy, especially with Harvard, and his influence on American critics made this a semi-academic volume. Certainly it presented readers with the academic Joyce: in particular, Eliot's selections were calculated to demonstrate both " 'the continuity of development' of Joyce's writing" and its autobiographical aspects, as Ira Nadel argues in his fine analysis of this edition. The anthology sold 16,000 copies by 1948, when it was superseded by Viking's 1947 anthology, *The Portable James Joyce* (in America) and *The Essential James Joyce* (in England), edited by Harry Levin.[135]

Harry Levin was an academic. He must have been chosen to write the introduction to the new anthology on account of his 1941 New Directions *James Joyce: A Critical Introduction,* the first American, academic, book-length study of the writer. His introduction to the Viking anthology opens by announcing that Joyce is a "classic":

> A long and hazardous period of probation seems to face a writer when, ceasing to be a contemporary, he becomes a classic. But in Joyce's case, perhaps because he was so rigorously tested during his lifetime, this further trial has been cut short.[136]

Though Levin did not recognize it, Ernst's defense of *Ulysses* cut Joyce's probation more than any test by a reading public, as I discussed in Chapter 3. And, as I discussed in Chapter 2, Huebsch's and Cerf's packaging contributed as well. Levin's chief label for Joyce—"the Writers' Writer"[137]—reflects Pound's and Eliot's characterization of the author. Levin implicitly invited his readers to add Joyce to the pantheon of artist-martyrs:

> The characteristics that enabled him to sustain his [artistic] purpose are apparent in his very death mask. Delicately but firmly molded, the head is long and narrow, the forehead high, the chin strong, and the eyes are closed. It is the face of Stephen Dedalus, of the perennial student, of a man who carries to the verge of his sixtieth year the agility, the curiosity, the sensibility of his youth.[138]

Levin characterized Joyce's artistry in the mystical, pseudoreligious terms appropriate to genius: Joyce's characters "are forever transfixed in the poses he caught"; "Joyce created his monumental [literary] achievement" out of the "irreducible substances . . . [of] nationality, religion, and language"; "with the self-dedication of the priest Joyce took the vows of the artist"; "optimists will emphasize the creation of matter *ex nihilo* [in *Finnegans Wake*], and trust in the Word to create another world." Levin rounds out his introduction with the observation that, "because [Joyce's] self-portrait was so explicit, and his masterworks were so elaborate," readers are bound to misunderstand him.[139] It is particularly interesting that the Viking Portable Library was geared specifically to an unacademic audience. It was launched in 1943 by Morton Glick, and the first issue, a volume of Alexander Woollcott's poems, was aimed at servicemen.[140] So Levin was writing for a broad audience, perhaps many of the exservicemen then enrolled in college under the GI Bill, and this anthology, though not strictly an academic publication, should be seen as an extension of the academy's influence on Joyce's readers.[141]

The true academic editions of *Dubliners* and *Portrait,* published in the 1960s, present Joyce as the New Critical genius artificer, always coherent and consistent throughout his career. Both texts bear the indelible stamp of Ellmann, though he was not much involved in either project. Chester Anderson, who studied under Tindall at Columbia, had worked on the text of *Portrait* for his 1962 dissertation. Viking gave Columbia the right to publish a new, corrected text of *Portrait,* but apparently Lionel Trilling soured the deal. Catherine Carver at Viking suggested that Anderson try the press at Cornell, but it turned the book down also. Anderson tried to peddle the project to Minnesota University Press, and after they declined Viking decided to bring out the corrected text itself.[142] Anderson reported that Ellmann "was asked to act as arbiter, and reviewed the final selection" of corrections to the Viking Compass (1964) edition of the novel, which was the text used in the Critical Edition of 1967 (*P*, 254). I presume Viking recruited Ellmann because his name had come to indicate a certain authority by the 1960s. But Anderson did not welcome the help. Recently invited to provide the text for the Bedford *Portrait*, Anderson writes,

> [T]here were errors made in carrying out [the editorial] rationale [of the 1964 edition]—most of them my own, though Mr. Ellmann's vetoes added to them substantially.[143]

Anderson did not know that Ellmann was going to get any credit for the book until after publication, and he would have credited Ellmann only with marring the text further. After the edition was published, Anderson immediately began working to bring out a better text:

> I found these errors as best I could and corrected them. But even though Marshall Best, then the pleasant executive vice president at Viking, was willing to make the changes, Mr. Ellmann was not. When I visited him in New College, Oxford, in 1972, he scolded me with his usual cheeriness for not being Hans Walter Gabler.[144]

Anderson goes on to thank Bedford Books for allowing him finally, thirty years later, "to get these corrections into print for the first time."[145]

The critical edition of *Dubliners* was the result of a collaboration between A. Walton Litz and Robert Scholes, two young critics recruited by Viking for the project.[146] Scholes, whose fine and exacting work on the text of *Dubliners* led to the 1967 Viking Compass edition (which is the text used by the Critical Edition of 1969), praised Ellmann warmly for his help: "In establishing the methodology for this edition, the editor has benefited greatly from the advice of Richard Ellmann" (*D*, 226). Nevertheless, Litz, who wrote the annotations, preface, and the introduction to criticism in the Critical Edition, thought Ellmann was unhelpful, basing his editorial selections on his own notion of what "sounded" most Joycean.[147] I do not mean to impugn Ellmann's sincerity of judgment. But, as I have established above, Ellmann's ear was tuned particularly to the pitch of American liberalism, and it is likely that such prejudices influenced his judgment. But I am speculating here. I do not know exactly which changes Ellmann authorized, and therefore I have no way of proving the degree to which the official academic texts of *Dubliners* and *Portrait* represent Ellmann's version of Joyce. Many of his decisions were probably fairly innocuous—the deletions of commas, for instance. Others might have been more substantial. For example, some probably concerned "thirty-seven substantive changes" made by Joyce for the aborted Maunsel edition of the *Dubliners*. Scholes incorporated these changes on the assumption that they were among the changes Joyce made to proofs ignored by Grant Richards's printer in 1914.[148] In his 1992 book, *In Search of James Joyce*, Scholes is refreshingly frank about his editorial assumptions:

> The "final intention of the author" is often a fiction for textual editors as well as for literary interpreters; and last thoughts may be final simply because the author was not given time for others, not because they are best. When an author's reputation has actually been made in texts held to be "imperfect," bibliographers should at least acknowledge that textual perfection may be less important than they would like it to be. In preparing editions we need to follow the author's wishes, so far as they can be determined; but they can never be determined so fully as to obviate the need for literary judgment on the part of editors.[149]

Scholes remarks that, "[d]uring the recent debates [over Gabler's *Ulysses*] I was asked how I had decided what format to follow for the use of dashes to introduce direct discourse in *Dubliners*." His answer is a perfect illustration of the judicious "literary judgment" editors must employ to construct their fiction of an author's last intention:

> Somewhat to the dismay of purer theoretical bibliographers, I replied that I simply took the format finally accepted by Joyce in the published *Ulysses* and followed it for *Dubliners* because I could find no clear justification for any other format and saw no need to multiply variations in the published texts. . . . Joyce wanted some alternative to quotation marks but had not really worked out exactly what he wanted when *Dubliners* was published by Grant Richards—who, in any case, did not let Joyce have his way.[150]

Scholes discussed this matter in one of his *Studies in Bibliography* articles in 1964, noting that the future editor of *Dubliners* will need to decide how to punctuate direct discourse:

> [W]ill he want to follow Joyce's habitual manuscript procedure and place a dash both before and after a paragraph in which direct discourse appears, or will he adopt the procedure of the published ver-

sions of *Portrait* and *Ulysses* and use the opening dash only? I am inclined to favor the latter, as representing Joyce's final procedure—but the question is certainly arguable.[151]

Of course that future editor was Scholes himself, and he did indeed favor the latter, a decision, no doubt, approved by Ellmann.

That decision significantly influenced Joyce's reputation. I read *Dubliners* for the first time in 1979. Trying to encourage literary pursuits, my parents gave me for Christmas a deluxe set of Joyce, which included the 1967 Viking Compass text of *Dubliners* prepared by Scholes. The set is bound in three handsome volumes—*Dubliners* and *Portrait* together in one volume, *Ulysses,* and *Finnegans Wake.* The uniform physical character of the set suggests continuity, but, more importantly, the uniform punctuation does also. I assumed that Joyce continuously insisted that direct discourse be indicated only by an opening dash. Later, in graduate school, I discovered that, against Joyce's wishes, the first edition of *Dubliners* used quotation marks. I believed that the change adopted by Scholes for the Viking text was the one Joyce authorized, and I have to admit that Scholes's judgment in this matter is perfectly reasonable. But we cannot deny that it is not the punctuation Joyce used. And it is also undeniable that Scholes's decision, which he based on the principal of continuity, contributes in a subtle but powerful way to our apprehension of continuity throughout Joyce's career. By using *Ulysses* to authorize his editorial decision regarding *Dubliners,* Scholes helped establish what we naively take as a given today: that Joyce's early technique was identical to his technique in his later work.

Brenda Maddox's recent Bantam Classic edition of *Dubliners* bears this out. She practically disowns the edition in her introduction:

> I wrote this introduction to *Dubliners* in the summer of 1989 in the expectation that the edition would observe Joyce's textual instructions that the dash be used to introduce direct dialogue. Joyce detested quotation marks and did not use them in his later work.[152]

Apparently, Brenda Maddox has fallen under the influence of Scholes, for she ignores Joyce's instructions that the dash be used to end direct dialogue. She implies that Joyce punctuated *Dubliners* the way he punctuated *Ulysses.* The publishers explained in their own apology that they had to use quotation marks because the text with introductory dashes was still under copyright.

The issue of copyright indicates another vested interest: so long as the Joyce estate can keep book buyers convinced that Joyce meant to use only introductory dashes, it can retain the profits on the sale of *Dubliners*. To avoid infringing the estate's copyright, Bantam used the text of the first American edition of *Dubliners*. Perhaps Bantam could have gotten around the copyright by using concluding dashes in addition to introductory dashes—that would have been a riddle for the lawyers to solve. But that punctuation does not seem to have been considered. Nowhere in the edition's prefaces is there a description of the punctuation Joyce actually used in *Dubliners*. We are left with Maddox's disavowal and Bantam's apology, which perpetuate the fiction that Joyce's technique was consistent throughout his career, a fiction compatible with New Criticism.

Looking back on the 1960s, Litz says that he was solidly New Critical.[153] By 1969 Scholes had already made himself a reputation as an expert textual scholar through a series of articles on *Dubliners* in *Studies in Bibliography,* and his critical orientation was a bit more complex:

> My generation of graduate students in English was mostly male and largely innocent of its own cultural construction. Most of us, finishing graduate school at the end of the 1950s, had been originally trained as New Critics, oriented to poetry rather than fiction or drama, and we believed, with almost touching simplicity, in the absolute value of literary study as an end in itself. . . . [T]he narrative structure that fits neatly over my life as a literary scholar finds me beginning as a somewhat rebellious New Critic and moving through structuralism and semiotics toward cultural criticism.[154]

He studied under René Wellek, M. H. Abrams, and R. S. Crane, but it was William M. Sale, Jr., who steered him toward bibliography. Scholes's dissertation, a catalogue of the Mennen Collection at Cornell (which houses many Joyce papers deriving from Stanislaus) ensured that he would appreciate extratextual evidence in the scholarly tradition. As a bibliographer, he had a healthier respect for authorial intention than the typical New Critic: "I seem always to have had, even when not fully aware of it, a hermeneutic desire to understand the Joycean text (and many another text) as an act of communication from an author to a reader. . . . I refused to give up the fiction of intentionality as a necessary criterion or protocol of reading."[155]

The critical apparatus of the 1969 *Dubliners* reflects the impulses of both the textual scholar and the critic. Scholes provided the reader with relevant extratextual evidence: biographical data, drafts, epiphanies, even pertinent letters. Scholes had published the letters from Grant Richards in *Studies in Bibliography* six years earlier, and the slant of his editorial introduction in that article moved Joyce away from the myth of genius. All in all, Scholes tried to diminish Richards's reputation as a bungling publisher impeding the progress of great literature (a reputation convenient to Joyce critics who used the correspondence to tout Joyce's image as the heroic, misunderstood artist). Scholes pointed out that Richards's "advice to Joyce in 1904 [about offensive passages] was not unsound in terms of the temper of the times," and he gives Richards his due among "those small publishers who were so influential in British literary developments around the turn of the century."[156] He included the letters in the critical edition of *Dubliners,* at least in part, to deflate Joyce's mythic stature:

> Here we can find Joyce's own thoughts on the purpose of his book, its style and its plan. We can see the author as a young man of twenty-two or -three, beginning to compare himself to other English and Continental writers of fiction and to measure his work against theirs. *We can get a sense of Joyce the man in these letters which should help us to understand the meaning of his work.* (D, 257) [emphasis added]

Here we can see evidence of Scholes's later claim that he "sought to read Joyce's work as the work of . . . a real person who lived a certain life and hoped to communicate important things through his writing."[157] The letters, which frankly discuss Joyce's intentions (many of which are manifestly anti-New Critical, as I argued in Chapter 1) are reproduced without interpretive commentary.

Nevertheless, the main thrust of critical apparatus in the 1969 *Dubliners* tends to promote Joyce the Genius rather than Joyce the Man. When he wrote the introduction to the criticism section of the book, Litz clearly was conscious of the antagonism between what he characterized as naturalistic readings and symbolic readings of the stories, another version of the "poetry/propaganda" dichotomy. Litz believed that the "turning point" in criticism about *Dubliners* occurred when the "unsatisfactory" early notices gave way to sophisticated, appreciative criticism, "when critics who had become skillful at tracing the symbolic motifs in the later works returned to *Dubliners* and found the same patterns adumbrated there" (D, 299). Litz does call for "other forms of criticism which will emphasize the nonsymbolic dimensions of the stories without sacrificing the achievement of the 'symbolic' critics," and he does give credit to readers like Stanislaus, who treated the text as referential (*D*, 300). These points suggest that Litz posed as an arbiter between two apparently extreme methods of reading:

> [T]he gold coin in "Two Gallants" may be a symbol of various subtle "betrayals," but it is first and last a fact of economic life. Any symbolic reading of *Dubliners* that compromises the realistic integrity of the stories should fall under immediate suspicion. (*D*, 300)

Such a statement seems extraordinary in 1969, or at least unusual, and Litz must be given credit for the tolerance of his view. It may be that by 1969, New Criticism had moved well beyond the polemical stage in which Marvin Magalaner first attacked Stanislaus.

Yet, despite the broadness of his view, ultimately Litz adhered to the general New Critical axiom of symbolic coherence. He might have reserved some place for historical interpretation, but he reinforced the supremacy of New Critical reading practices:

> The moral would appear to be that we must use all our tact, and all our knowledge of Joyce's materials and methods, to discriminate between details of "surface" and details with symbolic overtones, or between overtones and a full-fledged pattern of intricate symbolism. The stories of *Dubliners* gain enormously when we bring to them an understanding of Joyce's mature art, but we must never forget to confront them first on their own terms. (*D*, 301)

His biases are quite evident. If Joyce's "maturer" art is *Ulysses* and *Finnegans Wake,* to the degree that *Dubliners* is realistic it is "immature." If we must never forget to confront the stories first on their own terms, we also, unfailingly, must find symbolic patterns later. Litz equates "Joyce's artistic development" to his increasing "symbolic sophistication"—a development he claims is evident in the two drafts of "The Sisters" (*D*, 299). According to this characterization, the maturity of the artist is measured by the degree of symbolism we can discover in his or her text. More subtly, the metaphor of "surface" and its counterpart— presumably the "underneath" of a story—make it impossible for readers to be satisfied with a historical reading. To remain on the surface is to fail to dig deep and mine the stories for all they are worth. Built into the critical vocabulary is a bias that cannot be avoided, no matter how sensitive Litz was to "other forms of criticism that emphasize the nonsymbolic dimensions of the stories." Given his critical metaphors, it was impossible to imagine, let alone express, that the stories might lose, rather than gain, enormously by treating them like Joyce's "maturer" art.

Scholes and Litz composed the "Topics for Discussion and Papers" one weekend at Litz's house, taking turns at the typewriter and pacing the room.[158] Presumably, they were conscious of the demands of the classroom in 1969, and so the topics are slanted toward questions of form: recurrent themes, symbolic interpretations, matters of technique, etc. One topic does treat Joyce as satirist engaged in social criticism (D, 446). Another asks what forces paralyzed Eveline (D, 448). A third asks for the significance of the harp in Kildare Street in "Two Gallants" (D, 448). Yet these three remain exceptions to the rule. "Ivy Day," for example, an overtly political story, occasions one historical topic sandwiched by topics concerning Joyce's "method of presentation" and "the dramatic function of Mr. Hynes's poem" (D, 450).

While the notes to the stories raise the issue of Joyce's realism, they reflect a fairly New Critical attitude toward realism. Explaining his notes, Litz wrote,

> Although some of the place-names are fictitious, most of the local references are scrupulously exact; they are part of a "realism" which existed as much for Joyce's benefit as for ours. These references often suggest the social nuances of Dublin life, or they may indicate the "tone" of a particular place or area. . . . [W]e have supplied information where the significance of these references appears to extend beyond a sense of local "realism." (D, 462)

It is difficult to tell exactly what Litz meant by "a sense of local 'realism,'" but it is clear that when Joyce's place names fail to extend beyond the social nuances of Dublin life they would not be glossed. Such glosses, obviously, would enable a historical reading of the text, while their absence would discourage it. Litz did not always adhere to this principle. For example, he glosses the reference to the "National School boys" in "An Encounter":

> the government-sponsored National schools were feared by Catholic educators, since they pursued an English and nonsectarian theory of education. They were also considered to be socially inferior. (D, 465)

But Litz's preference for items that go "beyond a sense of local 'realism'" encouraged a symbolic treatment of the text. Litz also wrote that,

Although the stories do not have the density of reference and allusion found in Joyce's later works, they do pose a number of problems in symbolic interpretation. In these notes we have tried to avoid explicit interpretations, preferring to provide the raw materials from which such interpretations may be constructed. (*D,* 462)

In other words, the editors meant to supply students with enough information to mine their own symbolic patterns. Litz's explanation about National School boys was not meant to foreground the class conflict between the new Catholic middle class and their "inferiors"—the "ragged troop" of younger boys who take the narrator and Mahoney for Protestants. Nor was it meant to illustrate the role of education in the ideological indoctrination of the narrator, as I suggested in Chapter 1. Litz's note was meant to go beyond these "local" issues and supply students with the raw material of a New Critical interpretation.

The editorial apparatuses, as we would expect, provide the material required by the scholarly critic. In the critical *Portrait,* for example, Chester Anderson reproduced draft materials from *The Workshop of Daedalus* and *Stephen Hero* that give students some experience in the genetic method. He brought together essays in the scholarly critical venue by Maurice Beebe, William York Tindall, Richard Ellmann, Harry Levin, Hugh Kenner, and Wayne Booth, first published in journals like *The Sewanee Review, The Kenyon Review,* and *PMLA.* While two of eight topics for general classroom discussion seem to violate New Critical dicta, eleven of twelve "Special Topics for Discussion and Short Papers" and all topics "For Longer Papers" emphasize aesthetics and form.[159]

As early as 1964, Thomas Staley was working to establish an academic edition of *Ulysses* published by a university press.[160] That project would not come to fruition until Gabler's *Ulysses* was published in 1984, and the controversy over that edition has reminded us that academics have a variety of motivations, not all of them enlightened, when they seek to extend their authority over texts. Charles Rossman's study of the Joyce estate's role in Gabler's project demonstrates that one motive for exercising "authority" is money.[161] And John Kidd's criticism of Gabler's version of *Ulysses* illustrates that authority has definite consequences: "No one interested in the interplay of fiction and history," John Kidd writes, "will find the 'genetic apparatus' [of Hans Gabler's 1984 *Ulysses*] adequate."[162] Gabler's change of the "runner-up in the quarter-mile flat handicap in the Trinity Races" from H. Thrift to H. Shrift replaces a historical person with a wholly fictional character. Henceforth the real-life H. Thrift has disappeared from our consideration, or at least from the consideration of Dublin readers who realized the character referred to their own bursar at Trinity College.[163] History no longer impinges on the text at that point. The loss is small. It is only one of thousands of historically accurate details that swell the enveloping action of the novel. But by pointing it out Kidd reminds us that Joyce meant for readers to place his fiction in a real historical context. The thrust of Kidd's arguments imply that Gabler would have us treat *Ulysses* as a wholly fictional and in no way historically referential text.

According to Scholes, the critical edition of *Dubliners* has sold a thousand or so copies each year since its first publication.[164] Anderson says that he refused any royalties on the Compass *Portrait* and that he makes fewer than ten cents per copy of the Critical *Portrait,* so money clearly was not a motivation in either the Critical *Dubliners* or *Portrait.* Since sales figures for other editions are not available, it is impossible to gauge the influence of the Viking Critical *Dubliners* and *Portrait,* but I think it would be safe to consider these, coupled with Levin's *The Portable James Joyce,* as the standard classroom texts. The recent explosion of editions, which followed the lapse of copyright, has challenged the ahistorical Joyce. Bernard McGinley's recent annotated edition of *Dubliners,* for example, thoroughly glosses the "local" references. Though that book, handsomely illustrated and fairly expensive, does not really remove *Dubliners* from the authority of academics, it does reflect changes in the academy, changes that are also reflected in the MLA's *Approaches to Teaching Joyce's "Ulysses."*[165] Aimed at college professors and so, presumably, of some influence in many classrooms, that book includes Jeffrey Segall (on the culture, politics, and reception of *Ulysses*), Bonnie Kime Scott (on a feminist approach to the book), Mary Lowe-Evans (on a New Historicist approach), Joseph Heininger (on popular culture), and Kathleen McCormick (on the history of *Ulysses*'s production and reception).

Conclusion: The Trouble with Genius

I do not mean to attack the Joyce Industry indiscriminately. As David Hayman pointed out to me,

> If by Industry, we mean a system that cranks out dissertations, articles, and books in great numbers, I suppose we had one. . . . [But] [o]n the whole, the "custodianship" [of Joyce] was a good one since

there was a healthy sense of humor and a general openness to ideas, even a nice sense of internal feuding pretty early on.[166]

It has not been my purpose to point out the good effects of the Industry, though I have touched on a few. Not the least of these is the sense of collaboration fostered by journals like *MFS* and *JJQ*. I have tried in this chapter to establish a necessary connection between scholarly critical reading practices and the image of Joyce as a genius. I hope to have demonstrated that ever since Pound first wrote to Joyce in 1913, the framers of Joyce's reputation have consistently moved him toward "genius." Pound's and Eliot's egoist, Ernst's classical author, and Ellmann's Joyce all march toward the academy. The composition of the academy in the 1950s and 1960s, which deflected attention away from the social context of literature, required "genius" authors, so the industry continued to supply them.

Criticism has come a long way since the early days of the Joyce Industry. In fact, the careers of many of the founders of the Joyce Industry reflect those changes. Already I have mentioned Robert Scholes's *In Search of James Joyce*, which details his movement toward cultural criticism. Many others in the Joyce Industry have helped move criticism away from the autonomous text and toward history. For example, Bernard Benstock, in his last article in the *James Joyce Quarterly*, argues that part of Joyce's intention in *Ulysses* was to severely criticize bourgeois morality.[167] Despite these changes in Joyce critics, Joyce's reputation as a genius has remained.

I want to emphasize that I am not arguing that Joyce was not a genius. That issue is, I believe, beside the point of criticism today. Rather than ask whether he was or was not a genius, we ought to ask, Who benefits from that image? In his lifetime no doubt Joyce benefited. And Bennett Cerf did. Morris Ernst did. After his death, Richard Ellmann and, as I hope to have proved in this chapter, a generation of American scholarly critics benefited also.

What happened to Joyce is not unique. Jane Thompkins and Richard Brodhead have recently argued that "the rise of a new formation of the professoriate"[168] employed "a complex system of promotion, publicity, and politics" to canonize Nathaniel Hawthorne.[169] As Jan Gorak puts it, "canonical works ally themselves with a spectrum of vested interests that include male dominance, Anglo-Catholic orthodoxy, national self-definition, and professional aggrandizement."[170] Much of Gorak's admirable book, *The Making of the Modern Canon*, tempers the attack on the excluding function of the canon, which emerges as a paper tiger in his study. Nevertheless, Gorak's chapter on "The Modern History of the Canon" does detail how canons have always served the needs of canon formers, from Thomas Wilson's *The Arte of Rhetorique* in 1553 to the present. The modern canon, we should not be surprised to learn, benefited its manufacturers, the modern professoriate. But they have benefited at large expense. As I hope I have demonstrated, Joyce's texts were denied any direct influence on their readers. To restore such power to Joyce's books we must abandon "genius" as a category of literary reputation.

If we accept that authors are merely images projected onto writers by readers, and if we project those images to justify our own habits of reading, then it could be argued that no image of the author can claim any more authority than another. We are stuck in the vicious circle that Barbara Herrnstein Smith describes in her treatment of how one set of beliefs succeed another: the hermeneutic circle that holds that no evidence is independent of belief. Beliefs do not change by bumping into "autonomous, observer-independent reality" like "facts, rocks, bricks, and texts-themselves" because we cannot observe anything without being prejudiced by our beliefs.[171] In that case, it would be beside the point to argue that one reputation is more accurate than another. To abandon Joyce the Genius for some other image is not to get closer to truth. It is merely to substitute my own beliefs regarding evidence for someone else's.

Smith escapes this sort of relativism by ascribing value according to the "serviceability" and "congeniality" of beliefs. She holds that "total escape from circularity may not be possible, [and] it may also not be, under all conditions and from all perspectives, either necessary or desireable."[172] As conditions change, beliefs are modified to accommodate those changes. Beliefs that were once serviceable and congenial become an impediment, so they are modified. This is a clever solution that would let me squirm out from under the implications of my own argument, for the belief that certain writers are geniuses was serviceable and congenial to critics for years, and I am pointing out that this belief—the belief in genius—no longer serves the academy.

But I cannot fail to notice that institutional forces—some of which are the very same I have sought to expose—may have directed me. For example, I said in my introduction that I chose these four "episodes" in the history of Joyce's reputation because they are particularly important. I do not retract that assertion, but I would be hypocritical if I failed to entertain the possibility that these episodes seem important because information about them was available to me and still largely unexploited by others. If Ellmann, thinking his papers were trivial, had tossed them in the trash; if they had never made their way to the University of Tulsa; if the University of Texas had never collected Ernst's papers; if Thomas Staley had thrown away the *JJQ* papers; if none of these materials had been available and waiting to be researched, I might never have felt that these particular episodes were important. The very availability of the materials begs scholars to make something of them. Likewise, my own habit of reading, which, following a general trend in criticism, puts literature into contexts, must influence my own beliefs about intention. No doubt there are other forces to which I am blind, which are best left to others to point out, if they feel my argument is worth correcting.

Even so, I do not think we need to despair of improving our view of writers' reputations. According to John Rodden,

> One of the most difficult problems for literary and cultural historians is to cast light on the making of a reputation as a social process while not ignoring that intrinsic, sometimes indefinable, aesthetic attributes of works contribute to authors' reputations. For we should neither reduce reputation merely to an interaction among institutional forces nor presume cynically that all established judgments are largely groundless, the products of ruling class "mystifications" which demand "unmasking" and "demythologizing." [173]

No doubt Smith would say that Rodden's trust in "intrinsic, sometimes indefineable, aesthetic attributes" betrays a naïveté. She might argue that Rodden begs the question of his own beliefs, to borrow Smith's phrase, because such judgments assume an autonomous, observer-independent aesthetic. So be it. My study breaks out of the hermeneutic circle by appealing to certain historical data as if they were facts, rocks, bricks. I have presented this evidence in a sincere (if naive) belief that a more accurate view of Joyce is possible.

Notes

Introduction

1. Frank Budgen, *James Joyce and the Making of "Ulysses"* (Bloomington: Indiana University Press, 1960), 115–116.

2. G. Thomas Tanselle, "Textual Criticism and Literary Sociology," *Studies in Bibliography* 44 (1991): 89.

3. Jerome McGann, *The Beauty of Inflections* (Oxford: Clarendon Press, 1985), 21.

4. Ibid., 24.

5. Jerome McGann, "The Monks and the Giants: Textual and Bibliographical Studies and the Interpretation of Literary Works," in *Textual Criticism and Literary Interpretation* (Chicago: University of Chicago Press, 1985), 192.

6. McGann, *Beauty of Inflections,* 24.

7. McGann, "Monks," 192.

8. Michel Foucault, *The Foucault Reader,* ed. Paul Rabinow (New York: Pantheon Books, 1984), 138.

9. Ibid., 127.

10. John Rodden, *The Politics of Literary Reputation: The Making and Claiming of "St. George" Orwell* (New York: Oxford University Press, 1989).

11. McGann, "Monks," 193.

12. Jon P. Klancher, *The Making of English Reading Audiences, 1790–1832* (Madison: University of Wisconsin Press, 1987), 9.

13. G. Thomas Tanselle suggests this analogy is appropriate to a textual study of literature. "Textual Criticism," 87.

14. "The elementary maneuvers for studying, understanding, and finally teaching [literary] works involve, first, an elucidation of the textual history of the work, and second, an explication of the reception history." McGann, "Monks," 194–195.

15. Carolyn Porter, "Are We Being Historical Yet?" *South Atlantic Quarterly* 87 (1988): 770.

16. Frank Lentricchia, "Foucault's Legacy: A New Historicism," in *The New Historicism,* ed. H. Aram Veeser (New York: Routledge, 1989), 235, 242.

17. Richard Levin, "The Poetics and Politics of Bardicide," *PMLA* 105 (May 1990): 492–498. In a subsequent defense of his article, Levin claimed to be attacking not new historicists but "new Marxists" (316). His distinction seems to me to be too fine to be meaningful. (See his reply to Daniel Boyarin's letter, *PMLA* 106 (March 1991): 315–316.)

18. Richard Brown, *James Joyce and Sexuality* (New York: Cambridge University Press, 1985), 2, 4, 8, 11.

19. Ibid., 12.

20. Levin identified this tendency as a problem general to new historicists. "Unthinkable Thoughts in the New Historicizing of English Renaissance Drama," *New Literary History* 21 (1990): 434.

21. See, for example, A. Walton Litz's "Pound and Eliot on *Ulysses*: The Critical Tradition," in *"Ulysses": Fifty Years,* ed. Thomas Staley (Bloomington: Indiana University Press, 1974), and the conclusion to Jeffrey Segall's *Joyce in America: Cultural Politics and the Trials of "Ulysses"* (Berkeley: University of California Press, 1993), 170–188.

22. Emer Nolan, *James Joyce and Nationalism* (New York: Routledge, 1995); Robert Spoo, *James Joyce and the Language of History* (New York: Oxford University Press, 1994); Thomas Hofheinz, *Joyce and the Invention of Irish History* (New York: Cambridge University Press, 1995); Maria Tymoczko, *The Irish Ulysses* (Berkeley: University of California Press, 1994); Enda Duffy, *The Subaltern Ulysses* (Minneapolis: University of Minnesota Press, 1994); Vincent Cheng, *Joyce, Race, and Empire* (New York: Cambridge University Press, 1995); and James Fairhall, *James Joyce and the Question of History* (New York: Cambridge University Press, 1993).

23. Segall, *Joyce in America;* Edward L. Bishop, "Re: Covering Ulysses," *JSA* (1994): 22–55.

24. Bishop, "Re: Covering Ulysses," 36. My treatment of this same letter (in Chapter 3) comes to a different conclusion from Bishop's: I hold that Joyce's refusal to include the scheme was not an attempt to stand aloof from his work, but an attempt to regain control over it. Bishop also treats Woolsey's and Ernst's prefaces to the Random House *Ulysses,* concluding that they threaten to make a "social document" of the novel. I argue the opposite: that these prefaces confirmed its status as a classic and thus as a work irrelevant to contemporary society. But all in all I find Bishop's work admirable and inspiring.

Chapter One: Joyce the Propagandist

1. Cleanth Brooks and William K. Wimsatt, *Literary Criticism: A Short History,* vol. 2, *Romantic and Modern Criticism,* Phoenix Edition (Chicago: University of Chicago Press, 1978), 468. This book was first published in 1957.

2. Richard Levin and Charles Shattuck, "First Flight to Ithaca," in *James Joyce: Two Decades of Criticism,* ed. Seon Givens (New York: Penguin Books, 1969), 297–303. Thomas Jackson Rice suggests that this method of reading *Dubliners* through *Ulysses* actually began with Valery Larbaud's prepublication promotion of Joyce's 1922 novel. "The Geometry of Meaning in *Dubliners*: A Euclidean Approach," *Style* 25 (1991): 393.

3. Marvin Magalaner and Richard M. Kain, *Joyce: The Man, the Work, the Reputation* (New York: New York University Press, 1956), 57.

4. Marvin Magalaner, "The Other Side of James Joyce," *The Arizona Quarterly* 9 (1953): 5.

5. Brewster Ghiselin, "The Unity of Joyce's Dubliners," in *Dubliners: Text, Criticism, and Notes,* ed. Robert Scholes and A. Walton Litz (New York: Penguin Books, 1969), 316–332.

6. Brenda Maddox, introduction to *Dubliners,* by James Joyce (New York: Bantam Books, 1990), xvi, xiv.

7. John S. Kelly, afterword to *Dubliners,* by Hans Gabler (New York: Vintage Books, 1993), 236.

8. See "James Joyce's 'Dubliners,'" *Style* 25 (Fall 1991). Trevor Williams's essay, "No Cheer for the 'Gratefully Oppressed' in Joyce's *Dubliners*" (416–438), and J. P. Riquelme's "Joyce's 'The Dead': The Dissolution of the Self and the Police" (488–505) are the exceptions in this volume.

9. For example, in *JJQ*'s *Dubliners* issue (*JJQ* 28 [Winter 1991]), Lea Baechler speaks of the "deceptively transparent surface" of the stories (361), and Jane Miller (in an essay I admire for other reasons) begins by assuring us that the "'simple surface' [of "A Mother"] hides a complex and subtle story" (407). In the *Dubliners* issue of *Style,* Sonja Bašić writes that "the simplicity of *Dubliners* is a trap: "[critics are] led on by the deceptive transparency of the stories" (351).

10. Stanislaus Joyce, "The Background to *Dubliners,*" *The Listener* 51, no. 1308 (25 March 1954): 527.

11. As Grattan Freyer puts it, "poetry and prose by Irish writers must aim at being read largely by an English audience or not at all." *W. B. Yeats and the Anti-Democratic Tradition* (Dublin: Gill and MacMillan, 1981), 39.

12. Joyce's dispute with the Dublin publisher George Roberts confirms this impression. As Ellmann reports, Joyce had his "A Curious History" letter, which detailed his publication difficulties, circulated to the Irish press. The letter concludes by appealing to "Irish public opinion" in the matter (*JJ* 315).

13. One of these few exceptions is Trevor Williams, who argues that "paralysis is ultimately determined by the particular form of government these characters labor under . . . and that the church, through its pervasive ideological domination, is complicit with the dominating state force." "No Cheer," 424.

14. See Margaret Chestnutt's excellent article, "Joyce's *Dubliners*: History, Ideology, and Social Reality," *Eire* 14 (1979): 93–105. Chestnutt states that "It was Joyce's merit that he could transmit so sensitively and convincingly the alienation felt by a particular class at a particular place and time, but it is unjustifiable to understand or interpret *Dubliners* as containing universal human truths" (94).

15. Kevin Sullivan, *Joyce among the Jesuits* (New York: Columbia University Press, 1958), 18.

16. Thomas Kettle, *The Day's Burden: Studies, Literary & Political and Miscellaneous Essays by Thomas Kettle,* 2nd ed. (Freeport, N.Y.: Books for Libraries Press, 1968), 117. First published in 1918.

17. Ibid., 112.

18. See L. M. Cullen, *An Economic History of Ireland Since 1660* (London: B. T. Batsford Ltd., 1972), 134–171.

19. The state of Dublin between the fall of Parnell in 1891 and the Easter Rising in 1916 has not escaped the notice of commentators, nor has Joyce's influence on our impressions of that era. Joseph V. O'Brien's *"Dear, Dirty Dublin": A City in Distress* (Berkeley: University of California Press, 1982) begins with Joyce's version of the city. F. S. L. Lyons's "James Joyce's Dublin" (*Twentieth Century Studies* [November 1970]: 6–25) takes issue with Joyce's narrow view of the city.

And most recently, Fairhall's excellent *James Joyce and the Question of History* includes an entire chapter on "The Paralyzed City." My historical work in this chapter has benefited especially from Fairhall.

20. Cf. Yeats's "Easter, 1916": "I have met them at close of day / Coming with vivid faces / From counter or desk among grey / Eighteenth-century houses." Chandler could well have been one of those whom Yeats met. *W. B. Yeats: The Poems*, ed. Richard J. Finneran, New ed. (New York: Macmillan, 1983), 180.

21. Cullen, *An Economic History*, 166 (cited by Chestnutt, "Joyce's *Dubliners*," 96).

22. John Hutchinson, *The Dynamics of Cultural Nationalism: The Gaelic Revival and the Creation of the Irish Nation State* (London: Allen and Unwin, 1987), 258–260, 269. As Hutchinson reports, "In 1911 only 30,000 Catholics out of a total school-going population of 705,000 went into secondary education, and at . . . University College Dublin, no more than 100 graduated in any year during the 1890s" (226).

23. F. S. L. Lyons, *Ireland Since the Famine* (London: Fontana Press, 1973), 94–97.

24. Kevin Sullivan, *Joyce among the Jesuits* (New York: Columbia University Press, 1958), 152.

25. Ibid., 158–162. Cf. Joseph Lee, *The Modernisation of Irish Society: 1848–1918*, vol. 10, of *The Gill History of Ireland* (Dublin: Gill and MacMillan, 1973), 128–129.

26. Ibid., 172–173.

27. For a discussion of Hannah Sheehy, one of the neglected women of Irish history, see Bonnie Kime Scott's "Hanna and Francis Sheehy-Skeffington: Reformers in the Company of Joyce," in *Joyce and His Contemporaries*, ed. Diana A. Ben-Merre and Maureen Murphy (New York: Greenwood Press, 1989), 77–84. For a longer discussion of this generation of UCD students, see James N. Meenan's "The Student Body," in *Struggle with Fortune: A Miscellany for the Centenary of the Catholic University of Ireland 1854–1954*, ed. Michael Tierney (Dublin: Browne and Nolan, 1955), 103–120.

28. For a discussion of the competitive feelings between students at UCD and Trinity, see Ulick O'Connor, *Celtic Dawn: A Portrait of the Irish Literary Renaissance* (London: Hamish Hamilton, 1984), 172. The official history of UCD, compiled by the Jesuits, describes the relations between the two schools as more congenial, observing that, while the "official attitude of Trinity to its cheeky rival" was not "favorable," at least "the younger men of the staff and the undergraduates usually appeared pleased to meet the Catholic students." In "The Passing of University College," in *A Page of Irish History: The Story of University College Dublin, 1883–1909* (Dublin: Talbot Press, 1930), 581–587.

29. Hutchinson, *Dynamics of Cultural Nationalism*, 259–262, 270. Catholics were better represented in the less prestigious positions of the intelligentsia: civil service officers and clerks, 59 percent; and schoolteachers, 62 percent.

30. Alexander Humphrey, *New Dubliners: Urbanization and the Irish Family* (New York: Fordham University Press, 1966), 49.

31. Hutchinson, *Dynamics of Cultural Nationalism*, 271, 277. Joseph Lee

also faults UCD for failing to induce Irish youth to enter the much-needed social science careers (*Modernisation of Irish Society,* 128–129). Hutchinson calls this the "blocked mobility" theory, which helps explain why so many of the young Catholic elite embraced radical politics. Clearly it would have contributed greatly to Joyce's sense of paralysis in Ireland.

32. Lyons, *Ireland Since the Famine,* 212. James Fairhall ably demonstrates how Joyce attacks this new "democracy" in "Ivy Day." "Colgan-Connolly: Another Look at the Politics of 'Ivy Day in the Committee Room,'" *JJQ* 25 (1988): 289–304.

33. John M. Feehan, *An Irish Publisher and His World* (Cork: The Mercier Press, 1969), 19–20. The best studies of the Irish book industry before this century are by Richard Cargill Cole (*Irish Booksellers and English Writers: 1740–1800* [London: Mansell Publishing, 1986]) and M. Pollard (*Dublin's Trade in Books: 1550–1800,* Lyrell Lectures, 1986–1987 [Oxford: Clarendon Press, 1989]), who both focus on the eighteenth century. Histories of the industry in the nineteenth century are conspicuously nonexistent, because, as I will point out, there was little industry to speak of for most of those years.

34. Pollard, *Dublin's Trade in Books,* 197.

35. See Cole, *Irish Booksellers and English Writers,* 24–25.

36. Pollard, *Dublin's Trade in Books,* 217.

37. Ibid., 162.

38. See Cole, *Irish Booksellers and English Writers,* 148.

39. Pollard, *Dublin's Trade in Books,* 152.

40. Cole, *Irish Booksellers and English Writers,* 153.

41. Grattan Freyer, *W. B. Yeats and the Anti-Democratic Tradition* (Dublin: Gill and MacMillan, 1981), 38–39.

42. Cf. Maurice Colgan, "Exotics or Provincials? Anglo-Irish Writers and the English Problem," in *Literary Interrelations: Ireland, England and the World,* ed. Wolfgang Zach and Heinz Kosok, vol. 3 of *Studies in English and Comparative Literature* (Tübingen: Gunter Narr Verlag, 1987).

43. For information about the Cuala Press, see Liam Miller's *The Dun Emer Press, Later the Cuala Press,* New Yeats Papers VII (Dublin: Dolmen Press, 1973). I thank David Holdeman for pointing out this source to me.

44. Hutchinson, *Dynamics of Cultural Nationalism,* 163.

45. Hutchinson, *Dynamics of Cultural Nationalism,* 163. Young Ireland was the nationalist movement of Irish intellectuals, distinguished from Daniel O'Connell's program by its militancy, which led to the ill-fated 1848 insurrection. See Lyons, *Ireland Since the Famine,* 104–138 and R. F. Foster, *Modern Ireland: 1600–1972* (New York: Penguin, 1988), 310–317.

46. Freyer, *W. B. Yeats,* 39.

47. Hutchinson, *Dynamics of Cultural Nationalism,* 163. For Hyde's influence on Joyce, see R. Tracy, "Mr. Joker and Mr. Hyde: Joyce's Politic Polyglot Polygraphs," *LIT,* 1 (1989): 151–169.

48. Denis Donoghue, *We Irish: Essays on Irish Literature and Society* (New York: Alfred A. Knopf, 1986), 55–56. See also Yeats's notes for *Responsibilities* in *W. B. Yeats: The Poems,* ed. Richard J. Finneran (New York: Macmillan,

1983), 593–594. For a discussion of Yeats's "idea of class," see Elizabeth Cullingford's *Yeats, Ireland and Fascism* (New York: New York University Press, 1980), 64–84.

49. My own views derive, to a large extent, from these critics. See Field Day Theatre Company, ed., *Ireland's Field Day* (London: Hutchinson, 1985), which includes essays by critics Seamus Deane, Declan Kiberd, and Richard Kearney, as well as by poets Tom Paulin and Seamus Heaney. Kiberd and Deane have published a number of works re-evaluating the effect of the revival on Ireland, the most important, of course, the colossal three-volume *The Field Day Anthology of Irish Literature*, edited by Deane (Derry: Field Day Publications, 1991). I am surprised to find myself in disagreement with Seamus Deane over his introduction to "Araby," which claims the story "is neither 'realistic' nor 'symbolic.' It treads the previously invisible path between these apparently opposed modes of writing, thereby becoming a mode unique to itself" (Vol. III, 20). See also David Cairns and Shaun Richards's *Writing Ireland: Colonialism, Nationalism and Culture* (Manchester: Manchester University Press, 1988).

50. Margaret Chestnutt makes similar distinctions in her discussion of *Dubliners,* using "Jurgen Habermas's theory of the growth of bourgeois public opinion." See especially "Joyce's *Dubliners,*" 98–100.

51. Hutchinson, *Dynamics of Cultural Nationalism,* 152.

52. Ibid., 12.

53. Ibid., 4.

54. Ibid., 2, 9.

55. Ibid., 9.

56. Aubrey Gwynn, "The Jesuit Fathers and University College," in *Struggle with Fortune: A Miscellany for the Centenary of the Catholic University of Ireland 1854–1954,* ed. Michael Tierney (Dublin: Browne and Nolan, 1955), 46.

57. Clery, "Passing of University College," 585.

58. Eugene Sheehy, *May It Please the Court.* (Dublin: C. J. Fallon, Ltd., 1951), 19.

59. Hutchinson, *Dynamics of Cultural Nationalism,* 284.

60. Ibid.

61. Ibid., 282.

62. For a list of the salons, see Lyons, "Joyce's Dublin," 10.

63. George Russell, *Letters from AE,* ed. Alan Denson. (New York: Abelard-Schuman, 1961), 42.

64. Ibid., 43.

65. Ibid., 50.

66. Ibid., 55–56.

67. Ulick O'Connor, *Celtic Dawn: A Portrait of the Irish Literary Renaissance* (London: Hamish Hamilton, 1984), 177.

68. Deborah M. Averill, *The Irish Short Story from George Moore to Frank O'Connor* (Washington, D.C.: University Press of America, 1982), 15.

69. Richard Fallis, *The Irish Renaissance* (Syracuse: Syracuse University Press, 1977), 138.

70. Ibid., 138.

71. Ibid., 139.

72. Averill, *Irish Short Story,* 15.

73. Patrick Rafroidi, "The Irish Short Story in English. The Birth of a New Tradition," in *The Irish Short Story,* Cahiers Irlandais, nos. 7 and 8, ed. Terence Brown and Patrick Rafroidi (France: Publications de l'université de Lille III), 35.

74. John Wilson Foster, *Fictions of the Irish Literary Revival: A Changeling Art* (Syracuse, N.Y.: Syracuse University Press, 1987), xix.

75. See Foster, *Fictions of the Irish Literary Revival,* 155.

76. Lea Baechler, "Voices of Unexpected Lyricism in Two Dubliners Stories," *JJQ* 28 (1991): 361.

77. Ibid., 364.

78. See Lyons, *Ireland Since the Famine,* 207–216, and R. F. Foster, *Modern Ireland,* 434–436.

79. Russell, *Letters of AE,* 97.

80. For a description of conciliation, see Lyons, *Ireland Since the Famine,* 211–212, 217.

81. Lyons, *Ireland Since the Famine,* 50.

82. After *Dubliners* was composed, these acts were concluded with acts in 1907 and 1909 which compelled landlords to sell off their estates. Cf. Cullen, *An Economic History,* 154.

83. Cf. Brendan M. Walsh, "Marriage Rates and Population Pressure: Ireland, 1871–1911," *The Economic History Review* 23 (1970): 158; Lee, *Modernisation of Irish Society,* 14; and Lyons, *Ireland Since the Famine,* 51–52. See Cullen, *An Economic History,* 137–141, for an account of the increasing numbers of proprietary farmers in the five decades after the famine.

84. This proclamation is printed on the back cover of the 1902 Christmas issue of *The Irish Homestead* called *A Celtic Christmas.*

85. Facsimiles of these original stories have been republished in the *James Joyce Archive,* ed. Michael Groden, et al. (New York and London: Garland Publishing, 1978–).

86. See Lyons, *Ireland Since the Famine,* 207–216; and R. F. Foster, *Modern Ireland,* 434–436.

87. Henry Summerfield, introduction to *Selections from the Contributions to "The Irish Homestead" by G. W. Russell—AE,* vol. 1 (Atlantick Highlands, N.J.: Humanities Press, 1978), 31.

88. Hutchinson, *Dynamics of Cultural Nationalism,* 143.

89. Ibid., 138–139.

90. Lady Augusta Gregory, "A Story of the Country of the Dead," *The Irish Homestead: A Celtic Christmas.* (December 1902): 15.

91. Averill, *Irish Short Story,* 21. Cf. Vivien Mercier, "The Irish Short Story and Oral Tradition," in *The Celtic Cross: Studies in Irish Culture and Literature,* ed. Ray B Browne, et al. (Purdue: Purdue University Studies, 1964); and Declan Kiberd, "Story-Telling: The Gaelic Tradition," in *The Irish Short Story,* ed. Patrick Rafroidi and Terence Brown (Gerrards Cross, Buckinghamshire: Colin Smythe, 1979). Both of these are quoted in Averill's introduction, which provides a useful overview of the short story tradition in Ireland and how it has been defined.

92. Gregory, "Story of the Country," 15.

93. Averill, *Irish Short Story,* 21.

94. James Joyce, "After the Race," *The Irish Homestead* (17 December 1904): 1038.

95. James Joyce, "The Sisters," *The Irish Homestead* (13 August 1904): 676.

96. Ibid., 677.

97. Ibid.

98. James Joyce, "Eveline," *The Irish Homestead* (10 September 1904): 761.

99. Gregory, "Story of the Country," 16.

100. See also Albert Soloman's comparison of "Eveline" to George Moore's *Evelyn Innes,* "The Backgrounds of "Eveline," *Eire-Ireland* 6 (1971): 23–38, especially 31–36.

101. K. F. Purdon, "Match-Making in Ardenoo," *The Irish Homestead* (December 1902): 12–15.

102. Florence Walzl, "*Dubliners*: Women in Irish Society," in *Women in Joyce,* ed. Suzette Henke and Elaine Unkeless (Chicago: University of Illinois Press, 1982), 31–55.

103. Hugh Kenner writes: Joyce's "connection with the *Homestead* lapsed; not that implicit blasphemy was discerned, but there were letters of complaint. Readers of 'Our Weekly Story' were accustomed to a positive note." "Signs on a White Field," in *James Joyce: The Centennial Symposium,* ed. Morris Beja, et al. (Chicago: University of Illinois Press, 1986), 211.

104. Stanislaus Joyce, "Early Memories of James Joyce," *The Listener* 41, no. 1061 (26 May 1949): 896.

105. For a short discussion of Joyce's liberalism, see Sidney Feshbach's review of Dominic Manganiello's *Joyce's Politics, JJQ* 19 (1982): 208–213. Feshbach suggests that John Stuart Mill and John Ruskin strongly influenced Joyce's politics and art.

106. R. F. Foster, *Modern Ireland,* 428.

107. James Joyce, *Ulysses* (New York: Random House, 1961), 331.

108. Humphrey, *New Dubliners,* 195.

109. James Meenan, *The Irish Economy Since 1922* (Liverpool: Liverpool University Press, 1970), 16.

110. *CW,* 168, and Paul Delany, "Joyce's Political Development and the Aesthetic of *Dubliners,*" *College English* 34 (1972): 261.

111. Manganiello, *Joyce's Politics,* 85–86.

112. Paul Delany notes a similar sentiment in Joyce's 1907 lecture, "Ireland, Island of Saints and Scholars," except that it is the "individual initiative" that is paralyzed in Ireland, not economic prospects: "No one who has any self-respect stays in Ireland," Joyce wrote (*CW,* 171). As I argue, "individual initiative" was paralyzed not by "centuries of useless struggle and broken treaties" with England, as Delany would have it, but by the economic status of Joyce's class. "Joyce's Political Development," 257.

113. Hutchinson, *Dynamics of Cultural Nationalism,* 270.

114. Cullen, *An Economic History,* 147.

115. For a fuller treatment of "A Mother" in a similar vein, see Jane Miller's "'O, she's a nice lady!': A Rereading of 'A Mother,'" *JJQ,* 28 (1991): 407–426. Joe Valente's analysis of "A Mother," the best interpretation I have read, dis-

cusses gender conflict in the story, reflected in the clash of domestic and business discourses ("Joyce's Sexual Differend: An Example from *Dubliners*," *JJQ* 28 [1991]: 427–444). Mrs. Kearney's need to be "ladylike" would then designate a gender, not a class imperative. I do not think my reading contradicts Valente's. Indeed, the pseudo-feudal role of "lady" forced on women in a business-oriented society probably compelled middle-class women to assume identities that were untenable on two counts: a domestic identity in a world of public affairs and a feudal identity in a world of commerce.

116. David Pierce similarly treats *Dubliners* as Joyce's attack on class superiority in *James Joyce's Ireland*, (New Haven: Yale University Press, 1992), 98–103.

117. Chestnutt also attributes paralysis in *Dubliners* to the material conditions of the city. But ultimately she holds that *Dubliners* exhorts its readers to flee Ireland rather than to change society. "Joyce's *Dubliners*," 105.

118. James Fairhall, "Big-Power Politics and Colonial Economics: The Gordon Bennett Cut Race and 'After the Race,'" *JJQ* 28 (1991): 387.

119. Ibid., 389–395. Cf. Yeats's "To a Wealthy Man who promised a second Subscription to the Dublin Municipal Gallery if it were proved the People wanted Pictures," which similarly complains of a lack of philanthropy among Dublin's wealthy and holds up for example the capitalist patrons of art in Renaissance Italy. Yeats, *The Poems,* 107–108.

120. Fairhall, "Big-Power Politics," 391.

121. Ibid., 395.

122. Ibid., 389.

123. Lyons, *Ireland Since the Famine,* 274. Cf. Connolly, *Selected Political Writings of James Connolly,* ed. Owen Dudley Edwards and Bernard Ransom. Writings of the Left, gen. ed. Ralph Miliband (New York: Grove Press, 1973), 261–263.

124. Manganiello, *Joyce's Politics,* 128.

125. Robert Scholes, "Joyce and Modernist Ideology," in *Coping with Joyce: Essays from the Copenhagen Symposium,* ed. Morris Beja and Shari Benstock (Columbus: Ohio State University Press, 1989), 102.

126. Owen Edwards and Bernard Ransom, introduction to *Selected Political Writings of James Connolly,* 17.

127. Lyons, *Ireland Since the Famine,* 273.

128. Manganiello, *Joyce's Politics,* 126.

129. Fairhall discusses the Dublin Corporation's "reputation for malfeasance." In particular, he suggests that "Dublin's noxious tenements were the Corporation's heaviest responsibility." "Big-Power Politics and Colonial Economics: The Gordon Bennett Cut Race and 'After the Race,'" *JJQ* 28 (1991): 298.

130. Manganiello, *Joyce's Politics,* 127.

131. Brenda Maddox, *Nora: The Real Life of Molly Bloom* (Boston: Houghton Mifflin Company, 1988), 27.

132. Richard Brown, in *Joyce and Sexuality* (New York: Cambridge University Press, 1985), 50, argues that Joyce's fiction took part in the public, widespread, and ongoing debate over sexuality and marriage, and that he was influenced by advances in "the new science of sexuality."

133. Stanislaus Joyce, "Early Memories," 897.

134. Roy Gottfried recently analyzed Joyce's style in his article, "'Scrupulous meanness' Reconsidered: *Dubliners* as Stylistic Parody," in *Joyce in Context*, ed. Vincent J. Cheng and Timothy Martin (Cambridge: Cambridge University Press, 1992), 153–169. Gottfried's discussion is careful and thoughtful, but I think it repeats the familiar mistake of reading *Dubliners* through Joyce's later work.

Chapter Two: *The Egoist's Joyce*

1. The letter is published in *Pound/Joyce: The Letters of Ezra Pound to James Joyce, with Pound's Essays on Joyce,* ed. Forrest Read, (New York: New Directions, 1967), 17–18, and is reprinted in *JJ*, 349–350. A portion of this chapter was published in the *James Joyce Literary Supplement* (Spring 1933): 21–23.

2. Hugh Kenner, *The Pound Era* (Berkeley: University of California Press, 1971), 279.

3. Ezra Pound, *The Letters of Ezra Pound*, ed. D. D. Paige (London: Faber and Faber, n.d), 70–72.

4. Ibid., 82–83.

5. Ibid., 100–101.

6. *The New Freewoman,* 15 June 1913, 10.

7. Ibid., 5.

8. Ibid., 11.

9. Ibid., 12–15.

10. Ibid., 17–18.

11. See J. J. Wilhelm, *Ezra Pound in London and Paris: 1908–1925* (University Park: Pennsylvania State University Press, 1990), 118.

12. Shari and Bernard Benstock, "The Role of Little Magazines in the Emergence of Modernism," *The Library Chronicle* 20 (1991): 76.

13. *The New Freewoman,* 15 December 1913, 244.

14. *Letters of Ezra Pound,* 70.

15. Marsden's discussions of politics evolve from almost seditious exhortation in 1914 to a benign sort of criticism that does not much approve political action.

16. Ezra Pound, "The Serious Artist," *The New Freewoman,* 15 October 1913, 161–163; 1 November 1913, 194–195; and 15 November 1913, (213–214). Citations will refer to the reprint in *Literary Essays of Ezra Pound* (New York: New Directions, 1968), 41–57.

17. Ibid., 47, 56.

18. Ibid., 45, 46.

19. Ibid., 55, 57.

20. Ibid., 46.

21. Ibid., 45.

22. Ibid.

23. Frederick Hartt, *Art: A History of Painting, Sculpture, Architecture,* 3rd ed. (Englewood Cliffs, N.J.: Prentice-Hall, 1989), 198.

24. *Literary Essays of Ezra Pound,* 56.

25. *The New Freewoman,* 15 December 1913, 214.

26. *Letters of Ezra Pound,* 70–71.

27. *The New Freewoman,* 15 December 1913, 244–245.

28. Ezra Pound to R. Aldington, 16 March [1922], Texas.

29. Pound to Aldington, no date, Texas.

30. T. S. Eliot, *The Letters of T. S. Eliot, Volume I, 1898–1922*, ed. Valerie Eliot (New York: Harcourt Brace Jovanovich, 1988), 536, 598–603.

31. Ezra Pound, "On Criticism in General," *Criterion* 1 (January 1923): 143.

32. "Notice to Readers," *The Egoist*, December 1919, 71.

33. I should note that the emphasis this "Notice to Readers" gives to the duty of geniuses to explain themselves to the masses suggests that it was penned by Harriet Shaw Weaver, not by Eliot. As I hope to demonstrate, Eliot's views of the duties of geniuses were not nearly so democratic.

34. *The Egoist*, June–July 1918, 84.

35. "Ulysses, Order, and Myth," *Dial* 75 (November 1923): 481. Rpt. in *James Joyce: Two Decades of Criticism*. Ed. Seon Givens. (New York, Vanguard Press, 1948): 198–203.

36. "Tradition and the Individual Talent," *The Egoist* (September 1919): 55. Rpt. in Eliot's *The Sacred Wood* (New York: Methuen, 1983), 47–59.

37. Ibid.

38. Ibid.

39. *The Egoist*, December 1919, 72.

40. Ibid., 73.

41. Ibid., 72.

42. 41–42.

43. *The Egoist*, February 1917, 22.

44. *Literary Essays of Ezra Pound*, 402.

45. Ibid., 400–401.

46. Ibid., 401.

47. Ibid.

48. Stanislaus Joyce, "The Background to *Dubliners*," 526.

49. *Literary Essays of Ezra Pound*, 401.

50. *The Egoist*, February 1917, 22.

51. Lyons, *Ireland Since the Famine*, 282–284.

52. "Views and Comments," *The Egoist*, 1 January 1914, 4–5.

53. "England and Ireland," *The Egoist*, 1 June 1916, 84–85.

54. For details concerning the publication history of *Dubliners*, see John J. Slocum and Herbert Cahoon, *A Bibliography of James Joyce* (New Haven: Yale University Press, 1953), 12–18.

55. Archives of Grant Richards, 1897–1948 (Cambridge, England, 1979), reel 48, vol. 5.

56. The Egoist Press sold only 332 of 1,000 copies (500 unbound) before it "disposed of the book to Jonathan Cape in 1924." Slocum and Cahoon, *Bibliography of James Joyce*, 17.

57. Slocum and Cahoon, *Bibliography of James Joyce*, 16–22.

58. Timothy D. Murray, "The Modern Library," in *American Literary Publishing Houses 1900–1980: Trade and Paperback*, ed. Peter Dzwonskoski, *DLB* 46 (Detroit: Bruccoli Clark, 1986), 194.

59. B. W. Huebsch, "Footnotes to a Publisher's Life," *The Colophon* 2 (1936–1937): 406.

60. Ibid., 418.

61. See G. Thomas Tanselle, "In Memoriam: B. W. Huebsch," *Antiquarian Bookman* 36 (30 August 1965): 727–728.

62. Ann McCullough, "Joyce's Early Publishing History," in *James Joyce: The Centennial Symposium,* ed. Morris Beja, et al. (Chicago: Chicago University Press, 1986), 186–187.

63. Slocum and Cahoon, *Bibliography of James Joyce,* 17–19.

64. Murray, "The Modern Library," 242.

65. Slocum and Cahoon, *Bibliography of James Joyce,* 15.

66. Herbert Gorman, introduction to *A Portrait of the Artist as a Young Man* (New York: The Modern Library, 1928): vi.

67. Ibid., xi.

68. Ibid., xii.

69. *The Egoist,* March 1918, 39.

70. Ibid.

71. Ibid.

Chapter Three: Ernst's Joyce

1. Jane Heap, "Art and the Law," in *The Little Review Anthology,* ed. Margaret Anderson (New York: Hermitage House, 1953), 302. This article appeared originally in the September–December 1920 issue of *The Little Review.*

2. See Jackson R. Bryer, "Joyce, *Ulysses,* and the *Little Review,*" *South Atlantic Quarterly* 66(1967): 153. This article is the best study of the role of *The Little Review* in publishing *Ulysses.* I thank Jayne Marek for directing me to the article.

3. Margaret Anderson, *My Thirty Years War* (New York: Covici, Friede, 1930), 218.

4. See Edward de Grazia, *Girls Lean Back Everywhere: The Law of Obscenity and the Assault on Genius* (New York: Random House, 1992), 7; and Paul S. Boyer, *Purity in Print: The Vice Society Movement and Book Censorship in America* (New York: Charles Scribner's Sons, 1968), 56. Boyer's book remains the best history of the vice societies in America in the twenties and thirties.

5. After legally arresting one bookseller, a Mr. Seiffer, Sumner refused to allow him to call his lawyer and had two police officers escort him to his apartment building. The officers dragged him upstairs and forced him to let them into his apartment, where, in front of his mother, they searched and seized hundreds of volumes. The court transcript of this case is preserved in the Ernst collection, box 385. In nearly every case I have reviewed, Sumner overstepped his powers of seizure, and, when he was ordered to return property by the courts, he found ways to avoid doing so for years, to the great inconvenience of his victims.

6. One issue in 1917 was seized by the post office for a story by Wyndham Lewis, and Anderson unabashedly criticized publishers for capitulating to Sumner. See de Grazia, *Girls Lean Back,* 693–694.

7. The comparison to a farce is Anderson's. See *The Little Review Anthology,* 305.

8. Anderson, *My Thirty Years War,* 207. According to Pound, Yeats described Quinn as "the kindest, most generous, most irascible" of men (217).

9. Ibid., 216–217.

10. Ibid., 215.

11. Ibid., *My Thirty Years War*, 220.

12. He used this technique before in the celebrated 1919 *Jurgen* case, with equally lackluster results. See Boyer, *Purity in Print*, 76.

13. Irving Younger's *"Ulysses" in Court: The Litigation Surrounding the First Publication of James Joyce's Novel in the United States*, Classics of the Classroom 16 (Minnetonka, Minnesota: The Professional Education Group, 1988), 14. Younger's book is a transcript of his lecture on the *Ulysses* case and is told from Quinn's point of view. De Grazia suggests that Quinn lost the case because he was an old-school lawyer who did not argue the case on its constitutional grounds (de Grazia, *Girls Lean Back Everywhere*, 16n.), but it is as unjust to fault Quinn as it is to fault Anderson and Heap. No court would have ruled in his . favor on constitutional grounds in 1921. At any rate, Quinn hardly could have faulted Anderson and Heap for distributing Joyce, since, as Anderson has noted, he supplied them with a $1,600 endowment primarily to publish *Ulysses* (*My Thirty Years War*, 215). Younger probably based this argument on Quinn's letter to Pound, 16 October 1920, which makes the same point. This letter, quoted by Bryer (Bryer, "Joyce, *Ulysses*, and the *Little Review*," 156), is at the Northwestern University Library.

14. See Anderson, ed., *The Little Review Anthology*, 301.

15. Younger, *"Ulysses" in Court*, 9.

16. Anderson, *My Thirty Years War*, 220.

17. Anderson, *My Thirty Years War*, qtd. in de Grazia, *Girls Lean Back*, 11. As I'll discuss below, Ernst's defense of *Ulysses* twelve years later depended on his ability to raise this issue in court.

18. Anderson, *My Thirty Years War*, 212.

19. Anderson, *My Thirty Years War*, 214; and *The Little Review Anthology*, 299.

20. Anderson, ed., *The Little Review Anthology*, 297; and *My Thirty Years War*, 214.

21. Anderson, ed., *The Little Review Anthology*, 297.

22. See Bryer, "Joyce, *Ulysses*, and the *Little Review*," 153.

23. Anderson, ed., *The Little Review Anthology*, 303.

24. Anderson, *My Thirty Years War*, 228.

25. *New York Times*, 23 February 1921, 12. Qtd. in de Grazia, *Girls Lean Back*, 14.

26. Anderson, *My Thirty Years War*, 226.

27. Sylvia Beach, *Shakespeare and Company* (Lincoln: University of Nebraska Press, 1956), 87.

28. Ibid., 90–91.

29. See Ellmann, *James Joyce* (New York: Oxford University Press, 1959), 586, for the text of the petition.

30. See Beach, *Shakespeare and Company*, 96. Beach contends that the books "probably drowned like so many kittens in New York Harbor."

31. "Sumner Drive Traps Five as Obscene Booksellers," *New York Evening Post*, 17 September 1928.

32. W. G. Rogers, *Wise Men Fish Here* (New York: Harcourt, Brace, 1965), 146. In 1930, after Moss left Gotham, Steloff tried to establish a more cordial relationship with Sumner. When he saw a volume of *Venus and Tannhauser* in her catalogue, illustrated by the infamous Anne Tice, he wrote her a letter telling her it was actionable. She referred the letter to Greenbaum for advice and thanked Sumner sincerely for his courteous way of dealing with the matter. [Frances Steloff to Edward Greenbaum, 21 November 1930, Ernst collection, box 391]. Her overtures were not successful, for he had her arrested the next year for selling *Hsi Men Ching* and *From a Turkish Harem,* as I will discuss below.

33. Ernst collection, box 391.

34. John Sumner to Norman Levy, 8 September 1928, Ernst collection, box 391.

35. Sumner to Greenbaum, 28 March 1929, Ernst collection, box 391.

36. Sumner to Greenbaum, 2 May 1930, Ernst collection, box 391.

37. Kenneth Stevens writes, "Roth avoided difficulties with the censors by bowdlerizing Joyce's text." Moscato and LeBlanc, eds., *"Ulysses* on Trial," in *The United States of America v. One Book Entitled "Ulysses" by James Joyce* (Frederick, Maryland: University Publications of America, 1984), 61. First published in *Library Chronicle* 20/21 (1982). I have not been able to find a transcript of Knox's opinion against Roth in this case, and, since it was a relatively minor matter, a transcript probably was not made.

38. Sumner to Greenbaum, 2 May 1930, Ernst collection, box 391.

39. Greenbaum to Sumner, 23 May 1930, Ernst collection, box 391.

40. Beach, *Shakespeare and Company,* 201.

41. This information is culled from a typescript of a number of 1961 interviews with Ernst concerning his family history. The typescript, which I will call "Family History," is in box 877 of the Ernst collection. This quotation is from page 9.

42. Years after the *Ulysses* trial, he invited Woolsey, another yachtsman, to sail with him down to the Caribbean. Woolsey declined the invitation.

43. The quotations are taken from Blanchard's syndicated column that appeared in newspapers around the country on 22 December 1933. The column, without accompanying bibliographic information, is preserved in the Ernst collection, box 243. Ernst's impact on New York society is confirmed by Younger, *"Ulysses" in Court,* 20–21.

44. Younger, *"Ulysses" in Court,* 20.

45. Morris Ernst, "Family History," 387. Ernst collection, box 877.

46. See, for example, his and William Seagle's *To the Pure . . . A Study of Obscenity and the Censor* (New York: Viking, 1929); and his and Alan U. Schwartz's *Censorship: The Search for the Obscene* (New York: Macmillan, 1964). For more recent, but certainly derivative, accounts, see Charles Rembar's introduction to *Obscenity: The Complete Oral Arguments Before the Supreme Court in the Major Obscenity Cases,* ed. Leon Friedman (New York: Chelsea House, 1970), ix-xxii; Frederick F. Schauer, *The Law of Obscenity* (Washington, D.C.: The Bureau of National Affairs, 1976); Jay E. Daily, *The Anatomy of*

Censorship (New York: Marcel Dekker, 1973); Edward de Grazia's *Censorship Landmarks* (New York: Bowker, 1969) and *Girls Lean Back*.

47. Part of this decision is reprinted in Ernst and Schwartz, *Censorship*, 12–13. Unless otherwise noted, this brief review of obscenity law is culled from that book.

48. Ibid., 23–24. American obscenity law, which depends so heavily upon precedent, borrows freely across the Atlantic, and such tests as the Lord Campbell Act and the later Hicklin rule were adopted readily by American judges.

49. The appointment was unpaid, but, in accordance with the practice of sheriff appointments, Comstock secured a percentage of the fines levied in cases he brought before the court.

50. Ernst claims the book was *Sister Carrie* (Ernst and Schwartz, *Censorship*, 53), though it seems more probable that it was *The Genius*, as Paul Boyer reports (*Purity in Print*, 86).

51. With this strategy Ernst consciously followed the lead of a 1921 case involving *A Young Girl's Diary*, which included a preface in which Sigmund Freud declared its supreme importance as a document of adolescent female psychology. See Boyer, *Purity in Print*, 79–81.

52. *Brief: Magistrate's Court*, 3, 8, Ernst collection, box 90.

53. Ibid., 8.

54. *People v. Brewer and Warren, Inc.*, Ernst collection, box 90.

55. Materials concerning these cases are in the Ernst collection, box 94.

56. Ironically, this is the same Samuel Roth who pirated *Ulysses* in the 1920s.

57. See the Ernst collection, box 94.

58. Ernst and Seagle, *To the Pure*, 191.

59. Ibid., 28–29.

60. Ibid., 59. Ernst's class analysis has been reaffirmed by recent writers.

61. The first *Index Librorum Prohibitorum* was established in 1559 (Ernst and Seagle, *To the Pure*, 141).

62. Ibid. 30.

63. As Raymond Williams has pointed out, the term "classic," even as applied to literature, is rooted in designations of social hierarchy. *Key Words: A Vocabulary of Culture and Society*. Rev. ed. (New York: Oxford University Press, 1983), 60–69.

64. Ernst and Seagle, *To the Pure*, 56.

65. The protection of women as a separate class from the poor is a further complication. Such protection is based, I suppose, not on their greater susceptibility to corruption but on a greater horror (in male judges and male secretaries of vice societies) at such "corruptions" when they do take place.

66. Quoted in "Re: Covering *Ulysses*," *JSA* (1994): 22. Jerome J. McGann, ed., *Historical Studies and Literary Criticism* (Madison: University of Wisconsin Press, 1985), 4.

67. M[orris] L[.] E[rnst] to B. W. Huebsch, 21 October 1931. Rpt. in Moscato and LeBlanc, eds., *United States v. "Ulysses,"* 100. Unless otherwise noted, letters and memos concerning the *Ulysses* case of 1931–1934 are preserved in the Ernst collection, boxes 269–270 at the Harry Ransom Humanities Research

Center of the University of Texas at Austin. Nearly without exception these are reprinted in Moscato and LeBlanc.

68. I do not know what Ernst had against Guinzberg. Possibly they had had a falling out over the publication of Ernst's own *To the Pure*, which Viking had brought out three years earlier.

69. In a letter dated 19 July 1931, Joyce described that offer to Beach, another from Harpers, and his English and American contracts for *Work in Progress*, and said, "If you dislike or disapprove of Vikings [*sic*] offer wire me so early on Monday as I must sign or decline that afternoon." *James Joyce's Letters to Sylvia Beach*, ed. Melissa Banta and Oscar A. Silverman (Bloomington: Indiana University Press, 1987), 173–174.

70. A facsimile of this contract appears in Beach's *Shakespeare and Company*, 203.

71. Ibid., 204.

72. Stuart Gilbert, *Reflections on James Joyce: Stuart Gilbert's Paris Journal*, ed. Thomas Staley and Randolph Lewis (Austin: University of Texas Press, 1993), 43.

73. Beach, *Shakespeare and Company*, 202.

74. Ernst to Bennett Cerf, 21 December 1931, Ernst collection, box 269.

75. Beach, *Shakespeare and Company*, 205.

76. Ibid., 204. The spokesman was probably Robert Kastor, the brother of Joyce's daughter-in-law Helen (see Bennett Cerf, "Publishing *Ulysses*," *Contempo* 3 (15 February 1934): 2 [qtd. in de Grazia, *Girls Lean Back*, 28]).

77. Beach, *Shakespeare and Company*, 204–205.

78. Ellmann does not cite his source, but it probably was Cerf's, "Publishing *Ulysses*."

79. Cerf, "Publishing *Ulysses*," 2. Qtd. in de Grazia's *Girls Lean Back*, 28.

80. In *At Random*, Cerf gives Ernst a little more credit: "I had heard Morris Ernst, the great lawyer, say one night that the banning of *Ulysses* was a disgrace and that he'd like to wage a fight to legalize it. So in March, 1932, I had lunch with Ernst and said, 'If I can get Joyce signed up to do an American edition of *Ulysses*, will you fight the case for us in court?'" (New York: Random House, 1977), 90. Obviously this remark contradicts his other story about Kastor.

81. Cerf sent this contract to Kastor with a lengthy letter explaining its provisions. Both are published in Moscato and LeBlanc, eds., *United States v. "Ulysses,"* 102–107.

82. See also Cerf, *At Random*, 94. Their fear of multiple prosecutions was not paranoia: after losing a case in one venue under one set of obscenity laws, Sumner sometimes prosecuted in another venue under parallel laws. For example, in 1933, he lost in an attempt to hold the Vanguard Press liable for publishing *Female*, but then won in his prosecution of a bookstore for selling the same book. The difference was location: the press was in Manhattan, while the bookstore was in Queens. (See the Ernst collection, box 94, for papers concerning *Female*.)

83. See Cerf, *At Random*, 94.

84. Moscato and LeBlanc include a list of these experts as Exhibit A in the "Petition for Release and Admission of Book into the United States on the Ground that it is a Classic" (*United States v. "Ulysses,"* 190–192). Moscato and

LeBlanc's reprint of the *Preliminary Memorandum* does not include attached documents, but almost certainly those documents included this list. I discuss this exhibit—and its implications for the constitution of Joyce's audience—in greater detail below.

85. Cerf, *At Random*, 92–93.

86. See the Ernst collection, box 94.

87. All the records regarding *The Story-Teller's Holiday* are in the Ernst collection, box 95.

88. Assistant Collector of Customs to Ernest Bates and Greenbaum, Wolff, and Ernst, Ernst collection, box 95.

89. Petition for the importation of *The Story-Teller's Holiday* as a classic, Ernst collection, box 95.

90. Ibid.

91. Frank Dow, Acting Commissioner of Customs, to the Collector of Customs, 29 December 1932, Ernst collection, box 95.

92. Alexander Lindey to the National Council on Freedom from Censorship, 30 December 1932, Ernst collection, box 95.

93. Assistant Collector of Customs to Alexander Lindey, 31 January 1933, Ernst collection, box 95.

94. Lindey to Collector of Customs, 3 February 1933, Ernst collection, box 95.

95. Lindey to the National Council on Cenorship [*sic*], 8 September 1934, Ernst collection, box 95.

96. Material pertaining to the petition to the secretary of the Treasury for the admission of *Ulysses* as a classic are in the Ernst collection, box 93.

97. The statement is reproduced in Moscato and LeBlanc, eds., *United States v. "Ulysses,"* 227–229, though the exhibits are not included.

98. This brief is reproduced in Moscato and LeBlanc, eds., *United States v. "Ulysses,"* 235–272.

99. Unfortunately, no transcript of the arguments was preserved. For accounts of the oral arguments, see Morris L. Ernst, "Reflections on the *Ulysses* Trial and Censorship," *JJQ* 3 (1965): 3–11; Ernst and Schwartz, *Censorship*, 93–107; Younger, *"Ulysses" in Court*; and *"Ulysses* Case Reaches Court after 10 Years," an article in the *New York Herald-Tribune*, 26 November 1933 (reprinted in Moscato and LeBlanc, eds., *United States v. "Ulysses,"* 284–287). The Supplementary Memorandum is reproduced in Moscato and LeBlanc, 289–292.

100. Ernst and Seagle, *To the Pure*, 5.

101. See Boyer, *Purity in Print*, 104–107.

102. Ernst and Seagle, *To the Pure*, 9.

103. *Dictionary of American Biography*, s.v. "Woolsey, John."

104. Lindey, who got the names from Cerf, reported this to Ernst just hours after Woolsey handed down his decision. See Moscato and LeBlanc, eds., *United States v. "Ulysses,"* 317.

105. *Dictionary of American Biography*, s.v. "Canby, Henry Seidel."

106. "Early in November [1921] Joyce lent [Valery] Larbaud, as the previous year he had lent [Carlos] Linati, an intricate scheme for *Ulysses* which showed its Odyssean parallels and its special [narrative] techniques" (*JJ*, 519). Stuart Gilbert

published a version of this scheme in his influential 1930 *James Joyce's "Ulysses,"* and it has been the official unofficial key to the book ever since.

107. William S. Brockman, "American Librarians and Early Censorship of *Ulysses*: 'Aiding the Cause of Free Expression'?" *JSA* (1994): 57.

108. The map is reproduced in Moscato and LeBlanc, eds., *United States v. "Ulysses,"* 422, and Brockman, "American Librarians," 70.

109. George Bowerman to Cerf, 14 May 1932, Ernst collection. Ten years earlier Bowerman had been publicly upbraided by M. E. Ahern in *Public Libraries* for opposing censorship (Boyer, *Purity in Print,* 115). Perhaps this incident made him wary of being quoted in Cerf's letter. As his further correspondence with Cerf indicates, if he was opposed to censorship, he was circumspect in his voicing of that opposition.

110. Lindey to Cerf, 19 May 1932, Ernst collection.

111. Draft of letter from Cerf to Bowerman, 19 May 1932, Ernst collection.

112. Bowerman to Cerf, 27 May 1932, Ernst collection.

113. These responses are in boxes 269 and 293, Ernst collection. The responses were separated in Ernst's files according to whether they would find a cheap edition "of value," and they remain separated in the Ernst collection today.

114. Lindey to Peter Pertzoff, 26 October 1933, Ernst collection, boxes 269 and 270.

115. Eventually the thesis did prove helpful. Lindey cribbed extensively from Pertzoff's bibliography.

116. Pertzoff to Lindey, 25 October 1933, Ernst collection, boxes 269 and 270.

117. Lindey to Pertzoff, 26 October 1933, Ernst collection.

118. Harry Hanson, "The First Reader," *New York World Telegram,* 25 January 1934 (reprinted in Moscato and LeBlanc, eds., *United States v. "Ulysses,"* 12). Cerf wrote to Paul Leon on 17 January that the first copies arrived in his office and that he was sending six to Paris right away so Joyce could receive them by 2 February, the anniversary of the first edition (*M,* 357).

119. See also Stevens, *"Ulysses* on Trial," (reprinted in Moscato and LeBlanc, eds., *United States v. "Ulysses,"* 68–69).

120. Ernst and Schwartz, *Censorship,* 94.

121. Daily, *Anatomy of Censorship,* 16–17.

122. Schauer, *Law of Obscenity,* 24.

123. Moscato and LeBlanc, eds., *United States v. "Ulysses,"* 69.

124. Lindey to Bates, 9 November 1934, Ernst collection, box 95.

125. Cerf, *At Random,* 94.

126. Ibid., 93.

127. Ira Nadel, "The American *Ulysses*: A Lasting Boom," *JJQ* 28 (Summer 1991): 972.

128. See de Grazia, *Girls Lean Back,* 16n.

129. Quoted by Boyer, *Purity in Print,* 110, 90, 111, 112.

130. De Grazia, *Girls Lean Back,* 18.

131. Paul Vanderham, "Lifting the Ban on *Ulysses*: The Well-Intentioned Lies of the Woolsey Decision," *Mosaic* 27 (December 1994): 180, 195. The "well-intentioned lies" Vanderham refers to are Woolsey's lies about the function of lit-

erature, not Ernst's lies about evidence. Though I would dispute certain details of Vanderham's argument, we agree on many points, such as the fact that "Woolsey's *l'homme moyen sensuel* is really a projection of Woolsey himself, a man distinguished from the average man by, among other qualities, a high degree of literary sophistication" (193). I thank Bradley Clissold for bringing Vanderham to my attention.

132. Quoted by Boyer, *Purity in Print,* 113.

133. Ibid., 88.

Chapter Four: Ellmann's Joyce

1. Segall, *Joyce in America* (Berkeley: University of California Press, 1993), 175.

2. Edmund Wilson, *Axel's Castle: A Study in the Imaginative Literature of 1870–1930* (New York: Charles Scribner's Sons, 1931), 193, 211, 236.

3. Ibid., 223.

4. Magalaner and Kain, *Joyce: The Man, the Work, the Reputation,* 43.

5. I will discuss New Criticism and its influence on literary biography in more detail in the next chapter.

6. Stanislaus Joyce, "James Joyce: A Memoir," *The Hudson Review* 2 (1950): 485–514, and *Recollections of James Joyce by His Brother Stanislaus Joyce* (New York: The James Joyce Society, 1950).

7. Stanislaus Joyce, "James Joyce: A Memoir," 485.

8. Stanislaus Joyce, *Recollections,* 3. Thomas O'Grady recently reiterated the attack on Stanislaus Joyce: "the more reasonable contributions to the discussion [about "A Little Cloud"] share only one point in common: general disagreement with Stanislaus Joyce's dismissive declaration that his brother's story is simply a portrayal 'of married life.'" "Little Chandler's Song of Experience," *JJQ* 28 (1991): 399. O'Grady misrepresents Stanislaus, who was dismissing critics, not Joyce's story, with his declaration.

9. Stanislaus Joyce to Ellsworth Mason, 5 May 1952. This letter and some related correspondence quoted throughout are part of a private collection in the hands of Thomas Staley. Oliver Gogarty's article, entitled "They Think They Know Joyce," appeared in *The Saturday Review of Literature* 33, no. 11 (18 March 1950): 8–9, 35–37.

10. As they began collaboration on what was to become *The Early Joyce: The Book Reviews, 1902–1903,* ed. Ellsworth Mason (Colorado Springs: The Mamalujo Press, 1955), Mason admitted the boost it would give his career (Mason to Stanislaus Joyce, 18 April 1954, private collection). In fact, most of Mason's publications about Joyce depended on his association with Stanislaus. Besides Stanislaus Joyce's *Recollections* and *The Early Joyce,* Mason's "Mr. Stanislaus Joyce and John Henry Raleigh," *Modern Language Notes* 70 (March 1955): 187–191; his introduction to Joyce's journalism, "James Joyce's Shrill Note— The *Piccolo Della Sera* Articles," *Twentieth Century Literature* 2 (October 1956): 115–119; and his introduction and notes to *James Joyce: The Critical Writings* (New York: Viking, 1959) all directly resulted from his association with Stanislaus. Even so, as Mason's career matured, Joyce really became a sideline. His most distinguished accomplishments, and he had many, were as a librarian.

11. Mason to Stanislaus Joyce, 2 June 1953, private collection. The article by Raleigh is "'My Brother's Keeper'—Stanislaus Joyce and *Finnegans Wake*," *Modern Language Notes* 68 (1953): 107–110.

12. Stanislaus Joyce to Mason, 8 June 1953, private collection.

13. Mason, "Mr. Stanislaus Joyce and John Henry Raleigh," 187.

14. Ibid., 187–188.

15. Mason to Mr. Wynn, 10 November 1952, private collection. Stanislaus Joyce's "Open Letter to Dr. Oliver Gogarty" finally appeared in *Interim* 4 (1954): 49–56.

16. Mason to Stanislaus Joyce, 10 August 1952, private collection.

17. Mason to Stanislaus Joyce, 23 August 1953, private collection.

18. Mason to Stanislaus Joyce, 28 June 1953, private collection.

19. Mason to Stanislaus Joyce, 17 November 1954, private collection.

20. Mason to Stanislaus Joyce, 22 February 1953, private collection.

21. Mason to Stanislaus Joyce, 12 February 1955, private collection.

22. Mason to Stanislaus Joyce, 16 June 1955, private collection.

23. Mason to Stanislaus Joyce, 28 June 1953, private collection. Marvin Magalaner's article is "The Other Side of James Joyce," *The Arizona Quarterly* 9 (1953): 5–16.

24. Stanislaus Joyce, "The Background to *Dubliners*," 526.

25. Stanislaus Joyce, "Joyce's Dublin," *The Partisan Review* 19 (1952): 104, 107.

26. Stanislaus Joyce, "Early Memories of James Joyce," *The Listener* 26 (May 1949): 897.

27. Stanislaus Joyce, *Recollections*, 19, 21.

28. Magalaner and Kain, *Joyce: The Man, the Work, the Reputation*, 90.

29. Magalaner, "The Other Side of Joyce," 15.

30. Ibid.

31. Ellsworth Mason, "Joyce's Categories," *The Sewanee Review* 61 (1953): 427, 432. Mason's conception of the author projects on Joyce the concern Frank H. Ellis voiced in his 1951 *PMLA* article, which defined the New Critical dictum against the biographical fallacy ("Gray's *Elegy*: The Biographical Problem in Literary Criticism," *PMLA* 66 [1951]: 971).

32. Mason to Stanislaus Joyce, 2 June 1953 and 4 November 1953, private collection.

33. Mason to Stanislaus Joyce, 22 February 1953, private collection.

34. Mason to Stanislaus Joyce, 18 April 1954, private collection.

35. Mason, "Mr. Stanislaus Joyce and John Henry Raleigh," 188.

36. Ellsworth Mason, "*Ulysses*, the Hair Shirt, and Humility," *The CEA Critic* 14 (February 1952): 6.

37. Ellsworth Mason, "James Joyce: Moralist," *Twentieth Century Literature* 1 (January 1956): 205–206.

38. Stanislaus Joyce, "Early Memories of James Joyce," 897.

39. Mason to Stanislaus Joyce, 23 August 1953, private collection.

40. Ellsworth Mason, "Ellmann's Road to Xanadu," in *Essays for Richard Ellmann: Omnium Gatherum*, ed. Susan Dick, et al. (Montreal: McGill-Queen's University Press, 1989), 10.

41. Ibid.

42. Ibid., 5.

43. Mason to Richard Ellmann, 28 January 1948, The Richard Ellmann collection, McFarlin Library, the University of Tulsa. Letters from this collection will be cited as "Tulsa."

44. Mason to Ellmann, 5 July 1952, Tulsa.

45. Mason to Ellmann, 5 July and 11 December 1952, Tulsa.

46. Mason to Ellmann, 11 December 1952, Tulsa.

47. Ellmann to Mason, 20 June 1953, Tulsa.

48. Ellmann to Mason, 7 December 1953, Tulsa.

49. Mason to Ellmann, 26 June 1955, Tulsa.

50. Brenda Maddox, in her otherwise superb history of the provenance of Joyce's and Stanislaus's papers, implies that Stanislaus embraced Ellmann as his editor: "For Stanislaus, nearing seventy, the opportunity [of entrusting his papers to Ellmann] was irresistible." *Nora: The Real Life of Molly Bloom* (Boston: Houghton Mifflin, 1988), 389. Ira Nadel makes the same claim. "The Incomplete Joyce," *JSA* 2 (1991): 91. In fact, Stanislaus never took Ellmann into his full confidence.

51. Mason to Ellmann, 26 September 1955, Tulsa.

52. Ellmann to Mason, 6 March 1956, Tulsa.

53. Mason to Ellmann, 5 March and 10 March 1956, Tulsa.

54. Ellmann to Mason, 21 March 1956, Tulsa.

55. Maddox, *Nora,* 389.

56. For example, on 5 March 1958, Ellmann informed Mason that he had finished a 918-page draft but asked Mason not to speak of it as it would only spur on the other biographers (letter from Ellmann to Mason, Tulsa).

57. Mason to Ellmann, 11 December 1952, Tulsa.

58. Mason to Ellmann, 5 July 1952, Tulsa.

59. Mason to Ellmann, 11 December 1952, Tulsa.

60. Mason to Ellmann, 26 October 1954, Tulsa.

61. Mason to Ellmann, 11 December 1952, Tulsa.

62. See Richard Ellmann, "Joyce and Yeats" *Kenyon Review* 13 (1950): 618–638.

63. Mason to Stanislaus Joyce, 25 October 1954, private collection.

64. Mason to Ellmann, 26 October 1954, Tulsa.

65. Mason to Ellmann, 20 March 1955, Tulsa.

66. On 17 July 1956 Mason wrote to Ellmann, "The more you comment on my stuff, the more I realize that until your biography appears everything that is done is built on sand" (Tulsa).

67. Letters between Mason and Ellmann, December 1956, Tulsa.

68. Telegram from Mason to Ellmann, 27 December 1956, Tulsa.

69. Mason to Ellmann, 9 November 1958, Tulsa.

70. Ellmann to Mason, 20 November 1958, Tulsa.

71. Richard Ellmann, *Golden Codgers: Biographical Speculations* (New York: Oxford University Press, 1973), 3.

72. Ellmann to Mason, 3 November 1954, Tulsa.

73. Richard Ellmann, *James Joyce* (New York: Oxford University Press, 1982),

3; first published in 1959; issued in paperback in 1965; revised edition published New York, 1982; revised edition issued in paperback with corrections in 1983. Citations to *James Joyce* will refer to the 1983 paperback edition, because an assessment of Joyce's biography would most logically examine the current edition.

74. Richard Ellmann, "Freud and Literary Biography," in *a long the riverrun* (London: H. Hamilton, 1988), 261, 264, 266–267.

75. Phillip Herring, "Richard Ellmann's *James Joyce*," in *The Biographer's Art: New Essays*, ed. Jeffrey Meyers (London: Macmillan, 1989), 108.

76. Ellmann, *Golden Codgers*, 1.

77. Ellmann to Mason, 20 June 1953, Tulsa.

78. Ellmann to Richard Kain, 12 July 1953, Tulsa.

79. Ellmann is not alone in this method of biography. As Ira Nadel points out, the "interpretive [biography] where perspective, dimension, and point of view control the material" is one of two major trends of biography in the last 150 years. Ellmann to some degree joins such noted biographers as Lytton Strachey and Virginia Woolf, who advocated the use of "creative facts." See Ira B. Nadel, *Biography: Fiction, Fact and Form* (New York: St. Martin's Press, 1984), 7.

80. Ellmann, *Golden Codgers*, 16. Notably, this concession was voiced long after Ellmann's authority was established.

81. Maddox, *Nora*, xviii.

82. The portrait of the brothers gleaned here from various parts of *James Joyce* was first published, with essentially the same import, in 1955: Richard Ellmann, "The Grasshopper and the Ant: Notes on James Joyce and his brother, Stanislaus," *The Reporter* (1 December 1955): 35–38.

83. Introduction to *My Brother's Keeper: James Joyce's Early Years* by Stanislaus Joyce (New York: Viking, 1958), xi.

84. See Alessandro Francini Bruni, "Recollections of Joyce," in *James Joyce: Interviews and Recollections*, ed. E. H. Mikhail (New York: St. Martin's Press, 1990), 51.

85. See Eileen Joyce Schaurek, "Pappy Never Spoke of Jim's Books," in *James Joyce: Interviews and Recollections*, ed. E. H. Mikhail (New York: St. Martin's Press, 1990), 63.

86. Nadel, "The Incomplete Joyce," 91.

87. The letter, dated 6 August 1909, is reprinted in *JJ*, 280.

88. Herring, "Richard Ellmann's *James Joyce*," 116. The context for the letter to Herring was Hugh Kenner's attack on Ellmann's book, which Herring discusses.

89. Richard Ellmann, interview by John Francis Byrne, notes, Brevoort Hotel, Chicago, 22 March 1954, Tulsa.

90. Cosgrave certainly had some relationship with Nora. The letter from which Ellmann discerned Cosgrave's grudge concerning the name Lynch was occasioned by a letter Cosgrave received from Nora. Cosgrave concludes his letter to Joyce by saying, "I write to Nora tomorrow" (*JJ*, 206).

91. John Francis Byrne to Ellmann, 29 January 1957, James Joyce Collection, Harry Ransom Humanities Research Center, the University of Texas at Austin. Letters in this collection will be cited as "Texas."

92. Byrne to Ellmann, 29 January, 1957, Texas. To be fair, I must point out

that Stanislaus made a similar complaint against Byrne. In a letter to Stuart Gilbert he called Byrne's *The Silent Years* "a mass of misrepresentations" (14 July 1954, Texas).

93. Ellmann to Byrne, 2 February 1957, Texas.

94. Byrne to Ellmann, 1 February 1958, Texas.

95. Byrne to Ellmann, 26 May 1958, Texas. Brenda Maddox cites this letter in *Nora*, 396.

96. So William Noon called it in his "A Delayed Review," *JJQ* 2 (1964): 11.

97. John Francis Byrne, "Thistles in the Wheat Field," *America* (7 November 1952): 159.

98. Stanislaus Joyce, "Open Letter to Dr. Oliver Gogarty," 55. Joyce's letter to Stanislaus dated 16 October 1906 may contradict this account: "When he [Gogarty] wrote to me from New York it was you [Stanislaus], not I, that wished he should get a cordial answer." But the same letter implies that Stanislaus accused Joyce of being too weak in brushing off Gogarty's overtures of reconciliation (*Letters II*, 183).

99. Stanislaus Joyce, *My Brother's Keeper*, 179, 235, 254. Ellmann's notes concerning an interview with Stanislaus indicate that Joyce did keep a notebook of his friends' habits, although he may not have written it until he was in Trieste. Stanislaus claimed to have contributed to it. Richard Ellmann, typed notes of 12 August [1953], box 52, Tulsa.

100. Stanislaus Joyce, *The Dublin Diary of Stanislaus Joyce*, ed. by George Harris Healey (Ithaca: Cornell University Press, 1962), 35.

101. Mimeo radio broadcast transcript of *Portrait of James Joyce, Part I: A Portrait of Joyce as a Young Man*, produced by Maurice Brown (February 1950): 18. The transcript was published as "A Portrait of Joyce as a Young Man," in *Irish Literary Portraits*, ed. W. R. Rodgers (London: BBC, 1972), 22–47, but Stanislaus's dispute was deleted.

102. J. B. Lyons also disputes the likelihood of this account in his *James Joyce and Medicine* (New York: Humanities Press, 1974), 58.

103. Maddox, *Nora*, 398.

104. See for example, Jerome McGann, *Beauty of Inflections*.

105. William Empson complained of this defect in Ellmann's *James Joyce* as early as 1959. "The Joyce Saga: Before Bloomsday and After," *New Statesman* (31 October 1959): 585–586. But the critical community did not question Ellmann's authority on the matter until quite recently. In "Richard Ellmann's *James Joyce*," Phillip Herring candidly confesses his "naive reliance on the Ellmann biography" while repudiating his own "Joyce's Politics" *New Light on Joyce from the Dublin Symposium*, ed. Fritz Senn (Bloomington, IN: Indiana University Press, 1972), 3–14. He cites Dominic Manganiello's *Joyce's Politics* and Colin MacCabe's *James Joyce and the Revolution of the Word* (London: Macmillan, 1978) as two works that take a different view from Ellmann's. Manganiello's book attests either to Ellmann's evolving view of Joyce or to the breadth of his acceptance of other views, since it was a project undertaken under Ellmann's tutelage. See also Robert Scholes, "Joyce and Modernist Ideology," 91–110.

106. Nadel, *Biography: Fiction, Fact and Form*, 173–174.

107. Oliver St. John Gogarty, "James Joyce: A Portrait of the Artist," *Tomor-*

row 6 (1947): 22. Reprinted in *Mourning Became Mrs. Spendlove* (New York: Creative Age Press, 1948).

108. Oliver St. John Gogarty, *Many Lines to Thee: Letters to G. K. A. Bell from the Martello Tower at Sandycove, Rutland Square, and Trinity College Dublin 1904–1907,* ed. James F. Carens (Ireland, 1971), 33.

109. Ulick O'Connor, *The Times I've Seen: Oliver St. John Gogarty, A Biography* (New York: I. Obolensky, 1963), 85.

110. Ellmann, *James Joyce,* 174, and Stanislaus Joyce, *Dublin Diary,* 69.

111. Arnold Goldman, "Stanislaus, James and the Politics of Family," in *Atti del Third International James Joyce Symposium* (Trieste: Università degli Studi Facolta di Magistero, 1974), 61.

112. George Harris Healey, Introduction to *Dublin Diary,* by Stanislaus Joyce, 10.

113. Ellmann to George Healey, 18 March 1969, Tulsa.

114. C. P. Curran, *James Joyce Remembered* (London: Oxford University Press, 1968), 75.

115. See Stanislaus Joyce, *Recollections,* 14.

116. Gogarty, "James Joyce: A Portrait of the Artist," 25. Ellmann does refer to Gogarty's belief that the tower incident was a joke, but he only does so thirty-two pages later (207), and even then to dismiss Gogarty's assertion that the event was innocent.

117. Cf. Mason's universalizing of Bloom.

118. Ellmann to Stanislaus Joyce, 12 April 1954, Tulsa.

119. William Empson, "The Joyce Saga," 585.

120. Frank Kermode, "Puzzles and Epiphanies," *The Spectator* (13 November 1959): 675.

121. Robert Martin Adams, "In Joyce's Wake," *Hudson Review* 12 (1959–1960): 630; Stephen Spender, "All Life was Grist for the Artist," *The New York Times Book Review* (25 October 1959): 1, 58, and *The New Yorker* (2 April 1960): 32.

122. Magalaner and Kain, *Joyce: The Man, the Work, the Reputation,* 65n.

123. Richard Ellmann, quoted in subheadline to "Ellmann Rejoycing," *The New York Times Book Review* (19 September 1982): 7. A preview of the revised edition of James Joyce.

124. Thomas Jackson Rice, *James Joyce: A Guide to Research* (New York: Garland Publishing Company, 1982): 26.

125. For an indication of Ellmann's financial benefits from editing Joyce's work, see Herring, "Richard Ellmann's *James Joyce,*" 125–126.

126. Magalaner and Kain, *Joyce: The Man, the Work, the Reputation,* 65n.

127. T. S. Eliot, preface to *My Brother's Keeper,* by Stanislaus Joyce, edited by Richard Ellmann (New York: The Viking Press, 1958), ix.

128. For a thorough and long overdue treatment of this dissent, see Phillip Herring's "Richard Ellmann's *James Joyce,*" 112–118. In addition to those I discuss here, Herring also summarizes objections made by Joseph Prescott, Chester Anderson, Arnold Goldman, and Niall Montgomery.

129. Herring cites both of these reviews, Robert Scholes's attack on Noon,

and Ruth von Phul's rebuttal of Scholes in successive issues of *James Joyce Quarterly* (2 [Summer 1965]: 310–313; and 3 [Fall 1965]: 69–72). Scholes's defense of Ellmann is particularly ironic (and perhaps it illustrates the hasty praise heaped on Ellmann in the 1960s) in light of his recent criticism of Ellmann's treatment of Joyce's politics. I thank Jean Kimball for drawing my attention to this exchange. I might add to that dissent a review of the 1982 edition by Bernard MacCabe (*The Nation* [20 November 1982]: 527), which complains that, "In the 1980s we expect a more thorough attention . . . to social and political life in Joyce's Ireland."

130. Hugh Kenner, "The Impertinence of Being Definitive," *Times Literary Supplement* (17 December 1982): 1384.

131. See Kenner, "Impertinence of Being Definitive," 1384, and Noon, "A Delayed Review," 8.

132. Nadel, "The Incomplete Joyce," 97.

133. Herring's "Richard Ellmann's *James Joyce*," 115, n 23.

134. Ibid., 126.

135. Nadel, "The Incomplete Joyce," 98.

136. For an early critique of the impression of Joyce's politics given in Ellmann's biography, see William Empson's review, "The Joyce Saga," 585.

137. Richard Ellmann, *The Consciousness of Joyce* (London: Faber and Faber, 1977): 86.

138. Ibid., 88–89.

139. Ibid., 89.

140. Jeffrey Segall, "Between Marxism and Modernism, or How To Be a Revolutionist and Still Love *Ulysses*," *JJQ* 25 (Summer 1988): 442.

141. Seamus Deane, *Celtic Revivals: Essays in Modern Irish Literature, 1880–1980* (Boston: Faber and Faber, 1985), 92, 96, 99, 105.

142. MacCabe, *James Joyce and the Revolution of the Word*, 5, 28–30.

143. Margot Norris, "The Consequence of Deconstruction: A Technical Perspective of Joyce's *Finnegans Wake*," in *Critical Essays on James Joyce*, ed. Bernard Benstock (Boston: G. K. Hall and Co., 1985), 207. Cf. Vicki Mahaffey's *Reauthorizing Joyce* (New York: Cambridge University Press, 1988), which discusses Joyce's language in terms of authority.

144. Manganiello *Joyce's Politics*, 31, 36.

145. Ibid., 38–39.

146. Ibid., 40.

147. Ellmann, *Consciousness of Joyce*, 95.

Chapter Five: Our Joyce

1. See *JJ*, 520–524, and Beach, *Shakespeare and Company*, 73–74.

2. See *Letters III*, 232–233 and Stuart Gilbert's *Reflections on James Joyce*, 43.

3. Gerald Graff cites a few isolated exceptions in *Professing Literature: An Institutional History* (Chicago: University of Chicago Press, 1989), 124–126.

4. Ibid., 148.

5. Segall, *Joyce in America*, 117.

6. Graff, *Professing Literature,* 148–149. See also René Wellek, "Literary Scholarship," in *American Scholarship in the Twentieth Century,* ed. Merle Curti (Cambridge: Harvard University Press, 1953), 121.

7. Wellek, "Literary Scholarship," 116–120.

8. Graff, *Professing Literature,* 74.

9. Ibid., 153–154.

10. Wellek, "Literary Scholarship," 122.

11. Graff, *Professing Literature,* 153.

12. John Crowe Ransom, "Criticism, Inc.," in *Selected Essays of John Crowe Ransom,* ed. Thomas Daniel Young and John Hindle (Baton Rouge: Louisiana State University Press, 1964), 98.

13. Graff, *Professing Literature,* 145.

14. Ransom, "Criticism, Inc.," 94.

15. Ibid., 94–95, 102–103.

16. Ibid., 97.

17. Ibid., 94.

18. See Graff, *Professing Literature,* 152–153.

19. Ibid., 228.

20. Ibid.

21. Ibid., 238.

22. Ibid., 233. Graff feels that every reform succumbs to routine: "jaded observers of the profession's history [deconstructionists] merely prove once more that 'the whole of literature' can all too readily be made to 'respond' to techniques that validate themselves tautologically" (241). Ultimately, he predicts that, "Whether the cycle can be broken in a way that maximizes the theoretical awareness and minimizes the routinization may well depend on matters of institutional organization. For . . . the routinization of critical discourses is a function of institutional arrangements that do not require these discourses to confront one another" (242–243).

23. William K. Wimsatt and William Beardsley, "The Intentional Fallacy," in *The Verbal Icon: Studies in the Meaning of Poetry* (Lexington: University of Kentucky Press, 1954). First published in *The Sewanee Review* 54 (Summer 1946): 468–488.

24. Ibid., 5.

25. Eliot, *The Sacred Wood,* 110.

26. Amy Tan, "In the Canon, for All the Wrong Reasons," *Harper's Magazine* 293 (December 1996): 27–28.

27. George Kittredge, "The Dramatic Principle in the *Canterbury Tales,*" in *The Canterbury Tales: Nine Tales and the General Prologue, Authoritative Text, Sources and Backgrounds, Criticism,* ed. V. A. Kolve and Glending Olson (New York: Norton, 1989), 520. Reprinted from *Chaucer and His Poetry* (Cambridge: Harvard University Press, 1915). Ironically, Kittredge was an early "scholar," not a "generalist" (see Graff, *Professing Literature,* 66).

28. Wellek, "Literary Scholarship," 125–126.

29. Graff, *Professing Literature,* 193.

30. "Bibliography, Texts, Libraries: The Changing Shape of the Humanities."

Plenary Address at the South Central Modern Languages Association. New Orleans, Louisiana, 27 October 1989. Typescript, 16–17.

31. Maurice Beebe, "Modern Fiction News Letter," *MFS* 1 (May 1955): 39.

32. Beebe, "Modern Fiction Newsletter," *MFS* 3 (1957–1958): 362.

33. Beebe, "Modern Fiction Newsletter," *MFS* 4 [1957–1958]: 38.

34. Graff, *Professing Literature*, 60.

35. Beebe, "Modern Fiction Newsletter," *MFS* 7 (1961): 177–178.

36. I must emphasize the imprecision of these numbers. As the number of Ph.D.'s exploded, *Dissertation Abstracts* frequently was obliged to change its format, which makes yearly comparisons difficult. For example, in the 1950s dissertations were indexed under group headings, which allowed a count of all Ph.D.'s in a certain field. But these divisions were modified from year to year, and they were abandoned altogether in 1961. Someone else making a similar count might come up with different exact numbers, but the general proportions would be the same.

37. Of course this tally does not take into account students who were steered away from modern studies by their professors. But I do not see any way of documenting the extent of such diversions besides anecdotal evidence.

38. Robert Bierman, "White and Pink Elephants: *Finnegans Wake* and the Tradition of "Unintelligibility," *MFS* 4 (1958): 62. Bob Perelman's *The Trouble With Genius: Reading Pound, Joyce, Stein, and Zukofsky* (Berkeley: University of California Press, 1994) quotes this same passage—while arguing that Ezra Pound was a "genius" despite all the "mistakes" he made (28).

39. A. Walton Litz, "Joyce's Notes for the Last Episodes of *Ulysses*," *MFS* 4 (1958): 4.

40. Ibid., 17.

41. Hugh Kenner, introduction to *James Joyce and the Making of "Ulysses,"* by Frank Budgen (Bloomington: Indiana University Press, 1960), ix.

42. Patrick McCarthy, "Stuart Gilbert's Guide to the Perplexed," in *Re-Viewing the Classics of Joyce Criticism*, ed. Janet Egleson Dunleavy (Urbana: University of Illinois Press, 1991), 27.

43. W. G. Rogers, *Wise Men Fish Here: The Story of Frances Steloff and the Gotham Book Mart* (New York: Harcourt, Brace, 1965), 92.

44. Rogers, *Wise Men Fish Here*, 200, 225.

45. Ibid., 113.

46. Frances Steloff, "In Touch With Genius" *Journal of Modern Literature* 4 (1975): 848–856.

47. Ibid., 850.

48. Bruce Arnold, *The Scandal of "Ulysses": The Sensational Life of a Twentieth-Century Masterpiece* (New York: St. Martin's Press, 1991), 89.

49. Edmund L. Epstein, foreword to *James Joyce Review* 1 (2 February 1957): 1–2.

50. Ibid.

51. Edmund L. Epstein, review of *Joyce and Shakespeare*, by William M. Schutte, *James Joyce Review* 1 (16 June 1957): 42, 43.

52. Thomas Staley, interview by author, 14 July 1993.

53. Herbert Howarth to Thomas Staley, 9 February 1963, *JJQ* Archive.

54. Fred Higginson to Staley, 23 May 1963, *JJQ* Archive.

55. Staley, interview.

56. Clive Hart to Staley, 25 January 1963, *JJQ* Archive.

57. Hart to Staley, 12 February 1963, *JJQ* Archive.

58. David Hayman to Staley, 26 February 1963, *JJQ* Archive.

59. Staley to Hayman, 14 March 1963, *JJQ* Archive.

60. Howarth to Staley, 9 February 1963, *JJQ* Archive.

61. Joseph Prescott to Staley, *JJQ* Archive.

62. Memo from Staley to Hart, et al., n.d., *JJQ* Archive.

63. Memo from Staley to Hart, et al., n.d., *JJQ* Archive.

64. *JJQ* Archive.

65. Hart to Staley, 20 June 1963, *JJQ* Archive.

66. Fritz Senn to Staley, 9 June 1963, *JJQ* Archive.

67. Memo to Professor Fleischman, et al., n.d., *JJQ* Archive.

68. Harry Levin to Staley, 17 May 1963, *JJQ* Archive.

69. Staley to Ellmann, 6 March 1964, *JJQ* Archive.

70. Higginson to Staley, 23 May 1963, *JJQ* Archive.

71. Warren Frend to Staley, 23 July 1963, *JJQ* Archive.

72. Philip Lyman to Staley, 25 July 1963, *JJQ* Archive.

73. S. A. Golden to Staley, 22 October 1963, *JJQ* Archive.

74. Janet Salisbury to Staley, 15 July 1963, *JJQ* Archive.

75. J. S. Atherton to Staley, 24 June 1963, *JJQ* Archive.

76. Fleischman to Staley, 15 May 1963, *JJQ* Archive.

77. Hart to Staley, 20 June 1963, *JJQ* Archive.

78. Vivien Mercier to Staley, 10 September 1963, *JJQ* Archive.

79. John Kelleher to Staley, 1 August 1963, *JJQ* Archive.

80. Thomas Staley, "Notes and Comments," *JJQ* 1 (1963): 1.

81. Adeline Glasheen, review of *A Concordance to "Finnegans Wake,"* by Clive Hart, *JJQ* 1 (1963): 36.

82. Maurice Beebe to Staley, 3 July 1963, *JJQ* Archive.

83. Beebe, *Modern Fiction Studies* 9 (1963): 179.

84. Beebe to Staley, 13 November 1963, *JJQ* Archive.

85. Beebe to Staley, 6 May 1964, *JJQ* Archive.

86. Staley to Beebe, 11 May 1964, *JJQ* Archive.

87. Beebe to Staley, 16 August 1964, *JJQ* Archive.

88. Russell Cosper to Staley, 12 February 1968, *JJQ* Archive.

89. Hayman to author (by e-mail), 12 September 1993.

90. Staley, "Notes and Comments," *JJQ* 3 (Fall 1965).

91. Staley, "Notes and Comments," *JJQ* 4 (Fall 1966).

92. Staley, interview by author, 16 July 1993.

93. Staley, interview by author, 14 July 1993.

94. Staley, "Notes and Comments," *JJQ* 1 (Winter 1964): 1.

95. Richard Kain, "A Ghost on Bloomsday," *The Guardian,* 17 June 1967, 7.

96. Bernard Benstock, untitled typescript, 2. Morris Beja very kindly supplied me with a copy of this colorful memoir.

97. Richard J. Finneran, ed., *Anglo-Irish Literature: A Review of Research*

(New York: The Modern Language Association of America, 1976), 367. For other examples of this self-consciousness among Joyce scholars, see Staley's *An Annotated Critical Bibliography of James Joyce* (New York: St. Martin's Press, 1989) and his "James Joyce and the Dilemma of American Academic Criticism," *Dublin Magazine* 6 (Spring 1967): 38–45; Bernard Benstock's "The James Joyce Industry," *The Southern Review* 2 (1966): 210–228; Robert Martin Adams, "The Bent Knife Blade: Joyce in the 1960's," *Partisan Review* 29 (1962): 507–518; A. Walton Litz, "Pound and Eliot on Ulysses: The Critical Tradition," 5–18; Litz's "*Ulysses* and Its Audience," in *James Joyce: The Centennial Symposium,* ed. Morris Beja, et al. (Chicago: University of Illinois Press, 1986), 220–229; William Chace, "Joyce and the Professors," in *James Joyce: The Centennial Symposium,* ed. Morris Beja, et al. (Chicago: University of Illinois Press, 1986), 3–8; Segall, *Joyce in America;* and Janet Egleson Dunleavy, ed., *Re-Viewing Classics of Joyce Criticism* (Urbana: University of Illinois Press, 1991).

98. Magalaner and Kain, *Joyce: The Man, the Work, the Reputation,* 209. I thank William Brockman for drawing my attention to this early use of the term.

99. Willard Godwin kindly provided me with this bibliography: Hugh Kenner, "Smokeless Industry," *Prairie Schooner* 31, no. 1 (Spring 1957): 8–10, and "Turning New Leaves," *The Canadian Forum* 39, no. 469 (February 1960): 261–262; Vivien Mercier, "In Joyce's Wake: A Booming Industry," *New York Times Book Review* 66 (30 July 1961): 5, 20–21.

100. Anthony Burgess, "Dear Mr. Shame's Voice," *The Spectator* (27 November 1964): 731. This article was also published in New York's *Atlas.*

101. Burgess, "Dear Mr. Shame's Voice," 732.

102. Arnold, *The Scandal of "Ulysses": The Sensational Life of a Twentieth-Century Masterpiece,* 90.

103. Ibid., 88.

104. Arthur Power, qtd. in Chace, "Joyce and the Professors," 3.

105. Burgess, "Dear Mr. Shame's Voice," 731.

106. Adams, "The Bent Knife Blade," 518.

107. Burgess, "Dear Mr. Shame's Voice," 731.

108. Adams, "The Bent Knife Blade," 512–513.

109. William Noon, review of *Re-Joyce,* by Anthony Burgess, *JJQ* 3 (Spring 1966): 218–219.

110. Bernard Benstock, review of *A Shorter Finnegans Wake,* edited by Anthony Burgess, *JJQ* 4 (Winter 1967): 138.

111. Staley, "Notes and Comments," *JJQ* 3 (Winter 1965): 94.

112. Kain to Staley, 24 May 1963. *JJQ* Archive.

113. Staley to Maralee Frampton, 21 November 1966, *JJQ* Archive.

114. Rivers Carew to Staley, 12 December 1966, *JJQ* Archive.

115. Staley to Senn, Benstock, and Frampton, 10 April 1967, *JJQ* Archive.

116. Senn to Staley, 18 December 1966, *JJQ* Archive.

117. Senn to Staley, 28 December 1966, *JJQ* Archive.

118. Morris Beja, "Synjoysium: An Informal History of the International James Joyce Symposia," *JJQ* 22 (1985): 114.

119. Bernard Benstock, typescript, June 1986: 2.

120. Ibid., 4.

121. Terence Killeen, "Irish (Men) Recuperate Joyce," *JJLS* 7 (Fall 1993): 16.

122. Bruce Arnold, review of *Ulysses,* introduced by Declan Kiberd; *A Portrait of the Artist as a Young Man,* edited by Seamus Deane; *Dubliners,* introduced by Terence Brown; and *Poems and Exiles,* edited by J. C. C. Mays, *JJQ* 29 (Spring 1992): 698.

123. David Hayman, *Books Abroad* 42 (1968): 215.

124. Benstock, typescript, 1.

125. Hayman, *Books Abroad,* 216.

126. Ibid., 215.

127. Beja, "Synjoysium," 114.

128. W. L. Webb, "A Ghost on Bloomsday," *The Guardian,* 17 June 1967, 7.

129. Ibid.

130. Benstock to Staley, Senn, and David Ward, 6 October 1967, *JJQ* Archive.

131. Staley to Benstock, Senn, and Ward, 14 December 1967, *JJQ* Archive.

132. Staley, "Dilemma of American Academic Criticism," 38–45.

133. This library, originally intended for the Joyce Tower, is now housed at Southern Methodist University.

134. Ward to Joyceans, 17 March 1968, *JJQ* Archive.

135. Ira Nadel, "Anthologizing Joyce: The Example of T. S. Eliot," *JJQ* 27 (Spring 1990): 510, 514.

136. Harry Levin, ed., introduction to *The Portable James Joyce,* rev. ed. (New York: Viking Penguin, 1968), 1.

137. Ibid., 3.

138. Ibid., 2.

139. Ibid., 3, 8, 12–13.

140. Elizabeth Dzwonkoski, "The Viking Press," in *American Literary Publishing Houses 1900–1980: Trade and Paperback,* edited by Peter Dzwonskoski, *DLB* 46 (Detroit: Bruccoli Clark, 1986), 366.

141. According to Martha Sue Bean, the Viking Portable series, which numbered fifty-seven titles by 1967, "won a place both with general readers and in the college market." "A History and Profile of the Viking Press" (master's thesis, University of North Carolina, Chapel Hill, 1969), 36–37.

142. Chester Anderson, interview with author, 3 February 1995.

143. Chester Anderson, "About This Text," in *A Portrait of the Artist as a Young Man,* Case Studies in Contemporary Criticism (New York: Bedford Books of St. Martin's Press, 1993), ix.

144. Anderson, interview.

145. Anderson, "About This Text," ix-x.

146. A. Walton Litz, telephone interview by author, 26 August 1993; and correspondence by e-mail from Robert Scholes to the author, 21 August 1993.

147. Litz, telephone interview.

148. Robert Scholes, *In Search of James Joyce* (Chicago: University of Illinois Press, 1992), 226. Apparently, the printer ignored about two hundred of one thousand corrections Joyce made.

149. Ibid., 17.

150. Ibid., 16.

151. Robert Scholes, "Further Observations on the Text of *Dubliners*," in *In Search of James Joyce*, 35. Originally published in *Studies in Bibliography* 17 (1964).

152. Maddox, introduction to *Dubliners*, xxii.

153. Litz, interview conversation.

154. Scholes, *In Search of James Joyce*, 2–3.

155. Ibid., 3–4.

156. Robert Scholes, "Grant Richards to James Joyce," *Studies in Bibliography* 16 (1963): 139–140.

157. Scholes, *In Search of James Joyce*, 3.

158. Litz, telephone interview.

159. One of the two exceptions I noted ask students to discuss the "didactic purpose" of "Stephen's artistic aims," though perhaps Anderson would expect an apology for any didacticism. The other topic concerns the "social sphere" in the novel and its function (*D*, 557–558). Much more prominent are topics that require students to explicate symbols and themes, analyze Joyce's various techniques of narrative, and place Joyce's novel into the literary tradition.

160. Letter to Richard Kain, 24 February 1964. *JJQ* Archive.

161. See Charles Rossman, "The New *Ulysses*: The Hidden Controversy," *The New York Review of Books* (8 December 1988): 53–58.

162. John Kidd, "An Inquiry into *Ulysses: The Corrected Text*," *PBSA* 82 (December 1988): 493.

163. See John Kidd, "The Scandal of Ulysses," *The New York Review of Books*, 30 June 1988, 32.

164. Robert Scholes to author (by e-mail), 21 August 1993.

165. Kathleen McCormick and Erwin Steinberg, eds., *Approaches to Teaching Joyce's "Ulysses"* (New York: MLA, 1993).

166. David Hayman to author (by e-mail), 12 September 1993.

167. Bernard Benstock, "Middle-Class Values in *Ulysses*—and the Value of the Middle Class," *JJQ* 31 (Summer 1994): 439–454.

168. Richard Brodhead, *The School of Hawthorne* (New York: Oxford University Press, 1986), 5. Qtd. by Jan Gorak, *The Making of the Modern Canon* (Atlantic Heights, N.J.: Athlone, 1991), 3. Also see Jane Thompkins, *Sensational Designs* (New York: Oxford University Press, 1985).

169. Gorak, *Making of the Modern Canon*, 2.

170. Ibid., 3.

171. Barbara Herrnstein Smith, "Belief and Resistance: A Symmetrical Account," in *Questions of Evidence: Proof, Practice, and Persuasion across the Disciplines*, ed. James Chandler, Arnold I. Davidson, and Harry Harootunian (Chicago: University of Chicago Press), 140–141.

172. Ibid., 144.

173. Rodden, *The Politics of Literary Reputation*, ix.

Bibliography

Archives

Ernst collection The Morris Ernst papers housed at the Harry Ransom Humanities Research Center at the University of Texas at Austin.

JJQ Archive Extensive collection of correspondences and other materials related to the *James Joyce Quarterly*. These uncatalogued papers are housed at the offices of the *James Joyce Quarterly* at the University of Tulsa.

Private collection Collection of letters in the possession of Thomas Staley, between Ellsworth Mason and Stanislaus Joyce, consisting of nineteen letters from Mason to Stanislaus Joyce from 16 June 1952 to 16 June 1955; nineteen letters from Stanislaus Joyce to Mason from 5 May 1952 to 6 March 1955; and five letters between Mason, Mr. Wynn and G. Costigan regarding "Open Letter to Dr. Oliver Gogarty," 10–30 November 1952.

Texas James Joyce Collection at the Harry Ransom Humanities Research Center, the University of Texas at Austin.

Tulsa Richard Ellmann Collection at the McFarlin Library, the University of Tulsa.

(Note: Other previously unpublished materials consist of letters to the author and interviews conducted by the author.)

Published Works

Adams, Robert Martin. "The Bent Knife Blade: Joyce in the 1960's," *Partisan Review* 29 (1962): 507–518.

———. "In Joyce's Wake," *Hudson Review* 12 (1959–1960): 627–632.

———. *Surface and Symbol: The Consistency of James Joyce's Ulysses*. New York: Oxford University Press, 1962.

Althusser, Louis. "Ideology and Ideological State Apparatuses (Notes Towards an Investigation)." In *Lenin and Philosophy and Other Essays,* translated by Ben Brewster, 127–186. New York: Monthly Review Press, 1971.

Anderson, Chester. "About This Text." In *A Portrait of the Artist as a Young Man*. Case Studies in Contemporary Criticism, edited by R. B. Kershner. New York: St. Martin's Press, 1993.

Anderson, Margaret. *My Thirty Years War*. New York: Covici, Friede, 1930.

———, ed. *The Little Review Anthology*. New York: Hermitage House, 1953.

Arensburg, Conrad M., and Solon T. Kimball. *Family and Community in Ireland.* 2nd ed. Cambridge: Harvard University Press, 1968.

Arnold, Bruce. Review of *Ulysses,* introduced by Declan Kiberd; *A Portrait of the Artist as a Young Man,* edited by Seamus Deane; *Dubliners,* introduced by Terence Brown; and *Poems and Exiles,* edited by J. C. C. Mays. *JJQ* 29 (Spring 1992): 695–698.

———. *The Scandal of Ulysses: The Sensational Life of a Twentieth-Century Masterpiece.* New York: St. Martin's Press, 1991.

Averill, Deborah M. *The Irish Short Story from George Moore to Frank O'Connor.* Washington, D.C.: University Press of America, 1982.

Baechler, Lea. "Voices of Unexpected Lyricism in Two Dubliners Stories." *JJQ* 28 (1991): 361–376.

Baker, James. "Ibsen, Joyce, and the Living-Dead: A Study of Dubliners." In *A James Joyce Miscellany,* edited by Marvin Magalaner, 19–32. Carbondale: Southern Illinois University Press, 1962.

Bašić, Sonja. "A Book of Many Uncertainties: Joyce's Dubliners." *Style* 25 (Fall 1991): 351–377.

Beach, Sylvia. *Shakespeare and Company.* Lincoln: University of Nebraska Press, 1956.

Bean, Martha Sue. "A History and Profile of the Viking Press." Master's thesis, University of North Carolina, Chapel Hill, 1969.

Beck, Warren. *Joyce's Dubliners: Substance, Vision, and Art.* Durham, N.C.: Duke University Press, 1969.

Becker, George J., ed. *Documents of Modern Literary Realism.* Princeton: Princeton University Press, 1963.

Beja, Morris. *James Joyce: A Literary Life.* Columbus: Ohio State University Press, 1992.

———. "Synjoysium: An Informal History of the International James Joyce Symposia." *JJQ* 22 (1985): 113–130.

Belinsky, Vissarion. *Belinsky, Chernyshevsky, and Dobrolyubov: Selected Criticism.* Edited by Ralph E. Matlaw. Bloomington: Indiana University Press, 1976.

Benstock, Bernard. "The James Joyce Industry." *The Southern Review* 2 (1966): 210–228.

———. "Middle-Class Values in Ulysses—and the Value of the Middle Class." *JJQ* 31 (Summer 1994): 439–454.

Benstock, Shari, and Bernard Benstock. "The Role of Little Magazines in the Emergence of Modernism." *The Library Chronicle* 20 (1991): 68–87.

Bierman, Robert. "White and Pink Elephants: Finnegans Wake and the Tradition of 'Unintelligibility.'" *MFS* 4 (1958): 62–70.

Bishop, Edward L. "Re: Covering Ulysses." *JSA* (1994): 22–55.

Bourdieu, Pierre, and Jean-Claude Passeron. *Reproduction in Education, Society and Culture.* Translated by Richard Nice. London: Sage Publications, 1990.

Boyd, Ernest. *Ireland's Literary Renaissance.* 1916. Reprint, New York: Barnes and Noble, 1968.

Boyer, Paul S. *Purity in Print: The Vice Society Movement and Book Censorship in America.* New York: Charles Scribner's Sons, 1968.

Brockman, William S. "American Librarians and Early Censorship of Ulysses: 'Aiding the Cause of Free Expression'?" *JSA* (1994): 56–74.

Brodhead, Richard. *The School of Hawthorne.* New York: Oxford University Press, 1986.

Brooks, Cleanth, and William K. Wimsatt. *Literary Criticism: A Short History.* Vol. 2, *Romantic and Modern Criticism.* Phoenix Edition. Chicago: University of Chicago Press, 1978.

Brown, Malcolm. *The Politics of Irish Literature: From Thomas Davis to W. B. Yeats.* London: George Allen and Unwin Ltd., 1972.

Brown, Richard. *James Joyce and Sexuality.* New York: Cambridge University Press, 1985.

Bryer, Jackson R. "Joyce, Ulysses, and the Little Review." *South Atlantic Quarterly* 66(1967): 148–164.

Budgen, Frank. *James Joyce and the Making of "Ulysses."* Bloomington: Indiana University Press, 1960.

Burgess, Anthony. "Dear Mr. Shame's Voice," *The Spectator* (27 November 1964): 731–732.

Byrne, J. F. *The Silent Years.* New York: Farrar, Strauss, and Young, 1953.

———. "Thistles in the Wheat Field." *America* 7, no. 6 (November 1959): 159.

Cairns, David, and Shaun Richards. *Writing Ireland: Colonialism, Nationalism and Culture.* Manchester: Manchester University Press, 1988.

Calahan, James M. *The Irish Novel: A Critical History.* Boston: Twayne Publishers, 1988.

Cerf, Bennett. *At Random.* New York: Random House, 1977.

———. "Publishing Ulysses," *Contempo* 3 (February 15, 1934).

Chace, William. "Joyce and the Professors." In *James Joyce: The Centennial Symposium,* edited by Morris Beja, et al., 3–8. Chicago: University of Illinois Press, 1986.

Cheng, Vincent. *Joyce, Race, and Empire.* New York: Cambridge University Press, 1995.

Chestnutt, Margaret. "Joyce's Dubliners: History, Ideology, and Social Reality." *Eire* 14 (1979): 93–105.

Cixous, Hélène. "Joyce: The (r)use of writing." In *Post-Structuralist Joyce: Essays from the French,* edited and translated by Derrick Attridge and Daniel Ferrer, 15–30. New York: Cambridge University Press, 1984.

Clery, Arthur. "The Passing of University College." In *A Page of Irish History: The Story of University College Dublin, 1883–1909,* compiled by the Fathers of the Society for Jesus, 120–121. Dublin: Talbot Press, 1930.

Cole, Richard Cargill. *Irish Booksellers and English Writers: 1740–1800.* London: Mansell Publishing, 1986.

Colgan, Maurice. "Exotics or Provincials? Anglo-Irish Writers and the English Problem." In *Literary Interrelations: Ireland, England and the World,* edited by Wolfgang Zach and Heinz Kosok, 35–40. Vol. 3 of *Studies in English and Comparative Literature.* Tübingen: Gunter Narr Verlag, 1987.

Collins, Irene. "Liberalism in Nineteenth Century Europe." In *From Metternich to Hitler: Aspects of British and Foreign History 1814–1939,* edited by W. N. Medlicott, 25–46. New York: Barnes and Noble, 1963.

Colum, Padraic. Introduction to *Dubliners*, by James Joyce. New York: The Modern Library, Inc., 1926.

Colum, Padraic, and Mary Colum. *Our Friend James Joyce*. Garden City, New York: Doubleday & Company, Inc., 1958.

Connell, K. H. *Irish Peasant Society: Four Historical Essays*. Oxford: Clarendon Press, 1968.

———. "Peasant Marriage in Ireland: Its Structure and Development Since the Famine." *Economic History Review* 14(1962): 502–503.

Connolly, James. *Selected Political Writings of James Connolly*. Edited by Owen Dudley Edwards and Bernard Ransom. Writings of the Left, ed. Ralph Miliband. New York: Grove Press, 1973.

Cullen, L. M. *An Economic History of Ireland Since 1660*. London: B. T. Batsford Ltd., 1972.

Culler, Jonathan. *Structuralist Poetics: Structuralism, Linguistics, and the Study of Literature*. Ithaca, New York: Cornell University Press, 1975.

Cullingford, Elizabeth. *Yeats, Ireland and Fascism*. New York: New York University Press, 1980.

Curran, C. P. *James Joyce Remembered*. London: Oxford University Press, 1968.

Daily, Jay E. *The Anatomy of Censorship*. New York: Marcel Dekker, 1973.

Deane, Seamus. *Celtic Revivals: Essays in Modern Irish Literature, 1880–1980*. Boston: Faber and Faber, 1985. "Literary Myths of the Revival" is found on pages 28–36. The chapter "Joyce and Nationalism" was originally published in *James Joyce: New Perspectives*, edited by Colin MacCabe, 168–183. Bloomington: Indiana University Press, 1982.

———. "Civilians and Barbarians." In *Ireland's Field Day*. Edited by the Field Day Theatre Company, 33–44. London: Hutchinson, 1985.

———. "Heroic Styles: The Tradition of an Idea." In *Ireland's Field Day*. Edited by the Field Day Theatre Company, 45–60. London: Hutchinson, 1985.

———, ed. *The Field Day Anthology of Irish Literature*. Derry: Field Day Publications, 1991.

———, ed. *Nationalism, Colonialism, and Literature*. A Field Day Company Book. Minneapolis: University of Minnesota Press, 1990.

de Grazia, Edward. *Censorship Landmarks*. New York: Bowker, 1969.

———. *Girls Lean Back Everywhere: The Law of Obscenity and the Assault on Genius*. New York: Random House, 1992.

Delany, Paul. "Joyce's Political Development and the Aesthetic of Dubliners." *College English* 34 (1972): 256–266.

Derrida, Jacques. "Signature Event Context" *Glyph* 1 (1977): 172–197.

Desnoyers, Fernand. "On Realism." In *Documents of Modern Literary Realism*, edited by George J. Becker, 80–88. Princeton: Princeton University Press, 1963.

Dobrolyubov, N. A. "When Will the Real Day Come?" In *Belinsky, Chernyshevsky, and Dobrolyubov: Selected Criticism*, edited by Ralph E. Matlaw, 176–226. Bloomington: Indiana University Press, 1976.

Donoghue, Denis. *We Irish: Essays on Irish Literature and Society*. New York: Alfred A. Knopf, 1986.

Duffy, Enda. *The Subaltern Ulysses.* Minneapolis: University of Minnesota Press, 1994.

Dunleavy, Janet Egleson, ed. *Re-Viewing Classics of Joyce Criticism.* Urbana: University of Illinois Press, 1991.

Dzwonkoski, Elizabeth. "The Viking Press," In *American Literary Publishing Houses 1900–1980: Trade and Paperback,* edited by Peter Dzwonskoski. *DLB* 46. Detroit: Bruccoli Clark, 1986.

Edwards, Owen Dudley, and Bernard Ransom, eds. Introduction to *Selected Political Writings of James Connolly.* Writings of the Left, ed. Ralph Miliband, 15–44. New York: Grove Press, 1973.

The Egoist: An Individualist Review. 5 vols. New York: Kraus Reprint Corporation, 1967.

Ellis, Frank H. "Gray's Elegy: The Biographical Problem in Literary Criticism." *PMLA* 66(1951): 971–1008.

Eliot, George. "On Realism." In *Documents of Modern Literary Realism,* edited by George Becker, 112–116. Princeton: Princeton University Press, 1963. Reprint of *Adam Bede.* The Best Known Novels of George Eliot. New York: Random House, n.d.

Eliot, T. S. *The Letters of T. S. Eliot, Volume I, 1898–1922.* Ed. Valerie Eliot. New York: Harcourt Brace Jovanovich, 1988.

———. Preface to *My Brother's Keeper: James Joyce's Early Years,* by Stanislaus Joyce, edited by Richard Ellmann. New York: The Viking Press, 1958.

———. *The Sacred Wood.* New York: Methuen, 1920.

———. "Ulysses, Order, and Myth," *Dial* 75 (November 1923): 480–483. Rpt. in *James Joyce: Two Decades of Criticism,* edited by Seon Givens, 198–203. New York, Vanguard Press, 1948.

Ellmann, Richard. *The Consciousness of Joyce.* London: Faber and Faber, 1977.

———. "Cranly's Memoirs." *The Saturday Review.* 36 (13 March 1954): 18, 19, 46. Review of Byrne's *The Silent Years.*

———. "Ellmann Rejoycing." *The New York Times Book Review.* (19 September 1982): 7, 24. A preview of the revised edition of James Joyce.

———. "Freud and Literary Biography." In *a long the riverrun,* 256–270. London: H. Hamilton, 1988. First published in *Freud and the Humanities,* edited by P. Horden. Gerald Duckworth & Co., 1985.

———. *Golden Codgers: Biographical Speculations.* New York: Oxford University Press, 1973.

———. "The Grasshopper and the Ant: Notes on James Joyce and his brother, Stanislaus," *The Reporter* (1 December 1955): 35–38.

———. Introduction to *My Brother's Keeper,* by Stanislaus Joyce. New York: The Viking Press, 1957,

———. *James Joyce.* New York: Oxford University Press, 1959. Issued in paperback in 1965; revised edition published, New York: Oxford University Press, 1982; rev. ed. issued in paperback with corrections in 1983. Portions of this book had been published earlier in the *Kenyon Review, Sewanee Review, Reporter, Yale Review, Commonweal, My Brother's Keeper,* and *Critical Writings of James Joyce.*

————. "Joyce and Yeats" *Kenyon Review* 13 (1950): 618–638.

————, ed. *Letters of James Joyce*, Vol. II and III. New York: The Viking Press, 1966.

————, ed. *Selected Letters of James Joyce*. New York: The Viking Press, 1975.

————, and Ellsworth Mason. Introduction to *Critical Writings of James Joyce*. New York: The Viking Press, 1959. Reprinted: Ithaca, N.Y.: Cornell University Press, 1989.

Empson, William. "The Joyce Saga: Before Bloomsday and After." *New Statesman* (31 October 1959): 585–586.

Epstein, Edmund L. Foreword to *James Joyce Review* 1 (2 February 1957): 1–2.

————. Review of *Joyce and Shakespeare*, by William M. Schutte. *James Joyce Review* 1 (16 June 1957): 43.

Ernst, Morris L. "Reflections on the Ulysses Trial and Censorship." *JJQ* 3(1965): 3–11.

Ernst, Morris L., and Alan U. Schwartz. *Censorship: The Search for the Obscene.* New York: Macmillan, 1964.

Ernst, Morris L., and William Seagle. *To the Pure . . . A Study of Obscenity and the Censor.* New York: Viking, 1929.

Faherty, Michael. "Heads and Tails: Rhetoric and Realism in Dubliners" *JJQ* 28 (1991): 377–386.

Fairhall, James. "Big-Power Politics and Colonial Economics: The Gordon Bennett Cut Race and 'After the Race.'" *JJQ* 28 (1991): 387–398.

————. "Colgan-Connolly: Another Look at the Politics of 'Ivy Day in the Committee Room,'" *JJQ* 25 (1988): 289–304.

————. *James Joyce and the Question of History.* New York: Cambridge University Press, 1993.

Fallis, Richard. *The Irish Renaissance.* Syracuse: Syracuse University Press, 1977.

Feehan, John M. *An Irish Publisher and His World.* Cork: The Mercier Press, 1969.

Feshbach, Sidney. Review of *Joyce's Politics,* by Dominic Manganiello. *JJQ* 19 (1982): 208–213.

Field Day Theatre Company, ed. *Ireland's Field Day.* London: Hutchinson, 1985.

Flaubert, Gustave. "On Realism." In *Documents of Modern Literary Realism,* edited by George J. Becker, 89–96. Princeton: Princeton University Press, 1963.

Foster, John Wilson. *Fictions of the Irish Literary Revival: A Changeling Art.* Syracuse University Press, 1987.

Foster, R. F. *Modern Ireland: 1600–1972.* New York: Penguin Books, 1989.

Foucault, Michel. *The Foucault Reader.* Edited by Paul Rabinow. New York: Pantheon Books, 1984.

Francini-Bruni, Allesandro. "Recollections of Joyce." In *James Joyce: Interviews and Recollections,* edited by E. H. Mikhail. 51–56. New York: St. Martin's Press, 1990.

Freely, John. "James Clarence Mangan in Joyce's 'The Dead.'" *English Language Notes* 20 (1983): 27–30.

Freyer, Grattan. *W. B. Yeats and the Anti-Democratic Tradition.* Dublin: Gill and MacMillan, 1981.

Ghiselin, Brewster. "The Unity of Joyce's Dubliners." In *Dubliners: Text, Criti-*

cism, and Notes, edited by Robert Scholes and A. Walton Litz, 316–332. New York: Penguin Books, 1969.

Gilbert, Stuart. *Reflections on James Joyce: Stuart Gilbert's Paris Journal*. Edited by Thomas Staley and Randolph Lewis. Austin: University of Texas Press, 1993.

Giovanelli, Felix, trans. "James Joyce: A Memoir." By Stanislaus Joyce. *The Hudson Review* 2 (1950): 485–514.

Glasheen, Adeline. Review of *A Concordance to "Finnegans Wake,"* by Clive Hart. *JJQ* 1 (Fall 1963): 36.

Gogarty, Oliver St. John. "James Joyce: A Portrait of the Artist." *Tomorrow* 6 (1947): 20–27. (Reprinted in *Mourning Became Mrs. Spendlove*. New York: Creative Age Press, 1948.)

———. *Many Lines to Thee: Letters to G. K. A. Bell from the Martello Tower at Sandycove, Rutland Square, and Trinity College Dublin 1904–1907*. Edited by James F. Carens. Ireland, 1971.

———. "They Think They Know Joyce." *The Saturday Review of Literature* 33, no. 11 (18 March 1950): 8–9, 35–37.

Goldman, Arnold. "Stanislaus, James and the Politics of Family." In *Atti del Third International James Joyce Symposium*. Trieste: Università degli Studi Facolta di Magistero, 1974.

Gorak, Jan. *The Making of the Modern Canon*. Atlantic Heights, N.J.: Athlone, 1991.

Gorman, Herbert. Introduction to *A Portrait of the Artist as a Young Man*. New York: The Modern Library, 1928.

———. *James Joyce*. New York: Farrar & Rinehart, 1939.

———. *James Joyce: His First Forty Years*. London: G. Bles, 1926.

Gottfried, Roy. " 'Scrupulous meanness' Reconsidered: Dubliners as Stylistic Parody." In *Joyce in Context*, edited by Vincent J. Cheng and Timothy Martin, 153–169. Cambridge: Cambridge University Press, 1992.

Graff, Gerald. *Professing Literature: An Institutional History*. Chicago: University of Chicago Press, 1989.

Gregory, Lady Augusta. "A Story of the Country of the Dead." *The Irish Homestead: A Celtic Christmas* (December 1902): 15–16.

Groden, Michael, et al., eds. *The James Joyce Archive*. New York and London: Garland Publishing, 1978–.

Gwynn, Aubrey. "The Jesuit Fathers and University College." In *Struggle with Fortune: A Miscellany for the Centenary of the Catholic University of Ireland 1854–1954*, edited by Michael Tierney, 19–50. Dublin: Browne and Nolan, 1955.

Hanson, Harry. "The First Reader" *New York World Telegram* (25 January 1934). Reprinted in Moscato, *United States of America v. One Book Entitled "Ulysses,"* 12.

Hartt, Frederick. *Art: A History of Painting, Sculpture, Architecture*. 3rd ed. Englewood Cliffs, N.J.: Prentice-Hall, 1989.

Hayman, David. "Joyceans Wake at a Funeral in Dublin." In *Books Abroad* 42 (1968): 214–217.

Healey, George Harris. Introduction to *The Dublin Diary of Stanislaus Joyce*, by Stanislaus Joyce. Ithaca: Cornell University Press, 1962.

Heap, Jane. "Art and the Law." In *The Little Review Anthology,* edited by Margaret Anderson, 301–304. (New York: Hermitage House, 1953).

Herr, Cheryl. *Joyce's Anatomy of Culture.* Urbana: University of Illinois Press, 1986.

Herring, Phillip. "Joyce's Politics." In *New Light on Joyce from the Dublin Symposium,* edited by Fritz Senn, 3–14. Bloomington, IN: Indiana University Press, 1972.

———. "Richard Ellmann's *James Joyce.*" In *The Biographer's Art: New Essays,* edited by Jeffrey Meyers, 106–127. London: Macmillan, 1989.

Herrnstein Smith, Barbara. "Belief and Resistance: A Symmetrical Account." In *Questions of Evidence: Proof, Practice, and Persuasion across the Disciplines,* edited by James Chandler, Arnold I. Davidson, and Harry Harootunian, 139–153. Chicago: University of Chicago Press, 1994.

———. "Circling Around, Knocking Over, Playing Out." In *Questions of Evidence: Proof, Practice, and Persuasion across the Disciplines,* edited by James Chandler, Arnold I. Davidson, and Harry Harootunian, 162–167. Chicago: University of Chicago Press, 1994.

———. *Contingencies of Value: Alternative Perspectives for Critical Theory.* Cambridge: Harvard University Press, 1988.

Hoffman, Frederick J. "The Authority of the Commonplace: Joyce's Bloomsday." *Kenyon Review* 22(1960): 316–323.

Hofheinz, Thomas. *Joyce and the Invention of Irish History.* New York: Cambridge University Press, 1995.

Huebsch, B. W. "Footnotes to a Publisher's Life," *The Colophon* 2 (1936–1937): 406–426.

Humphrey, Alexander J. *New Dubliners: Urbanization and the Irish Family.* New York: Fordham University Press, 1966.

Hutchinson, John. *The Dynamics of Cultural Nationalism: The Gaelic Revival and the Creation of the Irish Nation State.* London: Allen and Unwin, 1987.

Joyce, James. "After the Race." *The Irish Homestead* (17 December 1904): 1038–1039.

———. *The Critical Writings of James Joyce.* Edited by Ellsworth Mason and Richard Ellmann. Ithaca, New York: Cornell University Press, 1989. (First printed in 1959.)

———. *Dubliners: Text, Criticism, and Notes.* Edited by Robert Scholes and A. Walton Litz. New York: Penguin Books, 1976. (This edition was first published by Viking in 1969.)

———. *The Early Joyce: The Book Reviews, 1902–1903.* Edited by Ellsworth Mason. Colorado Springs: The Mamalujo Press, 1955.

———. "Eveline." *The Irish Homestead* (10 September 1904): 761.

———. *James Joyce's Letters to Sylvia Beach.* Edited by Melissa Banta and Oscar A. Silverman. Bloomington: Indiana University Press, 1987.

———. *Letters of James Joyce.* Vol. 1. Edited by Stuart Gilbert. New York: Viking Press, 1957; reissued with corrections in 1966. Vols. 2 and 3, Richard Ellmann. New York: Viking Press, 1966.

———. "The Sisters." *The Irish Homestead* (13 August 1904): 676–677.

———. *Stephen Hero.* Edited by John J. Slocum and Herbert Cahoon. New York: New Directions, 1944, 1963.

———. *Ulysses.* New York: Random House, 1961.

———. *Ulysses,* edited by Hans Walter Gabler with Wolfhard Steppe and Claus Melchior. New York: Random House, 1986.

Joyce, Stanislaus. "The Background to *Dubliners.*" *The Listener* 51, no. 1308 (25 March 1954): 526–527.

———. *The Dublin Diary of Stanislaus Joyce,* edited by George Harris Healey. Ithaca: Cornell University Press, 1962. Republished with additions as *The Complete Dublin Diary of Stanislaus Joyce* in 1971.

———. "Early Memories of James Joyce." *The Listener* 41 (26 May 1949): 896–897.

———. "James Joyce: A Memoir," *The Hudson Review* 2 (1950): 485–514.

———. "Joyce's Dublin," *The Partisan Review* 19 (1952): 103–109.

———. *My Brother's Keeper: James Joyce's Early Years,* edited by Richard Ellmann. New York: The Viking Press, 1958.

———. "Open Letter to Dr. Oliver Gogarty" *Interim* 4 (1954): 49–56.

———. *Recollections of James Joyce by His Brother Stanislaus Joyce.* Translated by Ellsworth Mason. New York: The James Joyce Society, 1950.

Kearney, Richard. "Myth and Motherland." In *Ireland's Field Day.* Edited by the Field Day Theatre Company, 61–82. London: Hutchinson, 1985.

Kelly, John S. Afterword to *Dubliners,* by Hans Gabler. New York: Vintage Books, 1993.

Kelly, Timothy, and Joseph Kelly. "Searching the Dark Alley: New Historicism and Social History," *Journal of Social History* 25 (1992): 677–694.

Kenneally, Michael. "Joyce, O'Casey, and the Genre of Autobiography." In *Joyce and His Contemporaries,* edited by Diana A. Ben-Merre and Maureen Murphy, 105–112. New York: Greenwood Press, 1989.

Kenner, Hugh. "The Impertinence of Being Definitive." *Times Literary Supplement* (17 December 1982): 1383–1384.

———. Introduction to *James Joyce and the Making of "Ulysses,"* by Frank Budgen, ix–xv. (Bloomington: Indiana University Press, 1960).

———. *The Pound Era.* Berkeley: University of California Press, 1971.

———. "Signs on a White Field." In *James Joyce: The Centennial Symposium,* edited by Morris Beja, et al., 209–220. Chicago: University of Illinois Press, 1986.

Kermode, Frank. "Puzzles and Epiphanies." *The Spectator* (13 November 1959): 675–676.

Kettle, Thomas. *The Day's Burden: Studies, Literary & Political and Miscellaneous Essays by Thomas Kettle.* 2nd ed. Freeport, N.Y.: Books for Libraries Press, 1968. (First published in 1918.)

Kiberd, Declan. "The Perils of Nostalgia: A Critique of the Revival." In *Literature and the Changing Ireland,* edited by Peter Connolly, 1–24. Totowa, N.J.: Barnes and Noble, 1982.

———. "Story-Telling: The Gaelic Tradition." In *The Irish Short Story,* edited by Patrick Rafroidi and Terence Brown, 13–25. Gerrards Cross, Buckinghamshire: Colin Smythe, 1979.

Kidd, John. "An Inquiry into Ulysses: The Corrected Text," *PBSA* 82 (December 1988): 411–584.

———. "The Scandal of Ulysses." *The New York Review of Books,* 30 June 1988, 32.

Killeen, Terence. "Irish (Men) Recuperate Joyce," *JJLS* 7 (Fall 1993): 16.

Kittredge, George. "The Dramatic Principle in the *Canterbury Tales.*" In *The Canterbury Tales: Nine Tales and the General Prologue, Authoritative Text, Sources and Backgrounds, Criticism,* edited by V. A. Kolve and Glending Olson, 518–523. New York: Norton, 1989. Reprinted from *Chaucer and His Poetry.* Cambridge: Harvard University Press, 1915.

Klancher, Jon P. *The Making of English Reading Audiences, 1790–1832.* Madison: University of Wisconsin Press, 1987.

Lee, Joseph. *The Modernisation of Irish Society: 1848–1918.* Vol. 10 of *The Gill History of Ireland.* Dublin: Gill and MacMillan, 1973.

Lentricchia, Frank. "Foucault's Legacy: A New Historicism." In *The New Historicism,* edited by H. Aram Veeser, 231–242. New York: Routledge, 1989.

Levin, Harry, ed. Introduction to *The Portable James Joyce.* Rev. ed. New York: Viking Penguin, 1968. Originally published in 1947.

———. *James Joyce: A Critical Introduction.* New York: New Directions, 1941.

Levin, Richard. "The Poetics and Politics of Bardicide," *PMLA* 105 (May 1990): 491–504.

———. "Unthinkable Thoughts in the New Historicizing of English Renaissance Drama." *New Literary History* 21 (1990): 433–447.

Levin, Richard, and Charles Shattuck. "First Flight to Ithaca." In *James Joyce: Two Decades of Criticism,* edited by Seon Givens, 47–94. New York: Vanguard Press, 1948.

Litz, A. Walton, and Robert Scholes, eds. Introduction to Criticism Section, *Dubliners: Text, Criticism, and Notes,* by James Joyce. New York: Penguin Books, 1969.

———. "Joyce's Notes for the Last Episodes of Ulysses." *MFS* 4 (1958): 3–20.

———. "Pound and Eliot on *Ulysses:* The Critical Tradition." In *"Ulysses": Fifty Years,* edited by Thomas F. Staley, 5–18. Bloomington: Indiana University Press, 1974.

———. "Ulysses and Its Audience." In *James Joyce: The Centennial Symposium,* edited by Morris Beja, et al., 220–229. Chicago: University of Illinois Press, 1986.

Lodge, David. *The Modes of Modern Writing: Metaphor, Metonymy, and the Typology of Modern Literature.* Chicago: University of Chicago Press, 1977.

Lyons, F. S. L. *Ireland Since the Famine.* London: Fontana Press, 1973.

———. "Joyce's Dublin," *Twentieth Century Studies, Ireland* (November 1970): 6–25.

Lyons, J. B. *James Joyce and Medicine.* New York: Humanities Press, 1974.

MacCabe, Bernard. Review of *James Joyce* (rev. ed.), by Richard Ellmann. *The Nation* (20 November 1982): 527.

MacCabe, Colin. *James Joyce and the Revolution of the Word.* London: Macmillan, 1978.

MacDonald, Dwight. "A Hero of Our Time." *The New Yorker* 35 (12 December 1959): 213–234.

Maddox, Brenda. Introduction to *Dubliners,* by James Joyce, vii–xxiii. New York: Bantam Books, 1990.

———. *Nora: The Real Life of Molly Bloom.* Boston: Houghton Mifflin Company, 1988.

Magalaner, Marvin. "The Other Side of James Joyce," *The Arizona Quarterly* 9 (1953): 5–16.

———. Review of Patricia Hutchinson's *James Joyce's World,* James Joyce Review 1 (16 June 1957): 42.

———, and Richard M. Kain. *Joyce: The Man, the Work, the Reputation.* New York: New York University Press, 1956.

Mahaffey, Vicki. *Reauthorizing Joyce.* New York: Cambridge University Press, 1988.

Manganiello, Dominic. *Joyce's Politics.* London: Routledge and Kegan Paul, 1980.

———. "Through a Cracked Looking Glass: The Picture of Dorian Gray and A Portrait of the Artist as a Young Man." In *Joyce and His Contemporaries,* edited by Diana A. Ben-Merre and Maureen Murphy, 89–96. New York: Greenwood Press, 1989.

Marsden, Dora. "England and Ireland," *The Egoist* (1 June 1916): 81–85.

Mason, Ellsworth. "Ellmann's Road to Xanadu." In *Essays for Richard Ellmann: Omnium Gatherum,* edited by Susan Dick, et al., 4–12. Montreal: McGill-Queen's University Press, 1989.

———. Introduction and notes to *The Early Joyce: The Book Reviews, 1902–1903.* Colorado Springs: The Mamalujo Press, 1955.

———. Introduction and notes to *James Joyce: The Critical Writings.* New York: The Viking Press, 1959. rpt. Ithaca: Cornell University Press, 1989.

———. "James Joyce: Moralist," *Twentieth Century Literature* 1 (January 1956): 196–206.

———. "James Joyce's Shrill Note—The *Piccolo Della Sera* Articles," *Twentieth Century Literature* 2 (October 1956): 115–119.

———. "Joyce's Categories," *The Sewanee Review* 61 (1953): 427–432.

———. "Mr. Stanislaus Joyce and John Henry Raleigh," *Modern Language Notes* 70 (March 1955): 187–191.

———. "*Ulysses,* the Hair Shirt, and Humility," *The CEA Critic* 14 (February 1952): 6.

———, trans. *Recollections of James Joyce by his Brother Stanislaus Joyce.* New York: The James Joyce Society, 1950.

McCarthy, Patrick A. "Stuart Gilbert's Guide to the Perplexed." In *Re-Viewing the Classics of Joyce Criticism,* edited by Janet Egleson Dunleavy, 23–35. (Urbana: University of Illinois Press, 1991).

McCormick, Kathleen, and Erwin R. Steinberg, eds. *Approaches to Teaching Joyce's "Ulysses."* New York: MLA, 1993.

McCullough, Ann. "Joyce's Early Publishing History." In *James Joyce: The Centennial Symposium,* edited by Morris Beja, et al., 184–192. Chicago: Chicago University Press, 1986.

McGann, Jerome. *The Beauty of Inflections*. Oxford: Clarendon Press, 1985.

———. Introduction to *Historical Studies and Literary Criticism*, edited by Jerome J. McGann, 3–21. Madison: University of Wisconsin Press, 1985.

———. "The Monks and the Giants: Textual and Bibliographical Studies and the Interpretation of Literary Works." In *Textual Criticism and Literary Interpretation*, edited by Jerome J. McGann, 180–199. Chicago: University of Chicago Press, 1985.

———. "Theory of Texts," *London Review of Books*. (18 February 1988): 20–21.

McKeon, Michael. *Origins of the English Novel: 1600–1740*. Baltimore: Johns Hopkins Press, 1987.

Meenan, James. *The Irish Economy Since 1922*. Liverpool: Liverpool University Press, 1970.

———. "The Student Body." In *Struggle with Fortune: A Miscellany for the Centenary of the Catholic University of Ireland 1854–1954*, edited by Michael Tierney, 103–120. Dublin: Browne and Nolan, 1955.

Mercier, Vivien. "The Irish Short Story and Oral Tradition." In *The Celtic Cross: Studies in Irish Culture and Literature*, edited by Ray B. Browne, et al., 98–116. Purdue: Purdue University Studies, 1964.

Miller, Jane. " 'O, she's a nice lady!': A Rereading of 'A Mother.' " *JJQ* 28 (1991): 407–426.

Miller, Liam. *The Dun Emer Press, Later the Cuala Press*. New Yeats Papers VII. Dublin: Dolmen Press, 1973.

Moscato, Michael, and Leslie LeBlanc, eds. *The United States of America v. One Book Entitled "Ulysses" by James Joyce*. Frederick, Maryland: University Publications of America, 1984.

Murray, Timothy D. "The Modern Library." In *American Literary Publishing Houses 1900–1980: Trade and Paperback*, edited by Peter Dzwonskoski, 242–245. *DLB* 46. Detroit: Bruccoli Clark, 1986.

Nadel, Ira. "The American Ulysses: A Lasting Boom," *JJQ* 28 (Summer 1991): 967–981.

———. "Anthologizing Joyce: The Example of T. S. Eliot," *JJQ* 27 (1990): 509–516.

———. *Biography: Fiction, Fact and Form*. New York: St. Martin's Press, 1984.

———. "The Incomplete Joyce," *JSA* 2 (1991): 86–100.

Nelson, James G. *Elkin Mathews: Publisher to Yeats, Joyce, Pound*. Madison: University of Wisconsin Press, 1989.

The New Freewoman: An Individualist Review. Nos. 1–13. New York: Kraus Reprint Corporation, 1967.

Nolan, Emer. *James Joyce and Nationalism*. New York: Routledge, 1995.

Noon, William T., "A Delayed Review." *JJQ* 2 (1964): 7–12.

Norris, Margot. "The Consequence of Deconstruction: A Technical Perspective of Joyce's Finnegans Wake." In *Critical Essays on James Joyce*, edited by Bernard Benstock, 206–221. Boston: G. K. Hall and Co., 1985. First printed in *ELH* 41 (1974): 206–220.

O'Brien, Joseph V. *"Dear, Dirty Dublin": A City in Distress*. Berkeley: University of California Press, 1982.

O'Connor, Ulick. *Celtic Dawn: A Portrait of the Irish Literary Renaissance*. London: Hamish Hamilton, 1984.

———. *The Times I've Seen: Oliver St. John Gogarty: A Biography*. New York: Ivan Obolensky, Inc., 1963.

O'Grady, Thomas. "Little Chandler's Song of Experience." *JJQ* 28 (1991): 399.

A Page of Irish History: The Story of University College Dublin, 1883–1909. Compiled by the Fathers of the Society for Jesus. Dublin: Talbot Press, 1930.

Perelman, Bob. *The Trouble with Genius: Reading Pound, Joyce, Stein, and Zukofsky*. Berkeley: University of California Press, 1994.

Pierce, David. *James Joyce's Ireland*. New Haven: Yale University Press, 1992.

Pollard, M. *Dublin's Trade in Books: 1550–1800*. Lyrell Lectures, 1986–1987. Oxford: Clarendon Press, 1989.

Porter, Carolyn. "Are We Being Historical Yet?" *South Atlantic Quarterly* 87 (1988): 743–786.

Pound, Ezra. *The Letters of Ezra Pound*. Edited by D. D. Paige. London: Faber and Faber, n.d.

———. *Literary Essays of Ezra Pound*. New York: New Directions, 1968.

———. "On Criticism in General," *Criterion* 1 (January 1923): 143–156.

———. *Pound/Joyce: The Letters of Ezra Pound to James Joyce, with Pound's Essays on Joyce*. Edited by Forrest Read. New York: New Directions, 1967.

Purdon, K. F. "Match-Making in Ardenoo." *The Irish Homestead* (December 1902): 12–15.

Rafroidi, Patrick. "The Irish Short Story in English. The Birth of a New Tradition." In *The Irish Short Story*, Cahiers Irlandais, nos. 7 and 8, edited by Terence Brown and Patrick Rafroidi, 27–38. France: Publications de l'université de Lille III.

Raleigh, John Henry. " 'My Brother's Keeper'—Stanislaus Joyce and Finnegans Wake," *Modern Language Notes* 68 (1953): 107–110.

Ransom, John Crowe. "Criticism, Inc." In *Selected Essays of John Crowe Ransom*, edited by Thomas Daniel Young and John Hindle, 93–106. Baton Rouge: Louisiana State University Press, 1964.

Rembar, Charles. Introduction to *Obscenity: The Complete Oral Arguments Before the Supreme Court in the Major Obscenity Cases*, edited by Leon Friedman, ix–xxii. New York: Chelsea House, 1970.

Rice, Thomas Jackson. "The Geometry of Meaning in Dubliners: A Euclidean Approach," *Style* 25 (1991): 393–404.

———. *James Joyce: A Guide to Research*. New York: Garland Publishing Company, 1982.

Riquelme, J. P. "Joyce's 'The Dead': The Dissolution of the Self and the Police." *Style* 25 (Fall 1991): 488–505.

Rodden, John. *The Politics of Literary Reputation: The Making and Claiming of 'St. George' Orwell*. New York: Oxford University Press, 1989.

Rodgers, W. R. "A Portrait of Joyce as a Young Man." *Irish Literary Portrait*, 22–47. London: BBC, 1972.

Rogers, W. G. *Wise Men Fish Here: The Story of Frances Steloff and the Gotham Book Mart*. New York: Harcourt, Brace, 1965.

Rossman, Charles. "The New *Ulysses*: The Hidden Controversy," *The New York Review of Books* (8 December 1988): 53–58.

Russell, George. *Letters from AE.* Edited by Alan Denson. New York: Abelard-Schuman, 1961.

Schauer, Frederick F. *The Law of Obscenity.* Washington, D.C.: The Bureau of National Affairs, 1976.

Schaurek, Eileen Joyce. "Pappy Never Spoke of Jim's Books." In *James Joyce: Interviews and Recollections,* edited by E. H. Mikhail, 60–69. New York: St. Martin's Press, 1990.

Schenker, Daniel. "Stalking the Invisible Hero: Ibsen, Joyce, Kierkegaard, and the Failure of Modern Irony." *ELH* 51(1984), 153–183.

Scholes, Robert. "Grant Richards to James Joyce," *Studies in Bibliography* 16 (1963): 139–160.

———. *In Search of James Joyce.* Chicago: University of Illinois Press, 1992.

———. "Joyce and Modernist Ideology." In *Coping with Joyce: Essays from the Copenhagen Symposium,* edited by Morris Beja and Shari Benstock, 91–110. Columbus: Ohio State University Press, 1989.

———. Letter to the Editor. *JJQ* 2 (Summer 1965): 310–313.

Scott, Bonnie Kime. "Hanna and Francis Sheehy-Skeffington: Reformers in the Company of Joyce." In *Joyce and His Contemporaries,* edited by Diana A. Ben-Merre and Maureen Murphy, 77–84. New York: Greenwood Press, 1989.

Segall, Jeffrey. "Between Marxism and Modernism, or How To Be a Revolutionist and Still Love Ulysses." *JJQ* 25 (Summer 1988): 421–444.

———. *Joyce in America: Cultural Politics and the Trials of "Ulysses."* Berkeley: University of California Press, 1993.

Sheehy, Eugene. *May It Please the Court.* Dublin: C. J. Fallon, Ltd., 1951.

Slocum, John J., and Herbert Cahoon. *A Bibliography of James Joyce.* New Haven: Yale University Press, 1953.

Smidt, Kristian. "Joyce and Ibsen: A Study in Literary Influence." *Edda* 70(1970), 85–103.

Smith, Paul Jordan. *Key to "Ulysses."* Chicago: P. Covici, 1927.

Soloman, Albert. "The Backgrounds of "Eveline." *Eire-Ireland* 6 (1971): 23–38.

Spender, Stephen. "All Life was Grist for the Artist." *The New York Times Book Review* (25 October 1959): 1, 58; and *The New Yorker* (2 April 1960): 32.

Spoo, Robert. *James Joyce and the Language of History: Dedalus's Nightmare.* New York: Oxford University Press, 1994.

Staley, Thomas. *An Annotated Critical Bibliography of James Joyce.* New York: St. Martin's Press, 1989.

———. "A Beginning: Signification, Story, and Discourse in Joyce's 'The Sisters.'" In *Critical Essays on James Joyce,* edited by Bernard Benstock, 176–190. Boston: G. K. Hall and Co., 1985. First published in *Genre* 12 (Winter 1979): 533–549.

———. "Bibliography, Texts, Libraries: The Changing Shape of the Humanities." Plenary Address at the South Central Modern Languages Association. New Orleans, Louisiana, 27 October 1989. Typescript.

———. "James Joyce." In *Anglo-Irish Literature: A Review of Research,* edited by Richard J. Finneran, 366–435. New York: The Modern Language Association of America, 1976.

———. "James Joyce and the Dilemma of American Academic Criticism." *Dublin Magazine* 6 (Spring 1967): 38–45.

———. "Notes and Comments," *JJQ* 1 [Winter 1963]: 1.

———. "Notes and Comments," *JJQ* 3 [Winter 1965]: 93–94.

———. "Notes and Comments," *JJQ* 4 [Fall 1966]: 1–2.

Steloff, Frances. "In Touch With Genius." *Journal of Modern Literature* 4 (1975): 848–856.

Stevens, Kenneth. "Ulysses on Trial." *The Library Chronicle* 20/21 (1982): 90–105. Reprinted in Moscato, *United States of America v. One Book Entitled "Ulysses,"* 59–72.

Sullivan, Kevin. *Joyce among the Jesuits.* New York: Columbia University Press, 1958.

Summerfield, Henry. Introduction to *Selections from the Contributions to the Irish Homestead by G. W. Russell—AE.* Vol. 1, 31–34. Atlantick Highlands, N.J.: Humanities Press, 1978.

Taine, Hippolyte. "The World of Balzac." In *Documents of Modern Literary Realism,* edited by George J. Becker, 105–111. Princeton: Princeton University Press, 1963.

Tan, Amy. "In the Canon, for All the Wrong Reasons." *Harper's Magazine* 293 (December 1996): 27–31.

Tanselle, G. Thomas. "In Memoriam: B. W. Huebsch." *Antiquarian Bookman* 36 (30 August 1965): 727–728.

———. "Textual Criticism and Literary Sociology," *Studies in Bibliography* 44 (1991): 83–143.

Tate, Allen, and Caroline Gordon, eds. *The House of Fiction: An Anthology of the Short Story.* New York: Charles Scribner's Sons, 1960.

Theoharis, Theoharis C. "Hedda Gabler and 'The Dead.'" *ELH* 50(1983): 791–809.

Thompkins, Jane. *Sensational Designs.* New York: Oxford University Press, 1985.

Tierney, Michael, ed. *Struggle with Fortune: A Miscellany for the Centenary of The Catholic University of Ireland 1854–1954.* Dublin: Browne and Nolan, n.d.

Todorov, Vladimir. *Introduction to Poetics.* Translated by Richard Howard. Theory and History of Literature 1. Minneapolis: University of Minnesota Press, 1981.

Townshend, Charles. *Political Violence in Ireland: Government and Resistance since 1848.* London: Clarendon Press, 1983.

Tracy, R. "Mr. Joker and Mr. Hyde: Joyce's Politic Polyglot Polygraphs." *LIT* 1 (1989): 151–169.

Tymoczko, Maria. *The Irish Ulysses.* Berkeley: University of California Press, 1994.

Valente, Joseph. "Joyce's Sexual Differend: An Example from Dubliners," *JJQ* 28 (1991): 427–444.

Vanderham, Paul. "Lifting the Ban on *Ulysses:* The Well-Intentioned Lies of the Woolsey Decision," *Mosaic* 27 (December 1994): 179–197.

von Phul, Ruth. Letter to the Editor. *JJQ* 3 (Fall 1965): 69–72.

Walsh, Brendan M. "Marriage Rates and Population Pressure: Ireland, 1871–1911." *The Economic History Review* 23 (1970): 148–162.

Walzl, Florence. "Dubliners: Women in Irish Society." In *Women in Joyce,* edited by Suzette Henke and Elaine Unkeless, 31–55. Chicago: University of Illinois Press, 1982.

Watt, Ian. *The Rise of the Novel: Studies in Defoe, Richardson, and Fielding.* Berkeley: University of California Press, 1959.

Webb, W. L. "A Ghost on Bloomsday," *The Guardian* (17 June 1967): 7.

Wellek, René. "Literary Scholarship." In *American Scholarship in the Twentieth Century,* edited by Merle Curti, 111–145. Cambridge: Harvard University Press, 1953.

Wilhelm, J. J. *Ezra Pound in London and Paris: 1908–1925.* University Park: Pennsylvania State University Press, 1990.

Williams, Raymond. *Key Words: A Vocabulary of Culture and Society.* Rev. ed. New York: Oxford University Press, 1983.

Williams, Trevor. "No Cheer for the 'Gratefully Oppressed.'" *Style* 25 (Fall 1991): 416–438.

Wilson, Edmund. *Axel's Castle: A Study in the Imaginative Literature of 1870–1930.* New York: Charles Scribner's Sons, 1931. Reprinted in 1969.

Wimsatt, William K., and William Beardsley. *The Verbal Icon: Studies in the Meaning of Poetry.* Lexington: University of Kentucky Press, 1954. "The Intentional Fallacy" was originally published in *The Sewanee Review* 54 (Summer 1946): 468–488.

Yeats, W. B. *W. B. Yeats: The Poems.* Edited by Richard J. Finneran. New ed. New York: Macmillan, 1983.

Younger, Irving. *"Ulysses" in Court: The Litigation Surrounding the First Publication of James Joyce's Novel in the United States.* Classics of the Classroom 16. Minnetonka, Minnesota: The Professional Education Group, 1988.

Zola, Emile. "The Experimental Novelist." In *Documents of Modern Literary Realism,* edited by George J. Becker, 161–198. Princeton: Princeton University Press, 1963.

Index

Bestow, Fred, 128
Bible, 101–102
Bierman, Robert, 192, 194
biographical fallacy, 192, 246n.31
Bishop, Edward L., 11, 102, 228n.24
Blackmur, R. P., 183
Blanchard, Julia, 93
Blount, Godfrey, 65
"Boarding House, The," 15–16, 60
Boccaccio, Giovanni, 111
Bodkin, Michael, 168
Boni, Albert, 80–82, 137
Booth, Wayne, 221
Bord Failte, 207, 211
Boswell, 22
Bowerman, George, 124–125, 127, 129, 244n.109
Boyarin, Daniel, 227n17
Boyd, Ernest, 117
Boyer, Paul, 137–138, 238n.4, 241n.50
Briffault, Robert, 121
Brockman, William S., 123, 255n.98
Brodhead, Richard, 223
Brodsky, Judge C. M., 111
Brooks, Cleanth, 13, 149, 182, 184–185
Brown, Richard, 7–8, 235n.132
Brown, Terence, 209
Browne, Arthur, 22
Bryer, Jackson R., 238n.2
Buckley, William, 57
Budgen, Frank: and draft of "Scylla and Charybdis," 1–3; influence on Joyce criticism of, 193; and Richard Ellmann, 149
Burgess, Anthony, 204–206
Byrne, John Francis, 150, 156, 158–163, 175, 249n.92

Cahoon, Herbert, 144, 149
Callanan, Mary Ellen, 169
Callanan, Mrs. (Joyce's great aunt), 169
Campbell, Joseph, 194
Campbell, Lord, 95
Canby, Henry Seidel, 108, 119–121

Carew, Rivers, 207, 211
Carson, Edmund, 78
Carver, Catherine, 213
catholicism. See Ireland, Roman Catholic Church in
Catholic middle class. See Ireland, Catholic middle class in
"Cattleman's Spring Mate," 82–83
Celtic revival. See literary revival
Cerf, Bennett: colleges and universities solicited by, 128–129; consequences of Ulysses decision for, 133–134; Dubliners and Portrait published by, 80, 212; Joyce's reputation influenced by, 79, 179, 223; liberalism of, 139; librarians' opinion solicited by, 123–126, 244n.109; and the Linati scheme, 11, 135–136; Modern Library bought by, 81; negotiations with Ernst of, 242n.80; rights to Ulysses bought by, 104–106; testimonials about Ulysses solicited by, 107–108, 131; Ulysses donated to Columbia University by, 134; Ulysses published by, 131–134, 212–213, 244n.118; U. S. Customs' seizure of Ulysses described by, 109; Woolsey decision advertized by, 133
Cervantes, Miguel de, 120
Chamber Music, 58, 163
Chaucer, Geoffrey, 81, 135, 188
Cheng, Vincent, 11
Chestnut, Margaret, 13, 229n.14, 232n.50, 235n.117
Clancy, George, 20
classic, 10, 79–84, 101, 110–116, 118, 121, 136, 139–140, 212
"Clay," 15, 39, 48, 145–146
Clean Books League, 117
Cleland, John, 94
Clery, Arthur, 20, 26
Clissold, Bradley, 245n.131
Cockburn, Lord Chief Justice, 95
Cohn, Alan, 196, 199–200, 207
Cole, Richard, 21–22
Coleman, Judge, 110

"Little Cloud, A"; "Mother, A";
"Painful Case, A"; Pound, Ezra,
Dubliners reviewed by; "Sisters,
The"; "Two Gallants")
Duffy, Enda, 11

Edel, Leon, 194
Edward VII, King, 55–56, 75
Egoist, The, 9, 64–66, 68, 71–75,
77–80
Egoist Press, The, 71, 73, 237n.56
Einstein, Albert, 89
Eliot, T. S.: aesthetics of, 71–73,
81, 237n.33; essay on Ben Jonson
by, 186–187; Joyce anthology
published by, 212; Joyce criticism
influenced by, 212; Joyce's reputation influenced by, 9–10, 71, 73,
75–76, 83–84, 179, 213, 223; *My
Brother's Keeper* introduced by,
172; New Criticism initiated by,
183; obscenity discussed by, 82–83;
patrons of, 69–70; Pound's discovery of, 64, 77; Ransom's book
about, 185; *Ulysses* adopted at
Harvard by, 129; *Ulysses* defended
by, 71
Ellis, Frank H., 246n.31
Ellis, Havelock, 97
Ellmann, Richard: association with
James Joyce Quarterly of, 199, 206;
authority over Joyce's work of, 4,
165, 172–174, 213–216; background of, 148–149; biographical
method of, 154–156, 163–165,
175; canonization of, 172–174;
critics of, 174–175, 249n.105,
250–251n.128; *Critical Writings*
edited by, 153; Dora Marsden described by, 66; Ellsworth Mason's
advice received by, 151–154;
Jacques Benoît-Méchin interviewed
by, 180; John Francis Byrne interviewed by, 160; Joyce criticism
influenced by, 9, 15, 143, 173–174,
221; Joyce's politics described by,
54, 176, 178–179; Joyce's reputa-

tion influenced by, 10, 141–142,
168–172, 223; meetings with
Stanislaus Joyce of, 148–150, 152,
247n.50, 249n.99; and Nelly Joyce,
150–151; papers of, 225; reliance
on Stanislaus Joyce of, 10,
156–157, 159–163, 166–168,
172, 174; and sale of Stanislaus
Joyce papers, 153; support for
Nora's biography of, 155–156;
treatment of Oliver Gogarty by,
159–160, 162–168, 170, 175,
250n.116; treatment of Vincent
Cosgrave by, 158–162, 166, 168,
170, 175, 248n.90; *Ulysses* negotiations described by, 105
Elwood, John, 163
Emmet, Robert, 163
Empson, William, 171–172, 175,
249n.105
"Encounter, An," 45, 54, 202, 220
Ennis, Mr., 113
Epstein, Edmund, 195–196, 198, 207
Ernst, Morris: background of, 92–93;
Cerf's negotiations with, 242n.80;
consequences of Woolsey decision
for, 133; Edmund Wilson's influence on, 141; fear of juries of,
117–118; Frances Steloff defended
by, 111; Joyce's reputation influenced by, 103, 179, 223; liberalism
of, 138–139; Maria Stopes defended by, 98–99, 103; Mary Ware
Dennett defended by, 97–98, 103;
on the masthead of *James Joyce Review*, 195–196; Menken discussed
by, 241n.50; obscenity linked to
class prejudice by, 98–102; papers
of, 225; *Pay Day* defended by, 97;
Treasury petitioned by, on behalf of
The Story-Teller's Holiday, 111–
113; Treasury petitioned by, on behalf of *Ulysses*, 113–115; *Well of
Loneliness* defended by, 96–97,
103; *What Happens* defended by,
93–94; Woolsey decision advertized
by, 133, 136–137; Woolsey deci-

sion assessed by, 132, 228n.24;
Woolsey influenced by, 134–135;
Woolsey invited to go yachting by,
240n.42; *Ulysses* defended by,
9–10, 103–110, 115–131, 140,
212, 239n.17, 245n.131
Essential James Joyce, The. See
Portable James Joyce, The
"Eveline," 15, 36–38, 54, 234n.100
Explicator, The, 185, 205

Faherty, Michael, 31
Fairhall, James, 11, 13, 50–51, 55,
230n.19, 231n.32, 235n.129
fallacy of genius, 188, 192, 223, 224
Farrell, James T., 141, 176
Faulkner, William, 81
Feshbach, Sidney, 202, 234n.105
Field Day, 24, 232n.49
Finnegans Wake: abridged edition of,
206; biographical use of, 156; con-
troversial paper on, 209; criticism
of, 145, 147, 190, 192; Ellmann's
influence on, 174; Viking edition of,
194 (*see also* Joyce, James, inten-
tions for *Finnegans Wake* of)
Fitzgerald, F. Scott, 120, 137, 202
Flanagan, Thomas, 200
Flaubert, Gustave, 75–77
Fleischman, Bernard, 198, 200
Ford, Judge John, 138
Forster, E. M., 81
Foster, R. F., 41
Foucault, Michel, 3–4, 187
Fowler, Julian, 126
Frampton, Maralee, 207
Francini Bruni, Alessandro, 157
Freewoman, The, 65
Frend, Warren, 199
Freud, Sigmund, 154, 241n.51
Freyer, Grattan, 23, 229n.11
Friede, Donald, 137
Frost, Robert, 64

Gabler, Hans Walter, 214–215,
221–222
Gaelic revival. *See* literary revival

Garland, Hamlin, 138
Garvin, John, 208
Gautier, Theophile, 96
Gest, Morris, 89
Ghiselin, Brewster, 14
Gibbon, Edmund, 22
Gilbert, Stuart, 4, 104, 115, 118,
135–136, 149, 161, 193, 195,
243n.106, 249n.92
Giovanelli, Felix, 143–144
Gissing, George, 57, 59–60
Gladstone, William, 40
Glasheen, Adeline, 201, 206
Glick, Morton, 213
Godwin, Willard, 255n.99
Gogarty, Oliver: appearance in
Ulysses of, 159, 166, 171; attack
on English chastity of, 56–57; eco-
nomic status of, 29; Ellmann's
citations of, 156; Ellmann's review
of, 199; estrangement from Joyce
of, 167–168; John Francis Byrne's
opinion of, 162; loyalty to Arthur
Griffith of, 164; Stanislaus Joyce's
opinion of, 143, 162–163,
249n.98 (*see also* Ellmann,
Richard, treatment of Oliver
Gogarty by)
Gohdes, Clarence, 191
Goldman, Arnold, 167, 250n.128
Goldsmith, Oliver, 22
Gorak, Jan, 223–224
Gore-Booth, Eva, 34
Gorman, Herbert, 82, 115–116, 119,
135, 143–144, 149, 151, 163
Gotham Book Mart, 90, 110, 194,
198–199, 203, 240n.32
Gottfried, Roy, 236n.134
"Grace," 47
Graff, Gerald, 181–183, 185,
189–190, 251n.3, 252n.22
Greenbaum, Eddie, 90–93, 106,
138–139, 240n.32
Greene, David H., 200
Gregory, Lady Augusta, 27–29, 31,
34–37, 59
Grierson, Francis, 65

Griffith, Arthur, 29, 42, 54, 57, 75, 164, 176, 178
Guinzberg, Harold, 79, 81, 103

Habermas, Jürgen, 232n.50
"Hades," 73
Hall, Radclyffe, 9, 97, 103, 107, 115
"Hallows Eve," 15, 38
Halsey, Raymond, 96, 132
Hand, Judge Augustus, 132
Hand, Judge Learned, 82, 96, 132
Harding, Warren G., 138
Hardy, Thomas, 59–60
Harris, Frank, 90
Hart, Clive, 190, 197–201, 206
Hawthorne, Nathaniel, 223
Hayes, Will, 100
Hayman, David, 197–198, 202, 206, 209–210, 222
Healy, George, 167
Healy, Justice, 91
Heaney, Seamus, 232n.49
Heap, Jane, 85–87, 90, 99, 117–118, 239n.13
Heinemann, William, 15
Heininger, Joseph, 222
Hemingway, Ernest, 89, 137
Herring, Phillip, 155, 159, 175, 249n.105, 250n.128
Heymoolen, A., 90
Hicklin rule, 95–96, 98–99, 130, 132, 241n.48
Higginson, Fred, 197, 199, 206
Hitler, Adolph, 175
Hodgart, Matthew, 206
Hofheinz, Thomas, 11
Holdeman, David, 231n.43
Holmes, Justice Oliver Wendell, 108
Holmes, Peter, 94
"Holy Office, The," 27, 166
Homer, 117, 142, 169, 181
"Home Rule Comet," 41
Hoover, Herbert, 118, 139
Horace, 102
Howarth, Herbert, 197–198
Howe, Irving, 141, 176
Hudson Review, The, 143–144

Huebsch, Ben, 79–80, 89, 92, 103–106, 137, 139, 195, 212–213
Humphrey, Alexander, 43
Hutchinson, John, 18, 24–26, 230n.22, 231n.31
Hutchinson, Patricia, 195
Huysman, Joris Karl, 59
Hyde, Douglas, 24, 26, 28, 34

I. A. O. S. See Irish Agricultural Organization Society
Ibsen, Henrik, 13, 28, 40, 57, 61, 81
"Ibsen's New Drama," 58
intentional fallacy, 185–186, 192
International James Joyce Symposia, 11, 203, 207–212
Ireland: Catholic middle class in, 9, 18–21, 23–25, 29–33, 43–44, 49–57, 63–64, 221, 231n.31; economic condition of, 17–18, 32–34, 46–51, 56, 76; education in, 19, 45; local government of, 21, 55; marriage in, 8; publishing industry in, 15, 21–24; Roman Catholic Church in, 40, 43, 56, 76, 145, 148
"Ireland, Island of Saints and Sages," 41–42
Irish Agricultural Organization Society, 32–34, 46
Irish Homestead, The, 15, 31–39, 234n.103
Irish Land League, 175
Irish Literary Society, 23
Irish Literary Theatre, 24, 27–29
Irish party. See Parliamentary party
Irish Peasant, 34
Irish Socialist Republican party, 51, 54, 56
Irish Times, 50
"Ivy Day in the Committee Room," 16, 52, 54–56, 220

James, Henry, 183, 191
James Joyce, 153–154, 156, 158–163, 165–166, 168, 171–174, 181
James Joyce Industry. See Joyce Industry

149, 155, 172–173, 196, 198, 203, 207
Kastor, Robert, 105, 242nn.80,81
Kavanagh, Patrick, 204
Kearney, Richard, 232n.49
Kelleher, John, 200
Kelly, John S., 14
Kennedy, Hugh, 20
Kenner, Hugh, 9, 38, 64, 175, 193, 204, 206, 221, 234n.103
Kenyon Review, 152, 185, 221
Kermode, Frank, 172
Kettle, Mary Sheehy, 169
Kettle, Thomas, 17, 19
Kiberd, Declan, 176, 209, 232n.49, 233n.91
Kidd, John, 221–222
Killeen, Terence, 209
Kimball, Jean, 251n.129
Kinkeldey, Otto, 126
Kipling, Rudyard, 80
Kittredge, George, 188, 206, 252n.27
Klancher, Jon, 5
Klopfer, Donald, 105–106, 131
Knox, Judge, 92, 109–110, 240n.37

Larbaud, Valery, 193, 243n.106
Larkin, James, 77
Lawrence, D. H., 80, 137, 194
Lee, Joseph, 230n.31
Lennon, John, 203
Lennon, Michael J., 114
Lentricchia, Frank, 6
Leon, Paul, 11, 104, 107–108, 111, 134–136, 244n.118
Leslie, Shane, 117
"Lestrygonians," 85
Levin, Harry, 141, 196, 211–213, 221
Levin, Richard, 6–7, 14, 199, 227n.17, 228n.20
Levy, Norman, 90
Lewis, Wyndham, 64, 77, 238n.6
liberalism, 4, 25, 40, 85, 137–142, 175–179, 190, 214
librarian survey, 123–128
Library Journal, 139

Linati, Carlos, 243n.106
Linati scheme, 11, 121, 135–136, 142, 180–181, 243n.106
Lindey, Alexander: Edmund Wilson's influence on, 141; liberalism of, 138; Treasury petitioned by, on behalf of *The Story-Teller's Holiday*, 111–113; Treasury petitioned by, on behalf of *Ulysses*, 113–115; Woolsey decision advertized by, 133; *Ulysses* defended by, 103–110, 115–131
literary revival, 23–26, 35, 37, 39, 56, 75, 78, 140
"Little Cloud, A," 23, 245n.8
Little Review, The, 71, 80, 82–83, 85–86, 89, 91, 108
Litz, A. Walton, 14, 192–194, 206, 214, 217–218, 220–221
Liveright, Horace, 80, 137
Lord Campbell's Act, 95, 111, 241n.48
Lovett, Robert Morss, 120
Lowe-Evans, Mary, 222
Lowell, Amy, 64, 68
Lyman, Philip, 199
Lynch, Edmund, 119
Lyons, Freddie, 169
Lyons, F. S. L., 19, 21, 32–33, 51, 229n.19
Lyons, Mrs. (Joyce's great aunt), 169

MacCabe, Colin, 177–178, 249n.105
MacCarvill, Eileen, 208
MacNelly, Leonard, 163
Macrae, President of E. P. Dutton, 112
Maddox, Brenda, 14, 57, 151, 155, 164, 216–217, 247n.50
Magalaner, Marvin, 14, 142–143, 145–147, 169, 172–173, 195, 203, 219
Mahaffey, Vicki, 251n.143
Mallarmé, Stéphane, 59
Mangan, James Clarence, 41, 171
Manganiello, Dominic, 42, 44, 52, 54–55, 178–179, 249n.105

Staley, Thomas, 189, 196–203, 207, 209, 211, 221, 225
Steinberg, Erwin, 196
Steloff, Frances, 90, 110–111, 149, 194, 240n.32
Stendhal, Henri Beyle, 75
Stephen Hero, 53, 221 (*see also* Joyce, James, intentions for *Stephen Hero* of)
Stephens, James, 29
Sterne, Laurence, 22
Stevens, Kenneth, 132, 240n.37
Stevenson, Robert L., 80
Stone, Harlan Fiske, 138
Stopes, Maria, 98–99, 103, 107–108, 115
Strachey, Lytton, 248n.79
Stuart, H. C., 111
Studies in Philology, 190
Sullivan, Kevin, 17, 19
Summerfield, Henry, 34
Sumner, John: attacked by Ernst, 105; battle lost to Ernst by, 133; conservatism of, 137; *Hsi Men Ching* and *From a Turkish Bath* seized by, 110–111; methods of, 238n.5; "Nausicaa" seized by, 85–87; relations with Steloff of, 240n.32; *Ulysses* seized by, 90–92; Vanguard Press prosecuted by, 242n.82
Swift, Jonathan, 120, 187
Synge, John Millington, 31, 60, 170

Tan, Amy, 188
Tanselle, G. Thomas, 2
Tate, Allen, 182–183
Thompkins, Jane, 223
Thoreau, Henry David, 169
Tice, Anne, 240n.32
Time, 133
Tindall, William York, 194–195, 206, 213, 221
Tolstoy, Leo, 13, 28, 57
"Tradition and the Individual Talent," 72, 81
transition, 194

Trench, Samuel Chenevix, 167
Trilling, Lionel, 141, 176, 213
"Two Gallants," 16, 48–49, 202, 219–220
Tymoczko, Maria, 11

UCD. *See* University College, Dublin
Ulysses: Adrienne Monnier's bookshop reading of, 180; in American colleges, 128–131, 180; Anderson's defense of, 88–89; appeal of U. S. District Court trial of, 98; biographical use of, 152, 163, 167, 175; complaints in *The Little Review* about, 88; covers of, 102; criticism of, 14, 141–142, 145, 147, 181, 203–207, 223; direct discourse in, 215–216; *The Egoist* publication of, 71, 73, 79; Ellmann's influence on, 174; Gabler's edition of, 215, 221–222; humor in, 205; *The Little Review* publication of, 83, 85–86; New York Special Sessions trial of, 85–89, 91, 117–118, 239n.13; petition to Secretary of Treasury on behalf of, 113–115; prefigured by *Portrait*, 82; Random House edition of, 81, 131–134, 137, 193, 212, 228n.24; Roth edition of, 89–90, 92, 102, 104, 241n.56; seizure from Gotham Book and Art of, 90–92; seizure in Minnesota of, 90; Shakespeare and Company edition of, 89–90, 102–104; U. S. District Court trial of, 10, 103–110, 115–131, 139, 239n.13, 240n.42 (*see also* Eliot, T. S., *Ulysses* defended by; Joyce, James, intentions for *Ulysses* of; "Lestrygonians"; "Nausicaa"; "Oxen of the Sun"; "Penelope"; "Scylla and Charibdis"; "Wandering Rocks")
"*Ulysses*, Order, and Myth," 72
Unionism, 19, 25–26, 32–33, 41, 78
United Irishmen, 29, 42, 56